DATE DUE

GAYLORD			PRINTED IN U.S.A.

CRIME POLICY IN AMERICA

Laws, Institutions, and Programs

Shahid M. Shahidullah

Foreword by Albert R. Roberts

University Press of America,® Inc.
Lanham · Boulder · New York · Toronto · Plymouth, UK

Copyright © 2008 by
University Press of America,® Inc.
4501 Forbes Boulevard
Suite 200
Lanham, Maryland 20706
UPA Acquisitions Department (301) 459-3366

Estover Road
Plymouth PL6 7PY
United Kingdom

Library of Congress Control Number: 2008925824
ISBN-13: 978-0-7618-4098-5 (clothbound : alk. paper)
ISBN-10: 0-7618-4098-2 (clothbound : alk. paper)
ISBN-13: 978-0-7618-4099-2 (paperback : alk. paper)
ISBN-10: 0-7618-4099-0 (paperback : alk. paper)
eISBN-13: 978-0-7618-4251-4
eISBN-10: 0-7618-4251-9

™ The paper used in this publication meets the minimum
requirements of American National Standard for Information
Sciences—Permanence of Paper for Printed Library Materials,
ANSI Z39.48—1984

This book is dedicated to my wife Sufia
and our daughter Ashley

TABLE OF CONTENTS

FOREWORD

Significant changes have taken place after the enactment and implementation of crime policies, criminal law and juvenile law statutes, and illicit drug policies. Criminal justice policy-makers, administrators and practitioners must understand crime policies in order to seek and support policy changes, and advance the interests of the criminal justice profession. This is the first up-to-date book to provide an overview and discussions of the shaping of federal, state and local criminal justice policies throughout American Society. This excellent book increased my knowledge of the social, political, psychological, and economic context of criminal justice policies.

I have been a criminal justice professor and researcher for 37 years, and I evaluate a new book based on what, if anything, I have learned from it. I congratulate Professor Shahidullah for his comprehensive and all inclusive review of every important federal and state crime policy developed between 1770 and 2007. More specifically, I have learned about recent federal and state drug enforcement policies, sex offender apprehension and sentencing policies, cyber crime and child pornography policies, as well as counter-terrorism and homeland security legislation.

The most important contribution that Professor Shahidullah has made to criminal justice knowledge-building is his comprehensive examination of the strengths and limitations of crime policies. This comprehensive review traces the Sumerians in 2060 B.C. to the Hammurabi Code in Babylonian times (1700 B.C.) to the U.S. Omnibus Crime Control Act of 1968 and the implementation of the Federal Law Enforcement Assistance Administration (LEAA) and state planning agencies, to the 1994 Violent Crime Control and Law Enforcement Act to recent federal policy initiatives such as the 2001 Faith-Based Community Initiatives, the Cyber-crime Security Enhancement Act of 2002, the Amber Alert Act of 2003, Violence Against Women Act (VAWA III) of 2005, and the Adam Walsh Child Protection and Safety Act of 2006.

With many millions of victims and offenders involved as clients of criminal justice programs nationwide each year, the coming decade brings multiple challenges to all criminal justice clients and professionals. Therefore, I highly recommend this book to criminal justice students and practitioners, legislators, lobbyists, advocates, librarians, and educators.

Albert R. Roberts, Ph.D.
Professor of Criminal Justice, School of Arts and Sciences
Rutgers-The State University of New Jersey

PREFACE

There are three major sectors in criminal justice—police, court, and corrections. The nature, role, and functions of these sectors depend on laws and statutes made by legitimate political and governmental actors and institutions. The power of police search, the nature of search and seizures, the nature of trial and convictions, the types and essence of sentencing, the nature of corrections—all depend on laws, statutes, and policy developments. The nature of crime and justice in a country, in other words, is the reflection of the nature of its policy-making. This book is about policy-making in crime and justice in America. It has examined the growth of federalization in America's crime and justice, and the nature and evolution of laws and statutes in the areas of illicit drugs, juvenile crimes, sex crimes, and cyber crimes. The book, in general, is about the birth of America's criminal justice and its rapid maturation, particularly since the 1970s.

There are many books and other literature on the issue of drug crimes, juvenile crimes, sex crimes, and cyber crimes. But there are not many systematic works on how laws and statutes have evolved in these areas, and what kinds of institutional and organizational impacts they have on America's criminal justice as a whole. Books exist on many discrete issues such as mandatory sentencing, mass incarceration, drug sentencing, juvenile transfer laws, and rape and incest. But books written on those and other issues from the perspective of policy studies and policy analysis are still few and far between.

The issue more common in crime policy literature is the debate about the competing—conservative v. liberal—strategies of crime control. Sometimes, students in criminal justice are more aware of the debates than the subject debated. Who makes the laws and statutes to define what crime is and how crime has to be punished? When are these laws and statutes made and in what contexts are they made? How do they change from time to time, and what impacts do they have on the system of crime and justice? This book is about these actors, processes, and impacts of policy-making in crime and justice. It examines how ideology plays a dominant role in crime policy-making, but it also examines the role of science, philosophy, and morality. The book addresses the issues of criminalization in different areas of actions and behaviors, and the growth of crime control laws, statutes, institutions, and organizations. It examines and expands the role that different federal and state policy-makers play to make those laws and statutes and the impacts they have on the evolving system of crime and justice in America.

When Congress passes new crime legislation and it becomes a federal statute, new areas and definitions of crime emerge, new structures and methods of sentencing are proposed and imposed, many new federal and state organizations are established, new programs are created, and new justice dollars flow in criminal justice research and administration. Each crime legislation passed by Congress, and each decision related to crime and justice made by the federal courts, particularly the U.S Supreme Court, defines and extends the boundaries of crime, control, and punishment. They also define and set the limits of the roles and functions of various criminal justice actors, organizations, and processes. The nature of crime, criminality, and punishment cannot be clearly understood unless these myriad forms of laws and statutes are systematically examined.

This book will be a valuable reference for students in criminal justice specializing in court and criminal law, crime policy, judicial policy-making in crime and justice, and criminal justice management and administration. The book will also be immensely beneficial and informative for criminal justice experts, educators, and professionals. Criminal justice today is an expanding area of education and the professional work force in the United States, Europe, and other developing countries. This book will give these arenas a sense of how America's system of criminal justice was born, how it has grown, and where it is going.

ACKNOWLEDGEMENT

The idea of this book was born about seventeen years ago when I was at the University Center for International Studies and at the Graduate School of Public and International Affairs, University of Pittsburgh. The profession of criminal justice at that time was still in its infancy, and crime policy was at the periphery of interests for policy analysts. At that time, I had several discussions on crime policy with Burkart Holzner, William N. Dunn, B. Guy Peters, Phyllis D. Coontz and many others from the Policy Analysis Group of the Graduate School of Public and International Affairs.

My journey in crime policy analysis began with my journey in science and technology policy at the University Center for International Studies of the University of Pittsburgh. At the University Center for International Studies, I was privileged to work with Burkart Holzner, Donald Campbell, Nathan Sivin, Joseph Ben-David, Samuel Eisenstadt and many others on issues of global science policy. From the Center, in connection with science policy projects funded by the National Science Foundation and the Westinghouse Foundation, I was fortunate to travel to many countries in Europe to explore the nature and mechanism of European science and technology policy, particularly of the European Union. The origin of the present work of trying to bring a policy perspective to the understanding of crime and justice in America goes back in time to my associations with some of world leaders in science policy and best minds in America's policy analysis. I am grateful to all of them for instilling in me a genuine curiosity for understanding the nature and mechanism of policy-making and for giving me an opportunity to meet with policy-makers "close to power" on both sides of the Atlantic.

I am also thankful to many of my colleagues at Virginia State University, particularly of the Criminal Justice Program of the Department of Sociology, Social Work, and Criminal Justice. I am particularly indebted to Dr. Mokerrom Hossain, Dr. Jay W. Malcan, Dr. James F. Hodgson, Dr. C. Nana Derby, Dr. Isis N. Walton, Dr. David B. Stein, Dr. David L. Spinner, Dr. Nicolle Parsons-Pollard, Dr. Cheryl Stampley, Dr. Zaccheus Ogunnika, and Dr. Ghyasuddin Ahamed for their thoughtful comments and advice. This work would not have been possible without the help and logistical support from the Criminal Justice Program of the Department of Sociology, Social Work, and Criminal Justice at Virginia State University. Dr. Mokerrom Hossain, as Chair and founder of both undergraduate and graduate programs in criminal justice at Virginia State University, has been extremely generous in lending the needed logistics for this work and supporting my research through travel grants and flexible teaching schedules.

I also want to express my deep gratitude to Dr. Albert R. Roberts, Professor of Criminal Justice at Rutgers-The State University of New Jersey and Editor-in-Chief of *Victims and Offenders: Journal of Evidence-Based Policies and Practices*, for kindly agreeing to write a Foreword for this work. I had several discussions with Dr. Roberts about different issues in criminal justice and how policy-makers are increasingly demanding the use of evidence-based knowledge in policy-making. His insights about the emerging science-driven trend in policy-making in crime and justice have been extremely helpful and enlightening.

Dr. Rita Dandridge, Professor, Department of Languages and Literature, Virginia State University, kindly agreed to edit this book, and she did it with a high degree of interest, sensitivity, and competence. Her editorial help and comments have enriched this work. Many thanks also to Dr. Michael Sugg, Assistant Professor, Department of Sociology, Social Work, and Criminal Justice, and Dr. Freddy Thomas, Professor and Chair, Department of Languages and Literature, Virginia State University, for lending me editorial help for this work.

Ms. Patti Belcher, Acquisition Editor of the University Press of America, has been very patient, helpful, and cooperative. This book would not have been possible without her active interest in pursuing this project, and keeping me awake with frequent emails for the completion of this project. Many thanks also to Ms. Lynda Phung, Ms. Sarah Fell, and Mr. Brian DeRocco who reviewed the manuscript and provided technical help and guidance.

During the last four years, when I was closely working on this project, I stole hundreds of hours from our family time. It was particularly hard on my 10-year old daughter, Ashley. This book owes a great deal to my family, and it is dedicated to them.

However, none of the people mentioned above are responsible for the mistakes that remain. For the all the mistakes that remain, I am to blame. I very much believe in Nobel Laureate Herbert Simon's theory of "bounded rationality"—a theory that is at the core of modern policy analysis. There is always a limit to human perfections. In making decisions, do not try to be perfect, just try to satisfy. I also believe in what renowned mathematician Jacob Bronowski once said: "All information is imperfect. We have to treat it with humility. That is the human condition, and that is what quantum physics says."

CHAPTER 1

CRIME POLICY: MEANING, NATURE, ACTORS, AND CONTEXTS

1.1 Crime Policy: Historical, Theoretical, and Philosophical Roots

Crime Policy: Historical Notes

One of the major tasks and responsibilities of a modern government is the maintenance of law and order. A government defines, ensures, and protects the territorial boundary of a country, and it also defines and delineates the boundaries of crime, law, and justice for domestic peace and tranquility. The instrumentality of government and the policy-making for crime and justice has been with us since the beginning of human civilization. The Sumerians first built the institutions of civilization on the banks of Euphrates and Tigris Rivers of Iraq about 5500 years ago. They developed a thriving agricultural economy, kingdoms, city-states, science, law, and government. It was in the Sumerian kingdoms and city-states that a rudimentary form of policy-making in crime and justice began. "The earliest recorded examples of conscious efforts to analyze public policy are found in Mesopotamia. The ancient Mesopotamian city of Ur, situated in what is now Southern Iraq, produced one of the first legal codes in the twenty-first century B.C., some two thousand years before Aristotle (384-322 B.C.)" (Dunn, 1981, p.

9). Ur-Nammu, the king of the third Sumerian dynasty around 2060 B.C., was the first king who developed a systematic policy of law, crime, and justice. "Ur-Nammu was the promulgator of the oldest code of law yet known, older by about three centuries than the code of Hammurabi" (The Columbia Electronic Encyclopedia, 2003, p. 1). The Code of Ur-Nammu consists of seven laws defining the nature of crime and justice in the Sumerian kingdom. Archeologists have found that the Code of Ur-Nammu developed the earliest notions of judicial specialization, testimony under oath, restorative justice, victim compensation, and the proportionality of crime and punishment.

Policy-making in crime and justice was further advanced three hundred years later through the development of what is historically known as the Code of Hammurabi. Hammurabi was a Babylonian king around 1700 B.C., and he developed an elaborate code of written laws containing 282 provisions for the governance of his kingdom. Some of the major provisions of the Code of Hammurabi included the notions of justice and fairness, contractual obligation, restorative justice, retributive justice, judicial control, royal responsibility, welfare of the poor and the slaves, the private ownership of land, parental roles and responsibilities, and spousal roles and obligations. The modern western notion of *mens rea* (a mental component) as an element of criminal liability can be traced back to the Code of Hammurabi.

The history of policy-making in crime and justice from the dawn of civilization to the development of modern nation-states and governments is mostly a history of the development and evolution of law and legal structures. At different periods of history, as Table 1 describes, kings and emperors promulgated different codes of law and justice. Policy-making in the historical kingdoms and empires was not the function of any specialized branch of a government as it is today. There were, however, royal courts, royal scholars of law, and institutions of law enforcement. In addition to secular legal codes, pre-modern societies were also governed by the codes of religious law. Hinduism, Buddhism, Confucianism, Judaism, Christianity, and Islam respectively developed elaborate systems of religious laws for their believers. Until the advent of modern governments, there were no clear boundaries of secular and divine laws. In the West, the Catholic Church was the dominant policy-maker in crime and justice for almost fifteen hundred years.

Crime Policy: Theoretical Justifications

Policy-making in crime and justice has been a major preoccupation of politics and governance since the beginning of civilization because it is a domain of governance that is vital for social order and stability. Thomas Hobbes (1588-1679) was one of the first philosophers and political theorists who theorized about why policy-making in crime and justice is of compelling necessity in a government. Hobbes came to a theory of crime and justice through his theory of human nature. "Hobbes's first problem, therefore, was to state the law of human nature and to formulate the condition upon which a stable society is possible" (Sabine & Thorson, 1973, p. 427).

Table 1: Major Legal Historical Codes and the Roots of Modern Policy-Making in Crime and Justice

Time	Name of the Code	Major Policy Contributions
2050 BC	Ur-Nammu's Code	Developed the notions of judicial role and specialization, testimony under oath, and the proportionality between crime and punishment
1700 BC	Code of Hammurabi	Developed the notions of restorative and retributive justice. The earliest code of written and Public Laws
1300 BC	Ten Commandments	Divine laws came to Moses that became a part of the Old Testament. Birth of the notion of retributive justice—"eye for an eye, tooth for a tooth"
621 BC	Draco's Law	The word "draconian" came from the name of Draco, an Athenian citizen chosen to make laws against crime.
550 BC	Solon's Law	Recommended for democratizing justice by making courts more accessible to citizens
536 BC	The Book of Punishment	A legal code from China. It developed the idea of alternative sentencing including such punishments as tattooing and castration
450 BC	The Twelve Tables	Foundation of Roman Law and modern public and private laws
529 AD	Justinian Code	The word "justice" came from the name of this Byzantine Emperor. The Code refined the Roman law with more legal principles
1215	Magna Carta	The Code signed by King John of England established for the first time the notion of judicial autonomy. It laid the foundation of English Common Law
1791	The American Bill of Rights	Established the foundation of modern criminal justice in the new Republic

Source: Compiled by the Author from Time Table of World Legal History

Hobbes theorized that human society is inherently fragile because humans are inherently selfish and competitive. Competition, diffidence, and glory are basic to human nature. Humans are restless for power, sex, and wealth. This intrinsic nature of humans makes war, crime, domination, exploitation, and violence inevitable in human society. Without a common power, such as a government, social order becomes inherently fragile. Hobbes believed that "given such stupidity and selfishness as men habitually display, the only way to preserve the peace and prevent them from destroying each other was to concentrate all power in the hand of a single individual, the sovereign" (Jones, 1952, p. 653). Hobbes provided a theoretical foundation for a modern government, and made public policy-making in crime and justice a theoretically compelling necessity for maintaining a stable social order.

An equally compelling argument for policy-making in crime and justice is found in the social and psychological theories of Sigmund Freud (1856-1939). Freud theorized that human nature is inherently anti-social. Humans are instinctually driven by passions for pleasure and gratification. Crime and violence are, therefore, endemic in human society. Civilization is possible only through the development of the institutions of collective control and culture (Freud, 1989). Culture and civilization, for Freud, means the growth of the institutions of control, punishment, and repressions. Control and punishments will never be able to change the human nature seeking for unbounded pleasure and gratification. But they protect the boundaries of culture and civilizations. Under the control of culture and civilizations, some are destined to be neurotic and psychopathic, and it is for them that the growth of civilization, in view of Freud, is intimately connected with the growth and expansion of the institutions of control and repressions.

The need for policy-making in crime and justice in modern societies and modern governments has remained very prominent also in sociological theories. Sociologists firmly believe that humans cannot be completely socialized. Social order is possible through the internalization of the rules and standards of social behavior. French sociologist Emile Durkheim theorized that humanity is a social construction. Humans are not born social. They become social by learning and internalizing the standards of social and cultural behavior. But this process of internalization is problematic and unpredictable. There is always a probability that some have not internalized the social rules very well. The classical sociologists of the nineteenth century such as Auguste Comte, Karl Marx, Emile Durkheim, Max Weber, Georg Simmel, and Ferdinand Tonnies, therefore, predicted that concerns for control will remain prominent in the governance of modern societies characterized by urbanization, industrialization, market economy, consumerism, individualism, and secularization. The classical sociologists envisioned the birth of modern criminal justice and the need for a new system of control through their concerns about the problems of modernization—the disintegration of communities, the decline of traditional family values, the rise of alienation, and the growth of materialism (Nisbet, 1969; Berger, Kellner, & Berger, 1973; Riesman, Glazer, & Denney, 2001).

Crime Policy and Philosophical Issues

Policy-making in crime and justice is vitally important in a modern government also because of the philosophical foundations of modernity. No domain of policy-making is so intimately connected with philosophy, as is the domain of crime and punishment. The core vision for policy-making in crime and justice is the creation of a good society. Since the beginning of secular philosophy in ancient

Greece, philosophers have been debating about the nature of a good society—the nature of justice, authority, fairness, responsibility, obligation, control, and punishment. Policy-makers in crime and justice in a modern government have to deal with these philosophical issues in a very fundamental way.

Modern liberal democratic governments emerged in the nineteenth century on the basis of the philosophy of Enlightenment. The notion of the application of science and reason for growth and governance and the separation of politics from religion in policy-making are two of the major philosophical ideas of the Enlightenment. The enlightenment concerns were for equality, secularity, freedom, and rationality in relations between the ruler and the ruled. Cesare Beccaria (1738-1794), an Italian social philosopher, brought the philosophy of the Enlightenment to the center of policy-making in crime and justice. In 1764, about thirty years before the birth of the Bill of Rights in the American Constitution, he published a book titled *On Crimes and Punishments*. Beccaria theorized about human nature in terms of free will and rationality and proposed the rationalization of law, court, and punishment (Beccaria, 1995). He advocated that a rationally devised system of crime control and prevention should remain as one of the distinctive roles and rights of a modern government. Beccaria laid the foundation for the Bill of Rights in the American Constitution which is the foundation of America's criminal justice.

1.2 Crime Policy as Legal, Political, and Moral Documents

Public policy and modern governments are intimately connected and inseparable. No governments can be understood without studying the policies they make, and no policy studies will make sense without understanding the nature of the government that makes them. Public policies are decisions made by legitimate political and governmental authorities for the attainment of public good. "Etymologically, the term policy comes to us from Greek, Sanskrit, and Latin languages. The Greek and Sanskrit root *polis* (city-state) and *pur* (city) evolved into the Latin *politia* (state) and later, into the Middle English *Policie*, which referred to the conduct of public affairs or the administration of government" (Dunn, 1981, p. 7).

Public policies are the hallmarks of modern governments. From economics to environment, school to sex, and water to welfare, almost all realms of life in modern governments are influenced by public policies. Public policies are the mirrors of a modern government. They show its degree of achievement and activism, working of its democracy, and the nature of its progress towards modernity and open society. Public policies in a given domain of governance do not exist in isolation. Rather, they form a complex totality. Different policies of a government such as foreign policy, welfare policy, and health policy "are in fact complex bundles of individual policies, often quite disparate in subject matter or significance and affecting a range of different populations" (Meehan, 1981, p. 184). For the sake of analysis, we can pick up a single policy issue such as sentencing policy or hate crime policy. But they are a part of America's crime policy as a whole. America's crime policy is the bundle of laws, statues, rules, and programs that pertain to the whole domain of crime and justice in America. Crime policy defines the nature of criminalization and decriminalization, shapes the boundaries of acceptable standards of acts and behavior, and determines the modalities of justice, control, and punishment.

Crime Policy as a
Legal Document

Crime policy as a body of authoritative decisions is a document of highly complex nature. First and foremost, crime policy is a legal document. The Executive Orders given by the Presidents and state governors, the enactments passed by Congress and state legislatures, programs and regulations developed by federal and state executive agencies, decisions made by federal and state judiciaries, particularly by the U.S. Supreme Court, and laws and ordinances passed by city and local government councils related to crime and justice are primarily the main components of crime policy. Crime policy must have the enforcement of law and justice. Policies and decisions that do not provide the enforcement of law are not a part of public policy. For example, there are many groups and think-tanks that advocate and recommend for the legalization of marijuana. But those policy recommendations do not have the enforcement of law and they are not a part of America's drug Policy. The mandatory sentencing disparity between crack and powder cocaine, on the other hand, is a part of America's drug policy because it is authorized by the Congress. There are many think-tanks and citizen-groups that recommend for the removal of the disparities in drug sentencing, particularly because of their adverse effects on the minorities. But those recommendations are not a part of drug policy because the Congress has not yet passed a Bill to remove drug sentencing disparities.

Crime Policy as a
Political Document

The issues of legality and legitimacy make crime policy also highly politically divisive. Few areas of policy-making are politically more sensitive than the area of crime and justice. Crime policy is not just a body of laws and statutes. It also embodies the political expressions and ideologies of those who make it legal and legitimate, and those who debate and dispute it (Beckett, 1999; Gest, 2001; Marion, 1994; 2007; Meier, 1994; Wilson, 1983). The understanding of the nature and the roots of crime, and the choice and preference of crime control strategies by policy-makers are broadly based on two competing political philosophies or ideologies—conservatism and liberalism. Conservatives believe that crime is primarily an individual phenomenon. It is the result of the lack of individual responsibility that, in turn, is the result of inadequate socialization and the lack of moral and religious training. "Moral poverty," "poverty of being without loving, capable, responsible adults," "poverty of being without parents, guardians, relatives," and "poverty of growing up surrounded by deviant, delinquent, and criminal adults in chaotic, dysfunctional, fatherless, godless, and jobless settings," the conservatives believe, are the roots of crime and criminality (Dilulio, 1996; Rubin & Dilulio, 1998)). Conservative theorists claim that those who commit crime make a rational choice to do so by weighing its rewards and punishments. Crime is a matter of rational choice for those who commit crime. Law breakings and rule breakings are acts that are intentional, deliberate, and purposeful in nature. Conservatives hold the view that punishment is a major deterrent for reducing crime. Crime control strategies must be based on incarceration, incapacitation, and just deserts (Wilson, 1997; Shahidullah, 2002).

Liberals, on the other hand, believe that crime is a social phenomenon. It is related to a variety of social structural factors such as poverty, community disorganization, economic dislocations, structured inequalities, powerlessness, and social and economic exploitations (Currie, 1986; 1994). Some liberals believe that crime could also be biogenic in nature. In view of the liberals, therefore, crime cannot be reduced only through incarcerations and incapacitation strategies. Crime must be prevented through community revitalization, community empowerment, and the extension of social and economic opportunities for all groups of people. It must be prevented also through the extension of mental health treatments. These two competing political ideologies shape and inform crime policy debates and policy-making not just in the United States but in almost all countries of the world. They shape and inform the ideas about crime and justice not only of the policy-makers but also of different political role players such as lawyers' associations, women's groups, gay and lesbian organizations, human rights' organizations, victim rights' advocacy groups, child advocacy groups, and religious organizations.

Crime Policy as a
Philosophical and Moral Document

In a legal sense, crime is a violation of law that is backed by punishment. But the issues of crime, justice, and punishments are also moral and philosophical in nature. Law, philosophy, and morality are intimately connected. To make laws, particularly criminal laws, means to set the limits of moral choices and preferences (Braswell, Pollock, & Braswell, 2005). The process of criminalization in a society, in a deeper sense, is a process of articulating the acceptable boundaries of its morality. Every society has a boundary of what is moral and immoral, right and wrong, acceptable and unacceptable. The issues of morality are both sacred and secular. The sacred issues of morality come from religion, and the secular issues are related to philosophy. In reality, they are intertwined and interdependent. For instance, by legalizing same-sex marriage, the Supreme Judicial Court of Massachusetts in 2004 secularized the sacred boundary of marriage by bringing in the issues of rights and equality. The crime policy of a country shapes and molds the boundaries of its morality. In a modern society, crime policy seeks to expand, particularly the boundaries of secular morality. The issues of privacy, rights, justice, fairness, equality, and responsibility are the issues of secular morality or secular philosophy. Crime policies on many areas such as domestic violence, child abuse, sexual abuse, internet child pornography, and cyberstalking are deeply moral and philosophical in nature (Claster, 1992). These policies have set the limits of the boundaries of moral tolerance in those areas. Crime policies also raise many moral and philosophical questions. Mandatory sentencing guidelines, truth-in-sentencing laws, juvenile transfer laws, sex offender registration and notification laws, sex offender civil commitment statutes, disparities between crack and powder cocaine sentencing, abolition of parole, felony disenfranchisement, mandatory extraction of DNA profiles from convicted felons, death penalty—all have raised many moral and ethical questions.

Crime policy is intellectually more intriguing probably because of its moral and philosophical nature. It keeps space for debates on competing moral arguments. One of the most crucial indicators of modernity in a society is not its rate of crime, but its policy on crime and justice. The crime rate in most of the industrialized countries of the West is high because their systems of crime and justice are largely based on the principles of the philosophy of enlightenment. The philosophy of enlightenment based on the notions of justice and fairness and reason and rationality creates a tension between control and freedom. Crime policy is a legal and political document. It is a moral and philosophical document as well.

1.3 Crime Policy Actors: Presidents, Congress, and the Federal Judiciary

The Constitution and Crime Policy

Modern American policy-making in crime and justice historically began at the inception of this Republic. At the core of the birth of the American Republic is the doctrine of constitutionalism—the doctrine of limited government. The doctrine of limited government means that the executive, legislative, and judicial branches of the government are limited and constrained by constitutional principles. The constitution is the ultimate maker and guarantor of the laws of the land. Article VI of the U.S. Constitution states: "This Constitution and the laws of the United States which shall be made in Pursuance thereof; and all Treaties made, or which shall be made, under the Authority of the United States, shall be the supreme Law of the Land." Article VI expands the notion that the members of the Congress, officers of the Executive, and the members of the judiciary "shall be bound by Oath or Affirmation, to support this Constitution." The nature of power, authority, and responsibilities of the three branches of the government is thus defined and limited by the constitution.

The Bill of Rights, the first ten amendments of the constitution ratified in 1789, is at the core of America's law and justice. It is, in fact, the first modern document of crime policy. It is the first modern document that translated Becaria's philosophy of crime and punishment into the language of laws and the constitution. The Bill of Rights was ratified more than two hundred years ago, but still there hardly goes a day in American law and the court when it is not cited, raised, and debated to address issues related to crime and justice.

The Bill of Rights sets the framework of procedures within which law and justice must be rendered. The First Amendment argues that the Congress does not have the power to make laws that will infringe on the rights of free speech, free press, and the freedom of religion. The U.S. Supreme Court has ruled against many Congressional crime enactments because of their violations of the First Amendment principle of free speech. The Second Amendment is about the right to bear arms. It has been at the center of debates about gun controls from the beginning of the Republic. The Fourth Amendment is about the procedure of police search and seizures. The Fourth Amendment states that the "right of people to be secure in their persons, houses, papers, and effects, against unreasonable searches and seizures, shall not be violated, and no Warrants shall issue, but upon probable cause, supported by Oath or Affirmation, and particularly describing the place to be searched, and the persons or things to be seized." Hundreds of criminal convictions are appealed every year in federal courts for violations of the Fourth Amendment. The federal exclusionary rule—the rule that evidence collected through unusual search and seizures is not admissible in the court of law—is based on the principles of the Fourth Amendment. The Fifth Amendment is about due process of law and criminal indictment on the basis of the grand jury. The Six Amendment includes the rights to have a counsel and a jury trial. The Six Amendment states that "In all criminal prosecutions, the accused shall enjoy the right to a speedy and public trial, by an impartial jury of the State and district wherein the crime shall have committed." The Seventh Amendment protects the right of jury trial in criminal cases. It states that "In Suits at common law, where the value in controversy shall exceed twenty dollars, the right of trial by jury shall be preserved, and no fact tried by a jury, shall be otherwise reexamined in any Court of the United States, than according to the rules of the common law." The Eighth Amendment prohibits cruel and unusual punishment. It states that "Excessive bails shall not be required, nor excessive fines imposed, nor cruel and unusual punishments inflicted." It was the firm conviction of the framers of the constitution and the Bill of Rights that all humans are born with certain "inalienable rights"—natural rights. Those who violate the laws must be punished, but their fundamental natural rights at every stage of criminal justice must also be protected. The Congress, the President, and the Courts do not have the authority to take away these fundamental rights even in cases of "infamous crime."

The Presidents and Crime Policy

A federal policy becomes a law when the President signs a Bill passed by Congress. Once a policy becomes a law, new appropriations are made, new programs are created, new organizations are established, new regulations are written, and the courts, judges, attorneys, and law enforcement people are informed and trained in administering the new law. A new law becomes a part of the existing body of laws and statutes that comprise the crime policy. The President not merely signs a crime Bill passed by the Congress or sends his proposals to the Congress for new Bills. He holds enormous power to shape and control the directions of crime policy. He can issue Executive Orders that can have the force of law. He nominates the judges and Justices of the federal courts, members of his cabinet, and the heads of the executive agencies. He can appoint independent crime commissions and develop new crime control programs in the White House. The President can also influence the governors, state legislatures, and mayors to support his crime agenda. Above all, the President shapes and makes the federal crime control budget, and through the federal crime control budget, the President impacts on state and local crime control initiatives. The vision of the American President about crime and crime control is, therefore, very important for America's crime policy.

There is not a single American president, as shown in Table 2, who did not have his own theory of crime and his own vision of crime policy. It is particularly noticeable from the days of Herbert Clark Hoover (1929-1933)—the thirty-first President of the United States. The Wickersham Commission, known as the National Commission on Law Observance and Enforcement, appointed by President Hoover in 1929, recommended the need for scientific approach, particularly a social scientific approach, to the study of crime and crime policy. The Commission's report on Criminal Statistics provided justifications of the need for Uniform Crime Reporting (UCR) that the Bureau of Investigation, now known as the Federal Bureau of Investigation, started in 1928. The Hoover's Commission reflected his technocratic vision of governance. "An engineer by training," Hoover, "had deep faith in the capacity of a democratic society to master social problems by mobilizing and applying scientific expertise" (Walker, 1997, p. 2).

During the next three decades from 1933-1963, there were four presidents: Franklin D. Roosevelt (1933-1945), Harry Truman (1945-53), Dwight D. Eisenhower (1953-1961), and John F. Kennedy (1961-1963). The role and involvements of the presidents with crime policy began to further increase from that time because of the rapid increase in crime from the beginning of the 1930s. During the Roosevelt administration, one of the major policy enactments was the Twenty-first Amendment and the repeal of the Eighteenth Amendment. The Eighteenth Amendment, passed during the presidency of Woodrow Wilson (1913-1921), prohibited drinking, manufacturing, sale, transportation, and the exportation of alcohol. The Twenty-First Amendment decriminalized alcohol in America.

When President Kennedy came to power in 1961, his vision of crime control took a new direction. President Kennedy's theory was that poverty and historically structured racial inequalities are at the roots of escalating crime in America. The Kennedy administration passed a number of legislations, with the active leadership of the then Attorney General, Robert Kennedy, to combat organized crime, reduce juvenile violence, and extend the basic right to have a legal counsel by all defendants. The Juvenile Delinquency and Youth Offenses Control Act of 1961 signed by President Kennedy greatly impacted on the enactment of the Juvenile Justice and Delinquency Prevention Act of 1974 (Marion, 1994). No significant institutional developments, however, were achieved during the presidencies of Franklin Roosevelt, Harry Truman, Dwight Eisenhower, and John F. Kennedy to translate the recommendations of the Wickersham Commission—to develop a national system of crime and justice.

Table 2: Selected U.S Presidents and their Crime and Justice Related Landmark Legislations: 1789-1989

Presidents	Year	Major Legislations/ Crime Policies
George Washington	1789-1797	Ratification of the Bill of Rights Birth of the U.S. Census Report
John Adams	1797-1801	Alien and Sedition Act (Criminalization of Free Speech)
Thomas Jefferson	1801-1809	Criminalization of slave trade
Abraham Lincoln	1861 -1865	Emancipation Proclamation
Andrew Johnson	1865- 1869	Ratification of the XIII and the XIV amendments
Grover Cleveland	1885-1889	Interstate Commerce Act
Woodrow Wilson	1913-1921	Ratification of the XVIII amendment; criminalization of alcohol
Herbert Hoover	1929-1933	Wickersham Commission
Franklin. Roosevelt	1933-1945	Ratification of the XXI Amendment and repeal of The XVIII Amendment
Dwight Eisenhower	1953-1961	Criminalization of racial segregation Brown vs. Board of Education Enforcement of racial integration
John Kennedy	1961-1963	Juvenile Justice Acts Laws against organized crime
Lyndon Johnson	1963-1969	Commission on Law Enforcement and the Administration of Justice Omnibus Crime Control & Safe Street Act of 1968
Richard Nixon	1969-1974	The Birth of the "War on Drugs" policy
Ronald Reagan	1981-1989	Expansion of the War on Drugs U.S. Sentencing Commission Crime Control Act of 1984

Source: Compiled by the Author

Systematic policy-making for a national crime and justice system in America began from the presidency of Lyndon B. Johnson in 1963. A year after he assumed power, President Johnson appointed a Commission on Law Enforcement and Administration of Justice. Attorney General Nicholas Katzenbach headed the commission, and it included members from the political arena, law enforcement, crime policy-making agencies, Urban League, and academia. Some of the key members of the Commission included Alfred Blumstein, James Vorenberg, and Lloyd Ohlin (Wellford, 1998). After two years of research, two hundred specific recommendations were developed and published in 1967 in the famous work known as *The Challenge of Crime in a Free Society.* President Johnson described the Commission report as "the most comprehensive and detailed program for meeting the challenge of crime ever proposed in this country" (as quoted in Vorenberg, 1972, p. 1).

Richard Nixon and the Beginning of Get-tough Crime Policy

America's crime policy, with the coming of Richard Nixon to power in 1969, entered into a new turning point. The three successive Presidencies of Richard Nixon (1969-1974), Ronald Reagan (1981-1989), and George Herbert Walker Bush (1989-1993) set a new trend of thought that is still a dominant paradigm in America's crime policy. This new trend is what many scholars described as the rise of "new penology" or the growth of conservatism in crime policy. The policy-makers commonly described it as the "get-tough" approach to crime and justice. The new paradigm was born in the backdrop of a number of social and historical forces growing from the beginning of the 1970's.

During the 1970s, America was deeply engaged in the Cold War to control and contain the expansion of Soviet communism. The Cold War brought a significant challenge to America's basic and best premises of freedom, liberty, and prosperity—a challenge to the liberal model of society. The rise of Soviet Russia as an undaunted nuclear power, the Soviet expansion in the countries of Eastern Europe and Indo-China, the rise and expansion of communism in China, the spread of communist ideology among the intellectuals and the insurgents in Asia, Africa, and Latin America, and America's deep involvement in the war in Vietnam—all kept the Nixon and Reagan administrations thoroughly engaged in thoughts for charting far-reaching policies in international affairs.

The 1970s was also a time of turmoil at home in America. The rise of the civil rights movement, women's movement, sexual revolution, and counter culture in 1970s created an enormous sense of complexity, uncertainty, and confusion in America's domestic politics. These also brought new waves of crimes, illicit drugs, sex crimes, and violence among the youths in American homes, schools, and streets. Many historians describe the 1970s as the era of the beginning of the crime boom in America. The 1970s was also an era of the beginning of a new thought in crime policy, and it started with the Presidency of Richard Nixon.

President Nixon, very much troubled by the problem of law and order in America from the beginning of his Presidency in 1969, prioritized crime control. In his acceptance speech delivered before the Republican National Convention on August 8, 1968, Nixon said, "The American Revolution was and is dedicated to progress. But our founders recognized that the first requisite of progress is order." In that speech, Nixon declared, "I pledge to you that our new Attorney General will be directed by the President of the United States to launch a war against organized crime in this country .... The wave of crime is not going to be the wave of the future in the United States of America (Nixon, August 8, 1968, p. 1).

Immediately after assuming the presidency, Nixon created an inner circle crime policy team at the White House. The team included John Mitchell (Nixon's new Attorney General), John Ehrlichman (counsel to Nixon), Egil Krogh (an associate of Ehrlichman), Daniel Patrick Moynihan (who was then a counsel for domestic affairs), and Donald Santarelli (Nixon's crime policy adviser during the 1968 campaign). This inner circle, under the leadership of the President, formulated a new vision for crime control in America. The core of the new vision was to get-tough on crime and the criminals by overhauling the whole system of law enforcement, court, prison, and punishment. The metaphor of the "war on poverty" of the previous administration was replaced by a new metaphor of "war on crime" or more specifically "war on drugs" under the Nixon Presidency (Marion, 1994; Stenson & Cowell, 1991).

Nixon's major crime policy initiatives included two sectors: drugs and organized crime. He signed seven Executive Orders related to crime policy during his term of office. Four of them were in the area of drug policy (see Table 3). Nixon also signed three major crime Bills: The Organized Crime Control Act of 1969, The Omnibus Crime Control Act of 1970, and the Comprehensive Drug Abuse Prevention and Control Act of 1970. The Organized Crime Control Act of 1969 created a number of institutional mechanisms to control organized crimes such as the provision of grand jury for organized crime investigations, and the authority of the court to detain uncooperative witness for up to 18 months. The Omnibus Crime Control Act of 1970 made it a major federal responsibility to make adequate appropriations to state and local law enforcement agencies for developing crime control and prevention programs. The Act further enlarged the scope and functions of the Office of the Law Enforcement Assistance Administration (LEAA) created under the Omnibus Crime Control and Safe Streets Act of 1968. The Comprehensive Drug Abuse Prevention and Control Act of 1970, on the other hand, laid the legal foundation for America's contemporary drug policy.

Ronald Reagan and the Expansion of
Get-tough Strategies

In the two successive Presidencies after Nixon—the Presidencies of Gerald Ford (1974-1977) and Jimmy Carter (1977-1981)—crime was not high on the agenda for policy-making. President Ford and President Carter had neither the commitment for reform in criminal justice nor strong ideological support for Nixon's war on drugs (Marion, 1994). President Ford continued to support the Nixon's policy strategies but without Nixon's emotional attachment to crime policy activism. During the Carter administration, "crime had not completely drifted from the institution of the presidency, there was, to be sure, a temporary 'lull'" (Oliver, 2003, p. 76; Marion, 1994). It was under the Reagan administration (1981-1989) that crime again became one of the major concerns for presidential policy-making. Reagan brought back both the vision and emotional commitment of Nixon for policy activism in crime and justice. During his presidency, Reagan signed eight major Executive Orders related to crime and justice (see Table 3). He also signed five major crime Bills passed by Congress: the Comprehensive Crime Control Act of 1984, The Sentencing Reform Act of 1984, National Narcotics Leadership Act of 1984, Anti-Drug Abuse Act of 1986, and the Anti-Drug Abuse Act of 1988.

Four areas of policy-making in crime and justice were largely shaped and impacted by the vision and ideology of President Reagan. These are: crime and drug connections, sentencing policy, victim's rights, and crime analysis. The Executive Orders and the legislations that he signed related to drugs and crime connections not only crowded the nation's prisons but also vastly enlarged the bureaucracy for the control and prevention of drugs in America. Nixon's war on drugs was mostly rhetorical. It was under Reagan that drug policy became an integral part of America's crime policy. Reagan shaped the contours of the drug policy, expanded the drug bureaucracy at home, and took the drug war abroad. The war on drugs was Reagan's emotional attachment for crime policy. Reagan, like Nixon, deeply believed and theorized that the war on crime and the war on drugs are essentially a culture war (Hunter, 1992). Crime is essentially a moral problem. The inner essence of his get-tough approach was that morality must be judicially enforced and strengthened.

George H. W. Bush and the Extension of
Get-tough Strategies

George H. W. Bush took over the presidency (1989-1993) at a time of great transformations in the political and ideological landscape of the world. The late 1980s saw the fall the Soviet regime and the end of the Cold War. Most of the political energies of the Bush administration were spent to address the emerging global issues of that time. Crime at home was not forgotten, but it was not high in Bush's policy agenda (Marion, 1994). Bush continued to pursue the Reagan legacy in crime policy—the war on drugs, mandatory sentencing, more incarcerations, more conservative judges in federal courts, and a moral crusade for the revitalization of family values.

During his presidency, Bush signed two major Executive Orders related to crime policy. Both of them were related to the President's Drug Advisory Council. The major crime Bill signed by Bush was the Comprehensive Crime Control Act of 1990. The request for comprehensive crime legislation was sent by the White House with a number of provisions to enlarge the scope of death penalty for federal crimes, reform habeas corpus, restrict plea bargaining, reform exclusionary rule, and enhance penalties for the use of firearms in the commission of a crime (Cowin, 1991). Although all of these reforms were not included in the Bill, the Crime Control Act of 1990 made some major substantive changes in the area of child abuse, sexual abuse penalties, victim's rights, and the enforcement of drug laws. Some of the commonly known policy innovations made by the Crime Control Act of 1990 include the requirement for referring child abuse victims to counseling centers within 24 hours, a court-appointed special advocate program to deal with child abuse cases, child abuse training for judicial personnel, transmission of the victims of child abuse testimony through closed-circuit TV in the court room, criminal background checks for child care employees, increased penalties for sexual exploitation of minors and the possession of child pornography, drug-free schools, and gun-free school zones.

William J. Clinton: The Search for a Middle Ground

William J. Clinton was elected president of the United States in 1993 on the basis of a new public philosophy to focus on domestic issues. The end of the Cold War, new forces of globalization, and the rise of the new information technology—all deeply impacted the American domestic economy, politics, and culture. President Clinton was elected for putting the domestic agenda ahead of international affairs. And crime was one of Clinton's major passions for policymaking throughout his presidency. As he said: "When I ran for President, I had the opportunity to travel all over this country and visit with police officers, and walk the streets of our largest cities and some of our small towns and talk to people about crime and drugs and what was happening to young people and the rising tide of violence in our country" (Clinton, June 29, 1995, p. 1). In his last Radio Address in 2001, Clinton again focused on the issue of crime and violence. He said: "Today, I want to talk about our progress in reducing youth violence and new steps we're taking to make our communities even safer" (Clinton, January 13, 2001, p. 1).

During his presidency, Clinton signed seven major Executive Orders related to crime and justice. Some of these include the National Drug Control Program (E-12880), President's Council on Counter-Narcotics (E-12993), Critical Infrastructure Protection (E-13010), Collecting Delinquent Child Support Obligation (E-13019), Control of the Assets of Narcotic Traffickers (E-12978), and Working Group on Unlawful Conduct on the Internet (E-13133). President Clinton's major contribution, however, was that he was the architect of the Violent Crime Control and Law Enforcement Act of 1994. Clinton took over the presidency in January of 1993. He sent the new crime Bill to the Congress in September of 1993. Both Houses of Congress passed the Bill by August of 1994. President Clinton signed the Bill in September of 1994 describing it as "the smartest crime Bill in our nation's history" (Clinton, August 22, 1994, p. 1). The Act was signed into a law with price tag of $30.2 Billion for the implementation of a number of crime control and justice strategies. One of the most innovative aspects of the new crime Bill was the creation of a special trust fund—Violent Crime Reduction Trust Fund. As the President described: "One of the most important elements of this crime Bill is the creation of a Violent Crime Reduction Trust Fund, which ensures that every crime fighting program in the Bill will be paid for by reducing the federal bureaucracy by more than 270,000 positions over the next six years" (Clinton, August 22, 1994, p. 2).

President Clinton himself summarized The Violent Crime Control and Law Enforcement Act 1994 in terms of three key policy sectors: police, punishment, and prevention. In the area of policing, the Act mandated to put 100,000 more police officers in community policing. One of Clinton's major legacies in crime policy has been this notion of community policing. Clinton passionately believed that we not only need to increase the number of police officers on the streets, but also introduce and expand the style of community policing for crime control. The idea of an alternative style and philosophy of policing in America is being debated since the recommendations of the Kerner Commission of 1967 and the President's Crime Commission of 1968 (Crank, 1995). The Violent Crime Control and Law Enforcement Act of 1994 for the first time proposed to put this philosophy into practice for crime control and prevention ((Oliver, 2001).

Table 3: Major Presidential Executive Orders Related to Crime Policy: From John F. Kennedy to George H. W. Bush

Presidents	Executive Orders	Policy Actions and Statements
J. F. Kennedy	E-10940, May 1961	President's Committee on Juvenile Delinquency and Youth Crime
L. B. Johnson	E-11234, July 1965	President's Commission on Crime in the District of Columbia
L. B. Johnson	E-11236, July 1965	President's Commission on Law Enforcement and Administration of Justice
L. B. Johnson	E-11365, July 1967	National Advisory Commission on Civil Disorder
Richard Nixon	E-11469, May 1969	Extension of the National Commission on the Causes and Prevention of Violence
Richard Nixon	E-11534, June 1970	The National Council on Organized Crimes
Ronald Reagan	E-12358, April 1982	Presidential Commission on Drunk Driving
Ronald Reagan	E-12360,	Task Force on Victims of Crime
Ronald Reagan	E-12368, June 1982	Drug Abuse Policy Functions
Ronald Reagan	E-12415, April 1983	Presidential Commission on Drunk Driving
Ronald Reagan	E-12425, June 1983	International Criminal Police Organizations
Ronald Reagan	E-12435, July 1983	President's Commission on Organized Crime
Ronald Reagan	E-12564, September 1986	White House Conference on Drug-Free Federal Work Place
Ronald Reagan	E-12595, May, 1987	White House Conference on Drug Free America
George H. W. Bush	E-12696, November 1989	President's Drug Advisory Council

Source: Compiled by the Author

After the 1994 Act, an Office of Community-Oriented Policing was created within the Department of Justice to help expand the community policing movement across the country. The Bureau of Justice Statistics reports that about 86 percent law enforcement agencies now practice community policing, and the number of community policing officers increased 400 percent between 1997 and 1999. Congress approved about $8.6 Billion by the year 2002 for the expansion of the COPS program (Peed, 2002). Some of the innovative COPS programs under experiment in different cities and local communities include public education and media relations, Neighborhood Watch Program, Foot/Horse Patrol, Fixed Patrol Assignments, Neighborhood Town Meetings, and Community Newsletters and Websites. The Office of Community Oriented Policing, through COP grants, created many Regional Community Policing Training Institutes in the country.

The second most important policy sector of the Violent Crime Control and Law Enforcement Act of 1994 is prison and punishment. Clinton subscribed to the view that violent crime is the function of a small group of career criminals, and a policy of incapacitation through punishment and imprisonment is the best way to deal with them. As he remarked : "I would like to make two points about that, as someone who started public career as a State Attorney General almost two decades ago now. First of all, an overwhelming percentage of really serious violent crimes are committed by a relatively few people .... Secondly, this law is ... directed against that narrow class of people" (Clinton, April, 11, 1994, p. 2). The Act of 1994 allocated $9.9 Billion for new prison construction, tightened the truth-in-sentencing requirements, mandated life imprisonment for repeat violent offenders (three-strikes law), banned 19 types of semiautomatic assault weapons, banned the ownership of handguns by juveniles, mandated the Megan's Law for state and local law enforcement agencies, approved additional penalties for hate crimes, and extended the death penalty to about sixty different types of federal crimes. The Act also made provisions for state and local law enforcement agencies to find alternative punishment for first-time, non-violent young offenders in the form of boot camps and other community-based correction programs.

The third policy sector of the Violent Crime Control and Law Enforcement Act is the area of prevention. In terms of punishment, the 1994 Act is an extension of the conservative trend of the get-tough approach adopted by Nixon, Reagan, and Bush. The novelty of the 1994 Act, however, resides in its approach to crime prevention. The Act made some remarkable departures from the Omnibus Crime Control Act of 1984 and The Crime Control Act of 1990 because it made crime prevention an integral part of the get-tough strategy. The Act mandated the participation of the federal government for developing and organizing evidence-based innovative crime prevention programs. President Clinton affirms that "Prevention is the first, critical step in my Administration's three pronged strategy for crime control. Accompanied by stringent law enforcement and by certain, appropriate punishment, prevention is one of our Nation's most effective weapons against crime" (Clinton, October 5, 1994, p. 1).

The novelty of the 1994 Act lies also in developing a number of legislations and innovative strategies in the areas of violence against women, hate crimes, sex crimes, child abuse, and child pornography. The Act vastly increased the boundaries of criminalization and expanded the federalization of crime and justice. The war on drugs was extended both at home and abroad. A year after, he took over the presidency, Clinton signed and elevated the Office of National Drug Control Policy (ONDCP) to a Cabinet-level status to enable it to work closely with other federal Cabinet agencies. In his remarks on the Swearing-In of National Drug Control Policy Director Lee Brown, Clinton summarized his overall strategy of war on drugs. "Our aim is to cut off the demand for drugs at the knees through prevention. That means better education, more treatment, and more rehabilitation. At the same time, we want to strangle supplies ... by enforcing the law in our communities, at our Nation's borders, and by helping our friends and allies to do the same thing beyond our borders" (Clinton, July 1, 1993, p. 2). Clinton also signed the Brady Bill in 1993 (mandated five-day waiting period for buying a handgun), the National Child Protection Act of 1993, Drug-Free Communities Act of 1997, and a number of legislations related to transnational crime.

Through his Violent Crime Control and Law Enforcement Act of 1994 and other legislations, Clinton created a new blended approach to crime control by combining the conservative and liberal approaches to crime and justice. He was passionately involved in expanding the Reagan legacy of get-tough approach to crime and justice. He extended the list of federal capital crimes, reformed the habeas corpus, and stiffened penalties for domestic abuse, drug violations, sex crimes, and child abuse. But Clinton also deeply believed that crime control policies must be ultimately based on economic growth and the expansion of economic benefits and opportunities to all groups and classes of people. "Our new Covenant," he said, "is a new set of understandings for how we can equip our people to meet the challenges of a new economy .... We must have dramatic change in our economy, our Government, and ourselves" (Clinton, January, 24, 1995). He further added that "we simply cannot jail our way out of America's crime problem. We are going to have to invest some more money in prevention. And I say that as somebody who started out in law enforcement as attorney general over 20 years ago" (Clinton, June 9, 1996, p. 3). His unique approach to combine the conservative and liberal approaches to crime policy is clearly manifested in his following remarks: "For too long, crime has been used as a way to divide Americans with rhetoric. It is time to use crime as a way to unite Americans through action" (Clinton, August, 11, 1993, p. 1).

George W. Bush: Back to Get-tough Crime Policy

For Richard Nixon, Ronald Reagan and George H. W. Bush, morality and crime policy were inseparable. They brought and signed much legislation in areas of crime and justice. But their core belief was that crime control needs a blending of both punishment and moral education. The decline of family, religion, morality, and values is ultimately related to crime, drugs, and alternative life-styles.

The Reagan conservatism in crime policy was expressed, however, through the first strand of thought—the punishment approach. And the same was true for Clinton's approach to crime and justice. Clinton took a part of the conservative approach—the punishment approach—but left the question of crime and morality largely untouched. George W. Bush brought the issues of both punishment and morality to the center of policy-making and policy discourses in crime and justice. In his inaugural address, Bush summarized his vision of governance in terms of four principles: civility, courage, compassion, and character. But all are based on his core belief that faith is the most crucial component of life. As he remarked in the Proclamation of January 21, 2001 as a National Day of Prayer and Thanksgiving: "Let us become a nation rich not only in material wealth but in ideals—rich in justice, compassion, and family love and moral courage" (Bush, January, 20, 2001, p. 1). He further added: "Faith is ... important to the civility of our country .... Civility does not require us to abandon our deeply held beliefs" (Bush, February, 1, 2001, p. 2)

Clinton came to White House in 1993 with a package of a crime Bill ready to be sent to the Congress. Bush came to the White House in 2001 with a blue print not of a law and order crime policy, but with a framework of thought about how crime policy should be pursued in his administration. As a governor of Texas, he was a great policy activist in crime and justice. Crime and violence, for Bush, is rooted primarily in moral bankruptcy. Crime is the result of the lack of love, affection, faith, spirituality, and compassion. The teaching of values, faith, and morality for cleansing the inner soul, Bush believes, is far more important than expanding and providing material opportunities. And those who can teach these values well are the faith-based groups and organizations. Therefore, his national crime policy initiatives began by efforts to bring faith-based groups into discourses for developing crime control strategies (Shahidullah, 2004). A month after he took over the presidency, Bush declared: "My administration will put the Federal Government squarely on the side of America's armies of compassion .... The days of discriminating against religious institutions, simply because they are religious, must come to an end" (Bush, February, 1, 2001, p. 2).

Bush signed two Executive Orders in January of 2001 related to Faith-Based Community Initiative. The first Executive Order created a new office at the White House—the Office of Faith Based and Community Initiatives. The Office was created to work as a central point of policy-making in the area of crime and justice (Bush, March, 3, 2001). John Dilulio, a Princeton Professor and a noted criminologist was appointed as its first Director. In appointing Dilulio, Bush said:" Professor John Dilulio will head the new office I am announcing today. He is one of the most influential social entrepreneurs in America .... He has a servant's heart on the issues that we will confront" (January 29, 2001, p. 2). The second Executive Order was given to create five Faith-Based Initiative Centers in the Departments of Justice, Housing and Urban Development, Labor, Education, and Health and Human Services—each to be headed by a Director. These centers were created both for policy-making and policy implementations in the area of faith-based initiatives.

The Bush presidency did not produce any comprehensive crime Bill like those of the Reagan and Clinton presidencies. There was, however, a considerable amount of policy activities in a number of micro areas in crime and justice during the Bush administration. One of the major achievements early in his administration was the signing of the Juvenile Crime Control and Prevention Act (HR 1900) authored by Rep. Jim Greenwood (R-PA) and co-authored by Rep. Bobby Scott (D-VA). The authorization of the Juvenile Justice and Delinquency Prevention (JJDP) Act, enacted by the Congress in 1974, ended in September of 1996, and the 104th, 105th, and 106th Congresses failed (HR 2215) to pass any major juvenile legislation until 2002. The HR 1900 incorporated the HR 2215, and both Houses of the Congress passed the amended version in 2002 after six years of gridlock for juvenile justice legislation. In November of 2002, President Bush signed the Bill into a law (House Committee on Education and Workforce, November 4, 2002). One of the important aspects of HR 1900 of the Act of 2002 is that it consolidated four juvenile justice programs—boot camps, mentoring, a treatment program for child abuse and neglect victims, and state challenge activities—into one Prevention Block Grant. The goal was to provide more flexibilities and incentives for state and local government initiatives in the area of juvenile crime. The HR 1900 reformed the mandates for juvenile justice funding for state and local governments.

The HR 2215 of the Act is the 21st Century Department of Justice Appropriations Authorization Act (PL 107-273). The HR 2215 spent about $ 17.6 Billion over the 2002-2006 periods for programs and agencies of the Department of Justice, Federal Bureau of Investigation, the Immigration and Naturalization Service, the United States Attorneys, and the Bureau of Prisons (Congressional Budget Office, 2001). Some of the key policy strategies and innovations in HR 2215 included the establishment of the Violence Against Women Office in the Department of Justice, drug-free prisons and jails, establishment of specialized drug courts, grants for the expansion and modernization of state and local juvenile justice systems, funding and development of faith-based programs to reduce recidivism, enforcement of judicial discipline, and provisions for safeguarding the integrity of the criminal justice system.

Bush's impact on America's crime policy will remain historically significant because he signed the USA PATRIOT Act (Uniting and Strengthening America by Putting Appropriate Tools Required to Intercept and Obstruct Terrorism Act) in 2001, and created the Department of Homeland Security in 2002. These two policy developments have permanently changed the structure and the nature of policy-making in crime and justice in America. After the destruction of the World Trade Center on September 11, 2001 that took the lives of approximately 3,000 men and women, the Bush administration started a new global war on terror. It is in the context of this war on terror that he signed the Homeland Security Act of 2002 and created the Department of Homeland Security combining the various federal agencies responsible for policy-making and policy implementation in many areas of crime and justice. He also created the Office of Homeland Security in the White House by signing an Executive Order (E-13228) in October, 2001, and the President's Homeland Security Advisory

Council by signing an executive order (E-13260) in March 2002. America's crime policy began to address global organized crime and terrorism first through the war on drugs strategies expanded by Ronald Reagan in the 1980s. The Bush administration, by enacting the USA PATRIOT Act of 2001 and creating the Department of Homeland Security in 2002, further internationalized the America's crime policy in the context of the war on terror.

The USA PATRIOT Act (PL 107-56) defines domestic and international terrorism as new domains of crime needed to be controlled with new laws and law enforcement strategies. That Act contains a number of provisions and gives extraordinary power to the Attorney General and other federal authorities to address the problems of terrorism both at home and abroad. The Act authorizes indefinite imprisonment without a trial for suspected non-US citizens who pose threats to national security. It denies the right to have a counsel for suspected terrorists or their informants. It permits law enforcement officers to conduct unannounced search and seizers anywhere in the United States. It allows wiretapping for intelligence gathering from anybody, anywhere, and any events in the world including from religious places and congregations. The Act also authorized the Department of Justice to create a data bank of DNA profiles for all convicted terrorists. The Act was renamed as the USA Patriot Improvement and Reauthorization Act in 2005. The Reauthorization made some provisions for Congressional oversights, but made most of the earlier laws of the USA PATRIOT Act of 2001 permanent. Title I of the USA PATRIOT Improvement and Reauthorization Act of 2005 "Repeals the sunset date (thus making permanent) the surveillance provisions of the USA PATRIOT Act" (Congressional Research Service, 2006, p. 1). After the enactment of the Intelligence Reform and Terrorism Prevention Act of 2004, Bush created a new separate office of the Director of National Intelligence for a more coordinated approach to gathering of national and international intelligence related to domestic and international terrorist activities.

In addition, Bush signed a number of new laws that strengthened punishments for child sexual trafficking and exploitation, child pornography, domestic violence, drug crimes, and cyber crimes. These include the Victims of Trafficking and Violence Protection Act of 2000, Cyber Crime Security Enhancement Act of 2002, PROTECT Act (Prosecutorial Remedies and Other Tools to End the Exploitation of Children Today Act) of 2003, Illegal Drug Proliferation Act of 2003, Unborn Victims of Violence Act of 2004, Violence against Women Act of 2005, and the Adam Walsh Child Protection Act of 2006. President Bush began policy-making in crime and justice with the conservative perspective of brining the notion of faith and morality at the center of law and legislations. But he also signed much legislation to strengthen punishment. Through the USA PATRIOT Act of 2001, the Juvenile Control and Prevention Act of 2002, the 21st Century Department of Justice Appropriations Authorization Act of 2002, the PROTECT Act of 2003, and the Adam Walsh Act of 2005, Bush increased the boundaries of criminalization, control, and punishment. And through the White House Office of Faith-Based Initiatives, the new Faith-Based Centers in federal agencies, and more importantly the Unborn Victims of Violence Act of

2004, the Bush presidency applied and upholds the other side of the conservative approach to crime and justice—the moral agenda.

The Congress and Crime Policy

Article I of the United States Constitution defines the structure and functions of Congress. Section I of Article I describes: "All legislative Powers herein granted shall be vested in a Congress of the United States, which shall consist of a Senate and House of Representatives." Section 8 of Article I of the Constitution gives Congress a broad range of power for policy-making in crime and justice. Congress shall have power: "To define and punish Piracies and Felonies committed on the high Seas, and Offenses against the law of Nations." Congress is the center for policy-making in crime and justice. All federal Acts and statutes are created by Congress. The President makes crime policies by creating Executive Orders, proposing Bills to Congress, creating new executive agencies, and signing Bills passed by Congress. The President can impact on policies of his choice through his vision and political views. But it is only Congress that has the authority to create programs and make budget appropriations. The President's Executive Orders are limited in scope and impact. The crime Acts and statutes made by Congress become a part of the body of federal criminal codes.

Policy-making within Congress is largely based on the role of committees and subcommittees of the Senate and the House of Representatives. Bills for crime and justice can be proposed by any member and from any committees of the Congress, but they are proposed mostly by specialized committees responsible for crime and justice issues. In the Senate, the Judiciary Committee is broadly responsible for crime and justice issues. In the 109th Congress (2006-2007), the Senate Judiciary Committee is composed of seven subcommittees. Two of them—Crime and Drugs subcommittee chaired by Senator Joseph Biden of Delaware, and Terrorism, Technology, and Homeland Security subcommittee chaired by Senator John Kyl of Arizona—are particularly responsible for crime and justice issues in the 109th Congress. In the 105th and 106th Congresses, there was a Senate subcommittee on Youth Violence. The 107th Congress renamed it as a subcommittee on Crime and Drugs. The Technology, Terrorism, and Government Information subcommittee of the 106th and 107th Congresses is renamed as Terrorism, Technology, and Homeland Security in the 109th Congress. The nature and the nomenclature of the Senate subcommittees thus change from time to time depending on issues that are prominent in the crime policy agenda of a particular Congress.

Like the Senate, the House also has a Committee on the Judiciary responsible for policy-making in crime and justice. The House Committee on Judiciary of the 109th Congress has five subcommittees—subcommittee on the Courts, Internet, and Intellectual Property; subcommittee on Crime, Terrorism, and Homeland Security; subcommittee on Immigration, Border Security, and Claims; subcommittee on Commercial and Administrative Law; and subcommittee on Constitution, Civil rights, and liberties. These Senate and House Judiciary Committees and their subcommittees are the centers of policy-making in crime and justice within Congress. Any senator or a House representative can propose a crime Bill, but it most probably will die prematurely if it is not accepted by the committees and subcommittees. It is only when crime Bills are proposed and favored by these committees and subcommittees that they are sent to executive agencies for written comments, policy hearings and debates are organized, and both Houses of Congress are given opportunities for debates and deliberations. In order to understand why certain crime policies are more favored than others, how different crime policies are approached by different members of the Congress, and how politics and ideology play a role in crime policy-making, it is vitally important to understand the inner workings of these crime and justice committees and subcommittees. The committee and subcommittee hearings, as Table 4 describes, have a particularly important role in shaping the nature of Congressional policy-making.

Table 4: Selected Senate Committee on the Judiciary Hearings on Crime and Justice Policy in the 107th and 108th Congress

Numbers	Policy Areas
107-342	DNA Crime Laboratories: Forensic Science Improvement Act
107-396	Racial and Geographical Disparities in Death Penalty System
107-657	Biometrics: Technologies in the Global War on Terror
107-719	Homeland Defense and Local Law Enforcement
107-852	Identity Theft and Personal Protection in the 21st Century
107-885	NARCO-Terror: Drugs and Global Terrorism
107-910	The Criminal Justice System and Mentally ill Offenders
107-911	Federal Cocaine Sentencing Policy
107-974	Stopping Child Pornography
108-137	The War Against Terrorism
108-323	Forensic Sciences: DNA and beyond

Source: U. S. Congress. (2004). Senate Committee on the Judiciary Hearings. Washington DC: Government Printing Office

The chairs and the majority of the members of the committees and sub-committees are usually drawn from the majority party in the Congress. In the Senate Judiciary Committee of the 109th Congress, for example, the chair was Arlen Specter, R-Pennsylvania. In the 110th Congress, the Committee is being chaired by Patrick Leahy, D-Vermont. In the 110th Congress, all the subcommittees of the Senate Judiciary Committee and the House Committee on Judiciary are also chaired by the democratic Senators and House of Representatives.

Because of the norms and rules of committee leadership, policy-making in crime and justice in the committees and the subcommittees of the Congress is based mostly on party lines. From 1994 to 2006, the Republicans had the majority in the Congress, and they were in the leadership of the Senate and House Judiciary Committees. Most of the major crime control legislations in that period were sponsored and largely supported by the Republican members of the Congress. The Jacob Wetterling Act of 1994, Megan's Law of 1996, Children's

Online Protection Act of 1998, Children's Internet Protection Act of 2000, Trafficking Victims Protection Act of 2000, Cyber Crime Security Enhancement Act of 2002, PROTECT Act of 2003, Amber Alert Act of 2003, Unborn Victims of Violence Act of 2004, USA Patriot Reauthorization Act of 2005, Adam Walsh Child Protection and Safety Act of 2006—all were sponsored by the Republican members of the Congress and were passed with a majority vote from the Republican members.

The Congressional voting record is one of the important indicators to know the crime and justice perspectives of the two political parties and the members of the Congress. The opinions of the members of the Congress on different crime and justice issues are expressed mostly along party lines and in terms of their respective political views and ideologies. The Republican and Democratic Senators differ sharply, as shown in Table 5, on drug penalty issues. The objective of the Amendment Bill (S 625) "Penalties for Drug Offenses," proposed by Republican Senator Orrin Hatch, for example, was to increase penalties for manufacturing and trafficking of amphetamines and methamphetamines and the possession of powder cocaine. The Bill also proposed increased penalties for selling drugs to minors and especially near schools. The Bill was narrowly passed in the Senate (50-49). Thirty-four Democratic Senators opposed the Bill and forty-seven Republican Senators were in favor. The Democrats opposed the Bill because, in their views, it would bring more minorities in prison for longer terms. The Senate Bill 2549 proposed to expand the definition of hate crimes to include gender, sexual orientation, and disability. Forty-four Democrats were in favor, and forty-one Republicans voted against the hate crime Bill.

Table 5: Senate Voting Records (1999-2004) of the Republicans and Democrats on Seven Crime and Justice Policy Bills

Bills	Policy Area	Republicans	Democrats
S 1805	Gun Liability	N= 48; Y=3	Y=5; N=41
S2549	Expanding Hate Crimes	Y=13; N=41	Y=44; N=1
S 3	Partial Birth Abortion	Y=48; N=3	Y=16; N=29
S 625	Penalties For Drug Offences	Y=47; N=7	Y=3; N=42
S2329	Victim's Rights Passage	Y=49; N=0	Y=46; N=1
HR 1997	Unborn Victims of Violence	Y=48; N=2	Y=13; N=35
S 151	Virtual Child Pornography	Y=47; N=0	Y=37; N=0
HR 5005	Homeland Security	Y=48; N= 0	Y=41; N=8
HR 3162	Anti-Terrorism Authority	Y=49; N=0	Y=48; N=1
S877	Unsolicited E-mails	Y=51; N=0	Y=45; N=0

Source: Project Vote Smart. Michigan: Phillipsburg. www.vote-smart.org

The Democrats are known to have been mostly in favor of pro-choice issues, and the Republicans have been for pro-life issues. This was clearly reflected in the voting of HR 1997, Unborn Victims of Violence Act of 2004. The Senate was sharply divided on this issue. Forty-eight Republican Senators voted for the Bill, and thirty-five Democratic Senators voted against the Bill. Thirteen democratic Senators went across party lines and voted for the Unborn Victims of Violence Act of 2004 (Project Vote Smart, 2002-2004). There are, however, many issues of crime and justice that receive bipartisan support from Congress such as the development and enforcement of anti-terrorism laws, laws against transnational organized crimes, child sexual abuse laws, deadbeat parenting laws, cyber crime issues, use of the DNA in criminal investigation, and child pornographic laws. The Senate Bill S151 is a case in point. The Bill, sponsored by Senator Orrin Hatch, proposed to make it a crime to indulge in and solicit child pornography over the Internet. Forty-seven Republican and thirty-seven Democratic Senators voted in support of the Bill (Project Vote Smart, 2002-2004).

Crime Policy and the Federal Judiciary

In addition to the President and the Congress, the federal judiciary is also a vital component of policy-making in crime and justice. Section 1 of Article III of the Constitution states: "The judicial Power of the United States shall be vested in one supreme Court and in such inferior Courts as the Congress may from time to time ordain and establish." The constitution extends a widely broad judicial power in the hands of the Supreme Court to include "all cases, in law and equity, arising under this Constitution, the laws of the United States" (Article III, Section 2). The Supreme Court was created to work as the guardian of the Constitution. Because the American government is based on the doctrine of constitutionalism, the role of the federal judiciary, and more importantly, that of the U.S. Supreme Court, affects policy-making in all realms of governance including crime and justice (Tarr, 2003).

The Judiciary Act of 1789 passed by Congress created the structure of the federal judiciary. The federal judiciary is composed of three tiers: the federal District Courts, the Circuit Courts, and the U.S. Supreme Court. There are at present 95 District Courts, 13 Circuit Courts including the District of Columbia, and one U.S. Supreme Court. The federal District Courts are the courts of general jurisdictions. The Circuit Courts have the appellate jurisdictions, and they mainly see the application of the established procedures of federal law in federal cases. It is the Supreme Court that plays the role of policy-making, and it plays the role of policy-making by way of judicial enforcement, interpretations, and invalidations. The Judiciary Act confers on the Supreme Court the final judicial authority in all matters related to the Constitution. The decisions of the Supreme Court are binding on those of the Presidency, the Congress, state constitutions, state governors, state supreme courts, and all departments and agencies of the government. In Federalist Paper No. 78, Alexander Hamilton states: "It is far more rational to suppose, that the courts were designed to be an intermediate body between the people and the legislature, in order, among other things, to keep the latter within the limits assigned to their authority. The interpretation of law is the proper and peculiar province of the courts." The *Marbury v. Madison* case of 1803 has particularly institutionalized the power of judicial review of the Supreme Court (Schwartz, 1993). In writing the majority opinion in *Marbury v.*

Madison, Chief Justice Marshall wrote: "It is emphatically the province and duty of the Judicial Department [courts] to say what the law is. Those [judges] who apply the rule [law] to particular cases, must of necessity, expound and interpret that rule. If two laws conflict with each other, the Courts must decide on the operation of each" (Legal Information Institute, 2007, p. 14).

The present Supreme Court is composed of nine Justices appointed for life. The Justices, like other federal judges, are nominated by the President, an authority given to the President by the Judiciary Act of 1789. The Presidential nominations are also to be ratified by two- thirds majority the Senate. The judicial philosophy, political views, and ideology of these nine men and women of the Supreme Court have significant impact on crime and justice in America. The Supreme Court does not pass broad enactments like those of the Omnibus Crime Control Act of 1984 or the Violent Crime Control and Law Enforcement Act of 1994. The Supreme Court makes judicial decisions on cases related to constitutional issues. These case-based decisions and legal precedents form the core of the Supreme Court's policy-making that has broad impact on crime and justice. The Supreme Court does not criminalize or decriminalize certain areas for the sake of creating substantive criminal laws. But its constitutional enforcement and interpretations create and expand the body of substantive criminal laws. The Bill of Rights is a document of procedural criminal law. It becomes a living document through the decisions and interpretations given by the Supreme Court.

The judicial scholars and policy analysts often debate whether the Supreme Court ought to be engaged in making public policies. One group of scholars suggests that legal doctrines and principles are universal and that the court is only supposed to make them clear through interpretations. The making of public policy in a democracy is the responsibility primarily of the elected representatives of the people. Another group of scholars suggests that judicial policy-making is an integral part of public policy-making in America. Judicial policy-making is a standard and legitimate function of the modern courts (Feeley & Rubin, 2000). From the perspective of the doctrine of constitutionalism and the constitutional principle of checks and balances, the separation between the judiciary and public policy-making, however, is somewhat misleading. In America, all public policies are to be made and implemented remaining within the framework of the constitution. A given public policy could be very innovative but constitutionality is the basis of its legitimacy, and, hence, the Supreme Court becomes an integral part of policy-making. "The constitution vests the whole power of the United States" wrote Chief Justice Marshall in *Marbury and Madison* in 1803," in one Supreme Court" (Legal Information Institute, 2007, p. 12).

The decisions and the interpretations of the Supreme Court, however, are not based on any universal and immutable laws and principles. They change from time to time and from court to court depending on social and economic changes, prevailing political contexts, ideological perspectives of the court and the Justices, and the general culture. In *Scott v. Sandford in 1857,* for example, the Supreme Court decided that since blacks were not U.S. citizens, they were not entitled to protection by the principles of the Bill of Rights. "A free negro of the African race, whose ancestors were brought to this country and sold as slaves, is not a "citizen" within the meaning of the Constitution of the United States" (Legal Information Institute, 2007, p. 1). The then Chief Justice Roger B. Taney declared that prohibition of slavery was a violation of the Fifth Amendment rights of slave owners. The Thirteenth and the Fourteenth Amendments set aside the *Scott v. Sandford* rulings in 1868.

In Plessy *v. Ferguson* in 1896, the Supreme Court, under the separate but equal doctrine, again ruled along the color lines (Legal Information Institute, 2007). In 1892, Plessy, a mixed-race man, was denied a seat on a train in Louisiana assigned to whites. When he refused to take a seat assigned for colored people, he was forcibly evicted and later convicted for violating the Act of the General Assembly of Louisiana. The U.S. Supreme Court ruled that the Louisiana statute requiring separate interstate rail cars for the white and colored races "neither abridged the privileges or immunities of the colored man, nor deprived him of the equal protection of the laws under the 14th Amendment" (Constitutional Law Center, 2005, p. 2). This "separate but equal" doctrine was the law of the land for sixty-two years until the *Brown v. Board of Education* in 1954 overturned the *Plessy v. Ferguson*. The U.S. Supreme Court in *Brown v. Board of Education* ruled that segregated schools are in violation of the Fourteenth Amendment. These and other landmark decisions show that the Supreme Court decisions change from time to time and court to court depending on social and cultural transformations and the prevailing ideological trajectories of the court and politics.

Judicial policy-making in crime and justice is particularly more responsive to the prevailing modes of culture, politics, and ideology. This is clearly evidenced by judicial decisions rendered by the Rehnquist Court on many issues of crime and justice in recent years. In 1986, the U.S. Supreme Court in the case of *Bowers v. Hardwick*, for example, ruled in favor of the criminalization of oral and anal sex between two consenting adults. The rulings uphold the constitutionality of the Georgia Sodomy Law (Legal Information Institute, 1986). After 17 years, in the case of *Lawrence et al. v. Texas* in 2003, the Supreme Court ruled that sodomy laws are unconstitutional on the basis of privacy rights and equal protection grounds. "The Texas statute making it a crime for two persons of the same sex to engage in certain intimate sexual conduct violates the Due Process Clause" (Legal Information Institute, 2003, p. 1).

In 1988, the Supreme Court, in *Thompson v. Oklahoma*, ruled that death penalty for a juvenile under the age of 16 is a violation of the Eighth Amendment's principle of cruel and unusual punishment. In *Stanford v. Kentucky* in 1989, the Supreme Court reversed the *Thompson* decision. In 2004, in *Roper v. Simmons*, the Supreme Court again reversed the *Stanford* decision and ruled that death penalty for a juvenile under the age of 16 and 17 is a violation of the Eighth Amendment. "The Eighth and Fourteenth Amendments forbid imposition of the death penalty on offenders who were under the age of eighteen when their crimes were committed" (Legal Information Institute, 2004, p. 1). In *Roper v. Simmons*, the majority decision of the Supreme Court (5-4) used the reasoning of the standards of decency about the death penalty for juveniles evolving in American culture.

1.4 State Governors,
Legislatures, and Judiciaries

Along with constitutionalism, decentralization is another fundamental principle of governance in America. One of the unique events in American history is that the federal government was created by the state governments comprising the thirteen colonies (Virginia, Massachusetts, New York, New Jersey, Pennsylvania, Connecticut, Rhode Island, New Hampshire, Delaware, Maryland, North Carolina, South Carolina, and Georgia). The Constitution defines the structures, roles, and the limits of power of the federal and state governments. Through their admissions into a union, the states agreed to surrender some powers, such as the powers to create a military, enter into treaties with foreign countries, and coin money to the federal government. However, the Constitution guarantees the autonomy of the states. Section 4 of Article IV of the Constitution states: "The United States shall guarantee to every State in this union a Republican Form of Government." The Constitution also guarantees to a state full control of its administration of crime and justice. Section 2 of Article IV states: "A person charged in any State with Treason, Felony, or other crime, who shall flee from justice, and be found in another State, shall on demand of the executive Authority of the State from which he fled, be delivered up, to be removed to the State having Jurisdiction of the Crime." The Sixth Amendment of the Bill of Rights also guarantees exclusive jurisdiction of states on the administrations of crime and justice. The Sixth Amendment, as mentioned before, explains: "In all criminal prosecutions, the accused shall enjoy the right to speedy and public trial by an impartial jury of the state and district wherein the crime shall have committed."

Crime and justice is one of the expanding and expensive domains of policy-making in the states. Around the same time in the 1970s when the federal government began to be more involved, states began to be more active in policy-making in crime and justice. During the last three decades, there has been an enormous increase in the policy-making activities of the state governors and legislators. Along with the increase of their prison populations, the crime and justice systems of the states also have rapidly expanded. Today, the states not only comply with federal criminal laws and statues, but also are engaged in a variety of policy innovations in crime and justice. In 2001, the United States spent about $167 billion for justice expenditures including police, corrections, and judicial and legal activities. Out of $167 billion, the states spent about $64 billion. The states in 2000 spent $38.4 billion for corrections, $10 billion for police and $15 billion for judicial and legal activities. Total justice expenditure of the states in 1982 was about $12 billion. In two decades (1980-2001), there was a 446.2 percent increase in expenditures for crime and justice in the states (Bureau of Justice Statistics, 2004, pp. 1-2).

About 2.3 million personnel worked for the nation's justice system in 2001. Out of 2.3 million, about 750,000 worked for the states. In two decades (1982-2001), state employees in the crime and justice sector increased 117 percent, whereas justice employees as a whole during the same period increased about 81 percent (Bureau of Justice Statistics, 2004, p. 1). Out of all sectors, the states have the highest increase in expenditures for corrections. In two decades, correction expenditures increased 534.8 percent—from about $6 billion to 38.4 billion. The state's expenditure for legal and judicial activities during the same period increased 425.6 percent.

Different states have different constitutions, and different structures of the executive, legislative, and judicial branches. Their social and economic contexts are different, crime rates and history are different, and they have governors with different philosophies of crime and justice. There is, however, a considerable amount of uniformity among the states in policy-making in crime and justice, and in their crime and justice systems. The National Governors Association, the Council of State Governments, The National Association of State Legislators, and a variety of other state and regional associations play a significant role in the crime policy-making of the states. Through these state-wide organizations, different states learn about the critical crime policy issues faced by the nation, make concerted response to federal crime policy laws and statutes, and share knowledge and experience of the best-practice models of policy-making in crime and justice.

Crime Policy and the State Governors

In all fifty states today, separate executive departments for governance in crime and justice exist. There are also specialized policy making commissions and task forces within the Offices of the Governors. The role of state governors in crime policy-making, like that of the U.S. President, is vitally important. Governors set the policy agenda, develop crime and justice Executive Orders, and impact on state crime legislations. The general directions of policy-making in crime and justice in the states significantly depend on the political views and ideology of state governors. From 1995, the majority of the state governors have been republicans. In 1995, there were thirty Republican Governors, nineteen Democratic Governors, and one Independent. In 2005, there were also thirty Republican Governors, nineteen Democratic Governors, and one from the Popular Democratic Party in Puerto Rico (National Governors Association, 2004). Since 1995, Democrats have not been the majority among state governors. This political context has considerably influenced the nature, directions, and policy activism in crime and justice in recent decades. Although all governors routinely make crime and justice policies as a part of their administration of law and order, some governors are more actively engaged in policy-making in crime and justice than in others. Some Republican Governors, such as Governor Bush of Florida, Governor Pataki of New York, Governor Perry of Texas, Governor Hunt of North Carolina, former governor George Bush of Texas, and former governor George Allen of the Commonwealth of Virginia made many headlines in recent years as policy activists in crime and justice. As crime policy activists, they put crime control high in their policy agenda, mobilized commissions and task forces, focused on cutting-age crime control issues and technology, signed innovative legislations, and provided a symbolic leadership to be tough on crime.

Crime Policy Activist Governor: John E. "Jeb" Bush of Florida

In Florida, "Since Governor Bush took office, public safety agencies have seen a $361.1 million (11.5%) increase in funding. Governor Bush has funded 3,432 additional prison beds to protect Floridians by incarcerating violent offenders—and state prisoners now serve over 60% of their sentences, up from 43% in 1994" (Florida Department of Law Enforcement, 2001, p. 3). Governor Bush allocated more funds for the war on drugs, criminalized domestic violence by signing the Family Protection Act of 2001, increased funds for juvenile justice by 14 percent, created a central DNA data bank, established the Florida Computer Crime Center, signed a major identity theft legislation, increased pay for correctional and probation officers, and made a new law described as the "Bryant Peney Act." The Bryant Peney Act makes resistance to law enforcement officers with violence a felony crime. Under the Act, a violent criminal will face the death penalty if his or her violent resistance acts result in the death of a police officer. In 2005, Governor Bush signed and made one of the toughest sex crime laws—the Jessica's law—that imposed a mandatory sentencing of twenty five years to life in prison, and enforced the lifetime wearing of satellite tracking devices for repeat violent sex offenders.

Crime Policy Activist Governor: George E. Pataki of New York

In 1994, George E. Pataki became a governor in New York with the promise of becoming tough on crime. Immediately after he took over his office, Governor Pataki legalized the death penalty in New York, a Bill that was vetoed by the two previous administrations of Governor Mario Cuomo. During the last several years, Governor Pataki has enacted tough gun control legislations, increased the penalty for assault crimes, extended the drug war, reformed the sentencing guidelines, ended the statutes of limitations for rape and sexual crimes, abolished parole, and expanded the hate crime laws to include sexual orientation. One of his major policy initiatives has been the prison expansion for housing more violent criminals through such measures as double bunking and double ceiling. Governor Pataki cut and reduced prison education and prison health programs to make more money available for prison beds and space. Under his administration's promise to implement the truth-in-sentencing laws, more violent criminals are serving longer times. In 2004, Governor Pataki, declared a new crime-fighting initiative described as Operation IMPACT (Integrated Municipal Police and Anti-Crime Teams), particularly for high crime cities and neighborhoods. The core idea of this policy strategy is to create rapid deployment crime fighting teams through collaborations among a number of law enforcement agencies and communities such as the state police, Community Narcotics Enforcement Team, Violent Crime Investigation Teams, Violent Felony Warrant Squads, and local police and communities. The core elements of the Operations IMPACT Model includes: active partnership, accurate crime data analysis, intelligence development and sharing, and the development of effective strategies (Office of the Governor of New York, 2004).

Crime Policy Activist Governors: Former Governor George W. Bush and Rick Perry of Texas

In Texas, Governor Perry is continuing the war on crime that was high on the policy agenda of Governor George W. Bush in the 1990s. Governor Bush, during his six years of office in Texas (1994-2000), was a policy activist in crime and justice. His tough approach to crime and justice made headlines in the nations for his support of the death penalty, mandatory sentencing, restrictions on Miranda Rights, the elimination of parole, the two strikes and you're out law, Megan's Law, protection of victim's rights, the lowering of the age of juveniles to be treated as adults to fourteen, the lowering of the legal blood alcohol level from .10 to .08 percent, and more public access to juvenile crime records. Parole approval in Texas under Governor Bush fell from 79 percent in 1990 to 20 percent in 1998 (Reynolds, 2000, p. 12). "Texas had 704 prisoners per 100,000 population in 1999, compared to 290 per 100,000 in 1990, a 143 percent increase in imprisonment. Texas imprisonment rate is 50 percent above the national rate of 468, and second in the nation to Louisiana" (Reynolds, 2000, p. 10). Governor Perry signed a major legislation in 2002 to create a Statewide Texas Amber Alert Network by promulgating an Executive Order (Number RP 16). The Network is created as a cooperative program involving the Office of the Governor, Texas Department of Public Safety, the Texas Department of Transportation, and the Texas Association of Broadcasters. In 2007, Governor Perry signed the Jessica's Law and made it legal to impose a mandatory sentencing of 25 years to life in prison for repeat and violent sex offenders. In the signing ceremony of the Jessica's Law (House Bill B), attended among others by Jessica Lunsford's father, Mark Lunsford, Governor Perry said: "With the signing of the House Bill B, we have sent a clear message that we will not tolerate these heinous crimes in Texas" (StandDown Texas Project, July, 2007, p. 1).

Crime Policy Activist Governor: George Allen and others of Virginia

In the mid-1990s, Governor George Allen, later elected as a U.S. Senator, became one of the major crime policy activists as a Governor in the Commonwealth of Virginia. George Allen became governor in 1993, and crime was at the top of his policy agenda. A few weeks after he became a governor, George Allen set up a commission on Parole Abolition and Sentencing Reform. He also called a special session of the General Assembly to explain his crime control agenda. In his own words: " My administration pushed through legislations, which took effect on January 1, 1995 that will impose penalties for rape, murder, and armed robbery more than twice the national average for those crimes" (Allen, 1995, p. 1). He enacted legislations to abolish parole for felony convictions, reform sentencing guidelines, establish truth-in-sentencing laws, institute three strikes laws, increase penalties for repeat violent offenders, treat violent juveniles as adults, and build more prisons. Governor Allen remarked about his philosophy of crime control in the following words: "Experience vindicates what common sense always told us: the only foolproof crime-prevention technique is incarceration" (Allen, 1995, p. 1).

In 1997, Governor Allen started an innovative program to control gun violence in Virginia—an initiative described as the Project EXILE. The core idea was the federalization of gun control prosecution. The project's goal was to bring all gun related prosecutions from the state to the federal level for maximum penalties. The Project EXILE became a catchword among many governors looking for tougher gun control strategies in the 1990s. In his State of the State Address in 2003, Robert Ehrlich, Governor of Maryland "passionately endorsed Project Exile" for the state of Maryland (Healy, February 12, 2003, p. 1). The Project Exile is currently under experiment in New York, Pennsylvania, and many other states.

When James Gilmore, Governor Allen's Attorney General, became a governor of Virginia in 1997, he promised to continue and expand the achievements of Governor Allen. Governor Gilmore's Anti-Crime Plan contained 21 initiatives including bail reform, DNA samples from out-of-state parolees, stricter penalties for gang related crimes, and laws requiring criminals to pay for their incarcerations. Gilmore (1998) said: "For too long, criminals have imposed too many costs on civil society …. It is time every prisoner be required to pay as much cost of incarceration as he can afford as part of his repayment to society" (p. 1). In Virginia, this innovative initiative is extended also to those who are in juvenile correction centers. Gilmore's policy was that "Even after a criminal is released from jail or prison, he should continue to pay the costs he imposed on society at large. If Virginia recoups only 20 percent of the total costs of incarceration, Virginia taxpayers would save over $140 million each year" (Gilmore, 1998, p. 1)

Governor Mark Warner (2002-2006), who succeeded Governor Gilmore, was not a crime policy activist like Governor Allen and Governor Gilmore. However, he signed some of the toughest DUI laws for the Commonwealth recommended by his Task Force. The new laws imposed increased penalties for drunk driving. A third conviction for drunk driving within five years carries a minimum penalty of 180 days in prison, up from 30 days in previous laws. The new laws made provisions for mandatory sentencing, driving license suspension, and the confiscation of the vehicles of the drivers who have more than three drunken driving convictions within five years (Nuckols, May 28, 2004).

In 2004, Governor Warner signed a Bill protecting fetuses from violent crime modeled after the Unborn Victims of Violent Crime Act signed by President Bush in 2004 (Nuckols, May 22, 2004). Governor Warner also signed a Bill that criminalizes and prohibits same sex marriage in the Commonwealth of Virginia. The law says: "A civil union, partnership contract or other arrangement between persons of the same sex purporting to bestow the privilege or obligations of marriage is prohibited" (Nuckols, May 22, 2004, p. A16). Under this law, any civil union, partnership or marriage between two persons of the same sex who entered into this union in other states "shall be void in all respects in Virginia and any contractual rights created thereby shall be void and unenforceable" (Nuckols, May 22, 2004, p. A16).

Governor Warner, however, made significant policies to return the civil rights of ex-felons. In Virginia, about 310,000 ex-felons are barred from voting rights for life, and more than fifty percent of those are African-Americans. Governor Warner, through an Executive Order restored the voting rights of about 1,108 ex-felons in two years (Hopkins, April 24, 2004). The new law reduced the waiting period to apply for the restoration of voting rights from 5 years to 3 years for nonviolent offenders and from 7 years to 5 years for violent offenders. Governor Warner "restored civil rights to more ex-convicts than any other governor in Virginia's modern history (Hopkins, April 24, 2004, p. A12).

While the activist governors lean more towards punishment and incarceration, non-activist governors look at crime from another perspective—from that of justice, rights, and prevention. In January, 2003, Governor Ryan of Illinois, a Republican Governor, who believes in the deterrent role of death penalty, granted clemency to all 167 death row inmates of Illinois. In 2000, 13 Illinois death row inmates were exonerated on the basis of new DNA evidence. Governor Ryan declared a moratorium on death penalty execution after those inmates were exonerated. He set up a Commission to study and review the Illinois death penalty cases, particularly the possibility of wrongful convictions. The 14 member Illinois Commission, chaired by Federal Judge Frank McGarr, U.S. Senator Paul Simon, and former U.S. Attorney, Thomas Sullivan, made 85 recommendations to reform death penalty and reduce the possibility of wrongful convictions. The Ryan Commission report has been seriously studied both by the federal government and the governors of the states that support death penalty.

Many states are currently experimenting with a variety of policies to reduce recidivism. Governor Rod R. Blagojevich of Illinois has recently developed an innovative program to this end—a program to create more opportunities for the rehabilitation of drug offenders. Governor Blagojevich's program converted the Sheridan Correctional Center as a state facility for the treatment and rehabilitation of drug offenders. In the words of the Governor: "For too long, our state has led the nation in drug crime. Today, we begin our efforts to lead the nation for drug crime prevention" (The Illinois Office of the Governor, January 2, 2004, p. 1). In the Sheridon facility, medium-security level drug offenders receive 6 to 24 months of intensive treatment, counseling, and vocational education. It is a project of incarceration for rehabilitation. Those who worked in the planning of this project believe that it has the potential to become "a national model of substance abuse treatment in corrections" (The Illinois Office of the Governor, January 2, 2004, p. 2).

Apart from these and other policy innovations by individual states, there are also many state-wide collective policy initiatives developed by the governors. The National Governors Association has a Center for Best Practices. Some of the current crime and justice projects of the Center include Governors Criminal Justice Policy Advisors Network, Criminal Justice Information Technology Integration Project, and Prisoner Reentry Policy Academy (National Governors Association, 2004). The Governors Criminal Justice Policy Advisors Network is a body of state policy advisors on crime and justice. Through this advisory network, governors share their knowledge of and experience with critical crime policy issues and crime control models and strategies. "Governors rely on a core of criminal and juvenile justice policy advisors in forming state criminal justice policy, including defining issues, developing strategies, coordinating agencies, engaging communities, and allocating resources" (National Governors Association Center for Best Practices, 2007, p. 1). This Policy advisory Network provides "an opportunity to engage in peer-to-peer discussions and to learn about current criminal justice research and best practice models" (National Governors Association Center For Best Practices, 2007, p. 1).

The goal of the Criminal Justice Information Technology Integration Project of the Center for Best Practices is the integration of information technology in the management of crime and justice in the states. This initiative, taken with the aid of the Office of Justice Programs and the Bureau of Justice Assistance of the Department of Justice, aims to bring together the federal, state, and local law enforcement agencies to improve crime and justice policy through the use of information technology. "The objectives of this project include bringing Governor's staff and policy makers from federal, state, and local governments and criminal justice agencies together to develop statewide plans to implement information technology solutions that integrate law enforcement, corrections, and criminal justice systems" (National Governors Association Center for Best Practices, 2004, p. 2). The Prisoner Reentry Policy Academy is a policy initiative currently of twelve states: Georgia, Indiana, Idaho, Maine, Massachusetts, Michigan, Minnesota, New Jersey, Pennsylvania, Rhode Island, Virginia, and Washington. The Academy brings a team of people from law enforcement and correction agencies of each state for policy innovations in prison reentry initiatives. "The goal of the academy is the development of statewide strategic action plans that coordinate services across agencies and improve reentry outcomes along a number of dimensions" (National Governors Association Center for Best Practices, 2007, p. 1).

Crime Policy and the State Legislators

The state legislators do not usually make national headlines, like those of the state governors, in policy-making in crime and justice. However, they play a vitally important role in the policy-making of the states. Each state has two branches of legislature, and each branch has a number of committees and subcommittees responsible for crime and justice. In Florida, for example, the Senate has a Committee on Criminal Justice, a Committee on Judiciary, and a Senate Appropriations Subcommittee on Criminal Justice. The Florida House of Representatives has a Committee on Public Safety and Crime Prevention that includes three Subcommittees—Subcommittee on Corrections, Subcommittee on Criminal Justice, and Subcommittee on Juvenile Justice. The Texas Senate has a Standing Committees on Criminal Justice and Jurisprudence. In the Texas House, there are five Committees primarily responsible for crime policy—Committee of Corrections, Committee of Criminal Jurisprudence, Committee of Juvenile Justice and Family Issues, the Committee of Judicial Affairs, and the Committee of Law Enforcement.

In the State of New York, crime policy in the Senate is the primary responsibility of three Committees—Committee of Alcoholism and Drug Abuse, Committee of Crime Victims, Crime and Correction, and the Committee of Judiciary. In California, the Senate Committees of Judiciary and Public Safety and the Assembly Committees of Judiciary and Public Safety are mainly concerned with crime policy. The California Assembly also has eight Select Committees that make crime policy: Committee on Cyber Fraud, Committee on Domestic Violence, Committee on Elder Abuse, Committee on Gang Violence and Juvenile Crime, Committee on Gun Violence, Committee on Hate Crimes, Committee on Human Trafficking, and the Committee on Megan's Law.

In the Senate of the Commonwealth of Virginia, there is a Standing Committee of Courts and Justice that has two Subcommittees—Tort Reform Subcommittee and DUI Subcommittee. In the Virginia House of Delegates, crime policy making is the responsibility of the Committee of the Court of Justice and the Committee of Public Safety. The Committee of the Court of Justice has three Subcommittees—Criminal Law, Civil Law, and Judicial Panel. The Public Safety Committee has three Subcommittees—Firearms, Public Safety, and Homeland Security. Although their titles and numbers vary and change from time to time, such committees exist in all states, and they are the centers of state policy activities in crime and justice.

The state legislators, like the National Governors Association, also have a major state-wide policy-making organization—the National Conference of State Legislators (NCSL). The NCSL, created in 1975, has 15 Standing Committees composed of state legislators and legislative staff. The Committees "meet three times each year and allow legislators and staff to benefit from the experience of other states in shaping public policy, experimenting with new laws, and managing the legislative institutions" (National Conference of State Legislatures, 2004, p. 1). One of the important standing committees of the NCSL is the Committee on Law and Criminal Justice. "The many state criminal justice issues under the Committee's jurisdiction include capital punishment, corrections, crime victims, drug crime, juvenile justice, law enforcement, probation and parole, and criminal sentencing" (National Conference of State Legislatures, 2004, p. 1).

One of the trends observed from the current policy activities of the NCSL is that the state legislatures are increasingly focusing on cutting-age issues of crime and justice such as the use of information technology in criminal justice, creation of DNA data banks, creation of inter-governmental information sharing structures, assessment of the impact of the federalization of crime and justice, cyber crime policies, internet pornographic issues, identity theft, counterterrorism strategies, critical infrastructures protection strategies, and the rights of the victims. The traditional issues of drugs, guns, gangs, and juvenile justice are not abandoned, but policy activities are increasingly focusing on some of the more challenging issues in crime and justice. Out of the many critical issues that the NCSL focused on in 2006, two were cutting-age issues—Crime Technology and Information Systems, and Terrorism and Homeland Security. After September 2001, many states such as Georgia, Idaho, North Carolina, Ohio, Oklahoma, South Carolina, Florida, New York, South Dakota, Tennessee, and Utah made laws to extend death penalty for terrorist acts of murder (Lyons, 2003, p. 1). "At least 33 states have passed legislations that amend criminal codes related to acts of terrorism. Some new laws are specific to weapons of mass destruction. North Carolina law makes it a felony punishable by 20 years to life without parole to manufacture, assemble, possess or acquire chemical or biological weapons of mass destruction" (Lyons, 2002, pp. 1-2). Similar laws were enacted in Pennsylvania, Tennessee, Utah, Maine, Connecticut, Maryland, Vermont, and other states.

In the area of information technology and state criminal justice, one of the major projects recently developed in Boca Raton, Florida is described as MATRIX (Multistate Anti-Terrorism Information Exchange) System. "MATRIX allows investigators to share information and query Billions of available state and public records" (National Conference of State Legislatures, 2004, p. 1). Another state-wide information technology project initiated by the National Conference of State Legislatures is the Integrated Justice Information Systems (IJIS). "IJIS uses technology to allow the seamless sharing of information. The information shared includes all criminal justice related data, including photographs, fingerprints, DNA identification records, case records, court calendars, electronic messages and documents" (National Conference of State legislatures, 2007, p. 1).

Important policy innovations by the states are also being made in many micro areas of crime and justice. One of the innovative policies is the policy of baby abandonment. Hundreds of babies are abandoned in non-hospital environments every year. Texas was the first state to make a law in 2000 to decriminalize baby abandonment—a law described as the "Baby Moses" Program. According to the Baby Moses Program, a parent can legally leave a living child in hospitals, police stations, or fire stations. The law was intended to reduce the deserting of unwanted babies in dumpsters, trashcans, and other hiding places. More than half of the states have adopted baby abandonment legislations in recent years.

Crime Policy and the State Judiciaries

Along with state governors and legislatures, state judiciaries, particularly the state supreme courts also play an important role in crime policy. The governors and legislators can make laws but those laws must comply with the principles of the state constitutions. The state lower courts can make judicial decisions on crime and convictions, but they must follow the rules of procedural criminal law. The state supreme court is the highest court of appeal in the state, the maker of the state law, and the highest authority to interpret the state constitution. Its decisions are binding on other courts and throughout the state. It is through this role that the state supreme courts become an integral part of policy-making in crime and justice in the states. In 44 states, the highest state court is called the Supreme Court. In Maine and Massachusetts it is called the Supreme Judicial Court. In Texas and Oklahoma, it is called the Court of Criminal Appeals, and in New York and Maryland, it is described as the Court of Appeals.

The composition, appointment, and tenure of the Supreme Court Justices are not the same in all the states (26 states have seven Justices, 18 states have 5 Justices, 6 states have 9 Justices, and one state—the state of Oklahoma—has 3 Justices). The Justices and the judges of the Supreme Court in 4 states are appointed by the Governors. In 3 states, they are elected by the legislatures. In 25 states, selections are based on merits and professional experience. In 11 states, selections are based on partisan elections. The modes of selection of the state judges and their political affiliations impact on judicial policy-making in crime and justice in many ways.

The impact of the state Supreme Courts in crime policy has recently come at the center of policy debates and discourses in the context of the decriminalization of same-sex marriage by the Supreme Judicial Court in Massachusetts. In February 2004, the Massachusetts's Supreme Judicial Court ruled (4-3) that the state ban on same-sex marriage is unconstitutional. The state ban violated the equal protection and due process principles of the state constitution. With this ruling, the State of Massachusetts became the first state in the nation to legalize and decriminalize same-sex marriage. More importantly, the Massachusetts's ruling has created enormous policy debates not only about the meaning of marriage in culture and religion, but also about the role of judicial policy-making in crime and justice in general. A month after the Massachusetts ruling, the Supreme Court of California ruled against the legalization of same-sex marriage, and blocked the actions of the city of San Francisco that issued 4000 marriage license to gay couples.

1.5 Crime Policy and Local Governments

In America, there are more than 80,000 county governments, and crime and justice is one of their important functions. During the last two decades, the local governments' functions and involvements in crime and justice have significantly increased. In 1982, the direct expenditure of local governments for crime and justice was about $21 billion. In 2004, it increased to about $97 billion. Local governments "spend more on criminal justice than state governments or the federal government" (Bureau of Justice Statistics, 2007, p. 1). In 2004, the total direct expenditure of the federal government for crime and justice was approximately $34 billion, and the total direct expenditure of state governments approached $61 billion. Between 1982 and 2004, the total direct expenditure of local governments for crime and justice functions increased 366 percent (Bureau of Justice Statistics, 2007). In 2004, much of this increase came when local governments employed about 65 percent of all justice employees (about 1.4 million people).

Local governments comprised mainly cities and counties. They have separate governmental structures, executive agencies, legislative councils, and judicial systems. There are about 240 cities with a population of more than 100.000. Each is run by an executive department headed by a Mayor and has an elected legislative branch. In some of the mega-cities with a population of more than a million such as New York (8.5 million), Los Angeles (3.7 million), Chicago (2.9

million), Philadelphia (1.6 million), Houston (2 million), San Diego (1.2 million), and Dallas (1.2 million), the governments are highly organized. Crime control is a vital part of the administration of these cities. The cities not only implement the federal and state crime laws and statutes but also make many innovative policy strategies relevant to their respective people and regions. In the 1990s, New York City, under the leadership of Mayor Juliani and his Police Commissioners, Lee Brown, Raymond Kelly, and William Bratton, for example, created a very effective model of policing for crime control. The New York innovation was the result of a combination of different strategies: community policing, computer mapping of police performance in different precincts, commander accountability, and the control of quality of life violations (Office of New York State Attorney General, 2004). Many cities are now experimenting with the New York model of policing.

The United States Conference of Mayors particularly plays an important role in making innovative crime control strategies for American cities (see Table 6). The United States Conference of Mayors, comprised of Mayors from 1,139 cities, has twelve standing committees, and Crime and Social Justice is one of most important. In 2007, the United States Conference of Mayors in its 75th Winter Meeting in Washington DC developed a 10-point plan described as "Strong Cities, Strong Families for a Strong America." The United States Conference of Mayors (2007) noted that through its 10-point plan "The mayors are calling for a federal fund to provide flexible resources for the deployment of law enforcement personnel, support local innovations, fight domestic violence and fund technology that helps fight crime" (p. 1)

Many innovative crime policies are also made by county governments. There are 3,066 counties in the United States, and 48 of the 50 states have operational county governments. Crime control or the maintenance of law and order is one of the most important tasks of the counties. Cities are located within the counties. County services and administrations are available mostly in areas that are not incorporated into cities. A particular county may have a number of cities such as the County of Los Angeles that has about 9.5 million people. There are, however, many overlapping functions and responsibilities between the cities and counties. The county Policy Chief, the Sheriff, is mainly responsible for the maintenance of law and order. Most of the counties are governed by elected county commissioners, and they have legislative authority to enact regulations and ordinances in all relevant matters including crime and justice.

The National Association of Counties (NACo), established in 1935, is a major national organization for innovative policy-making for the counties. It works both as a think-tank for the counties, and their lobbyist in the Congress. The NACo has 11 standing committees that focus on a variety of issues including crime control and public safety. One of the major policy initiatives recently taken by NACo, and the one that has made an important impact on national policy making, is its series of studies on the abuse of methamphetamine. NACo's study, "The Meth Epidemic in America: The Criminal Effect of Meth on Communities," is based on a survey of 500 county law enforcement officials (Kyle & Hansell, 2005). The study found that the abuse of methamphetamine is the number one drug problem in the American counties. More than 48 percent of the counties reported that the abuse of methamphetamine is the main drug problem—more than cocaine (22 percent), marijuana (22 percent), and heroin (13 percent).

Table 6: Selected Local Government Policy Innovations On Crime Control and Crime Prevention

City/County	Policy Project	Policy Objectives
City of Cleveland	Community-Wide Strategy	Community linkages with the Cleveland Division of Police
El Paso, Texas	Community-Wide Strategy	Community policing focused on prevention
Tucson, Arizona	After School Program For Latchkey Kids	Tutoring, recreation, and prevention education in community-based organizations
Middleburgh, Vermont	Positive Alternatives to Drugs	After school arrangements of job training, athletic contests, theater, puppet shows, and concerts
Cambridge, Massachusetts	Domestic Violence	Development of domestic violence free zones
Burlington, North Carolina	Crime Reporting for Monetary Rewards	Development of a crime tip reward system in collaboration with school administrators; and creation of a separate bank account for the reward money
Silverton, Oregon	Parental Responsibility Laws	City ordinances to make parents accountable for the actions of their children; parenting classes by local government agencies to teach the ordinance
St. Paul, Minnesota	Shaken Baby Awareness	Promoting awareness and prevention of Shaken Baby Syndrome through community-based education curriculum
Little Rock, Arkansas	Teaching Law-Related Education	Teaching law and sanctions to school children with community involvement

Source: Compiled by the Author from materials available from the National Crime Prevention Council. VA: Arlington

Another notable policy innovation of NACo that made national impact is the initiative on non-violent mentally ill inmates in county jails. Under this initiative, which Dallas County Commissioner, Kenneth Mayfield spearheaded in 2003, NACo officials visited a number of model diversion programs in different counties (National Association of Counties, 2003). The Commissioners' report recommended three policy strategies: diversion of the mentally ill offenders to organizations outside the criminal justice system, provision of long-term supervised housing programs for mentally ill offenders upon return to community, and education and training for county law enforcement officers in mental health areas for developing innovative adjudicating processes (National Association of Counties, 2004). This study has been largely responsible for the enactment of the Mentally Ill Offender Treatment and Crime Reduction Act by Congress in 2003. The Act was signed into law by President Bush in 2004. The Act authorized a $50 million federal grant program for the improvement of mental health treatment in county jails and the establishment of mental health courts. There are many similar examples of policy innovations made by both the United States Conference of Mayors and the National Association of Counties for crime control and crime preventions in the cities and counties.

1.6 Crime Policy Agenda: The Contexts of Policy-Making

The process of how a crime Bill becomes a law or how court decisions become a part of crime policy, and who are the key governmental actors in that process is relatively clearly understood. The process of how general concerns are turned into policy issues, and issues are turned into policy agenda, however, is much more complex. It is shaped and influenced by a number of policy issues, policy actors, and policy agencies. Those actors and agencies are like different streams of rivers that flow into an ocean. The process of policy-making "is highly fluid and loosely coupled, various streams—problems, policies, and politics—seem to flow through around the federal government largely independent of one another, and big policy change occurs when the streams join" (Kingdon, 1995, p. xiii). The policy-makers do not make policies in a vacuum. The larger social and cultural contexts shape and impact on policy-making.

Crime, Public Opinion, and the Media

In the last three decades, America's criminal justice system has seen unprecedented growth and expansion. Many factors contributed to this expansion, but the growth in crime has been one of the most important. From the 1970s, all forms of crimes, particularly violent crimes, have been consistently on the rise. In 1960, the violent crime rate was 160.9 per 100,000 population. In 1990, as Table 9 shows, the violent crime rate jumped to 731.8 per 100,000 population. Up to 1997, violent crime has consistently increased. Between 1997 and 2004, there was a declining trend, but violent crime started to increase again from 2005.

Since the 1970s, crime has become an endemic fear in the American mind. Even in the declining days of violent crime in the late 1990s, public fear of crime was high. From 1994 to 2000, public opinion in different surveys rated crime more important than economy for the government to address. Crime also was rated as one of the most important problems facing local communities. In response to a question about the most important problem facing by them, 23 percent of teenagers in 1999 said it was drugs. This response consistently remained high in the surveys of 2000 and 2002. The same type of response was reported when asked about the biggest problem facing public schools. Lack of discipline was cited as a problem more important than lack of financial support. Students between 12-18 years of age think that the biggest fear is school-related victimization. Regarding confidence in the police to protect residents from violent crime in 2002, only about 19 percent expressed a great deal of confidence, and about 39 percent expressed some confidence. In 2002, about 41 percent of people have agreed to have guns in their homes. This figure has remained consistent for the last four decades (Bureau of Justice Statistics, 1995). In 1959, 49 percent agreed to have guns at home. The growth of policy activism in crime and justice at all levels of government in the 1980s and 1990s was related to this escalating rate and fear of crime in America (see Table 7).

Table 7: U.S. Violent Crime Rate per 100, 000 Population, 40 Years Trend: 1960-2000

Country/States	Year	Index	Violent	Murder	Rape
U.S.	1960	1887.2	160.9	5.1	9.6
U.S.	1970	3984.5	363.5	7.9	18.7
U.S.	1980	5950.0	596.6	10.2	36.8
U.S.	1990	5820.3	731.8	9.4	41.2
U.S.	2000	4124.0	506.1	5.5	32.0

Source: The Disaster Center Data Compiled on the basis Uniform Crime Reports, 2004

That crime is the main context of crime policy is also evidenced through the history of some of the recent enactments such as the Jeanne Clery Act of 1990, Megan's Law of 1994, PROTECT Act of 2003 (Amber Alert Law), and the Unborn Victims of Violence Act of 2004. Each of these enactments was preceded by a crime episode that galvanized public opinion, created a new sense of crime fear, led the growth of new advocacy groups, and gave birth to new legislative initiatives. They brought new "windows of opportunity "for policy-makers to push for new legislations.

Jeanne Ann Clery was a freshman student at Lehigh University in Pennsylvania in 1986. She was raped and murdered while asleep in her residence hall on campus. Jeanne's parents later learned that the campus authority did not tell students and parents of Lehigh University that there were 38 major incidences of violent crimes on campus during the preceding three years. Jeanne's parents came up with a noble idea that each and every campus must be legally obligated to publicize their crime status and statistics. They began lobbying the state legislatures of Pennsylvania. In 1988, the Governor of Pennsylvania, Robert Casey signed a new Bill "mandating that all state colleges and universities publish three years' worth of campus crime statistics" (Epstein, 2001, p. 6). In 1990, this became a federal law under the Act of Student Right-to-Know and Campus Security Act signed by President George H. W. Bush. In 1998, President Clinton signed an amended version of the Bill extending more reporting requirements, and the Act was formally named in memory of Jeanne Ann Clery.

Abduction, rape, and murder of children have been a problem of crime and justice in America for a long time. But a crime episode in the state of New Jersey in 1994 has permanently changed the way America will view child sexual exploitation in particular and sex crimes in general in the 21st century. On July 29, 1994, a seven-year old New Jersey girl named Megan Kanka was lured to see a puppy in the house of a thirty-six year old man named Jesse Timendequas, who lived in the same neighborhood. Megan was raped and murdered and Jesse was found guilty and sentenced to death. Megan's parents and neighbors later found that Jesse had two prior child molestation convictions. Megan's parents and neighbors began to lobby for a law to make it mandatory for the states and local governments to notify people when ex-sex offenders move into their communities. The news of Megan's murder saddened the whole nation, media galvanized the news, and policy-makers found another window of opportunity for policy-making.

The Omnibus Violent Crime Control and Law Enforcement Act signed by President Clinton made it legal to create a National Registry of Sex Offenders. Under the new law, it became legally mandatory for a state to create a state-wide sex offender registry. In 1996, President Clinton formally named the legislation Megan's Law in memory of Megan Kanka. In his Weekly Radio Address on June 22, 1996, President Clinton remarked: "Too many children and their families have paid a terrible price because parents didn't know about the dangers hidden in their neighborhood. Megan's law ... will help to prevent more of these terrible crimes (Clinton, June 22, 1996, p. 11).

Closely related to Megan's Law is the Amber Alert Law signed by President George W. Bush in 2003. In 1990, the Department of Justice commissioned a study called the National Incidence Studies of Missing, Abducted, Runaway, and Throwaway Children (NISMART). According to that study, about 114,600 attempts for abduction of children are made every year of which about 4500 are successful. The study also reports that family members abduct about 345,000 children each year due to custody battles. "According to the U.S. Department of Justice, 74 percent of children who were abducted and later found murdered were killed within three hours of being taken" (California Amber Alert, 2000, p. 1). Child abduction, more than any other crime, galvanizes the nation within a very short period of time. The Amber Alert Law made it mandatory for law enforcement agencies to notify public and the media immediately after cases for missing children are reported.

In 1993, Polly Klaas, a twelve-year old, was abducted from her bedroom slumber party in Petaluma, California. The media galvanized the whole nation within an hour. All branches of law enforcement began a search with thousands of volunteers across the state and the nation. Polly was later found raped and murdered by a repeat sex offender named Richard Allen Davis. The law enforcement and the nation sunk into a deep sense of frustration.

Three years later in 1996, a similar episode happened in Arlington, Texas. A nine-year old girl named Amber Hagerman was kidnapped and brutally murdered. The kidnapping of Amber Hagerman, however, brought an innovative idea in the minds of the media and the broadcasters of Dallas Fort-Worth. They teamed up with local law enforcement people to develop an early warning system to help find the missing children (National Center for Missing and Exploited Children, 2003). The new program was named as Amber Alert in memory of Amber Hagerman. By 2003, Amber Alert was adopted in 41 states. In 2003, President Bush made Amber Alert a federal law and a federal program by signing the PROTECT Act. In the signing ceremony of the PROTECT Act in the Rose Garden, present among others were the mothers of Amber Hagerman and Elizabeth Smart and her family from Salt Lake City, Utah. Elizabeth smart—a fifteen-year old—was abducted from her bedroom in June, 2002, and was found alive and apparently unharmed in March 2003. In signing the Bill, President Bush remarked: "With my signature, this new law will formally establish the federal government's role in the Amber Alert system and will make punishment for federal crimes against children more severe" (Bush-Cheney'04, Inc., 2004, p. 1). He further added: "Amber Hagerman, whose mom is with us today—a good Texan, I might add—was nine years old when she was taken away from her parents. We are acting in her memory and in the memory of so many other girls and boys who lost their lives in innocence and acts of cruelty" (Bush-Cheney'04, Inc, 2004, p. 3).

In 2004, with Jeanne Cleary, Megan Kanka, Amber Hagerman, the name of another woman victim is permanently added to the history of the development of crime policy in America. Her name is Laci Peterson. On Christmas Eve in 2002, Laci Peterson, a 27-year old pregnant woman, disappeared from her home in Modesto, California. After four months, the badly decomposed bodies of Laci and her newborn son were found on the shore of San Francisco Bay. Laci Peterson's husband Scott Peterson was charged with double homicide. "More than two dozen states, including California, have adopted "fetal homicide statutes and prosecutors often will seek a double-murder charge when a pregnant woman is killed" (Jennings, 2003, p.1). However, until 2004, there was no relevant federal statute. It is estimated that about 2.1 million women become the victims of violent crime by their intimate partners every year. But neither the Department of Justice nor the Centers for Disease Control and Prevention has any reliable data on pregnant victims of intimate violence and homicide (United States General Accounting Office, 2002).

President Bush's signing of the Unborn Victims of Violence Act in 2004, has permanently changed the way America's criminal justice system will look at the victimization of pregnant women in future. The Act, dedicated in memory of Laci Peterson and her son Conner, is described as the "Laci and Conner Law." In signing the Bill in the East Room of the White House, where Laci Peterson's parents among others were present, President Bush remarked: "This act of Congress addresses tragic losses such as Sharon and Ron have known. They have laid to rest their daughter, Laci, a beautiful young woman who was joyfully waiting the arrival of a new son. They have also laid to rest that child, a boy named Conner" (The White House, 2004, p. 1). The President further added that the name of Conner "is forever joined with that of his mom in this statute, which is also known as Laci and Conner's Law" (The White House, 2004, p. 1). Under the Laci and Conner Law, the victimization of a pregnant woman will be automatically considered a double offense and a federal crime.

These four cases—Megan Kanka, Jeanne Clery, Amber Hagerman, and Laci Paterson that led to four major federal enactments suggest that crime, public opinion, and the media have significant impact on policy-making in crime and justice (Atwell, 2004; Brown, 2003; Gaubatz, 1995) All these cases galvanized public opinion, created a new sense of a national crisis, engulfed a new fear of crime, and mobilized people and resources from all corners of the country. The policy-makers found windows of opportunity for policy-making.

The Role of Policy Advocacy Groups

In addition to the context of crime, media and public opinion, policy-making in crime and justice is also impacted by different non-governmental groups and organizations, particularly by different policy advocacy groups. In any domain of policy-making, numerous think-tanks and advocacy groups debate and discuss different policy enactments. They study the nature, direction, and impact of different policy strategies. They mobilize public opinion and lobby Congress for legislations. Policy think-tanks and advocacy groups, however, are highly diverse. They have divided goals and competing choices and interests. They have diverse ideological preferences, and they represent diverse constituencies (see Table 8).

Table 8: Major Think-Tanks and Advocacy Groups on Crime and Justice Issues

Think-Tanks	Advocacy Groups
Cato Institute	Drug Policy Alternative
Hudson Institute	Hand Gun Control, Inc.
American Enterprise Institute	National Rifle Association
The Brookings Institution	American Bar Association
Heritage Foundation	Criminal Defense Lawyers
National Center For Policy Analysis	American Civil Liberties Union
Rand Drug Research Center	The Sentencing Project
National Crime Prevention Council	Center for Court Innovation
Criminal Justice Policy Foundation	Talk Left
Center For Policy Alternatives	American Society of Criminology
Koch Crime Institute	Criminal Justice Policy Foundation
Vera Institute of Justice	The Sentencing Project
National Center for State Courts	U.S. Justice Fund

Source: Compiled by the Author

In the area of crime and justice, there are groups, for example, who are for the death penalty, and there are groups who oppose the death penalty. Some advocacy groups claim that get-tough strategies work, but others claim that get-tough strategies do not have any significant impact on crime. Some want to protect the rights of the victims, and some advocate for the protection of the offenders' rights. Talk Left, for example, is a liberal crime policy advocacy group. Its analysis and ideas sharply differ from those of the National Center for Policy Analysis—a conservative think-tank. The views of the American Civil Liberties Union on crime and justice are sharply different from those of the Brookings Institution (liberal) or the Heritage Foundation (conservative). But the understanding of the role and perspectives of these diverse think-tanks and advocacy groups is vitally important to gain a critical understanding of the nature and evolution of crime policy (Covington, 1998).

The Context of Science and Crime Policy

The degree to which policy-making is done in the context of science and scientific research is also an intriguing question in policy studies. There are two issues concerning the impact of science on policy-making. One is the nature of the utilization of scientific research in policy-making. The other is the contributions of scientific research in the development of specific policy strategies and interventions. Hardly anyone in policy analysis today seriously believes that policy-making is exclusively a scientific and objective venture—that policy decisions are always based on rigorous and rational analyses of competing strategies (Fischer, 2003). Crime is real and objective. Megan Kanka was raped and killed. Jeanne Clery was raped and killed while asleep in her dorm. Laci Peterson and her son Conner were murdered. These are objective truths. But the policies made to control and contain these crimes are made by human actors and agencies, and they are not immune from their subjective beliefs and values about what is right and what is wrong, what is moral and what is not. Scientific research is used in policy-making, but its instrumental role is limited and uncertain. An enormous amount of research and information is collected and analyzed to make the draft of a Bill and to justify its different provisions and strategies. Science experts are often asked to testify before Congress. Many members of the Presidential Commissions and Task Forces come from the scientific community. But still the role of a specific scientific theory or a particular piece of scientific research in the making of a particular legislation is uncertain and ambiguous (Dunn, 1981; Kingdon,1995; Quade, 1982; Shahidullah, 1998). The policy-makers use science and scientific research mainly for knowledge and enlightenment (Weiss, 1991). Reviews of hundreds of federal policy-makers and policy initiatives have shown that policy-makers use scientific research mainly for conceptual clarification, knowledge of scientific debates, and general intellectual enlightenment.

The role of scientific research in crime and justice systematically began first through the development of the Uniform Crime Reports (UCR) in the 1930s. Today, the UCR, in addition to the National Crime Victimization Survey (NCVS), and the National Incidence-Based Reporting System (NIBRS), is one of the most developed and reliable sources of information on crime data. In recent years, criminological research and the working criminologists with the UCR have greatly improved its methodology of collecting social and psychologically relevant individual-level crime data. On the basis of the UCR, NCVS,

NIBRS and other federal crime surveys "longitudinal study designs have become increasingly prevalent, thereby enabling researchers to investigate the dynamics of criminal behavior to a degree never possible" (Lafree, Bursik, Short, & Taylor, 2000, p. 8).

Almost all crime legislations enacted since the Omnibus Crime Control Act of 1968 emphasized the role of scientific research in policy improvement and made provisions for federal research grants. The 1994 Stop Violence against Women Act, for example, clearly mandated that "The Attorney General shall request the National Academy of Science, through its National Research Council, to enter into contract to develop a research agenda to increase the understanding and control of violence against women, including rape and domestic violence" (Subchapter III, Subpart 2, The Violence against Women Act of 1994). The Act further added that in "furtherance of the contract, the National Academy shall convene a panel of nationally recognized experts on violence against women, in the fields of law, medicine, [and] criminal justice" (Subchapter III, Subpart 2, The Violence Against Women Act of 1994).

During the last three decades, legislations in many areas such as drug and addictions, child abuse, domestic violence, media violence, child pornography, and sex crimes were enacted in the context of many issues raised by scientific research from criminology, sociology, psychology, psychiatry, behavioral neurology, medicine, and public health. The American Society of Pediatrics, for example, in several research studies has shown that abuse has serious negative impact on the development of the brain and behavior of children (De Bellis, 2005). Hundreds of empirical studies concluded that abuse and physical punishment of children are associated with children's aggressive and maladaptive behavior (Hooper, 2003; Kendel, 1992; Kilpatrick, Saunders & Smith, 2003; Mullen & Fleming, 1998; Putnam, 2003;). A large number of studies done by neurologists and brain researchers found that abuse and violence cause inadequate development of the frontal lobe of the brain—the region of the brain that is the center for morality, development, emotion growth, behavioral control, and attachment growth (Shahidullah, 2001). Research has shown that there are positive relations between female criminality and domestic violence, the use of drugs during pregnancy and the birth of under-weight babies with neurological disorders, and school bullying and teen violence. These and many other scientific studies in different ways in recent years set the contexts of bringing many new crimes on the policy agenda, and enacting many new crime legislations.

CHAPTER 2

FEDERALIZATION OF CRIME AND JUSTICE POLICY: HISTORY, TRENDS, AND PROCESSES

2.1 Federalization of Crime and Justice: 1770-1860

Crime and justice in America historically began as a local system. In the thirteen colonies before the birth of the Republic, thirteen different types of crime and justice systems existed depending on the colonies' specific nature of charters received from the British colonial government and their specific nature of economy, demography, politics, and culture. With the birth of the new republic and constitution, a new dual system of crime and justice began. The state is still the primary locus of crime control and justice, but there is also a vastly expanding federal crime and justice system. In fifty states, there are fifty different codes of criminal law. There is also a U.S. Code of criminal law which not only defines the boundaries of federal crime and justice but also significantly impacts on state crime and justice systems. The process of increasing expansion of federal criminal codes and expanding federal control on crime and justice is described as the process of federalization. Federalization in crime and justice has expanded from the 1970s, but its history began with the constitution and the birth of the Bill of Rights.

The Constitutional Doctrine of Federalism

The constitutional power given to Congress and the Presidency, the power of the Supreme Court to enforce and interpret the Bill of Rights, and the Fourteenth Amendment's limits imposed on the power of state and local governments established the roots of federalization in policy-making in crime and justice. One of the three primary principles of the American constitution is federalism. Through the principle or doctrine of federalism, the constitution mandates that national and local governments must share powers, except those on which the Congress, the Presidency and the U.S Supreme Court have exclusive jurisdictions. Section 8 of Article I of the constitution gives Congress a broad range of power in policy-making in all realms of life and activities including crime and justice. Section 8 of Article I also establishes what is described as the commerce clause. The constitution gives Congress the power "To regulate Commerce with foreign Nations, among the several States, and with Indian Tribes." The commerce clause has remained as one of the major constitutional justifications for federal expansion in policy-making crime and justice.

Section 8 of Article I also suggests the need for uniformity in law and justice throughout the United States. "The Congress shall have Power to lay and collect Taxes, Duties, Imposts, and Excises, to pay the Debts and provide for common defense and general welfare of the United States; but all Duties, Imposts and Excises shall be uniform throughout the United States." The constitutional mandate that Congress has the power to make laws for the "general welfare of the United States" creates a vast and undefined scope for federal involvement in crime and justice. During the last two hundred years, relations between the federal and state governments have evolved through different styles and strategies. In the domain of crime and justice, the history of federalization is a history of increased dominance of federal policy-making in crime and justice, and this history is as old as the Bill of Rights. It was through the Bill of Rights that the framers of the constitution laid the foundation of a national system of crime and justice.

The fundamental principles that guide the American system of crime and justice are the principles about the rights of the accused, the limits of power of the government and law enforcement, and the nature and extent of punishment. The principles of the due process of law, the rights of the accused to have a counsel, the limits of police search and seizures, the rights to have a speedy trial by an impartial jury, and checks against cruel and unusual punishment are the pillars of the America's criminal justice system. These principles make the American systems of crime and justice uniquely modern and qualitatively different from those of other countries of the world.

Birth of the Bill of Rights

The fundamental principles of the Bill of Rights were first formulated in the Virginia Declaration of Rights presented at the Virginia Convention in May 1776. Among the prominent architects of the Virginia Declaration of Rights were Edmund Pendleton, Patrick Henry, Archibald Cary, James Madison, Edmund Randolph, and George Mason (Tarter, 1987). The Virginia Declaration of Rights immediately became the basis of the framework of the constitutions of other states. "The Virginia Declaration of Rights stood as the lone beacon to the conventions of other states as they defined their rights and wrote their constitutions" (Tarter, 1987, p. 6).The federal constitution written in Philadelphia in 1787 created a strong central government, but it did not include the Bill of Rights. The new constitution, for many members of the Philadelphia Convention "raised the specter of governmental invasions of the liberties" (Tarter, 1987, p. 7), and George Mason "refused to sign the constitution and returned to Virginia determined to prevent its ratification" (Tarter, 1987, p. 8). James Madison sent a draft of the constitution to Thomas Jefferson who was then in France as the United States Minister in 1787. Jefferson replied to Madison "that a bill of rights is what the people are entitled to against every government on earth" (Jefferson Papers, 12, pp. 440, 556 as quoted in Tarter, 1987, pp. 8-9).

Fifteen years after the passage of Virginia Declaration of Rights, Congress passed the first ten amendments, and Virginia became the last state to ratify the constitution in December 1791. Through the ratification of the Bill of Rights, the Thirteen States gave the power to the federal government to protect and interpret the fundamental principles of law and justice in America. There was a debate in the beginning of the nineteenth century whether the actions of the state and local governments are also to be covered by the Bill of Rights. The Fourteenth Amendment passed in 1868 clearly made the Bill of Rights the supreme document of law and justice in the United States. Section I of the Fourteenth Amendment states: "No state shall make or enforce any law which shall abridge the privileges or immunities of citizens of the United States; nor shall any state deprive any person of life, liberty, or property without due process of law, nor deny to any person within its jurisdiction the equal protection of the laws." The Fourteenth Amendment gives a vast amount power to Congress to regulate the state and local governments with respect to issues related to the U.S. constitution. Section 5 of the Fourteenth Amendment states: "The Congress shall have power to enforce, by appropriate legislation, the provisions of this article."

Founding Fathers and the Concerns
For a Just Society

One of the issues prominent in the minds of the founding fathers and the framers of the constitution was the notion of justice. George Washington, in his first Inaugural Address on April 30, 1789 said that "the foundation of our national policy will be laid in the pure and immutable principles of private morality." Equal justice "ought to watch over this great assemblage of communities and interests." Public good and public prosperity depend on the union between "virtue and happiness; between duty and advantage; between the genuine maxims of an honest and magnanimous policy." A good society and a good administration, said George Washington in his first State of the Union Address on January 8, 1790, must "distinguish between oppression and the necessary exercise of lawful authority." A good government is a government that has "an inviolable respect to the laws."

The concern for law and justice in the new government was more central to the political philosophy of Thomas Jefferson. "Equal and exact justice to all men," said Jefferson in his First Inaugural Address on March 4, 1801, is one of the "essential principles of our Government." Jefferson did not articulate a crime policy in his Inaugural Address, but he pointed to its centrality in policy-making. "A wise and frugal government", in his view, "shall restrain men from injuring one another." The "will of the law," he said again, must be the fundamental basis for the achievement of common good. "All, too, will bear in mind this sacred principle, that though the will of the majority is in all cases to prevail, that will to be rightful must be reasonable; that the minority possess their equal rights, which equal law must protect, and to violate would be oppression." Jefferson described the new nation as "the strongest Government on earth." And it was the strongest because "I believe," he said, "it the only one where every man, at the call of law, would fly to the standard of law, and would meet invasions of the public order as his own personal concern." From the beginning of the republic, the dominant concerns of the founding fathers and the framers of the constitution were not about the governance of a particular region or a particular state of Union. Their main concern was the creation of a federal government structure on the basis of the constitution and the Bill of Rights. Their moral visions and political philosophies defined and described the essence of that governmental structure in the United States of America.

The visions and philosophies of the founding fathers, however, neither created immediately a national criminal justice system nor developed a federal agenda for policy-making in crime and justice. Nineteenth century America was primarily a country of physically loose structured states and localities largely isolated with no highways, electricity, and telecommunications of the kind we know today. In the first half of the nineteenth century, although federal judiciary was expanding and some new enactments were made, crime and justice were primarily a state and local responsibility. The federal government's, particularly the federal judiciary's involvement in crime and justice, was mainly with issues related to the constitution and the Bill of Rights. "There was nothing organized or bureaucratic about any part of the system" of criminal justice (Friedman, 1985, p. 276) in the first half of the nineteenth century. "The criminal justice system was, on the whole, not the professional business as it is today. Almost nobody involved in criminal justice was a full-time expert on the subject" ((Friedman, 1985, p. 286).

The Congress and the Judiciary in the Nineteenth Century

Some of the notable federal enactments of the late 18th and the first half of the 19th centuries related to crime and justice include the Bill of Rights, the Judiciary Act, and the Fugitive Slave Law signed by George Washington (1789-1797), Alien and Sedition Act signed by John Adams (1797-1801), and the criminalization of Slave Trade by Thomas Jefferson (1881-1809). The Judiciary Act enacted in 1789 was the first body of law and policies undertaken by the federal government to create a federal system of crime and justice. The Act established the Department of Justice in 1790. As a central law enforcement agency, the Department of Justice was established "in marked contrast with conditions existing in the individual states or in England from which it has drawn so large a part of its judicial institutions. The development of the department is thus a distinctly American product" (Langeluttig, 1927, p 1).

The Judiciary Act also set up the foundations of the federal judiciary system. It defined the roles and responsibilities of the Attorney General, described the structure of the federal judiciary, specified the qualifications for appointment of the federal judges and attorneys, and set forth the functions of the United States Marshal Service. The Act for Punishment of Certain Crimes against the United States, passed in 1790, further defined and expanded the roles and responsibilities of the U.S. Marshal Service. The U.S. Marshals were the earliest federal law enforcement officers responsible for pursuing federal criminals, putting convicted federal criminal in prisons, and executing federal death sentences.

Some of the landmark decisions of the Supreme Court in the first half of the 19th century came from the cases of *Marbury v. Madison* in 1803 and *Martin v. Hunter's Lessee* in 1816. In a unanimous decision (6-0) in *Marbury v. Madison*, the Marshall Court established the constitutional power of the Supreme Court for Judicial Review of federal enactments. *The Martin v. Hunter' Lessee*, a case related to Lord Fairfax of Virginia, established the Supreme Court's appellate jurisdiction over state courts. This landmark decision established the power of the Supreme Court, on the basis of the constitution and the 'Supremacy Clause," to establish a uniform system of justice throughout the United States.

2.2 Federalization of Crime and Justice: 1860-1930

The Contexts of the Growth of Federal Power

The growth of federal involvement in crime and justice and the expansion of the federal crime and justice system in every stage of American history have been related to prevailing social and economic transformations. The growth in federal power is intimately connected to the growth of social complexity and the progress of modernization. The first phase of modernization in America began in the 1830's, and some of the major forces that shaped the events of that time include territorial expansions, the rise and expansion of a political culture of democracy and nationalism, the rise of social reform movements, the growth of cities and industries, the invention of new technology, the growth in immigrant population, the civil war and the abolition of slavery, and the movement of progressivism. These modernizing processes brought new problems to and challenges for the new nation, and they contributed to the rise of federal power in all domains of governance including crime and justice.

Rise of a National Political Culture

In the political history of the nineteenth century, the Presidency of Andrew Jackson (1829-1837) is particularly remembered. The expansion of the federal political and territorial power and a culture of democracy and nationalism began more intensely during the Presidency of Andrew Jackson. The 1830s was a period of rapid expansion in national political participation. Jackson abolished the property qualification for voting and holding offices, and this expanded a new political culture. He abolished the spoils system that appointed federal bureaucrats on the basis of political patronage. This began the development of a professional federal bureaucracy. Jackson's economic and banking policy, for the first time, brought the federal government to the protection of an open and competitive economy. The 1830s also saw more territorial expansion of the United States in the Pacific regions and the India territories. All these developments created a new trust for the federal government in the minds of the common people. By the 1850s, the federal government was considerably stronger and ready to face the challenges of the issues rising from the emerging social and economic transformations of that time.

Growth in Immigration Population

One of the forces that always created complexities in governance in a society is the nature of demography. The historical creation of America on the basis of immigration has been an American dilemma since the Republic's beginning. In different periods of American history, different groups of immigrants arrived and created different trajectories of power, problems, and possibilities. Each and every generation of immigrants created new social problems, new tensions, new prejudices, and new issues for social and political inclusions. At the time of the first census in 1790, the total population of the United States was 4 million. In 1900, the population increased to 76 million. In the middle of the nineteenth century, about 2 million Irish immigrants, and 1.5 million German immigrants arrived. Even though the Irish and the Germans had many cultural and religious similarities with those of the early settlers, tensions and turbulence existed from the beginning. "The sudden arrival of hundreds of thousands of immigrants from 'heavy drinking' cultures heightened the concerns of temperance reformers" (Martin, Roberts, Mintz, McMurrry, & Jones, 1989, p. 303).

Populist Reform Movements

Populist reform movements began in the 1820s. Some of these movements were moral in nature, and some were social and cultural. Some were based on the principles of the Declaration of Independence, some were inspired by the ideas of religious revivalism, and some drew inspirations from the philosophy of Enlightenment. But all of them demanded political actions. In the 1920s, a vigorous national movement against drinking started in different parts of the country. Drinking was perceived as a moral degradation and the cause of many crimes and violence. The American Society for the Promotion of Temperance was created by a group of clergy and common citizens in 1826. In three years, 222 anti-drinking groups were formed across the country, and by 1835 "membership in temperance organizations had climbed to 1.5 million, and an estimated 2 million Americans had taken the 'pledge' to abstain from hard liquor" (Martin, Roberts, Mintz, McMurry, & Jones, 1989, p. 303). The temperance movement was followed by the birth of the movement for a humanitarian crime policy and prison reforms, the abolition of slavery, women's rights movement, and many movements for the creation of ideal communities. Historically, one of the most decisive of these was the movement for the abolition of slavery that quickly galvanized the nation and eventually led the nation to Civil War.

Economic Transformations and New Federal Power

From the middle of the nineteenth century, America began to move from agriculture to manufacturing economies, particularly in the north. This process was aided by territorial expansion in the pacific regions, the rise of new manufacturing technology, the growth of railways and modern means of communication, the advance of education, and the expansion of foreign trade. The invention of the telegraph by Samuel Morse in 1840, the expansion of railways in the 1860s, and the invention of telephone by Graham Bell in 1876 made remarkable impacts on the growing industrial economy in the late nineteenth century. In 1880, there were only 30 miles of telephone wires in the country. In 1900, these increased to about 2,000 miles, and by 1905 to about 5,780 miles (Bureau of the Census, 1975, p.786). In 1851, railways operated about 11 thousand miles of tracks. By 1870, the total miles operated increased to 52,922. In 1820, the total value of goods exported from America was $84 million. In 1860, the value increased to $438 million. In 1900, the total value of goods exported was more than $1 billion (Bureau of the Census, 1975, p. 865). The expanding industrialization and urbanization not only increased the size and the fiscal capability of the federal government, but also created many new challenges in national policy-making including crime and justice. The growing cities of Boston, Chicago, New York, and Philadelphia gave birth to new slums that became the hotbeds of many new crimes and violence (Adler, 2006; Friedman, 1993; Lane, 1997; 1979).

Civil War and New Federal Power

Historically, the Civil War (1860-1865) is one of the most decisive forces of modernization in America. The Civil War was not just about the abolition of slavery. It was the test of the nation—the federal government—to translate the principles of the Declaration of the Independence and the Bill of Rights into reality. It was the test of the government to uphold and continue to expand the process of building a modern nation that started in 1776. The triumph of the Union army was the triumph of the American experiment. The Emancipation

Proclamation by Abraham Lincoln ended slavery, but it also vastly proved the increased military and political power of the federal government to carry the American experiment. Federal policy-making during the era of Reconstruction greatly expanded in the areas of law and justice. The need for opening new opportunities for millions of emancipated slaves and containing their further dehumanization were the catalysts. Congress established the Freedman's Bureau in 1865, in the form of a modern welfare agency, to help organize emancipated slaves for social and economic inclusion into mainstream society. The Freedman's Bureau established 4,000 public schools to educate the new generation of children of the emancipated parents.

The Impact of Progressivism

In the late 1860s, America entered into a new phase of modernization. Abundant natural resources, expanding frontiers in the Pacific region, the arrival of new immigrants, and a series of technological and organizational innovations in the late nineteenth century led to a rapid growth of the national industrial economy and a rapid expansion of cities and towns both in the North and the South. The Transcontinental Railroad was completed in 1869. In 1879, there began a new era of the expansion of electricity after the invention of incandescent light bulb by Thomas Edison. John D. Rockefeller started the Standard Oil Company in 1881. Andrew Carnegie wrote the *"Gospel of Wealth"* in 1889, and J. P. Morgan founded United States Steel in 1901 (Martin, Roberts, Mintz, McMurry, & Jones, 1989). In 1909, Frederick Taylor wrote the treatise on the *Principles of Scientific Management* that remained as a dominant paradigm of modern corporate management until the 1970s. These social and economic transformations and technological innovations led to the growth of a new ideology of optimism in federal power known as the Progressive Movement in the late nineteenth century.
    Advocates of the Progressive Movement believed that the federal government is the catalyst to bring order to the chaos that came as a result of social and economic changes. From the late nineteenth century, the role that the federal government played in social and economic regulations became prominent. Paid civilian employees of the federal government in 1816 were about 4,837. In 1901, the number increased to 239,476. In Washington D.C. in 1816, there were only 535 paid civilian employees. In 1891, the number increased to 20,834. In 1908, the number of paid employees in Washington DC was 34,647. The number of competitive civil service employees of the federal government in 1884 was 13,780. In 1900, the number civil service employees increased to 94,893 (Bureau of the Census, 1975, pp. 1102-1103). The Interstate Commerce Commission, the first and the most important regulatory commission in U.S. history, was established in 1887. The Bureau of Corporations that later became the Federal Trade Commission, was established in 1903. The Federal Reserve Bank was established in 1913. These developments began to show signs of the advent of a new regulatory state in America (Denson, 2001; King 2007).

The Congress and Crime and Justice, 1860-1930

The regulatory nature of the federal government began to be prominent particularly in the area of crime and justice. The growth of the federal government that started with President Andrew Jackson and became more decisive after the Civil War further widened in the context of the rise of a regulatory state from the late nineteenth century. During the period from 1860 to 1930, Congress made some major enactments that began to bring the federal government increasingly into the realm of crime and justice. Some of the notable enactments of this period include the Thirteenth Amendment which abolished slavery in 1865, the Fourteenth Amendment which extended federal power to the states in 1868, the Fifteenth Amendment which extended civil rights to the emancipated Blacks in 1870, the Comstock Law of 1873, the Sedition Act of 1918, the Eighteenth Amendment of 1919, and the Twenty First Amendment of 1933.

The Thirteenth Amendment:
Criminalization of Slavery

In his 1862 Emancipation Proclamation, Abraham Lincoln declared that all persons held as slaves in the United States shall be forever free. In January 1865, the Congress passed the Thirteenth Amendment to criminalize slavery in the United States. The Thirteenth Amendment describes: "Neither slavery nor involuntary servitude, except as a punishment for crime where of the party shall have been duly convicted, shall exist within the United States, or any place subject to their jurisdiction." The Amendment was accepted with the ratification of 27 out of 36 states in December 1865. New Jersey, Texas, Delaware, and Kentucky ratified after the Amendment was passed. The State of Mississippi rejected the Amendment. The Thirteenth Amendment criminalized slavery and servitude not just of the Blacks but also of people of all races and colors. The Thirteenth Amendment obviously did not immediately solve all problems of racism, law, and justice, but it brought the country to a new turning point from the perspective of the philosophy of the Declaration of Independence.

The Fourteenth Amendment:
Federal v. State Powers

The Fourteenth Amendment passed in 1868 set the boundaries of authority between the states and the federal government, particularly with respect to the application of the Bill of Rights. Section I of the Fourteenth Amendment, as mentioned before, states: "No state shall make or enforce any law which shall abridge the privileges or immunities of citizens of the United States; nor shall any State deprive any person of life, liberty, or property, without due process of law; nor deny to any person within its jurisdiction the equal protection of the laws." The Fourteenth Amendment not only expanded federal power over the general regulation of state activities but also "opened the door to considerable supervision of criminal justice in the states by the federal courts" (Fellman, 1986, p.

516). The Fourteenth Amendment "has become the text upon which most twentieth-century constitutional law is a gloss" (Nelson, 1986, p. 757).

The Fifteenth Amendment and the
Criminalization of Discrimination

Before the Civil War and the ratification of the Thirteenth Amendment, the legal status of Blacks was almost exclusively within the states' jurisdiction. Before the enactment of the civil war legislations, the federal government did not have any significant policy directions for transformations in the social and legal status of the slaves. The Fifteenth Amendment was passed in 1870 to extend civil rights to free and emancipated Blacks. Section I of the Fifteenth Amendment stated: "The right of citizens of the United States to vote shall not be denied or abridged by the United States or by any State on account of race, color, or previous condition of servitude." The Fifteenth Amendment authorized Congress to criminalize discrimination based on race and color by enacting legislations. Between 1865 and 1877, Congress enacted five legislations: Civil Rights Act of 1866, Civil Rights Act of 1870, Force Act of 1871, Civil Rights Act of 1871, and Civil Rights Act of 1875. These enactments criminalized race discrimination, but the crimes of discrimination against Blacks grew and became more vigorous in the later part of the nineteenth century with the development of Black Codes and Jim Crow Laws in different Southern states. In *Plessy v. Ferguson* in 1896, as mentioned in Chapter I, the U.S Supreme Court upheld the segregation of Blacks and Whites in interstate rail travel on the basis of the doctrine of "separate but equal."

During the six successive presidencies from Theodore Roosevelt (1901-1909) to Herbert Hoover (1929-1933), no significant enactments were made to advance the civil rights for the Blacks. Theodore Roosevelt "was openly opposed to civil rights and suffrage for Blacks" (Tafari, 2002, p. 1). President Taft "publicly endorsed the idea that blacks should not participate in politics" (Tafari, 2002, p. 2). Virginian Democrat, Woodrow Wilson deliberately "encouraged the introduction and passage of discriminatory legislations" (Tafari, 2002, p. 3). During the Presidency of Woodrow Wilson, the House of Representatives passed a bill to make "interracial marriage in the District of Columbia a felony" (Tafari, 2002, p. 2). President Hoover "excluded blacks from federal offices and executive departments, and his administration would not allow blacks to work on federal construction jobs" (Tafari, 2002, p. 3).

The second generation of civil rights enactments to criminalize racial discrimination did not emerge until the middle of the 1960s. It took about one hundred years to translate the principles of the Fifteenth Amendment from papers to practice in a substantive and meaningful way, but throughout the century crime and justice policy and the further extension of federal rights remained intimately connected to civil rights issues. There was nothing more fundamental in terms of law and justice in the first half of the twentieth century than the issue of establishing and implementing laws to criminalize discrimination on the basis of race and color.

The Interstate Commerce Act and
Federal Power

After the Fourteenth and the Fifteenth Amendments, one of the significant Acts that remained the basis for justifying the extension of federal power in crime and justice in the whole of the twentieth century was the Interstate Commerce Act signed by President Grover Cleveland. Congress passed the Interstate Commerce Act in 1887. The Act created the Interstate Commerce Commission with power to regulate and control all commercial activities involving two or more state governments, the federal and state governments, the United States and foreign governments, and the state governments and foreign governments. This Act, framed as an extension of the Commerce Clause of the Constitution, opened up a new door for the federal government to regulate not just the fares and rates of the commercial carriers but also activities and behaviors related to the transportation of men, women, and children across the state lines. This brought a number of activities that cross the state lines such as the shipment of illegal drugs, child abduction, carjacking, shipment of pornographic and obscene materials, and terrorism within the definition of federal crime. The Interstate Commerce Act gave the federal government power for the "regulation of virtually any activity, down to the wearing of hats" (Reynolds, 1994, p. 20).

The Sedition Act:
Criminalization of Free Speech

The sedition Act was passed during America's involvement in the First World War. In 1917, the Bolsheviks, under the leadership of Lenin, took over the political power of Russia. The Bolshevik Revolution laid the foundation for the Union of Soviet Socialist Republic (USSR) and started the Cold War. During the First World War, the Wilson administration became concerned about the expansion of communism and left-wing organizations in America. The Espionage Act was passed in 1917 to stop opposition against the draft law. The Sedition Act was passed in 1918 to stop any criticism against the government and America's involvement in the war. The right to criticize the government or the constitution, and to oppose the draft laws and war activities either publicly or privately became a federal crime. Both the Espionage Act and the Sedition Act were repealed in 1921.

The Eighteenth Amendment:
Criminalization of Drinking

A group of young students working with the archaeological program of the University of Virginia recently made a startling discovery in the historic Jamestown about the history of drinking in America. Their excavation discovered a wine cellar complete with unbroken glass and bottles as old as 1680. (Uhde, 2004) Drinking has been a problem in America since the discovery of the New World. The Virginia Colonial Assembly ruled in 1629 that "Ministers shall not give themselves to excess in drinking." The Plymouth Colony prohibited the sale of alcohol in 1633. During the Temperance Movement in the nineteenth century, drinking was seen as a moral violation and a serious social problem. Before 1917, the federal government, however, did not intervene in matters related to drinking and alcoholism.

Congress passed the Eighteenth Amendment in 1917 to criminalize drinking. Thirty-six states ratified the Amendment by 1920. Section I of the Eighteenth Amendment made it a federal crime to manufacture, sell, or transport intoxicating liquors in the United States. On the basis of the Eighteenth Amendment, Congress passed the National Prohibition Act, known as Volstead Act, in 1919. The Act classified all beverages as alcoholic that contained more than .05 percent of alcohol by volume. The Bureau of Internal Revenue was given the power to enforce the Act. The Twenty-First Amendment passed in 1933, however, repealed the National Prohibition Act. Section I of the Twenty-First Amendment states: "The eighteenth article of amendment to the Constitution of the United States is hereby repealed." The Twenty-First Amendment gave the states "virtually complete control" over issues of liquor regulations.

The Lindbergh Law:
Kidnapping as a Federal Crime

Under the Common Law, kidnapping is a misdemeanor. In 1934, Congress made kidnapping, if state lines are crossed, a federal crime through the enactment of the Lindbergh Law. In 1932, an infant son of Charles and Anne Morrow Lindbergh was kidnapped and later brutally murdered. The convicted kidnapper, Bruno Hautmann, was electrocuted on April 3, 1936. The Lindbergh Law is the precursor of the present federal kidnapping statute (Title 18 of the U.S. Code, Section 1201). The present federal statute defines kidnapping as an unlawful seizure, confinement, abduction, and transportation in interstate commerce or foreign commerce of any person below the age of 18.

Landmark Supreme Court Decisions, 1860-1930

During the first half of the nineteenth century, the Supreme Court, under the leadership of Chief Justice John Marshall, vastly expanded the federal power through a series of judicial decisions. "The decisions of Marshall and his colleagues constructed federal supremacy upon so strong a base that it has never since been subject to successful *legal* attack" (Schwartz, 1993, p.133). Federal power during and after the Civil War further increased. During the Civil War, President Lincoln set aside many constitutional principles to conduct and win the war. "On his own authority he suspended the writ of habeas corpus and ordered wholesale arrests without warrants, detentions without trials, and imprisonment without judicial convictions" (Schwartz, 1993, p.127). Lincoln justified his wartime power because it was aimed to save the nation. He said if the nation is not saved, the constitution is disintegrated. "I felt," Lincoln said "that measures, otherwise unconstitutional, might become lawful, by becoming indispensable to the preservation of the constitution, through the preservation of the nation" (Schwartz, 1993, p. 129). During the Civil War "The Supreme Court did little more than passively confirm the measures taken by the government to cope with the Southern rebellion" (as quoted in Schwartz, 1993, p. 130). During the Reconstruction in the second half of the nineteenth century, the Supreme Court's position remained unchanged, and it was aptly summarized in the case of *Texas v. White* in 1869. In that case, the Supreme Court ruled that the "Constitution in all its provisions looks to an indestructible Union" (as quoted in Schwartz, 1993, p.136). During the period from 1860 to 1930, the Supreme Court made three significant rulings in the area of crime and justice. These rulings were made in the cases of *Reynolds v. United States* in 1879, *Weeks v. United States* in 1914, and *Powell v. Alabama* in 1932.

In the case of *Reynolds v. United States,* the Supreme Court ruled that polygamy is a crime in the United States. In 1878, the state of Utah charged George Reynolds, a man who belonged to the Mormon Church, with bigamy in violation of the state laws. He was found guilty by a jury, fined $500, and sentenced to prison for two years. The State Supreme Court affirmed the lower court ruling. The case came to the U.S. Supreme Court on the plea of Reynolds's belief in the Mormon religion that sanctifies polygamy. The Supreme Court upheld the lower court's decision and ruled that it was not a violation of the constitution because religious belief cannot be superior to the "law of the land." In *Weeks v. United States* in 1914, the Supreme Court, in a unanimous decision, declared that a police search without a warrant is a violation of the Fourth Amendment. *In Powell v. Alabama,* in 1932, the Supreme Court overturned the death penalty for seven Black defendants convicted of raping two White women because of the denial of the defendant's right to have a counsel. Through the *Weeks* and *Powell* decisions, the Supreme Court extended the Bill of Rights on criminal procedural laws of the states.

Executive Branch and Crime
and Justice Policy, 1860-1930

Throughout the nineteenth century, the power of the executive branch and the Presidency kept on growing. The end of the Civil War, the end of slavery, engagement in the process of reconstruction, economic expansion, technological growth, the rise of Progressive Movements, new internationalism, and participation in the World War I—all significantly strengthened the power of the executive branch. However, a federal criminal justice system in the sense of an interconnected complex of crime and justice institutions as a part of the executive branch was still in its infancy. In between 1790, when the Department of Justice and the United States Marshal Service were established, and 1909 when the Bureau of Investigation was created, for more than hundred years, there were no major institutional developments for criminal justice within the executive branch of the federal government. There were congressional enactments and judicial decisions on many crime and justice issues, but institutions to exercise power by the executive branch on crime control and investigation were almost non-existent, except the Department of Justice.

Birth of the Federal
Bureau of Investigation

The creation of the Bureau of Investigation in 1909 under the recommendation of President Theodore Roosevelt marked the beginning of a new era in the federalization of crime and justice. The Bureau of Investigation came out of the creation of a force of Special Agents in 1908 under the leadership of then Attorney General Charles Bonaparte. Before the creation of the Corp of Special Agents, the Department of Justice, for more than hundred years, did not have its own investigators. In 1909, the Corp of Special Agents was established as the Bureau of Investigation. In 1932, the Bureau of Investigation was renamed the United States Bureau of Investigation that included a Division of Investigation and the Bureau of Prohibition. The United States Bureau of Investigation was renamed the Federal Bureau of Investigation (FBI) in 1935.

The Bureau of Investigation started with 34 Special Agents in 1909. When Edgar Hoover was appointed as its Director in 1924, the Bureau of Investigation "had approximately 650 employees, including 441 Special Agents who worked in field offices in nine cities. By the end of the decade, there were approximately 30 field offices with Divisional headquarters in New York, Baltimore, Atlanta, Cincinnati, Chicago, Kansas City, San Antonio, San Francisco, and Portland" (Federal Bureau of Investigation, 2004, p. 2). Edgar Hoover started a process of modernization within the FBI from the beginning of his administration, and remained as the key architect to transform this organization as one of the most powerful agencies within the federal criminal justice system. Both President Roosevelt and his Attorney General Charles Bonaparte believed in federal involvement in crime and justice in the spirit of the Progressive Movement. As social complexities began to grow in the context of industrialization and urbanization, crimes of different kinds began to increase. Organized crimes and violent crimes escalated in the 1920s and 1930s. The national homicide rate in 1900 was 1.2 per 100,000 population. In 1910, the rate increased to 4.6. In 1920, it jumped to 6.8, and in 1930 to 8.8 per 100,000 population (Bureau of the Census, 1975, p. 414). Both the public and the federal government soon began to realize that it could be too costly to depend only on the states and localities for the establishment of law and justice. With the creation of the FBI, the federal government took a decisive move to step into the domain of national crime and justice.

Birth of the Uniform Crime Reports (UCR)

Until the 1850s, collection of data on crime and punishment in America was not a policy priority for the Department of Justice. The Bureau of the Census began collecting data on prison populations in 1850. It made the first nationwide collection of criminal statistics in 1926 and continued to do so up to the 1940s (Bureau of the Census, 1975). The creation of the system of Uniform Crime Reporting (UCR) by the International Association of the Chiefs of Police in 1930 brought a remarkable turning point in the collection of national statistics on crime and Justice. In 1930, Congress authorized the FBI to use the UCR and work as the national clearinghouse for the collection of crime data. The FBI has been collecting national crime statistics through the UCR from the beginning of the 1930s. The UCR "is a city, county, and state law enforcement program which provides a nationwide view of crime based on the submission of statistics by law enforcement agencies throughout the country" (Federal Bureau of Investigation, 2004, p. 1). The birth of the UCR, for the first time, made it possible for policy-makers to assess crime growth and trends both in different states and localities and in the nation as a whole.

Birth of Federal Prisons

A prison is an integral part of a criminal justice system. The idea of modern prison is an American innovation in the early nineteenth century. In 1831, Alexis de Tocqueville came to study America's prison innovation on behalf of the government of France. But America's early prison innovations were made mostly by the states. The Walnut Street Jail in Philadelphia, created in 1770, was the first innovation of a modern prison in the New World. The Walnut Street Jail was later turned into a state prison in Pennsylvania. New York created the Newgate state prison in Greenwich Village in 1796. "New Jersey completed its state penitentiary in 1797 and Virginia and Kentucky theirs in 1800. That same year, Massachusetts made an appropriation for the prison at Charlestown, and in short order Vermont, New Hampshire, and Maryland followed suit"(Rothman, 1995, p.115). The federal government did not build any prison before the late nineteenth century because it "housed prisoners convicted of federal crimes in state penitentiaries. In return, the state penitentiaries received boarding fees and were permitted to use the federal prisoners in their prison labor system" (Rotman, 1995, p. 186). It was only in 1891, when federal prison population began to increase, that Congress authorized the construction of federal prisons.

The first federal prison was built in Leavenworth, Kentucky in 1897. The second federal prison was built in Atlanta in 1902. The first federal prison for women was built in Alderson, West Virginia in 1928 (Rotman, 1995). In 1934, Alcatraz was transformed to a federal prison for high-risk federal prisoners. With the rise of federal crime in the late nineteenth and early twentieth centuries, the federal prison population began to grow. In 1885, there were about 1027 federal prisoners. In 1895, the number increased to 2,516 (Rotman, 1995). In 1926, the total number of federal prisoners rose to 6,803. At the end of the year 1930, the number of federal prisoners was 12,181 (Bureau of the Census, 1975, p. 420).

The increase in the federal prison population led to the growth of another federal institution for law and justice—the Federal Bureau of Prisons in 1930. In 1930, the Bureau operated 14 institutions with more than 13,000 federal prisoners. With the creation of the Federal Bureau of Prisons, a process of modernization began in the management of federal correctional institutions and correctional populations. "In 1937, the [Federal] Bureau of Prisons placed all prison employees under the Federal Civil Service, throwing off the last vestiges of political patronage" (Rotman, 1995, p. 187). The creation of the Federal Bureau of Investigation, the innovation and the beginning of the use of the Uniform Crime Reporting, and the birth of the Federal Bureau of Prisons in the first three decades of the twentieth century laid the foundation of a federal criminal justice system under the control of the Department of Justice. In the 1930s, the federal criminal justice system looked vastly different from what it is today. The system was loosely structured, and weakly organized. But it certainly began a new era of federal role in crime and justice that has rapidly grown and expended during the rest of the twentieth century.

2.3 Federalization of Crime and Justice: 1930-1970

From the 1930s, federal involvement in crime and justice policy entered into a new phase of growth and maturation. Many factors and forces shaped that phase of expansion. The first was the rise of urbanization and new crimes. The U.S. population in 1900 was 75 million. In 1930, the U.S. population increased to 123 million, and in 1970 to 203 million. About 250,000 immigrants arrived at the end of the 1930s, and about 374,000 immigrants arrived at the end of the 1970s. Urban populations doubled between 1900 and 1930. In 1900, they comprised 30 million, less than 50 percent of the total population. In 1930, they increased to 69 million. From the 1970s, about 70 percent of the population began to live in towns and cities. Urban populations in the 1970s increased to 150 million (Bureau of the Census, 1975).

The urban growth contributed to the spurt in the U.S. GDP (Gross Domestic Product). In 1900, the total value of U.S. GDP was $18.7 billion (according to 1994 price). In 1930, the GDP increased to $94.4 billion. In 1970, the total value of the GDP was $977.1 billion (Kurian, 1994). The rapid rise in population, the arrival of new immigrants, the growth of cities, the rise of new industrial manufacturing towns, and massive economic growth at the end of the decade of the 1920s brought new hopes for more freedom and prosperity. But new urbanism was also associated with the rise of many new crimes. Except for violent crime and homicide, all forms of crimes increased in the period between 1930 and 1970. The total number non-negligent murders reported in 1937 was 2,479. In 1957, the number increased to 2,533. The total number of rapes reported in 1937 was 3,047. In 1957, it increased to 6,752 (Bureau of the Census, 1975). The rise of new crimes created a new context for federal policy-making in crime and justice. From the beginning of the 1930s, "new forms of crimes called for new administrative organizations and new legislations" (Calder 1993, p. 2).

Herbert Hoover: The Birth of Modern Criminal Justice System

During Herbert Hoover's Presidency (1929-1933), serious policy deliberations began at the top of the administration for the creation of a national system of crime and justice. Hoover "was the first president to assemble a team of practitioners and scholars to comprehensively investigate the conditions under which federal, state, and local governments administered justice" (Calder, 1993, p. 3). In 1929, Hoover appointed, as mentioned in Chapter 1, a National Commission on Law Observance and Enforcement. George W. Wickersham, the former Attorney General under President Taft, chaired the commission. The Wickersham Commission of 1929 was "the first occasion in thirty administrations on which a federal commission was formed to examine comprehensively federal criminal justice" (Calder,1993, p. 77). Hoover was particularly interested in bringing the achievements of social and behavioral science into policy-making for crime and justice. The Commission's advisors "represented, indeed, a who's who of mid-twentieth-century criminologists, lawyers, and social and behavioral scientists. Every academic discipline demonstrating a published concern for crime and justice administration was included in some fashion within the main body of the commission" (Calder, 1993, p. 81). The Commission collected information about the different facets and issues of crime and justice from the field through "state-of- the-art survey research" (Calder, 1993, p. 85).

The Wickersham Commission Report, released in 1931, contained fourteen volumes of information on reforms in crime and justice. One of the major recommendations was to conceptualize justice administration as a system of interconnected and interdependent federal, state, and local justice institutions. The Commission strongly recommended the use of a scientific approach to design and reform the institutions of justice. It particularly recommended federal involvement in gathering crime statistics, and refining and expanding the UCR system in collaboration with state and local law enforcement agencies. The Commission's report on *The Causes of Crime* "marked the coming-of-age of American criminology" (Walker, 1997, p. 3). That report for the first time, after the growth of the classical and positivist schools of criminology in Europe, emphasized the need for a scientific, particularly a social scientific approach, to the study of crime in America. The two-volume reports on *The Causes of Crime* "played a major role in shaping the development of the field of criminology in the United States" (Walker, 1997, p. 3). The Commission report on *Penal Institutions, Probation and Parole* recognized rehabilitation as a model for criminal justice on the basis of the belief that science-based treatments can reform human behavior. The report on *Prosecution* recommended for emphasis on judicial experience, integrity, and professionalism in reforming the judicial system. Herbert Hoover's strong commitment to reform in crime and justice, and the recommendations of the Wickersham Commission did not immediately begin to create a new system. But they certainly brought a new perspective about the federal government's involvement in policy-making for crime and justice.

Johnson Era, 1963-1969: "The Challenge of Crime in a Free Society"

From the presidency of Franklin Roosevelt there began a process of fundamental change in the interventionist nature of the federal government. Franklin Roosevelt, during his twelve years of presidency, created the vision and the structure of a new regulatory state through his policy of New Deal. Based on the theory of Keynesian economics, the Roosevelt's New Deal gave birth to a new regulatory state in America that later expanded in all domains of governance including crime and justice. Harry Truman, Dwight Eisenhower, and John Kennedy further expanded the regulatory role of the federal government in their successive presidencies.

A number of factors and forces contributed to the rise of a new form of interventionist federal government since the presidency of Franklin Roosevelt. Most notable among those are the predicament of "Great Depression," the emergence of America as a nuclear power in the late 1940s in the context of the World War II, the rise of the Cold War in the 1950s, the growth of a variety of social movements, and increase in crime in the 1960s. The 1960s was particularly remarkable for federal involvement in crime and justice. In no period of American history, was the nation engulfed with so many challenges both at home and abroad as it was in the 1960s. When America became deeply entrenched with the Cold War abroad, radical social movements of different kinds and of disparate groups began to spread at home with utmost vigor and intensity. The Civil Rights Movement, the Women's Movement, the Sexual Movement, the New Left, and the Counter Culture began to challenge the traditional institutions of politics, culture, justice, and morality (Farber, 1994). In the 1960s, Crime and violence rapidly spread across the nation. The 1960s saw four major assassinations: John F. Kennedy in 1963, Malcolm X in 1965, Martin Luther King Jr. in 1968, and Robert Kennedy in 1968. The urban murder rate in the beginning of the 1960s was 4.7 per 100,000 populations. In 1970, the rate increased to 8.3 per 100,000 population (Bureau of the Census, 1975, p. 414). The rate of forcible rape in 1960 was 17 per 1,000 population. In 1970, it increased to 38 per 1,000 population (Bureau of the Census, 1975, p. 413). Between 1962 and 1963, the national crime rate increased 9 percent. Between 1958 and 1963, the crime rate increased five times faster than that of population growth. During the same period, street robbery increased 22 percent. In 1963, 400,000 cars worth about $369 million were stolen, and more than two million crimes were reported to law enforcement (Uniform Crime Reports, 1963).

The decade of the 1960s saw the enactment of a number of historical legislations for the expansion of civil and political rights. But it also saw a deep sense of concerns about escalating crime and violence and the problem of general order in society. The new regulatory state from the beginning of the 1960s came face to face with a new challenge of governance in the midst of affluence, diversity, and rising demands for social and political inclusions. Lyndon B. Johnson came to power in 1963 to preside over that period of extraordinary historical change and transformations. When Johnson took over the Presidency in 1963, a culture of fear was looming large in the horizon of the nation. The time was ripe for a President to bring crime control at the top of policy agenda (Braithwaite, 2000).

The Wickersham Commission, set up by Herbert Hoover, presented a blue print of ideas about the architecture of a modern criminal justice system. But the transformation of the Commission's ideas into policy-making did not systematically begin until Lyndon Johnson took over the Presidency. President Johnson, as mentioned in Chapter I, appointed a Commission on Law Enforcement and Administration of Justice in 1964 to recommend to him the measures to overhaul the nation's crime and justice system. The Commission's report *"The Challenge of Crime in a Free Society"* was published in 1967—a year before the assassinations of Martin Luther King Jr. and Robert Kennedy. The Wickersham Commission recommended thinking of crime and justice as a "system." The President's Commission recommended the "systems approach" as a new paradigm for crime and justice administration. In the early 1960s, the nation's law enforcement agencies "for the most part operated independently, with little coordination or over-all crime-fighting strategy" (Gest, 2001, p. 6). The idea behind the systems paradigm, a paradigm that was already dominant in science and organizational thinking in the 1960s, was to conceptualize different elements of federal, state, and local crime and justice—police, court, and corrections—as an interconnected and interdependent totality. The flow chart "A General View of the Criminal Justice System" presented by the Commission "has been reproduced in criminal justice text books more than any other crime graphic ... except perhaps the Uniform Crime Report's time clocks" (Wellford, 1998, p. 1). The Commission discovered "a new idea that has informed our thinking about crime and justice for the last 30 years, the concept of a criminal justice system" (Wellford, 1998, p. 1).

Today's vastly complex system of crime and justice with hundreds of federal, state and local organizations, interconnected through information technologies, owes its origin to this systems paradigm recommended by the President's Commission. The Commission also recommended that reforms in crime and justice must be based on science and scientific research. There was a strong belief among the members of the President's Commission that research-based professional knowledge can greatly improve government's capacity for crime control and justice administration. It was from the days of the President's Commission that criminal justice as a separate field of study began to expand and draw intellectual legitimacy from the domain of academia. Criminal justice emerged as a new field of study "based on law, social science, history, and policy analysis" (Wellford, 1998, p. 4). Like the Wickersham Commission of 1929, the President's Commission of 1965 also recommended that the criminal justice be based on the philosophy of rehabilitation, and the science of criminology be based on the study of the impact of social institutions and the lack of social opportunities and cultural capital in the creation of crime and criminality. As one observer of the President's Commission noted: "A centerpiece of the Commission's agenda was rehabilitation—not the old, 'failed,' medical model based on crime as mental illness, but the newer idea of reintegration based on a view of blocked opportunities for legitimate participation in society" (Clear, 1998, p. 6).

The President's Commission made a number of recommendations about the need for professional education for law enforcement officers, improvement in law enforcement technology, the creation of crime victim's statistics, expansion of community-based correction programs, community involvement in crime-fighting programs, judicial reforms for equal justice and fairness, and investment in social programs to reduce crime. On the basis of some of these recommendations, Congress passed the Omnibus Crime Control and Safe Street Act of 1968.

Omnibus Crime Control and Safe Street Act of 1968

The Omnibus Crime Control and Safe Street Act of 1968 was a turning point in the federalization of crime and justice, particularly with respect to the growth of a comprehensive national system of crime and justice (Stolz, 2002). Through this Act, the federal government established a federal grant-in-aid program to state and local agencies for the improvement of crime fighting strategies. But more importantly, the goal was the creation of an interconnected system of national crime and justice administration (see Table 9). The Act aimed "at improving the capability of government to manage continuing and complex social processes, rather than obtaining specific goals in the pursuit of soluble social problems" (Feeley and Sarat, 1980, p. 5). It created "entirely new agencies and procedures, and in the process generated new organizations and new coalitions to implement objectives" (Feeley and Sarat, 1980, p. 58).

Table 9: Major institutional Developments and Enactments Related to Crime and Justice, 1770–1970

Executive Agencies	Enactments
Department of Justice, 1789	Bill of Rights, 1789-1791
U.S. Marshal Service, 1790	Judiciary Act, 1789
Bureau of Investigation, 1909	Alien and Sedition Act, 1798
Wickersham Commission, 1929	XIV Amendment, 1868
Uniform Crime Report, 1930	XV Amendment, 1870
Federal Bureau of Prisons, 1930	Civil Rights Act, 1875
Bureau of Investigation, 1932	Comstock Law, 1873
FBI, 1935	Interstate Commerce Act, 1887
President's Commission, 1967	Mann Act, 1910
LEAA, 1969	XI Amendment, 1933
State Planning Agencies, 1969	Civil Rights Act, 1964
Regional Planning Units, 1969	Safe Street Act, 1968

Source: Compiled by the Author

Title I of the Safe Street Act created three interconnected sets of administrative and planning structures. As a federal umbrella organization, it created within the Department of Justice a separate organization—the Law Enforcement Assistance Administration (LEAA). The LEAA was entrusted with three major functions: 1) administration of federal grants; 2) advancement of basic and applied research on crime and justice under the newly created National Institute of Law Enforcement and Criminal Justice (NILEC); and 3) provision of technical assistance to the states.

At the state level, the Safe Street Act mandated the creation of State Planning Agencies (SPA). Each state receiving funding under the Act was required to create a state executive agency responsible for the administration of federal crime dollars and to develop a "comprehensive planning" for crime control. The key idea behind the creation of state planning agencies was to expand the federal role in building a national system of crime and justice. The Safe Street Act created a third tier of organization called Regional Planning Units. These units were created to foster local participation in planning for crime control strategies (Feeley & Sarat, 1980). These three organizational tiers went through a series of changes in the subsequent decades, but they signified a notable development in the process of thinking that started with the Wickersham Commission.

From the Wickersham Commission in 1929 to the President's Commission in 1967, the dominant thinking was to create a national system of crime and justice organizationally and professionally competent to address the challenges of increased crime and violence. The idea of a national crime and justice system was born through the recommendations of the Wickersham Commission. The President's Commission presented a blue print of that system. The Omnibus Crime Control and Safe Act of 1968 translated that blue print into action strategies and a set of nationally interconnected organizational structures. By 1970, an incipient system of national crime and justice system was in place to face the challenges of the coming decades. The process of federalization in crime and justice that started from the middle of the 1860s entered into a new phase of maturation in the context of the social economic transformations in the 1970s.

2.4 Federalization of Crime and Justice, 1970–2006

The contemporary history of federalization in crime and justice began from the 1970s. One of the major predicaments of the 1970s was the containment of crime, violence, and social disorder created by the social upheavals of the 1960s. The tasks that were dominant in the minds of the federal government in the 1970s were not only of expanding the boundaries of open society but also controlling its orderly unfolding through the enforcement of law and justice. The expansion of the Cold War and America's involvement in the war in Vietnam and Indo-China at that time made the expansion of federal power in containing domestic crime and violence a compelling and a justifiable necessity.

Crime and violence rapidly escalated in all cities and towns of the country in the 1970s and 1980s. The FBI reported that "In 1970 alone, an estimated 3,000 bombings and 50,000 bomb threats occurred in the United States." A major study on gangs conducted by the Office of Juvenile Justice and Delinquency Prevention (OJJDP) found that between 1970 and 1995, the number of gangs in American cities increased 640 percent, and the number of gangs in the counties increased 867 percent (Office of Juvenile Justice and Delinquency Prevention, 2001, p. 5). From the middle of the 1960s to the end of the 1970s, the homicide rate doubled. In 1980, it peaked to 10.2 per 100,000 population. With a slight decline during the mid-1980s, the homicide rate remained at 9.8 per 100,000 population in 1991.

Growth in Federal Crime Control Bureaucracies, 1970-2004

The federal system of crime and justice in the 1970s included the Department of Justice and its few agencies such as the FBI, Federal Bureau of Prisons, United States Marshals Service, and the Office of the Law Enforcement Assistance Administration created by the Safe Street Act of 1968. In 2006, the system is vastly different, and it includes a vast number of executive departments and agencies that operate a large number of crime control programs with state and local governments. The system is highly differentiated, professionalized, and is based on state-of-the-art information technology. Between 1982 and 2004, the direct justice expenditure of the federal government increased 704 percent. In 2004, the federal government's direct expenditure for criminal and civil justice was more than $34 billion. Between 1982 and 2003, the federal government's intergovernmental justice expenditure increased 2,612 percent. In 1982, the federal government's intergovernmental justice expenditure was about $182 million. In 2003, it rose to about 5,126 million (Bureau of Justice Statistics, 2007). The total number of justice employees between 1982 and 2003 increased 81 percent. The total number of federal justice employees during the same time increased 109 percent (Bureau of Justice Statistics, 2007).

Expansion of the FBI

The growth of federalization in crime and justice from the 1930s is intimately connected with the growth of the FBI. During the five decades of Director J. Edgar Hoover's leadership (1924-1972), and in the context of turbulent social and political transformations of the 1960s and 1970s, the FBI emerged as the leading institution of federal law enforcement. In the 1930s, the FBI was an infant organization without much professional and technological competency. At that time it had less than 500 hundred special agents and approximately 30 field offices, and the agents did not have the power of arrest and the authority to carry firearms. The FBI today is one of the most professionally and technologically competent federal organizations. It has a wide network of 56 major field offices, 400 resident-agencies, 4 technology centers, 1 Academy and Engineering Complex (located in Quantico, Virginia), 1 Fingerprint Identification and Criminal Justice Information Services Center (located in Clarksburg, West Virginia), and more than 45 foreign liaison offices. The FBI currently has jurisdiction over the violations of more than 200 categories of federal law (Federal Bureau of Investigation, 2004).

There has been a rapid evolution in the role and responsibilities of the FBI as the centerpiece of federal law enforcement since the 1930s. Its programs are now divided into four broad categories: Counterterrorism, National Security, Criminal Enterprises/Federal Crimes, and Criminal Justice Services. The FBI is no longer just a domestic crime investigation agency. With the rise of global organized crime and terrorism, and the expansion of international drug trafficking in the 1980s, the FBI has emerged as one of federal government's major agencies for tracking and investigating foreign crimes against the United States. "In 1986, Congress had expanded the FBI jurisdiction to cover terrorist acts against U.S. citizens outside the U.S. boundaries. Later, in 1989, the Department of Justice authorized the FBI to arrest terrorists, drug traffickers, and other fugitives abroad without the consent of the foreign country in which they resided" (Federal Bureau of Investigation, 2004, p. 2).

The federal government's expenditure for the FBI has also been consistently growing. In 2003, the federal budget for FBI's National Security Program was $673 million. In 2005, it reached about 781 million. The Criminal Justice and Federal Crime Control Program of the FBI received $1.7 billion in 2003. In 2005, the Program spent more than $2 billion. The Counterterrorism Program in 2003 received about $1.3 billion. In 2005, the Program's spending reached about $1.5 billion. Between 1993 and 2002, the FBI's budget increased by more than $1.27 billion, and the Bureau added 5,020 new agents, and more than 4,000 new support personnel (Federal Bureau of Investigation, 2004).

Some of the important centers and organizations within the FBI today include The National Center for the Analysis of Violent Crime established in 1984, Computer Analysis and Response Team (CART) created in 1991, Criminal Justice Information Services Division (established in 1992 by incorporating the FBI's Integrated Automated Fingerprint Identification System and the Uniform Crime Reports Program), The International Law Enforcement Academy established in Budapest in 1995, the National DNA Index System (NDIS) created in 1997 for electronic exchange of DNA profiles with state, local and even foreign law enforcement agencies, and the National Infrastructure Protection Center (NIPC) created in 1998 to control the growth of cyber crime.

Growth of the Federal Bureau of Prisons

In 1930, the Federal Bureau of Prisons operated 14 institutions with a prison population of 13,000. In 1970, the federal prison population increased to 20, 686 (see Table 10). In 2004, the Federal Bureau of Prisons operated 104 institutions with about 177,518 inmate populations. These 104 institutions are located throughout the country, and they are divided in terms of different levels of security and described in terms of different correctional goals. The total operating expenses for federal prisons in 2003 was $4 billion. In 2005, it rose to $4.5 billion. Between 1982 and 2003, federal correctional expenditures increased by 925 percent (Bureau of Justice Statistics, 2007).

One of the important organizations created after 1970 related to federal corrections is the National Institute of Corrections (NIC). It was established in 1974 within the Department of Justice. NIC is administered by a Director appointed by the Attorney General. It is primarily a research, training, and consulting organization created with the goal of bringing new knowledge and research into policy-making for corrections. NIC's research, training, and technical assistance programs assist federal, state, and local correction agencies. Currently five divisions exist within the NIC that perform a host of research and training programs: the NIC Academy, the Division of Community Corrections,

Division of Jails, the Prison Division, and Offender Workforce Development Division.

Table 10: Growths in Federal Correctional Population, 1970- 2000

Year	Total Sentenced Population	% Drug Offenders
1970	20,686	16.3
1980	19,023	24.9
1990	46,575	52.2
1995	76,947	60.7
2000	128,090	54.7

Source: Federal Bureau of Prisons, 2004

Growth of the Office of Justice Programs

The Office of Justice Programs was created within the Department of Justice in 1984. It was established as an extension of the Law Enforcement Assistance Administration (LEAA) created by the Safe Street Act of 1968. By the end of the 1970s, federal grants through the LEAA to state agencies more than tripled (see Table 11). This led to the need for a new organization within the Department of Justice for more control and accountability. Various amendments to the Safe Street Act in 1971, 1973, 1974, and 1975 "added new responsibilities to LEAA and SPAs, and each of them has broadened the sphere of participation for law enforcement and criminal justice agencies" (Feeley & Sarat, 1980, p. 60).

Table 11: LEAA Appropriations and Grants to selected State Agencies 1969-1975 (In thousands)

State	1969-71	1972	1973	1974	1975 (1/2)	Total
CA	72,368	60,447	64,390	64,260	57,198	318,663
FL	25,574	19,864	21,287	19,831	22,492	110,048
NY	59,860	53,310	60,823	55,205	57,015	286,153
TX	38,415	33,846	38,553	42,123	35,015	185,952
VA	16,146	12,572	14,508	13,923	13,800	70,949
Total	796,119	698,919	855,587	870,675	895,000	

Source: Crime Control Act of 1976 (PL 94-503)

In 1978, the Carter Administration proposed the creation of a national-level umbrella organization to further organize the three main functions performed by the LEAA—research, statistics, and grant administration. The new structure was named the Office of Justice Assistance. In the mid-1980s, the Reagan Administration extended the Office of Justice Assistance and created a new Office of Justice Programs within the Department of Justice. The Office of Justice Programs is now the main federal agency responsible for planning and directing national research on crime and justice; collection, storage and dissemination of national crime data; the administration of federal grants and justice assistance to state and local agencies; and policy-making in the emerging fields of crime and justice. The Office of Justice Programs includes five bureaus and offices: the Bureau of Justice Assistance (BJA), the Bureau of Justice Statistics (BJS), the National Institute of Justice (NIJ), the Office of Juvenile Justice and Delinquency Prevention (OJJDP), and the Office for Victims of Crime (OVC). The major activities of these bureaus and offices are grouped into six programs of Justice Assistance—Counterterrorism research and development, criminal justice system improvement, technology for crime identification, improvement of the juvenile justice system, substance abuse reduction program, and services for victims of crime. Two of the priority programs in Justice Assistance are criminal justice system improvement and technology for crime identification. The total federal budget for all the programs of Justice Assistance in 2003 was $636 million. In 2005, their total budget rose to about $1.8 billion (Office of Management and Budget, 2004).

Growth in Federal Law Enforcement Personnel

Federal law enforcement agents are located in various federal agencies responsible for crime and justice administration. There is no single department of federal policing except the United States Capitol Police created in 1828, the United States Marshals Service created in 1789, United States Secret Service created in 1865, and the United States Federal Protective Service Police (USFPS) created in 1971 within the General Services Administration. The federal police force is a vast collective body of agents and officers working in different federal agencies. In most federal agencies, such as the FBI, IRS, Customs and Border Protection, Border Patrol, Coast Guard, and Secret Service, they are described as special agents. In some agencies, the special agents are also described as police officers. In other agencies, they have specialized designations such as Deportation Officer at the Immigration and Customs Enforcement Agency, and Diversion Investigator at the DEA.

The Wickersham Commission of 1929 and the President's Commission of 1967 recommended that a modern police force be an integral part of a modern criminal justice system. In the 1970s, the growth of modern policing began with grants from Law Enforcement Assistant Administration (LEAA). From the 1970s, there also began throughout the country a public discourse for police modernization, particularly through the Knapp Commission of 1972 and the Mollen Commission of 1993 created to investigate police corruptions in New York.

Modernization in federal policing began with the establishment of the Federal Law Enforcement Training Center (FLETC) by an enactment of the Congress in 1970. The Center was established within the Department of Treasury as a state-of-the-art national facility to provide training to federal law enforcement agents and officers. FLETC has now four major facilities in the country. Its main facility is in Glynco, Georgia established in 1975 by moving the headquarters from Washington D.C. In 1989, FLETC created its second 2,200-acre campus in Artesia, New Mexico, to facilitate the training of the federal agents working in Western States and with the Department of Indian Affairs. In 1991, under a new enactment (PL 108-7), the third facility was established in Charleston, South Carolina. In 2001, FLETC constructed its fourth facility in Cheltenham, Maryland, for the training of federal agents from Washington D.C. area (Department of Homeland Security, 2003). In 2004, in the context of the war on terror and the new role of the federal government, FLETC was brought under the control of the Department of Homeland Security.

The federal mandate for FLETC is the creation of a cadre of federal agents and law enforcement officers professionally, technologically, culturally, and ethically competent to face the challenges of crime and justice in the 21st century. FLETC was created with a Memorandum of Understanding among 8 federal agencies in the 1970s. Today, FLETC, as an interagency national center, provides training to agents and officers from 75 federal departments and agencies including the United States Congress, Department of Justice, Department of Homeland Security, Department of Defense, Department of State, Department of Treasury, Department of Transportation, Department of Labor, Department of Interior, Central Intelligence Agency, Nuclear Regulatory Commission, United States Postal Service, and the United States Supreme Court. FLETC provides four categories of training: basic, advanced, specialized, and international. The basic training is mandatory for all entry-level federal law enforcement personnel. Advanced trainings are for the professional advancement of junior and senior-level law enforcement personnel. Specialized trainings are related to specific agency functions and are conducted by both FLETC and the related agencies (United States General Accounting Office, 2003). The international trainings are related to the development of technical and organizational expertise to protect the America's homeland from global criminal and terrorist activities. The international trainings are organized by the International Training and Technical Assistance Division (Federal Law Enforcement Training Center, 2006).

During the last two decades of federal expansion in crime and justice administration, FLETC vastly expanded its role and responsibilities. Many federal agencies have completely transferred their law enforcement training operation at FLETC. In 1999, the total budget of FLETC was 110 million. In 2003, it increased to 172 million. In 1999, FLETC trained 25,168 federal and state law enforcement personnel. In 2003, the number of trained personnel increased to 37,693. In 2005, FLETC trained more than 45,774 personnel (United States Department of Homeland Security, 2003). After September 2001, the demand for training from FLETC has rapidly grown. Between 1983 and 2002, the demand for training has grown 267 percent. From 1999 to 2002, the demand for training increased about 72 percent (United States General Accounting Office, 2003).

Federal Crimes and Congressional Enactments

The growth of federal bureaucracy in crime and justice during the last three decades is intimately connected with the growth of the boundary of federal crimes and congressional enactments. The Constitution provides the federal government the power to deal with only a limited number of crimes. Section VIII of the Article I of the Constitution states that the Congress shall have the power to "provide for the Punishment of counterfeiting the Securities and current Coin of the United States", and "define and punish Piracies and Felonies committed on the high Seas and Offenses against the Law of Nations." Section III of the Article III of the Constitution states: "The Congress shall have the power to declare the Punishment of Treason." Between the Judiciary Act of 1789 and the Omnibus Crime Control and Safe Street Act of 1968, the number of federal enactments in crime and justice were very limited. Within a period of 179 years, there were only ten major legislations enacted by Congress that were related to crime and justice. These are, the Alien and Sedition Act of 1798, XV amendment of 1870, Comstock Law of 1873, Interstate Commerce Act of 1887, Mann Act of 1910, the Espionage Act of 1917, the Sedition Act of 1918, XVIII Amendment of 1920, the XXI Amendment of 1933, and the Civil Rights Act of 1964.

The social, political and the cultural landscape of American society in those 179 years, however, did not remain the same. Between the evolutions from a simple agrarian society of the early nineteenth century to a global information economy of the 1970s, the American society has become vastly diverse, dynamic, and complex. In the 1970s, the challenges of crime and justice were quantitatively and qualitatively very different from those of the nineteenth century. These developments vastly impacted on the role of the Congress in matters of crime and justice. From the 1970s and the beginning of war on drugs by the Nixon Presidency, crime and justice have remained at the top of the federal agenda for policy-making. During the last thirty six years, Congress enacted hundreds of crime and justice legislations that criminalized thousands of acts and activities. A debate among criminal justice experts exists about the exact or even the approximate number of acts and behaviors defined as "criminal" by the U.S. criminal code. The American Bar Association's (1998) Task Force report "*The Federalization of Criminal Law*" estimated that about 3,300 criminal statutes exist on the federal books. Another study claims that there "are over 4,000 offenses that carry criminal penalties in the United States Code" (Baker & Bennett, 2004, p. 3).

It is relatively easy to count the number of congressional enactments in the area of crime and justice, but the number of federal crimes contained and defined by those enactments is much more complex. Each statute is divided into number of Titles, and each Title contains a number of Sections and Subsections. One particular statute may criminalize hundreds of acts and behavior. One "statute does not necessarily equal one crime. Often, a single statute contains several crimes" (Baker & Bennett, 2004, p. 4). For example, the U.S. Federal Code 1470 of Title 18 criminalizes the knowing transfer of obscene materials to juveniles. This definition could be drawn from a number of juvenile crime statutes. The U.S. Federal Code 1591 of Title 18 criminalizes sex trafficking of children. This definition is scattered throughout most sex crime statutes.

At the same time, one crime may have multiple definitions. For example, Chapter 96 of Part one of Title 18 provides a definition of racketeering activity.

It is defined in terms of a number of acts and violations. Racketeering means A) any act or threat involving murder, kidnapping, gambling, arson, robbery, bribery extortion, and dealing in obscene matter; B) any act indictable under Section 201 of Title 18 of the United States Code (mail fraud, wire fraud, financial fraud, misuse of passport, fraudulent citizenship papers, welfare fraud, and interstate murder-for-hire etc.); C) any act of embezzlement; D) any act of felonious manufacturing, importation, buying, and selling of controlled substance defined by the Controlled Substance Act; E) any act which is indictable under the Currency and Foreign Transaction Reporting Act; and F) any act which is indictable under the Immigration and Naturalization Act. Thus, the definition of a particular federal crime could be drawn from a number of federal statutes (Baker, 2005).

Title 18 of the U.S. Federal Code defines and describes the list of federal crimes. With the passage of each and every crime and justice enactment and amendment, the numbers of federal crimes are increased, and their definitions and meanings are changed. "The federal statutory law today is set forth in the 50 titles of the United States Code. Those 50 titles encompass roughly 27,000 pages of printed text. Within those 27,000 pages, there are approximately 3,300 separate provisions that carry criminal sanctions for their violation" (as quoted in Baker & Bennett, 2004, p. 13). Title 18 of the U.S. Code contains only about 1,200 criminal provisions, and "the remainder are scattered throughout the other 49 titles" (as quoted in Baker & Bennett, 2004, p. 13).

The American Bar Association's Task Force report claimed that the present body of federal criminal law is so large "that there is no conveniently accessible, complete list of federal crimes" (American Bar Association, 1998, p. 9). This process of the federalization in crime and justice by the Congress has become particularly intensive from the beginning of the 1970s. The number of acts and behavior "now potentially subject to federal criminal control has increased in astonishing proportions in the last few decades" (American Bar Association, 1998, p. 10). The report found that about 5 percent of 3,300 federal crimes were enacted before the 1900. Between 1970 and 1996—in 26 years—Congress enacted about 40 percent of all federal crimes. In the 105th Congress alone 1,000 crime bills were introduced by the end of July 1998 (American Bar Association, 1998).

After the Omnibus Crime Control and Safe Street Act of 1968 (PL 90-351), three comprehensive crime bills were enacted by Congress: the Comprehensive Crime Control Act of 1984 (PL 98-473), the Comprehensive Crime Control Act of 1990 (PL 101-647), and the Violent Crime Control and Law Enforcement Act of 1994 (PL 103-322). They are described as major landmarks in crime legislations because they covered a wide range of topical areas in crime and justice. The move from one comprehensive crime bill to another is essentially an evolutionary process. All comprehensive crime bills contain some new policy areas and new policy innovations. But many old policy provisions are also amended and retained. The change from one comprehensive crime bill to another is a process of policy evolution and policy innovations. With the enactment of each comprehensive crime Act, the process of federalization is enlarged and strengthened.

The Omnibus Crime Control and Safe Street Act of 1968, for example, is a major legacy that has been drawn and amended in almost all subsequent crime legislations. In creating new organizational structures of crime and justice or enacting new strategies of cooperation between federal and state law enforcement agencies, the Act of 1968 is always a major reference because it was in those areas that it made some major policy breakthroughs. The Act of 1968 laid the foundation of a national criminal justice system by institutionally and administratively integrating state and local law enforcement systems with federal crime and justice administration.

In the same way, in the area of sentencing reforms, victim's assistance, and insanity defense, the Crime Control Act of 1984 is always a major reference because it was in those areas that the Act made major policy innovations. One of the major innovations of the Act of 1984 is the creation of the United States Sentencing Commission and the development of mandatory federal sentencing guidelines which most states now follow. The Act of 1984 created the Victims of Crime Act of 1984. Almost all states have policies at present on victim assistance. The Act of 1984 made some major policy innovations on insanity defense. Those innovations now are followed in both state and federal courts. The Bail Reform Act of 1984 and the Comprehensive Forfeiture Act of 1984, in the same way, are enforced in both state and federal courts. Some of the major policy innovations achieved in the Crime Control Act of 1990 include the Victims of Child Abuse Act of 1990 (Title II), Child Protection, Restoration, and Penalties Enhancement Act of 1990 (Title III), Offenses Involving Children Act of 1990 (Title IV), Protection of Crime Victims (Title V), and Drug-Free School Zone (Title XV). Many of these policies became a part of the U.S. Code of Crimes against Children and juvenile justice. The federal Crime Control Act of 1990 and the U.S. Code of Crimes against Children largely impacted the state juvenile crime control policies of the 1990s.

With the enactment of the Violent Crime Control and Law Enforcement Act of 1994, the process of federalization was further intensified. The key policy innovations of the Act of 1994, as mentioned in Chapter I, are community policing, expansion of the federal death penalty to cover about 60 offenses, assault weapons ban, registration of sexually violent offenders (Megan's Law), adult prosecution of juveniles above the age of 13 charged with serious violent crimes, three-strikes law, increased penalties for repeat sex offenders, incentive grants to states to implement truth-in-sentencing laws, construction of new federal prisons, control of violence against women, incentive grants to states to implement the Brady Law, competitive grants to states for drug courts, crime prevention block grants to local governments, and competitive grants to states for the development of police corps. These policy innovations not only vastly expanded the number of federal crimes and the scope of federal justice administration, but they also expanded federal control of state and local crime and justice systems. After the enactment of the Violent Crime Control and Law Enforcement Act of 1994, most of the states enacted relevant crime legislations.

Apart from these landmark crime legislations, Congress during the last three decades also enacted numerous special legislations in the areas of drug policy, juvenile justice, sex crimes, cyber crime, gun control, federal rules of evidence, and improvement of the federal criminal justice system (see Table 12).

Table 12: Major Congressional Enactments in Some Selected Areas of Federal Crime Policy, 1970 –2006

PL	Enactment Title
	Drugs/ Alcohol
PL 91-513	Comprehensive Drug Abuse and Control Act of 1970
PL 91-513	Controlled Substance Act of 1970
PL 98-473	Comprehensive Crime Control Act of 1984
PL99-57	Anti-Drug Abuse Act of 1986
PL 99-570	International Narcotics Control Act of 1986
PL 99-570	National Drug Interdiction Act of 1986
PL100- 690	The Anti-Drug Abuse Act of 1988
PL 103-322	Violent Crime Control and Law Enforcement Act of 1994
PL 108-021	Illicit Anti-Drug Proliferation Act of 2003 (The RAVE Act)
	Juvenile Justice
PL 93-415	JJDP Act of 1974
PL 101-647	Crime Control Act of 1990
PL 103-322	Violent Crime Control and law Enforcement Act of 1994
PL 108-021	PROTECT Act of 2003: Amber Alert
	Sex Crimes
PL 103-322	Jacob Wetterling Act of 1994
PL 104-71	Sex Crimes against Children Prevention Act of 1995
PL 104-145	Megan' s Law—Sex Offender Registration Act of 1996
PL 104-236	Pam Lychner Act of 1996
PL 104-305	Drug-Induced Rape Prevention and Punishment Act of 1996
PL 106-366	Victims of Trafficking and Violence Protection Act of 2000
PL 109-248	Adam Walsh Child Protection and Safety Act of 2006
	Terrorism/Cyber Crime
PL 104-518	Anti-Terrorism and Effective Death Penalty Act of 1996
PL 107-56	USA PATRIOT Act of 2001
PL 104-294	National Information Infrastructure Protection Act of 1996
PL 107-296	Cyber Security Enhancement Act of 2002

Source: Compiled by the Author

One of the recent trends in federalization by Congress is that the federal government is becoming more involved in defining substantive criminal laws. As the American society becomes more global, diverse, and technologically complex, federal crime policies are moving more in the direction of criminalizing new substantive acts and behavior such as cyber crime, child pornography in the Internet, international money laundering, international trafficking of women and children, global terrorism, bio-terrorism, dealing with weapons of mass destructions, hate crime, violence against women, sexual harassment, child abuse, and identity theft. The nature of social change and transformations, the nature and dynamics of crime, and the nature and extent of federalization in crime and justice are intimately connected.

Federalization and the Role of Federal Judiciary

The history of the growth of federalization in crime and justice is the history of the growth of federal crime control bureaucracy and congressional crime enactments. But it is also related to the growth and transformation of federal judiciary. The federal judiciary, as discussed in Chapter I, is an integral part of the federal crime and justice administration and the national criminal justice system. The federal judiciary at present is comprised of 91 District Courts (678 judges), 13 Court of Appeals (including 11 Circuit Courts, one U.S. Court of Appeals for the Federal Circuit, and one U.S. Court of Appeals for the District of Columbia Circuit (179 judges), and one U.S. Supreme Court (9 Justices). The Constitution (Article III) empowers Congress to make laws for the organization and administration of the federal judiciary.

With the growth of social and economic transformations and the problem of crime and justice, the role and the responsibilities of the federal judiciary also changed. The Act of 1891, commonly known as Evans Act, created nine Court of Appeals (U.S. Circuit Courts) with jurisdictions over appeals from the U.S. District Courts. In 1893, the Congress created a Court of Appeals for the District of Columbia Circuit. Congress created the Tenth Circuit Court (Colorado, Kansas, New Mexico, Oklahoma, Utah, and Wyoming) in 1929 and the Eleventh Circuit Court (Alabama, Florida, and Georgia) in 1980. In 1982, the Congress created the U.S. Court of Appeals for the Federal Circuit combining the U.S. Court of Customs and Patent Appeals, and the U.S. Court of Claims.

Three judicial institutions make recommendations to Congress for administration of the federal courts and judicial policy-making. These are the Judicial Conference of the United States created in 1922, the Administrative Office of the U.S. Courts created in 1939, and the Federal Judicial Center created in 1967. The Judicial Conference of the United States is a body of senior circuit judges who advise Congress on matters of policy-making in federal law and justice. The Administrative Office of the U.S. Courts is responsible for budget and personnel management issues. The Judicial Center is responsible for research and the assessment of trends in development of judicial matters. These institutions were created to assure the independence of the federal judiciary from the control of the executive branch and the Congress.

During the last three decades of increased involvement of the federal government in crime and justice, the scope and functions of the federal judiciary have also considerably increased (Administrative Office of the U.S. Courts, 2006). In 1990, there were 168 judges in the U.S. Court of Appeals. In 2005, the number increased to 179. Between 1990 and 2005, the number of senior judges in the U.S. Court of Appeals increased 58.7 percent. The total number of judges in the U.S. District Courts in 1990 was 575. In 2005, the number increased to 678. Between 1990 and 2005, the number of senior judges in the U.S. District Courts increased 45.3 percent. During the same period, the number of fulltime magistrate judges in the U.S. District Courts increased 52.9 percent

The growth of federalization in crime and justice is also evidenced from the growth of criminal caseloads in federal courts. In 1990, a total of 40,893 cases were commenced in the U.S. Court of Appeals (excluding Federal Circuit). In 2005, the number increased to 68,473. In between 1990 and 2005, the number of cases commenced in the U.S. Court of Appeals increased 27.3 percent (Administrative Office of the U.S. Courts, 2006). The 2007 Judicial Business of the United States Courts reports that "Within an historical context, caseloads in the federal courts remain at high level .... Filings of appeals were at an all-time high in 2005 having risen for 11 consecutive years (Administrative Office of the U.S. Courts, 2007, p. 1). The growth of federalization in crime and justice has also lead to a rapid increase of criminal caseloads in the U.S. District Courts. In 1997, a total of 48,418 criminal cases were filed in the U.S. District Courts. In 2006, the number increased to 68,670. Between 1997 and 2006, the number of criminal cases filed in the U.S. District Courts increased 41.8 percent. During the same time, the number of criminal defendants filed in the U.S. District Courts increased 34.2 percent.

What is more important about the advancing trend of federal involvement in crime and justice since the 1970s is the growing trend of increased control of the judiciary by the Congress and the Executive. Since the beginning of the federalization, judicial appointments have become more politicized. Presidents who are tough on crime would like to have judges on the bench who are also tough on crime. The judicial autonomy is particularly challenged by the mandatory sentencing guidelines enacted by Congress. Under the sentencing guidelines, judges do not have much autonomy for judicial discretions. Under the PRO-TECT ACT of 2003, judges have been instructed to minimize the trend of "downward departures" and to justify its reasons in writing. In *Blakely v. Washington* in 2004 and *United States v. Booker* in 2005, the U.S. Supreme Court, for the first time in the twenty years of the history of mandatory sentencing, ruled that mandatory sentencing is in violation of the Sixth Amendment's right to trial by jury. The impact of these landmark decisions on federal mandatory sentencing and in the whole process of federalization in crime and justice remains to be seen.

CHAPTER 3

THE WAR ON DRUGS: EVOLUTION OF THE POLICY OF CRIMINALIZATION

The expansion of federalization in America's crime policy is particularly visible in what is metaphorically called the "war on drugs." During the last three decades, Congress enacted a wide array of legislations, created a large number of organizations, and authorized the spending of billions of dollars both at home and abroad for the war on drugs. More than 30 percent of federal criminal prosecutions at present are related to drug offenses alone. In 1981, the total federal spending on drug control programs was about $1.5 billion. In 2000, federal spending for drug control programs increased to about $18.4 billion. In 2006, the total federal spending for drug control was about $12.5 billion. This chapter will describe the nature and the extent of drug abuse in America, the assumptions behind the policy of criminalization, and the role of different national actors in the making of the drug policy.

3.1 The Nature and Extent of Illicit Drug Abuse in America

Drugs have remained with human societies since the beginning of the Agriculture Revolution and the rise of cities and urban civilizations about ten thousand years ago. Historians and archeologists found traces of drug use in all ancient civilizations—the Egyptians, Sumerians, Chinese, Indians, and the Greeks. During the late middle ages and the time of the expansion of European colonialism, opium and hemp production expanded in all most all the colonies of the old world (Booth, 2004). In the new colony of Virginia in 1619, cultivation of hemp was legally enforced. Throughout the nineteenth and the early part of the twentieth centuries, opium, heroin, morphine, marijuana, and hashish were legally bought and sold in the free market. They were locally produced, manufactured, distributed, marketed, and prescribed by doctors. "The opiates were commonly dispensed in patient medicines until shortly before World War I, and the number of persons in the United States addicted to opiates at the turn of the century was much larger than it is at present" (Clausen, 1963, p. 185). In the early part of the twentieth century "according to the best estimates available, there were between 200,000 and 500,000 opiate addicts in the United States" (Clausen, 1963, p. 187).

Systematic surveys on drug abuse in America did not begin until the 1970s. Even though drugs were used and abused in the past, systematic empirical data on the prevalence and trends of drug abuse across various social and demographic groups and various cities and regions, until recently, were not available. At present, empirical data on drug abuse in America are collected by the Bureau of Justice Statistics of the Department of Justice, White House Office of the National Drug Control Policy (ONDCP), Drug Enforcement Administration (DEA), National Institute on Drug Abuse(NIDA), and hundreds of other drug policy research and advocacy groups. More reliable drug abuse data today are gathered particularly by three organized surveys funded by the federal government: National Youth Risk Behavior Survey (YRBS), Monitoring the Future Survey (MTF), and the National Household Survey on Drug Abuse (NHSDA).

The YRBS is a part of the Youth Risk Behavior Surveillance System (YRBSS)—a project organized by the Centers for Disease Control and Prevention (CDC). The CDC has been conducting this survey of risk behavior among high school students across the country regularly every other year since 1991. The MTF survey is organized and conducted by the University of Michigan's Survey Research Center through grants from the National Institute of Drug Abuse. Since 1975, the MTF annually surveys 50,000 high school students drawn from various regions of America to assess the prevalence of drug use and the values and attitudes that contribute to such behavior.

The NHSDA survey is organized and funded by the Substance Abuse and Mental Health Services Administration of the Department of Health and Human Services. The NHSDA survey, conducted annually since 1971, "is the primary source of statistical information on the use of illegal drugs by the United States population" (Raub, 2000, p. 3). This survey, on the basis of representative samples drawn from a cross section of population of all the 50 states, conducts face-to-face interviews at the interviewees' place of residence. With the aid of computer-assisted survey instruments, the NHSDA has recently been able to increase its sample size to more than 70,000 individuals. These three surveys, funded by the federal government, "provide an unparalleled source of information to monitor and more fully understand trends in substance use and abuse" in America (Raub, 2000, p. 4).

The 2003 National Survey on Drug Use and Health (NSDUH), previously described as NHSDA, estimated that about 19.5 million Americans, or 8.2 percent of the population ages 12 and older, were current users (use of any illicit drug during the past thirty days before the survey) of illicit drugs (United States Department of Health and Human Services, 2003). According to the 2001

NSDUH survey, the estimated number of current users ages 12 and older was 15.9 million. On the basis of these two estimates, one can reasonably suggest that more than 20 million Americans used illicit drugs of some kind in 2006. Out of 19.5 million users in 2003, 14.6 million used marijuana, 2.3 million used cocaine (604,000 of whom used crack), and about 1 million used hallucinogenic drugs of different kinds (LSD, PCP, and MDMA).

Marijuana is the most commonly used illicit drug in America. Out of 19.5 million users of illicit drugs in 2003, about 75.2 percent were reported as current users of marijuana. The use of marijuana is rapidly increasing particularly among the youths. "There were an estimated 2.6 million new marijuana users in 2002. This means that each day an average of 7,000 Americans tried marijuana for the first time. About "two thirds (69 percent) of these new marijuana users were under the age of 18" (United States Department of Health and Human Services, 2003, p. 15). The 2003 NSDUH survey also reported that about 2.1 million Americans ages 12 and older used ecstasy (MDMA) during the past year. About 90 percent of ecstasy users also use other illicit drugs. About 58 percent of 12th graders surveyed said ecstasy is fairly or very easy to obtain. The 2002 NSDUH survey reported that there were more than 12 million people ages 12 and older who used methamphetamine at least once in their life-time. There are thousands of illegal methlabs in the country, particularly in the Western and Midwest states.

During the last three decades, illicit drug use has spread to all ages, genders, classes, races, occupations, and regions. According to the National Institute on Drug Abuse's 2002 Monitoring the Future Survey, 53 percent of high school seniors reported to have used illicit drugs at least once in their lives, 41 percent within the past year, and 25.4 percent within the past month (Office of National Drug Control Policy, 2003). The use of illicit drug is particularly high among youth between 12 and 17 years of age. In the 2003 NHSDA survey, 11.2 percent of youth 12-17 years of age are reported as current users of illicit drugs. The 2002 MTF survey found that 24.5 percent of 8th graders, 44.6 percent of 10th graders, and 53 percent of 12th graders used an illicit drug during their life-time (Office of National Drug Control Policy, 2003).

While males have the higher rate of use of illicit drugs of all kinds, females are also increasingly using them. The illicit drug use is more likely in females who are single, unemployed, divorced, separated or living with an unmarried partner (National Household Survey on Drug Abuse, October, 2004). "Females ages 12 to 17 are more likely than their male peers to report that cocaine, crack, LSD, and heroin were fairly or very easy to obtain" (National Household Survey on Drug Abuse 2001, October, p. 1). Out of about 7,000 Americans who are becoming new marijuana users each day, more than 53 percent are females (United States Department of Health and Human Services, 2003). The use of illicit drugs is also prevalent among pregnant women. The 1999 NHSDA survey found that about 91,000 or 4 percent of pregnant females aged 15 to 44 used illicit drugs including marijuana, hashish, cocaine, crack, heroin, PCP and LSD during their pregnancy (National Household Survey on Drug Abuse, July, 2001). The use of illicit drugs varies across the various racial and ethnic groups. Blacks are more likely to use illicit drugs in general than Whites, Hispanics, and Asians (United States Department of Health and Human Services, 2003). But Whites are more likely than Blacks, Hispanics and Asians to use marijuana, Ecstasy, and other hallucinogenic drugs. "Among youths, Blacks were less likely than Whites, Asians, and Hispanics to have used any hallucinogen in their life time" (National Household Survey on Drug Abuse, August, 2003, p. 1). Of all racial and ethnic groups, the American-Indians had the highest rate of illicit drug use in 2003.

The rate of illicit drug use also varies in terms of educational status, employment, and geographical area. The 2003 NSDUA survey found that high school dropouts are more likely to use drugs than high school graduates. High school graduates who did not enter college are more likely to use drugs than those graduates who did. But in the college-aged population, persons aged 18 to 22 years, education does not seem to have much impact on illicit drug use in any significant way. Unemployed persons are more likely to use illicit drugs, but most drug users in 2003 were employed. "Of 16.7 million illicit drug users aged 18 or older in 2003, 12.4 million (74.3 percent) were employed either full or part time" (United States Department of Health and Human Services, 2003, p. 32). The use of illicit drugs is slightly higher in Western and Northeast states. "Among persons aged 12 and older, the rate of current illicit drug use in 2003 was 9.3 percent in the West, 8.7 percent in the Northeast, 7.9 percent in the Midwest, and 7.4 percent in the South" (United States Department of Health and Human Services, 2003, p. 32). The rate of illicit drug use is also high in big cities and large metropolitan areas.

A recent report from the Office of National Drug Control Policy (2001) estimated that American "spent $67 billion on heroin, cocaine, methamphetamine, marijuana, and other illegal drugs in 2000" (p. 33) The report estimated that between 1989 to 1998, Americans used $65 billion to $108 billion per year for illicit drugs. In drug use estimate, the quantity used is sometimes more important than price estimates because of complexities arising from price fluctuation and inflations. In 2000, the ONDCP report estimated that Americans consumed about 259 metric tons of cocaine, 13.3 metric tons of heroin, 1047 metric tons of marijuana, and 19.7 metric tons of methamphetamine.

The patterns in the use of illicit drugs over the last two decades remained largely consistent. In 1988, Americans used 14.6 metric tons of heroins. In 2000, the amount decreased to only 13.3 metric tons (Office of National Drug Control Policy, 2002). In 1988, the amount of methamphetamine consumed was 22.7 metric tons. In 2000, the amount consumed decreased to only 19.7 metric tons. Some significant changes in patterns are seen in the consumption of cocaine and marijuana. In 1988, the total amount of cocaine consumed was about 660 metric tons. In 2000, the amount of cocaine consumed was about 259 metric tons. But during the same period, the consumption of marijuana significantly increased. In 1988, the total amount of marijuana consumed was about 894 metric tons. In

2000, the amount of marijuana consumed by Americans increased to 1047 metric tons. The United States is still the most attractive and profitable market for the illicit drug traffickers from South America, Europe, Asia, and Africa. "The illegal drug market in the United States is one of the most profitable in the world. As such, it attracts the most ruthless, sophisticated, and aggressive drug traffickers" (United States Drug Enforcement Administration, 2005, p. 1).

3.2 Criminalization of Illicit Drugs: The Policy Assumptions

The number of illicit drugs is more than the numbers mentioned above, and the extent of illicit drug use is much wider than we can comprehend from the numbers presented. The U.S. Code (Title 21, Section 812, Chapter 13, Subchapter 1, and Part B) classified hundreds of synthetic and non-synthetic drugs, described as controlled substances, into five categories or schedules ((see Table 13).

Table 13: Drug Policy: Schedules of Controlled Substances

Schedules	Criteria for Inclusion in the Schedules	Examples of Controlled Substances
Schedule I	Potential for high abuse No accepted medical use Lack of safety	Heroin, Marijuana Morphine, MDMA, PCP and MDA
Schedule II	High potential for abuse Restricted medical use Highly addictive	Opium extracts, Opium poppy, Powdered opium, Cocaine, Poppy Straw, and Methamphetamine
Schedule III	Accepted medical use Psychologically addictive	Anabolic steroids, Codeine, Testosterone, and Lysergic acid
Schedule IV	Potential for low abuse Accepted medical use Limited dependence	Xanax, Valium, Cathine, and Barbital
Schedule V	Potential for limited abuse Accepted medical use Low dependence	Codeine preparations, Opium preparations, and Difenoxin preparations

Source: U.S. Code (Title 21, Section 812, Chapter 13, Part B)

These schedules are not defined once and for all. Congress authorizes the Attorney General of the United States to revise and refine these schedules and their various provisions annually on the basis of new research and new issues of enforcement of the drug policy. As Section 812 of Title 21 of the U.S. Code describes: "There are established five schedules I, II, III, IV, and V. Such schedules shall initially consist of the substances listed in this section. The schedules established by this section shall be updated and republished ... on an annual basis." These schedules of illicit drugs and the punishment they carry for violations have evolved in the context of a series of legislations enacted by Congress since the beginning of the drug war in the 1970s.

The core of U.S. drug policy is the notion of criminalization. Drug policy is not merely a regulatory policy. It is a policy that centers in the notion of crime and punishment. Although there are provisions for drug education, treatment, and prevention in the policy package, its dominant paradigm is criminalization. Section 841 of Title 21 of the U.S. Code describes a complex array of actions and activities related to the drugs contained in the five schedules as unlawful, and hence, punishable by law. Subchapter I on Control and Enforcement of Section 844 of Title 21 of the U.S. Code details that "It shall be unlawful for any person knowingly or intentionally to possess a controlled substance." According to Subchapter 1, drug offense—chemical or narcotic—means "any offense which proscribes the possession, distribution, manufacture, cultivation, sale, transfer or attempt or conspiracy to possess, distribute, manufacture, cultivate, sell or transfer any substance the possession of which is prohibited under this subchapter."

As there are different categories of illicit drugs, there are also different categories of penalties and punishments, as shown in Table 14, depending on the nature of violations. Particularly significant are the mandatory sentencing guidelines developed during the last two decades by the United States Sentencing Commission under the directives of various Congressional enactments. In addition to fines and mandatory prison terms, as sections 853 and 881 of Title 21 of the U.S Code narrate, real estate properties, vehicles, boats, and aircrafts of those who violate drug laws can be forfeited. Section 862 of the U.S. Code describes that different federal benefits, such as student loans, grants, welfare benefits, housing benefits, and professional and commercial licenses can be denied to the violators of drug laws.

The Consequentialist Argument

The notion of criminalization is one of the most contentious and contested aspects of U.S. drug policy. A number of ideas and assumptions lie behind the model of criminalization. Some of these are scientifically grounded, and some are philosophical, ideological or moral in nature. One of the key assumptions is about the consequences of drug use (MacCoun & Reuter, 2001). There is a wide consensus among the policy-makers that drug use has multifaceted negative impacts on society, and this justifies the criminalization of drugs. Illicit drugs are physiologically damaging and individually and psychologically harmful. The use and the spread of illicit drugs are socially destructive and globally disruptive. A large number of studies from a variety of scientific fields, such as brain research, neurology, endocrinology, psychology, sociology, and criminal justice support this view about the negative consequences of drugs on society. Scientists have found that heroin, cocaine, marijuana, methamphetamine, PCP, MDMA and other hallucinogenic drugs can significantly impair the functions of the brain and memory by altering the brain waves, changing the functions of the brain cells, limiting the functions of brain chemistry, and recasting the role of the brain's neurotransmitters. "In fact, through the use modern imaging techniques, we now have direct evidence in humans to support the voluminous animal literature showing a decrease in a structural component of serotonergic or brain 5-HT neurons in human MDMA users" (Leshner, 2000, p. 1).

Table 14: Mandatory Sentencing Guidelines for Some Selected Drugs in the five Schedules

Drugs/ Schedule	Quantity	1st Conviction (Prison and Fines)	2nd Conviction (Prison and Fines)
Cocaine Schedule II	500- 4999g mixture	5 - 40 years 20 to life in case of death $2 Million	10 years to life $ 4 Million
Crack Schedule II	5 grams	5 – 20 years Up to $250,000	For 3 grams 5-20 years Fines up to $250,000
Cocaine Schedule II	5–100kg or more mixture	10 to life in prison If death, 20-life in prison $4 Million	20 to life If death, mandatory life
Heroin Schedule I	100-999g mixture	5 - 40 years 20 to life in case of death $2 Million	10 to life in prison If death, mandatory life
Heroin Schedule Schedule I	1kg or more mixture	10 to life in prison If death, 20-life in prison $4 Million	20 to life in prison If death, mandatory life $8 Million
Methamphetamine Schedule II	5-49g pure or 50-499g Mixture	5 to 40 years in prison If death, 20-life in prison $2 Million	10 to life in prison If death, mandatory life $4 Million
Methamphetamine Schedule II	50g- more pure	10 to life in prison If death, 20-life in prison $ 4 Million	20 to life in prison If death, mandatory life $8 Million
Marijuana Schedule I	1,000– more kg mixture	10 years to life If death, 20-life in prison $ 4 Million	20 years to life If death, mandatory life $8 Million

Source: U.S. Drug Enforcement Administration, 2005. www.dea.gov

Scientists have found that MDMA alters the normal supply and functions of serotonin — the neuron that regulates human mood, emotion, sleep, and behavior. In the brain, MDMA increases the "activity levels of at least three neurotransmitters: serotonin, dopamine, and norepinephrine. Much like the way amphetamines works, MDMA causes these neurotransmitters to be released from their storage sites in neurons resulting in increased brain activity" (Hanson, 2001, p. 2). Scientists working on fetal drug exposure now believe that human fetal liver and placenta, in contrast to sub-primate animals in general, develop drug-metabolizing enzyme activities during gestational maturation. Drug use can impair the normal growth of these activities (Chiang & Lee, 1985).

Research in modern psychology and psychiatry has found that drug use is related to depression, anxiety, aggressive behavior, addiction, sexual dysfunctions, and depressed cognitive functions. The relationships between marijuana and depression and suicidal behaviors are well established. "Longitudinal research conducted in the United States, Australia, and New Zealand has provided evidence of a connection between marijuana and depression. One 16-year study showed that individuals who were not depressed and then used marijuana were four times more likely to be depressed at follow-up. There is particularly a strong relationship between marijuana and schizophrenia" (Office of National Drug Control Policy, 2005, p. 1). According to a major recent study on the relationship between violence and substance abuse the "most general conclusion is that prevalence of the overlap between substance abuse and relationship violence is generally high" (Wekerle & Wall, 2002, p. 1-2).

The criminalization policy regarding drugs is particularly based on the understanding that they are also socially devastating. Illicit drug use is related to crime and violence. It seriously affects marriage, family, work, and education. It is economically harmful, and it leads to the transmission of serious infectious diseases such as AIDS, hepatitis B, and tuberculosis. All of those who use illicit drugs do not commit crime, and all are not offenders. But a substantial number of crimes are committed because of the use of drugs. Chronic use of drugs leads to addiction by changing the functions of the brain and endocrinology. Addiction lowers the capacity to understand the boundaries of right and wrong, legal and illegal, and moral and immoral. Many serious crimes of violence are committed under the influence of drugs. Addiction also leads to many economic crimes because it creates a sense of physiological and psychological desperation to have drugs at any cost. Addiction and economic desperation, in turn, create a life style that reinforces criminal behavior—a life style of participation in gangs, organized crimes, drug trafficking, prostitution, and gambling.

Research conducted by the National Survey on Drug Use and Health finds that in 2002 "the percentage of youths engaging in delinquent behavior was higher among past year marijuana users than among those who had not used marijuana. For all six categories of the delinquent behaviors examined, the percent of youths engaging in the behavior rose with increasing frequency of past year marijuana use" (National Survey on Drug Use and Health, 2004, p. 2). Links between youth violence and illicit drug use are found to be strong not just in the use of marijuana, but also in cases of the use of cocaine, crack, heroin, LSD, PCP, and other hallucinogenic drugs (National Household Survey on Drug Abuse, November, 2001).

The ADAM Program (The Arrestee Drug Abuse Monitoring Program) of the National Institute of Justice, every year, monitors the patterns of crime and drug connections by surveying, on the basis of personal interviews and urine analysis, the extent of drug use among the arrestees in 35 major sites from different states in the U.S. The urine analysis of the report of 2003 shows that about 67 percent (median) of adult males and 68 percent (median) of adult females arrestees tested positive for the use of any or multiple drugs or alcohol. Among the male arrestees, 30.1 percent tested positive for powder and crack cocaine, and 44.1 percent for marijuana. Among the female arrestees, 35.3 percent tested positive for powder and crack cocaine, 31.6 percent for marijuana, 8.8 percent for methamphetamine, and 6.6 percent for heroin (National Institute of Justice, 2003).

The use of illicit drugs has enormous social and economic costs. It is estimated that the overall cost of drug abuse in 1992 was S107.6 billion. In 1998, the cost increased to about $142.4 billion. Between 1992 and 2002, the overall coast of illicit drug use rose 5.3 percent increasing from 107.2 billion to 180.9 billion (Office of National Drug Control Policy, 2001). The illicit drug abuse cost is divided into three components: health care costs, productivity losses, and other costs. In 2002, "By for the largest component of cost is from the loss of productivity, at 128.6 billion. In contrast to other costs of drug abuse (which involve direct expenditures for goods and services), this value reflects a loss of potential resources" (Office of National Drug Control Policy, 2007, p, x). In 2002, "It is estimated that $107.8 billion, or almost 60 percent of total cost are related to crime" (Office of National Drug Control Policy, 2007, p. xii). Between 1992 and 2002, crime related costs of illicit drug use increased from $61.8 billion to S107.8 billion. "The most rapid growth in drug costs came from increases in criminal justice system activities, including productivity losses associated with growth in the population imprisoned due to drug abuse" (Office of National Drug Control Policy, 2007, p. xiii).

Illicit drugs have negative consequences not just on any single society, but also on the collective world societies. During the last decades, there has emerged an expanding network of global illicit drug suppliers in the world market, particularly in North America and Western Europe. The trading of illicit drugs is one of the major sources of income of the newly emerging organized criminal groups of Russia, South and Southeast Asia, Africa, and South America. Political corruptions, money laundering, illegal human migrations, international trafficking of women and children, and global terrorism are connected to the global trading of illicit drugs. The 2004 World Drug Report produced by the United Nations noted that there is a wide consensus among the world nations about illicit drugs. "Current level of illicit drug use, together with the health consequences and criminal activities associated with it, has consistently been deemed unacceptable by both policy makers and public opinion. This is why a multilateral drug control system continues to enjoy almost universal adherence" (United Nations, 2004, p. 7).

The Utilitarian Argument

The first policy argument that illicit drugs are individually and socially harmful leads to the second argument that the government has justifiable power to take a policy through which it can protect the rest of society from the harmful effects of illicit drugs. This second argument is defined in philosophy as utilitarianism. The utilitarian philosopher John Stuart Mill, in his classic work *On Liberty* published in 1859, developed a theory of harm principle. The theory of harm principle claims that the political power of a government to constrain the rights and liberties of its citizens is legitimate if those rights and liberties lead to actions that are socially harmful. The principle of liberty, for Mills, does not exist in a social vacuum. We have a right to do something as long as it does not infringe on the rights of others. In other words, there is no conception of rights beyond the boundaries of society. We have the rights to use any drugs we want to use as long as they do not harm others and our drug related activities do not transgress the rights of others. The government is responsible for the attainment of common good or the greatest happiness for all by limiting the harmful activities of the few.

In the area of drug policy, this leads to the question of whether the use of illicit drugs is socially harmful. The criminalization of drugs is justified on the basis of this argument of harm principle (MacCoun & Reuter, 2001). During the last three decades, the Drug Enforcement Administration, the Office of National Drug Control Policy, the Department of Justice, the Department of Health and Human Services and a variety of other governmental departments and agencies have set up a vast number of research programs and institutes, and spent billions of dollars to study and understand the depth and extent of harm caused by the use of illicit drugs. The utilitarian argument also leads to a question of whether the use of the harm principle in policy-making is based on scientific grounds. The use of illicit drugs is one of the most widely studied areas of scientific research both within the policy-making organizations of the federal government, and in the literature on crime and justice.

The Moral Policy Argument

Science alone, however, does not shape America's drug policy. The drug policy is intimately connected with the dynamics of American culture and politics, particularly from the beginning of the war on drugs in the 1970s (Bertram, Blachman, Sharpe, & Andreas, 1996; Gest, 2001; Meier, 1994; Musto & Korsmeyer, 2002). In the 1970s, while America was fighting the Cold War abroad, there was growing a culture war at home. This culture war has grown as a pervasive moral battle in American politics (Hunter, 1992). On one side of this culture war are those who believe that the lack of faith in God and the absence of the practice of traditional moral virtues are at the core of the growing social problems of drugs, sex, and violence in American society. The use of illicit drugs is the manifestation of the lack of individual responsibility—the lack of moral strength. Addiction results from the lack of self-control and self-discipline. Those who indulge in addiction project the absence of character—the lack of moral essence. Their souls are broken and fractured; they do not have a moral wholeness (DeGreiff, 1999; Lakoff, 1996). And this lack of moral strength and wholeness results primarily from the lack of respect for the traditional values of marriage and family. This moral discourse has always been with American politics (Becker, 1977; Greiff, 1999), but it became dominant in contemporary politics and policy-making, particularly in crime and justice.

On the other side of this political discourse of culture war are those who believe that the roots of America's growing social problems are not in the realm of morality, but in the evolving and historically embedded structures of unequal social arrangements and social opportunities for historically disadvantaged racial groups and classes. The policy of the criminalization of drugs, they argue, is further widening these structures of inequality by bringing a "race to incarcerate" (Mauer, 1999). This argument, however, is not dominant in policy-making for crime and justice, particularly in drug use. Policy-makers in drug use, from both conservative and liberal camps, agree on the policy of criminalization, even though they may have different views about the nature and extent of punishment and the strategies of drug law enforcement.

The Rational Choice Argument

The assumptions that drug use is harmful, that it is morally reprehensible, and that the government has legitimate power to protect the society from its harmful effects provide justifications for the policy of criminalization. The policy of criminalization, in turn, leads to the argument about the nature and justification of punishment for the users of illicit drugs. The policy of mandatory sentencing for violation of drug laws, based on the principle of deterrence, came from the classical theory of rational choice developed through writings of Cesare Beccaria and Jeremy Bentham in the late nineteenth century. The core argument of this theory is that humans are essentially rational beings endowed with free will. Human activities are based on rational calculations—a cost-benefit analysis of pain and pleasure. Humans will refrain from painful activities. Incarceration is one of the dominant forms of punishment for inflicting pains on humans, and it is justified both to reduce the probability of crime and to preserve the common good. The strategy of mandatory sentencing for drug law violators and drug related crimes is justified on the ground of its role as a deterrent. It is believed and argued that mandatory sentencing punishes law breakers, incapacitates lawbreakers through incarceration, and reduces the probability of future violation of drug laws.

3.3 Crimes of Illicit Drugs: Policy Developments, 1870-1970

Federal control and regulations of drug use in America did not begin until the end of the nineteenth century. Food and drug industries, medicine and medical practices, and people's behavior and moralities were largely unregulated in the nineteenth century. Although federal concerns for public health can be traced back to the creation of Marine Hospital Services by Congress in 1798, the present structure of the Office of U.S. Surgeon General did not evolve before 1875. Throughout the nineteenth century, European colonial traders freely traded opium in the New World. Around the same time when the slave trade from Africa became dominant, opium trade in America from India, China and other Asian colonies significantly expanded, particularly before the Opium War in China in 1840.

In the growing cities of the nineteenth century, Americans freely used opium, heroin, morphine and marijuana. Morphine was freely prescribed as painkillers for the soldiers wounded in the Civil War. In the Opium Dens of San Francisco, the Chinese, described as "coolies" brought in for the construction of railways in the middle of the nineteenth century, openly used opium for relaxation. Smoking marijuana was an exciting way to exotic relaxation in the tea pads of the cities of New Orleans, New York, Boston, and Chicago. Cocaine was publicly recognized as an ingredient in Coca Cola, and the use remained in force up to 1929. The harm principle of these drugs was unknown and unexplored in the nineteenth century. The issue of drug use was not in the policy agenda of the federal government of that time.

By 1870, however, the context of federal policy-making in drug use began to change. Two factors were important for involvement of the federal government in regulating drugs and drug use. The first was the dawning of a gradual but yet-to-be scientifically established notion of the harm principle. From the late nineteenth century, it began to be realized that some drugs are harmful. Heroin was isolated from morphine in 1874, and the Bayer Company of Germany began to widely commercialize heroin in America in the 1890s. By that time, heroin began to be doubted as an intensely addictive drug. In 1859, a scientist named Albert Niemann in Germany chemically isolated cocaine from coca leaves taken from South America. By the 1890s, chemists, pharmacists, and medical doctors began to find that cocaine is addictive. The second factor responsible for federal involvement in drug policy was the growing realization among middle and upper middle class people of the late nineteenth century cities, particularly among the advocates of the Temperance Movement and the reformers of the Progressive Era, that the use of drugs is a sign of a morally decadent society, and it is related to urban crime and urban underclass. The federal government in the late nineteenth century reacted to both these developments by bringing drug regulation in the agenda for policy-making.

The federal policy for the criminalization of drugs began with the promulgation of a law for banning the import of opium in 1887. In the late nineteenth century, social concerns began to grow against the spread of Chinese opium dens across the various cities, particularly in the Western states. The federal government responded to this problem by banning the import of opium, but the law was applicable only to the Chinese immigrants. Opium trade was still open and legal for other Americans, and it was a major source of federal revenue. In 1915, the second federal enactment restricted opium smoking in the American colony of the Philippines. When America, after the Spanish-American War, annexed the Philippines, the problem of opium smoking was rampant. American colonial administrators and missionaries convinced the federal government to put a ban on opium smoking in the new colony.

In 1909, opium smoking was banned in America by the enactment of the Smoking Opium Exclusion Act. In the same year, America agreed to the 13-nation Shanghai International Opium Commission Resolution to impose control on the global narcotic trade. In 1914, America was the leading nation in the Hague International Opium Convention. The Hague Opium Convention was a major attempt to develop an international code of law against the trading and use of illegal drugs and narcotics.

From 1887 to 1970, Congress enacted a number of legislations that expanded the boundary of the federal control of illicit drugs and created an incipient structure of organizations for the implementation of federal drug policy. Some of the important legislations of that period include the Harrison Act of 1915, the Jones-Miller Act of 1922, the Marijuana Act of 1937, Food, Drug, and Cosmetic Act of 1938, Opium Poppy Act of 1942, Narcotic Drug Act of 1956, and the Drug Abuse Control Act of 1965. Of all these legislations, the Harrison Act was the most comprehensive, and it was the one that largely shaped the federal drug policy for almost fifty years before the modern war on drugs began in the 1970s (Harrison, Backenheimer, & Inciardi, 1996; Musto, 1987).

The Harrison Act was primarily an Act of registration. The Act was passed to legalize the prescription, manufacturing, and the sale of narcotics through a process of registration with the Commissioner of Internal Revenue. The federal government at that time did not intend to criminalize the possession or the use of illicit narcotics. The Act simply stated that it would be unlawful to prescribe, manufacture, distribute, import, sell, and possess narcotics without one being registered with the government and paying taxes. Even though the framers of the Harrison Act knew about the growing problem of drug use as a social problem at that time, the Act did not directly address the issue of addiction and the criminalization of the use of drugs for recreations. "The Harrison Act required strict accounting of opium and coca and their derivatives from entry into the US to their dispensing to a patient. However, the patient paid no tax, needed no permit, and, in fact, was not allowed to obtain one. The term addict did not appear in the Harrison Act" (Cohen, 2004, p. 89). The Act was not based on the strict interpretation of the harm principle. It extended the notion of criminalization in the area of drug dispensation and drug trading, but not in the area of drug use and addiction, although many habitual drug users were chased and chastised by federal agents throughout the whole process of enforcement (Erlen & Spillance, 2004).

The Marijuana Tax Act of 1937 enacted by the 75th Congress was primarily an Act of taxation, but its impact on the use of marijuana was far more invasive. It was a landmark legislation that for the first time extended federal power to regulate almost all areas of activities dealing with marijuana. The Act did not criminalize the use of marijuana. It imposed taxes on the importers, manufacturers, producers, dealers, sellers, and users of marijuana. The Act also imposed taxes on doctors, dentists, and veterinarians who prescribed marijuana for medical use. As Section 2 of the Act described: "Every person who imports, manufactures, produces, compounds, sells, deals in, dispenses, prescribes, administers, or gives away marijuana shall pay special taxes." Tax for importers and manufacturers were $24 a year, and for others was $1-3 a year. The Act made it unlawful to send, ship, carry, and transport marijuana within the United States without paying taxes. Section 9 of the Act described: "Any marijuana which has been imported, manufactured, compounded, transferred, or produced in violation of any of the provisions of this Act shall be subject to seizure, and forfeiture."

Although the use of marijuana was not criminalized, all activities dealing with marijuana in general were brought under intense federal regulations by the Marijuana Act. As Section 10 of the Act described: "Every person liable to any tax imposed by this act shall keep such books and records, render under oath such statements, make such returns, and comply with such rules and regulations as the Secretary may from time to time prescribe." The Act was also punitive in nature. Section 12 of the Act proposed: "Any person who is convicted of a violation of any provision of this Act shall be fined not more than $2,000, or imprisoned not more than five years, or both in the discretion of the court." The Act brought marijuana into the same narcotic category with opium and heroin.

From the beginning of the 1950s, however, it was the harm principle that began to be more visible in policy-making for illicit drugs. The use of illicit drugs began to be seen, by both public and policy-makers, as the reason for increasing crime and violence, particularly the rise and expansion of organized crime in many American cities in the 1950s. The use of drugs also began to be associated with the rise of family violence, juvenile violence, sexual crimes, and mental illness. This led to the passage of the Narcotic Control Act by Congress in 1956. In contrast to the Harrison Act, the Narcotic Control Act of 1950 made registration for the users of drugs and drug addicts legally mandatory. The Act introduced the notion of mandatory sentencing for drug law violations and significantly increased the fines and penalties for the violators. While drug use and addiction continued to increase in the 1960s, there was also growing an increased understanding within the medical professions and public health experts about addiction as a medical problem. Congress responded to the new medical view through the passage of the Narcotic Addiction Rehabilitation Act (NARA) in 1966. The Act for the first time made systematic provisions for federally funded treatment as an alternative to incarceration for habitual drug addicts.

Up to the end of the 1950s, since federal drug policy was primarily a policy of control and regulation through registration and taxation, the tasks of policy implementation were mainly in the Department of Treasury. The Harrison Act of 1915 created the first federal drug enforcement agency—the Federal Bureau of Narcotics—within the Department of Treasury. The Federal Bureau of Narcotics was responsible to restrict access to narcotics through the enforcement of the laws of registration and taxation. In 1930, the Federal Bureau of Narcotics was renamed the Bureau of Narcotics, but it still remained within the Department of Treasury. The first Commissioner of the Bureau of Narcotics was Harry

J. Anslinger. During his three decades of tenure as a Commissioner, Anslinger was one of the earlier architects of America's drug policy. The Bureau of Narcotics was renamed as the Bureau of Narcotics and Dangerous Drugs (BNDD) in the federal reorganization plan of 1968. The creation of the Bureau of Narcotics and Dangerous Drugs in 1968 was a turning point because it brought drug policy-making and drug policy enforcement within the Department of Justice. Under the leadership of the Department of Justice in the late 1960s, drug policy began to move rapidly into an arena of criminalization (King, 1974).

3.4 Crimes of Illicit Drugs: Policy Developments, 1970-2006

From the beginning of the 1960s, the issue of drug use and addiction began to be prominent in policy discourses for crime and justice. Drug use began to be seen not just as a problem of registration and the control of trafficking, but also as a problem of antisocial behavior. "By the late 1960s, the relationship between heroin addiction and street crime was generally accepted as a fact, despite the absence of any careful research and documentation, heroin had become inextricably linked in the public's mind with the urban crisis" (Goldberg, 1980, p. 4). The idea of drug use as an antisocial behavior led to the development of a new policy perspective. Criminalization of all activities related to illicit drugs became a dominant policy agenda through the declaration of the war on drugs by President Nixon.

Drug Policy in the Decade of the 1970s

In 1969, Nixon asked his law partner then Attorney General, John N. Mitchell, to prepare a comprehensive drug Bill for Congress. Attorney General prepared a "comprehensive new measure to more effectively meet the narcotic and dangerous drug problem at the federal level by combining all existing federal laws in a single new statute" (King, 2005, p. 2). The Bill that Attorney General sent to the Congress in July 1969 "pulled together everything Congress had done in the drug field since the opium-smoking curbs of 1887" (King, 2005, p. 3). The final enactment of the Bill was titled the Comprehensive Drug Abuse Prevention and Control Act of 1970.

In June 1971, President Nixon sent a message to Congress: "If we cannot destroy the drug menace in America, then it will surely in time destroy us. I am not prepared to accept this alternative" (Goldberg, 1980, p. 10) In 1971, Congress set up a Commission under the chairmanship of Raymond Shaffer, former Republican Governor of Pennsylvania, to examine the scientific basis of putting marijuana into Schedule I under Title II of the Comprehensive Drug Abuse Prevention and Control. Having learned that the Commission was soft on marijuana, President Nixon reacted and said: "We need, and I use the word 'all out war', on all fronts ... we have to attack on all fronts" (Zeese, 2002, p. 2). In his State of the Union Address in 1973, Nixon charted his philosophy of a new war on crime in general in America. Nixon said: "Americans in the last decade were often told that the criminal was not responsible for his crime against society, but that society was responsible. I totally disagree with this permissive philosophy" (Nixon, 1973, p. 1). Nixon further added: "When we fail to make the criminal pay for his crime, we encourage him to think that crime will pay. Such an attitude will never be reflected in the laws supported by this administration" (Nixon, 1973, p. 1) Nixon declared in his speech that drug abuse is "public enemy number one in America." The federal drug budget in 1969 was $86 million. In 1970, it increased to $101.9 million. In 1971, the budget was doubled—it increased to 212.5 million (Goldberg, 1980).

The Comprehensive Drug Abuse and Control Act of 1970 was landmark legislation because it consolidated most of the drug laws and legislations of the past decades. Title II of the Comprehensive Drug Abuse and Control Act—the Controlled Substance Act of 1970 (CSA)—was the first document that created a description of all federally regulated controlled substances in terms of five schedules based on their "medical value, harmfulness, and potential for abuse or addiction. Schedule I is reserved for the most dangerous drugs that have not been recognized in medical use" (United States Drug Enforcement Administration, 2003, p.1). The Controlled Substance Act "is the legal foundation of the government's fight against the abuse of drugs and other substances" (United States Drug Enforcement Administration, 2003, p. 1). The laws and regulations of Chapter 13—Drug Abuse Prevention and Control—of Title 21 of the U.S. Code evolved from the Control Substance Act of 1970. The Act created a tougher and hierarchical sentencing system based on the hierarchical structure of the five drug schedules.

Another major institutional innovation brought by the Comprehensive Drug Abuse and Control Act of 1970 was the centralization of drug policy within the Department of Justice. The Attorney General was given the major responsibility to oversee the implementation of the new rules and regulations. The Act abolished the Bureau of Narcotics and Dangerous Drugs (BNDD) and created the Drug Enforcement Administration (DEA) in 1973. The DEA since then remained as the focal point of organizing and implementing the federal government's drug policy. Although almost all federal agencies have drug law enforcement activities, the DEA is primarily responsible for coordinating and directing the government's overall programs of drug policy both at home and abroad. The Act mandated the DEA to conduct scientific research on the additive nature of different drugs in the five schedules and to study the evolution of the patterns of illicit drug use in America for informed policy-making.

With the passage of the Comprehensive Drug Abuse and Control Act of 1970, drug policy-making began to be seen primarily from the perspective of harm principle. Through the new enactment, Congress began to emphasize the need for basic scientific research to understand the multifaceted harmful effects of dangerous drugs. Although criminalization was its dominant perspective, the Act of 1970 made drug prevention and education also a major federal responsibility. A new White House agency, Special Action Office for Drug Abuse Prevention (SAODAP), was set up by the Nixon administration in 1972 to direct and coordinate drug prevention and drug research activities. In the mid-1970s, there were about 135 federally funded drug treatment programs. After the creation of SAODAP, the number of treatment programs, particularly methadone treatment for heroin addiction, under the leadership of its first Director, Jerome Jaffe, increased to about 394 (Goldberg, 1980, p. 11). Of the $212.5 million of federal drug budget in 1971, $86.5 million was allocated for drug treatment and rehabilitation, $39.2 million for drug education, prevention and training, and $21.5 million for research. Law enforcement received an allocation of $66 million (Goldberg, 1980, p. 8).

The Nixon administration, from the beginning of the war on drugs, tried to develop a nationally comprehensive drug policy with uniform standards of enforcement and programs across various states and localities. In 1972, Congress enacted the Drug Abuse Office and Treatment Act. With the passage of this Act, the supply and demand approach was adopted, and new federal initiatives were taken to develop a national policy for illicit drug use prevention and control by bringing the state and local governments into drug policy planning (Goldberg, 1980). The Act also established a National Institute on Drug Abuse (NIDA) within the Department of Health, Education, and Welfare, presently titled as the Department of Health and Human Services. The mission of NIDA was to develop, organize, and provide leadership in federal drug treatment and prevention activities – the activities that were previously the responsibility of the National Institute of Mental Health.

During the Ford Administration, there was no significant change in the drug policy programs initiated by President Nixon. "Although the style was different and the goals less ambitious, the Ford administration's response to illicit drugs was largely predicated on the same assumptions about the innate harmfulness of illicit drugs that have guided the government's response to drugs throughout the twentieth century" (Goldberg, 1980, p. 19). President Ford, however, wanted more inter-agency control on federal drug policy and wanted to establish a Cabinet Committee for Drug Abuse Prevention. The Congress, after the abolition of the SAODAP in 1976, passed legislation and created a new White House Office of Drug Abuse Policy (ODAP). The ODAP was given broader power to coordinate drug policy activities both at home and abroad (Goldberg, 1980).

The first decade of the drug war ended with the Carter Presidency. During the Carter Administration, Congress did not pass any major drug legislation. President Carter abolished the ODAP in 1978 and supported the decriminalization of marijuana, but he brought no significant shift in drug policy in general. Carter's policy proposals "were conceptually indistinguishable from those made by Presidents Nixon and Ford; all sought to enact measures that would deter major drug traffickers in the hope of reducing the availability of illicit drugs at the street level" (Goldberg, 1980, p. 20). The Drug war entered into its second decade with more expansive programs of control and prevention with the coming of the Reagan Presidency. The federal drug budget in 1971 was $212.5 million. In 1978, the federal drug budget increased to about $885 million (Goldberg, 1980).

Drug Policy in the Decade of the 1980s

In America's history of the drug war, the decade of the 1980s was the decade of the "cocaine revolution." When President Reagan came to power in 1981, the cocaine and crack epidemic rapidly spread to American cities, suburbs, homes, and streets. With the rise of the Colombian Medallion Drug Cartel in 1981-1982, international trafficking of cocaine from South America greatly intensified. The seizure of 3,906 pounds of cocaine worth of about $100 million at the International Airport in Miami in 1982 created a new concern for the spread of international drug trafficking in America. In 1981, President Reagan ratified the U.S.-Colombian Extradition Treaty to control Colombian drug trafficking in America. In response and in revenge, the Medallion Cartel assassinated the Colombian Attorney General in 1984, and in 1985 killed about 95 people including 11 Superior Court Justices by viciously attacking the Colombian Palace of Justice—the institution responsible for executing the extradition treaty.

Along with the spread of drugs, violent crime also began to rise in the 1980s. "One in 30 Americans committed a criminally violent act in 1981, up 76 percent since 1969; the combined violent crime index ... rose 69 percent during the same period to 555.3 such crimes per 100,000 citizens" (Hallahan,1986, p. 1). It was in the context of these developments that the war on drugs further escalated both at home and abroad in the 1980s. As one author observed, "President Reagan launched a new and decidedly militant phase in the U.S. campaign to halt global narcotics trafficking when he addressed the Annual Meeting of the International Association of Chiefs of Police in September 1981" (Carpenter, 2004, p. 1). President Reagan placed the whole policy of war on drugs both at home and abroad "in the context of a larger 'crime epidemic' afflicting the United States" (Carpenter, 2004, p. 1).

In the 1980s, drug policy evolved and expanded through the passage of three major enactments by the Congress: Comprehensive Crime Control Act of 1984, Anti-Drug Abuse Act of 1986, and Anti-Drug Abuse Amendment Act of 1988. The Violent Crime Control Act of 1984 can be regarded as the beginning of a new era not just in drug policy but also in crime policy in general—the beginning of the era of mandatory sentencing. From the beginning of the 1980s, the Congress became skeptical about the efficacy of indeterminate sentencing, effectiveness of bail, role of parole and probation, and the overall capacity of prisons to rehabilitate the violent offenders. Title II of the Comprehensive Crime Control Act of 1984, known as Sentencing Reform Act of 1984, set up a new institution—United States Sentencing Commission—to develop mandatory sentencing guidelines for drug law offenders and violent criminals. While the Drug Abuse and Control Act of 1970 developed a comprehensive system of drug schedules, the Sentencing Reform Act of 1984 developed a comprehensive system of mandatory sentencing for drug related crimes and violence.

The Sentencing Reform Act severely limited judicial discretions in sentencing. Except some special reasons, the Act required the federal courts to follow the sentencing range and formula prescribed by the Sentencing Commission.

However, the special sentencing provisions by the court were eliminated for violent offenders, youth offenders, young adult offenders, and drug addicts. The Act abolished the parole system, set the maximum terms of imprisonment for five classes of felonies (A to E) and three classes of misdemeanors, and made provisions for annual Congressional review of the operation of the sentencing system.

Title III of the Comprehensive Crime Control Act of 1984—the Comprehensive Forfeiture Ac of 1984—gave special power to the Attorney General and the court to forfeiture the tangible and intangible personal property of those who gained them through racketeering activities including drug dealing and drug trafficking. The Attorney General was also authorized to transfer drug-related forfeited property to other federal, state and local agencies for assistance in law enforcement. Title V of the Comprehensive Crime Control Act of 1984—Controlled Substances Penalties Amendments Act of 1984—increased prison term to 20 years and fines to $250,000 for trafficking large amounts of Schedule 1 and II narcotic drugs. Penalties for violating Schedule III, IV and V drugs and selling and distributing drugs within 1,000 feet of elementary or secondary school property were also increased.

The same year that the Comprehensive Crime Control Act was passed, two specific drug legislations were enacted by the Congress—The Aviation Drug-Trafficking Control Act of 1984 and the Dangerous Drugs Diversion Control Act of 1984. The Aviation Drug-Trafficking Control Act authorized the Federal Aviation Authority to revoke airman certificates and aircraft registration if they are engaged in drug trafficking. The Dangerous Drugs Diversion Control Act provided emergency scheduling authority to the Attorney General to bring the drugs that are addictive and of serious public health concerns into Schedule I without the constraint of any judicial review.

In the middle of the 1980s, during the time of massive escalation of the crack epidemic at home and the massive mobilization of international drug trafficking groups, particularly in South America, the 99th Congress enacted the Anti-Drug Abuse Act of 1986 with the aim primarily of supply reduction. With the passage of this Act, the Drug war opened a number of new battlegrounds. In the home front, Title I of the Act—the Anti-Drug Enforcement Act—criminalized the simple possession of a controlled substance. The Act established enhanced penalties for drug violations by juveniles, extended the ban on drug distribution to college campuses, made the sale of controlled substances through the U.S. Postal Service a federal offense, and established the death penalty for violent and repeat drug offenders. Title I authorized enhanced budgetary allocation for drug enforcement operations, made provision for the use of federal buildings under the jurisdiction of the Department of Defense as detention centers for drug violators, and authorized the Director of the FBI to make federal grants available to state and local drug enforcement agencies.

In the international front of the drug war, Title II of the Anti-Drug Abuse Act of 1986—International Narcotics Control Act of 1986—established a number of new fighting strategies. With the passage of this legislation, the American drug war reached almost all regions of the world—from Afghanistan to Colombia to bust and destroy the growing centers of production and manufacturing of illicit narcotics. The Act made it legal for U.S. law enforcement officers and employees to participate in narcotic arrests in foreign countries, and it authorized the Secretary of State to help expand the activities of the DEA in foreign countries. The Act authorized the President and the Secretary of the State to explore new relations with the United Nations Commission on Narcotic Drugs and to seek help from international security related organization such as the North Atlantic Treaty Organization (NATO). The Act introduced a system of drug certification by the President for foreign assistance requests. The President, since then, is required annually to certify to Congress whether countries receiving American foreign assistance are complying with the U.S. drug control efforts. Title III of the Act—National Drug Interdiction Improvement Act of 1986 —authorized the Secretary of Defense to engage the military, along with the agents of the FBI, DEA, U.S. Customs, and U.S. Coast Guard, in the control and conduct of foreign drug operations.

The Anti-Drug Abuse Act of 1986 also made significant provisions for demand reduction. Through Title IV of the Act—Alcohol and Drug Abuse Amendments of 1986—Congress reorganized the federal drug research infrastructure. Congress authorized the Secretary of Health and Human Services, with increased budgetary allocations, to enhance drug related research activities of the National Institute on Drug Abuse, National Institutes of Mental Health, and other related agencies. The Drug-Free School and Communities Act of 1986 (subtitle B of Title IV) expanded the scope of drug prevention education by authorizing the Secretary of Education to provide federal grants to state and local drug education centers and initiatives.

Two years after the passage of the Anti-Drug Abuse Act of 1986, the 100th Congress passed major drug legislation—the Anti-Drug Abuse Act of 1988—to further address the issue of demand reduction. This Act "represents the Federal Government's attempt to reduce drug abuse by dealing not just with the person who sells the illegal drugs, but also with the person who buys it" (United States Drug Enforcement Administration, 2003, p. 8). Through the Anti-Drug Abuse Act of 1988, the assumptions of morality and personal responsibility came to be more visible in policy-making. "The purpose of user accountability is to not only make the public aware of the Federal Government position on drug abuse, but to describe new programs intended to decrease drug abuse by holding drug abusers personally responsible for their illegal activities" (United States Drug Enforcement Administration, 2003, p. 8). The responsibility assumption was forcefully demonstrated in Title V of the 1988 Act. Title V of the Act "declares the Congressional finding that the legalization of drugs is an unconscionable surrender in the war on drugs." On the basis of the assumption of responsibility, the Act established the National Commission on Drug-Free School, and set up regulatory and enforcement provisions against the use of illicit drugs in the workplace and public housing, The Act made provisions for the denial of federal benefits—grants, contracts, loans, licenses, and public housing—for up to five years for first time drug convictions, up to ten years for the second conviction, and life for the third conviction. The Act declared a drug-free America by 1995.

Another new direction was Title I of the Anti-Drug Abuse Act of 1988 that established the Office of National Drug Control Policy (ONDCP) in the Executive Office of the President with one Director, and two Deputy Directors—one for the Supply Reduction Program and the other for the Demand Reduction Program. The ONDCP was given the task to coordinate the drug control activities of different federal agencies, prepare a yearly budget for federal drug enforcement programs, and submit an annual report to Congress on National Drug Control Policy.

Title II of the Act—the Comprehensive Alcohol Abuse, Drug Abuse and Mental Health Amendments of Act of 1988—made many new provisions for state and local government agencies to set up innovative and peer reviewed drug education and prevention programs with the support of federal funds. Title II authorized the Secretary of Health to provide funds for the development of community-based intervention programs and demonstration projects for drug education. Title III made increased authorization for drug education and prevention programs for state and local agencies, related particularly to at-risk youths, members of youth gangs, and runaway and homeless youth.

Title IV of the 1988 Act—International Narcotic Control Act of 1988— further expanded the global reach of the drug war. It increased appropriations for American contributions to the United Nations Fund for Drug Abuse and Control, and Inter-American Drug Abuse Control Program of the Organization of American States (OAS). Provisions were made to increase foreign assistance to countries cooperating with the U.S. international narcotic control efforts. Title IV required the Secretary of the State to report to Congress annually on the nature and success of U.S. international supply reduction efforts. When President Reagan came to power in 1981, the federal drug control budget was about $1.5 billion. In 1989, at the end of the Reagan era, the federal drug control budget increased to about $6.7 billion. In 1981, the total budget for the DEA was $219.5 million and it had 1,964 special drug enforcement agents. In 1989, the DEA budget increased to $597.9 million, and it employed 2,969 special agents (United States Drug Enforcement Administration, 2005, p. 1).

In the early 1970s, President Nixon started the war on drugs. After the demise of the Nixon presidency in 1974, the drug war temporarily lost the vision of its architect. However, since the beginning of the 1980s, President Reagan again expressed a strong moral conviction and a deep policy commitment to expand the war on drugs both at home and abroad. The laws and regulations, programs and strategies, and the institutional complexes of today's war on drugs were built primarily through drug legislations of the 1980s. In the 1980s, as Reagan became the architect of America's policy for military and diplomatic engagement for the global war on drugs, First Lady Nancy Reagan at home became a prominent advocate of a vast social movement in America's homes, schools, and inner cities to "Just Say No" to drugs.

Drug Policy in the Decade of the 1990s

During the 1990s, Congress enacted four major bills related to drugs and crime: the Crime Control Act of 1990, the Alcohol, Drug Abuse, and Mental Health Administration Reorganization Act of 1992 (ADAMHA), the Violent Crime Control and Law Enforcement Act of 1994, and the Comprehensive Methamphetamine Control Act of 1996. Title XII of the 1990 Act increased penalties for crack possession from a fine or imprisonment to a term of imprisonment and a fine of not less than $1,000, and amended the Controlled Substance Act to increase penalties for the distribution or manufacturing of illicit drugs in or near schools. Title XV of the 1990 Act—the Drug-Free School Zone—amended the Drug-Free Schools and Communities Act of 1986 and made more provisions for increased involvement of both law enforcement and school personnel to develop drug-abuse prevention programs, mobilize local community resources, and punish the drug law violators. The Act instructed the United States Sentencing Commission to increase the penalty for smoking crystal methamphetamine. Title XIX of the 1990 Act—the Anabolic Steroids Act of 1990—amended the Controlled Substances Act of 1970 and placed anabolic steroids in Schedule III. Title XXIV imposed more penalties for interstate trafficking of drugs and drug paraphernalia.

Congress established ADAMHA in 1972 as a lead federal agency for research in substance abuse and mental health. In the Reorganization Plan of 1992, Congress abolished ADAMHA and created two structures: the National Institutes of Health (NIH) and the Substance Abuse and Mental Health Services Administration (SAMHSA). The National Institute on Drug Abuse (NIDA) and the National Institute of Alcoholism and Alcohol Abuse (NIAAA) were placed within the National Institutes of Health, and the activities of the ADAMHA were placed within the SAMHSA. Of all these agencies that are within the Department of Health and Human Services, the SAMHSA is now a leading federal agency for research on drug addiction and drug use.

The violent Crime Control and Law Enforcement Act of 1994 is one of the most comprehensive crime bills passed by Congress after the Omnibus Crime Control and Safe Streets Act of 1968. The 1994 Act did not bring any substantial change in the drug war. It rather expanded the war by putting more emphasis on demand reduction primarily through more training and education for law enforcement, the expansion of community policing, and more fines and prison terms for drug law violators. Title VI of the Act—Federal Death Penalty Act of 1994—extended the death penalty to twenty different kinds of federal crimes including violent drug related offenses. Title VII of the Act extended life imprisonment for a number of felonies including serious drug offenses. Title IX directed the United States Sentencing Commission to enhance penalties for distributing drugs in drug-free zones, and in federal prisons. The Act extended the boundary of drug-free zone to include not just schools and offices but also truck stops and rest areas. The Act authorized the Attorney General to establish a Rural Drug Enforcement Task Force. It also authorized the President to bring immediate federal assistance to state and local governments to address drug-related emergencies.

In 1993, President Clinton elevated ONDCP to cabinet-level status to make it able to work in a more collaborative way with other federal agencies in the direction and execution of drug policies. The 1994 Act further extended the size, roles and responsibilities of ONDCP. The Director of ONDCP was authorized to coordinate the drug budget and the drug prevention programs of all federal departments and agencies. The Act required the Director of ONDCP to conduct scientific research on effective methods and technology for drug education prevention.

In 1996, Congress also enacted a major bill to control the spread of methamphetamine—the Comprehensive Methamphetamine Control Act of 1996. The Act made a provision for ten years of imprisonment for dealing with the methamphetamine chemicals listed in Schedules 1 and II. The Act authorized the United States Sentencing Commission to consider the manufacturing of methamphetamine as a significant violation of the Controlled Substances Act, and to impose increased penalties for trafficking of methamphetamine and the possession of equipment and laboratory supplies used to manufacture methamphetamine. The Act established for the first time a federal Methamphetamine Interagency Task Force under the direction of the Attorney General.

The Crime Control Act of 1990, the Reorganization Plan of 1992, Violent Crime Control and Law Enforcement Act of 1994, and the Comprehensive Methamphetamine Control Act of 1996 extended and strengthened the strategies of the drug war developed in the 1980s. In the 1990s, the drug war further expanded the role of law enforcement, particularly in areas of demand reduction at home. There, however, began a trend to understand the problem of addiction and drug use on the basis of scientific research, and the problem of drug policymaking and policy implementations on the basis of scientific data. The Federal drug control budget in 1991 was about $10.9 billion. In 2000, it increased to about $18.4 billion. The total budget for the DEA in 1991 was $875 million. In 2000, the DEA budget was $1.5 billion.

Drug Policy, 2000-2006

From 2001 to 2004, the 106th, 107th and the 108th Congresses remained preoccupied with the "war on terror." But the war on drugs also kept expanding during the Bush administration. Presidents Bush's first Attorney General, John Ashcroft, immediately after he assumed the office, expressed his firm commitment to further expand and "escalate" the war on drugs. After the start of drug war in 1971, drug "control legislations were actively considered by every Congress, and the 108th Congress was no exception" (Congressional Research Service, 2005, p. 1). The 107th Congress did not come up with any new enactment but it "approved FY2002 funding for the war on drugs in the amount of $18.8 billion" (Congressional Research Service, 2005, p. 4).

One of the major enactments of this period is the Illicit Drug Proliferation Act of 2003—a new version of the Rave Act of 2002. The new law, included as a part of the PROTECT Act, authorized the United States Sentencing Commission to develop tougher penalties for the use of ecstasy, predatory drugs, and methamphetamine. The act made it unlawful for managers, employers, or owners of bars and nightclubs to make profit from the use, sale, and distribution of these drugs. The law made provisions to prosecute them if they fail to prevent drug use by their clients and customers. In 2001, an amendment to the Ecstasy Proliferation Act of 2000 authorized the United States Sentencing Commission to increase penalties for trafficking ecstasy. The new amendment increased the penalties for trafficking 800 pills of ecstasy by 300 percent, from 15 months to five years. For trafficking 8,000 pills, penalty was increased 200 percent—from 41 month to 10 years (Office of National Drug Control Policy, 2005). In addition to these legislations related to demand and supply reduction at home, the 108th Congress also made enactments to expand the drug war abroad. In 2001, three months after he took over the office, President Bush declared a broader regional initiative to control international drug trafficking—the Andean Counter Drug Initiative. The name was later changed to Andean Regional Initiative.

Key National Drug Policy Strategies: 2007

The laws and enactments made by Congress on illicit drug policy define primarily the boundaries of crime and punishment. Congress sets the legal boundaries, but the development of an overall national drug policy strategy is the function of the executive branch. Until the late 1990s, the national drug policy was made by different agencies of the federal government, such as the DEA, the Department of Justice, and the Department of Health and Human Services. It was in view of the lack of coordination among different federal agencies and the lack of an overall national drug policy strategy that Congress created ONDCP in 1988. ONDCP developed the first document of the national drug policy strategy in 1989. Every year ONDCP revises the policy document and submits it to Congress for appropriations. Thousands of laws and regulations about illegal drug abuse exist, and hundreds of drug education and prevention programs are present across the country, but the nation's key drug control policy strategies are outlined by this annual report produced by ONDCP (see Table 15).

The 2007 U.S. National Drug Control Policy includes three core strategies: demand reduction, harm reduction, and supply reduction. Each of these strategies contains a number of programs and each program contains a number of specific projects. The strategy of demand reduction described by ONDCP as "Stopping Use Before it Starts" is a plan to reduce the use of illicit drugs through the involvement of parents, schools, community organization, faith-based organizations, and the media. The strategy of harm reduction is described by ONDCP as "Healing America's Drug Users." The goal is to make drug treatments available through such channels as drug courts, hospitals, and even faith-based organizations. The supply reduction strategy is to control the expansion of the drug market and supply both at home and abroad and to attack the economic base of drug trafficking.

Table 15: U.S. National Drug Control Policy Strategies, 2007

Core Strategies	Core Programs	Drug Budget, 2006 (In millions)
Demand Reduction	Student Drug Testing Workplace Drug Testing School-based Programs Faith-Based Initiatives Community Coalition Program Anti-Drug Media Campaign Drug Free Community Program	$4,804.4 million
Harm Reduction	Access to Recovery Initiative Abstinence Through Drug Courts SBIRT Program Prescription Drug Safety Program	$1,862.6 million (This was out of total $4.804.4 million for demand reduction]
Supply Reduction	Priority Targeting Initiative Drug Enforcement Task Force Andean Counter Drug Initiative Attacking Transporter Networks Counterdrug Intelligence Program Targeting Synthetic Drugs Democracy in Afghanistan Central/Southwest Asian Operations	$8,194.8 million

Source: ONDCP: National Drug Control Policy, 2007

The total federal budget for the demand reduction strategy in 2001 was $4,431 million. In 2006, it increased to $4,808.4 million. In 2001, the federal government spent about 46.9 percent of its total drug budget for demand reduction strategies. In 2006, it dropped to 36.6 percent of the total drug budget. In 2001, the federal government spent 53.1 percent of its drug budget for supply reduction strategies ($5,023.8 million). In 2006, the federal government spent 63. 0 percent of its total drug budget for supply reduction strategies. In 2001, out of 46.9 percent of the drug reduction budget, 27.2 percent was used for drug abuse treatment and treatment research programs, and 19.7 percent was used for supporting drug use prevention programs. In 2006, budget allocations for both treatment and prevention programs decreased. It came down to 22.6 percent for treatment and 14.3 percent for prevention. Allocations for drug treatment and prevention programs have been decreasing, although not in any significant way, since fiscal year 2002. Since 2002, more emphasis has been given to drug supply reduction strategies. In 2006, out of 63.0 percent of the budget allocated for drug supply reduction, 27.4 percent was used for domestic law enforcement, 25.7 percent was used for drug interdiction programs, and 10.0 percent was used for drug reduction programs abroad (Office of National Drug Control Policy, 2007, p.12).

3. 5 Crimes of Illicit Drugs:
State and Local Policy Policy-Making

One of the earliest state enactments for drug control came from the state of Pennsylvania. Pennsylvania banned the use of morphine—an opium derivative—in 1860. In 1875, San Francisco, as mentioned before, enacted a legislation that banned opium smoking, applicable particularly to the Chinese Immigrants who came to California for work on gold mines and railroads. In 1876, Virginia City in Nevada passed an ordinance to ban opium smoking—an ordinance that became a law throughout the state in 1877. In 1881, California banned the use and opening of opium dens in the state (King County Bar Association, 2005). In the 1920s and 1930s, many states began to prohibit the sale and distribution of marijuana. "By 1937 when the federal government finally passed the Marijuana Act, all 50 states had their own laws forbidding the non-medical use of marijuana" (ImpacTeen Illicit Drug Team, 2002, p. 2; Balenko, 2000). From the beginning of the 1930s, most of the states also began to restrict the sale and distribution of cocaine primarily in the context of rising public opinion against the use of cocaine by the then Mexican immigrants. By 1931, "Thirty-six states had enacted legislation prohibiting unauthorized possession of cocaine and thirty-five prohibited unauthorized possession of the opiates and other restricted drugs" (Bonnie & Whitebread, 2005, p. 2).

The modern drug war did not begin in the 1930s, but a national drug policy began to evolve at that time particularly in the context of the enforcement of the Harrison Act of 1915 and the Marijuana Act of 1937. When different states began to develop different drug control strategies in addition to the enforcement of federal prohibitions, needs began to be felt for a more coordinated national approach to drug control. "The general lack of uniformity in anti-narcotic legislation, the weakness of state enforcement procedures, and the growing hysteria about dope fiends and criminality converged in several requests beginning as early as 1927 for a uniform state narcotic law" (Bonnie & Whitebread, 2005, p. 3). In response, the Federal Bureau of Narcotics drafted the Uniform Narcotic Drug Act, with assistance from the states, in 1932. Thirty-five states, by 1937, "had enacted the Uniform Narcotic Act" (Bonnie & Whitebread, 2005, p. 5).

The modern drug war began in the states around the same time when it became a major crime policy agenda for the federal government in the beginning of the 1970s. The drug war is not a war of the federal government alone. It is a war led also by all states, cities, and regions of the nation. Today, all 50 states have their own drug policy institutions and drug enforcement agencies. The core assumptions of the national drug policy—the harm principle, utilitarianism, moral argument, and the deterrence perspective—are shared by the policy-makers at all levels of government—federal, state, and local.

The expansion of the drug war in all 50 states is evidenced by the nature and degree of their compliance to national drug policy strategies, enforcement of drug laws, use and mobilization of resources for drug law implementations, and their engagement in policy-making for innovative drug legislations. According to the Uniform Crime Reports, from 1980 to 2003, state drug abuse violation arrests have consistently increased. In 1980, the total drug abuse violation arrests in all 50 states were about 600,000. The number increased to 1.3 million in 1990 and 1.7 million in 2003. In 1980, the number of persons in state correctional institutions for drug abuse violations was 19,000. The number increased to 148,600 in 1990, and 246,100 in 2001 (Bureau of Justice Statistics, 2002). In 2000, among the state agencies with 100 or more law enforcement officers, 71 percent operated a full time drug enforcement unit. Of local agencies with 100 or more officers in 2000, 87 percent of county police officers, 79 percent of municipal police departments, and 69 percent of sheriff officers had primary drug enforcement responsibility (Bureau of Justice Statistics, 2004). The state and local law enforcement officers also participate in multi-agency drug enforcement task force. In 2000, an estimated 21percent of local police departments had one or more officers assigned full time to multi-agency drug enforcement task force (Bureau of Justice Statistics, 2003). The National Governor Association's Center for Best Practices claims that about 13 percent of all state spending can be linked to substance abuse and addiction.

The states' participation in the drug war began more systematically after the enactment of the Anti-Drug Abuse legislation in 1988. The 1988 Act developed the Edward Byrne Memorial State and Local Law Enforcement Assistance Program. The Program was aimed to provide federal funds for the improvement of state and local criminal justice enforcement activities. For the last fifteen years, the Byrne Memorial Program remained a major tool to fight the drug war by state and local governments. In 2004, the Program provided about $476 million to all the 50 states including Puerto Rico, Virgin Islands, Guam, and American Samoa. Some of the major drug enforcement strategies mandated by the Byrne Memorial Program include demand-reduction education program, creation of a multi-agency and multi-jurisdictional drug enforcement task force, programs to control the domestic sources of drug production and drug manufacturing, programs to improve and use drug-control technology, programs to control drug abuse in public housing, development of innovative law enforcement strategies to control domestic drug trafficking, improvement of drug related data and information systems, and the development of community–based drug education and drug intervention programs. "The Byrne Program "places emphasis on violent and drug-related crime and serious offenders and on fostering multijurisdictional and multi-state efforts to support national drug-control priorities" (Gist, 1997, p.1). The states funded under this program are "required to develop a statewide strategy to improve the functioning of the state's criminal justice system, with an emphasis on drug trafficking, violent crimes, and serious offenders" (Gist, 1997, p. 4).

All fifty states comply with the broader provisions of federal drug legislations, and work within the three-tier framework of national drug policy strategies, but there are also many innovations and variations in their drug policies.

The Controlled Substances Act of 1970 broadly applies to all states, but many states have their own legislations related to drug scheduling, and penalties. "State legislatures' approaches to controlled substances scheduling of marijuana, cocaine, methamphetamine, Rohypnol, GHB, ecstasy and ketamine for the most part reflect the system set up by the Controlled Substances Act (CSA); yet variations from the CSA do exist" ((ImpacTeen Illicit Drug Team, 2002, p. viii). Instead of the five schedules of the CSA, Alaska, Arkansas, North Carolina, and Virginia, for example, adopted a six-schedule system of drug classification. South Dakota has introduced a four-schedule system and Tennessee developed a seven-schedule system (ImpacTeen Illicit Drug Team, 2002). Marijuana is in Schedule in 37 states, but six states—Colorado, Georgia, Illinois, South Dakota, Virginia, and Wisconsin—do not include it in schedules. In the CSA and in 36 states, ecstasy is in Schedule I. Eleven states do not classify it at all (ImpacTeen Illicit Drug Team, 2002).

Like the federal government, most state governments use their drug schedules as a basis for legislating penalty provisions. But there is a lack of uniformity in drug penalties across the states. "At the federal level, it takes 100 times the amount of powder cocaine to equal the same sentence as crack cocaine" (ImpacTeen Illicit Drug Team, 2002, p. 2). As of 2002, "only eleven states specify separate statutory penalties for the possession and/or sale of crack and powder cocaine. The data suggest that distinctions between crack and powder forms of cocaine may be of less importance at the state level, where the majority prosecutions take place" (ImpacTeen, Illicit Drug Team, 2002, p. 2). Most state statutes, however, have provisions for enhanced penalties for second and third conviction like that of the federal government. Five states—Delaware, Florida, New Jersey, Ohio, and Oregon—do not have statutory provisions for enhanced penalties. Most states, however, enacted legislations for enhanced penalties for the use and possession of club drugs—Rohypnol, GHB, and ecstasy. "Across the states, the statutorily-imposed maximum imprisonment for sale and possession of Rohypnol, GHB, and ecstasy ranges up to a maximum of lifetime imprisonment. The maximum statutorily-imposed fine for sale of Rohypnol, GHB, and ketamine is $750,000 while the maximum fine for the sale of ecstasy is $1 million" (ImpacTeen Illicit Drug Team, 2002, p. 25).

Policies about the criminalization of marijuana also vary across the states. In the CSA Act, marijuana is in Schedule I, and its violation (possession of 1000 kg or more mixture or 1000 or more plants) carries, for a first-time offender, 10 years to life in prison and a fine of $4 million. As of 2006, thirty states and the District of Columbia have laws that legalize the use and possession of marijuana for medical purposes. "Since 1996, 11 states have enacted laws that effectively allow patients to use medical marijuana despite federal law" (Marijuana Policy Project, 2006, p. 1). How these states will enforce their medical marijuana laws and provisions, however, remains to be seen in the context of the Supreme Court rulings in cases of *United States v. Oakland Cannabis Buyer's Cooperative in 2001*, and the *Raich v. Ashcroft* in 2005. In the first case, the Court ruled that the medical necessity provisions of the states do not apply to third party distribution of marijuana to patients. In the second case, the Court ruled that the federal government has the right, under the interstate commerce clause, to regulate marijuana.

During the 1990s, when the drug war entered into its third decade, both federal and state policy-makers began to reflect on the nature and the effectiveness of drug policy strategies across the various states. In 1992, Congress created a President Commission on Model State Drug Laws for a more comprehensive and balanced approach to drug control in the nation as a whole. The Commission's mission was to develop comprehensive model state laws through the effective use and coordination of prevention, education, treatment, and law enforcement (National Alliance For Model State Drug Laws, 1993). Commission members were drawn from state legislators, state attorney generals, police chiefs, city mayors, drug prevention specialists, and other experts. The Commission in its final report submitted to the National Governors Association, Conference of State Legislatures and the federal drug control community in 1993 submitted 44 model drugs laws and recommendations. The model recommendations were presented under five major titles: Economic Remedies, Community Mobilization, Crime Code Enforcement, Treatment, and Drug-Free School and Families. The Commission recommended for expanding and strengthening the law enforcement, but it focused "many of its legislative ideas on the front-end: prevention and education" (National Alliance For Model State Drug Laws, 1993, p. 3).

A change began to be observed in the direction of national drug policy from the middle of the 1990s, particularly the context of rising concerns about the impact of get tough approach to drug control on prison population, incarcerated families, minority population, and state budgetary allocations,. Both federal and state policy makers since then began to see the need for revisiting the drug sentencing guidelines and developing a more balanced approach combining the tools of law enforcement with education and treatment (Drug Policy Alliance, 2003). In 1995, Congress created a new organization—the National Alliance for Model State Drug Laws (NAMSDAL)—to assist the state governments in translating the recommendations of the President's Commission into laws and enactments. It is estimated that the "states have passed over 100 model laws, policies, or programs because of NAMSDAL's efforts" (Carnevale Associates LLC, 2005). Many of these laws are in the areas of drug education, drug treatment, community-based intervention strategies, school-based prevention programs, media literacy, broadening the drug-free zones, and the revision of the mandatory sentencing guidelines.

Many states in recent years created special policy-making agencies to address the issue of substance abuse in general from the new perspectives emerging from the studies on Model State Drug Laws and other science-based approaches. Connecticut, New York, Ohio, Oklahoma, and South Carolina have recently established cabinet level agencies for substance abuse policies. (National Governors Association Center for Best Practices, 2002). Many states such as Connecticut, Delaware Kentucky, Minnesota, Vermont, North Carolina, and South Carolina have enacted laws to require private insurers to pay for substance abuse treatment. "A program in Connecticut empowers judges to order a full continuum of treatment alternatives for low-risk, first-time offenders. Some alternatives even combine substance abuse treatment with community service requirements" (National Governors Association Center for Best Practices, 2002, p. 10). In 2000, California voters passed Proposition 36 that proposed the treatment-instead-of-incarceration initiative for first-time non-violent drug offenders solely for drug possession. In 2004, California enacted two innovative legislations. The first legislation made it legal for adults to buy sterile syringes without a prescription. The second legislation authorized the government to restore food stamps to drug offenders who served time and are drug-free (Drug Policy Alliance, 2003). A similar law allowing the purchase of sterile syringes without prescription was enacted in Illinois in 2003.

Different states are also revisiting their minimum mandatory drug sentencing guidelines. In the 1980s and 1990s, most states have enacted some form of minimum sentencing guidelines for drug offenders. From the beginning of the 1990s, most states are also rethinking their arrest-to-incarceration strategy. One of the earliest programs in this direction is the Alternative to Incarceration Program (AIP) developed in Connecticut in 1990. Under this program, judges were allowed to give discretionary sentencing for first time drug offenders. In the state's Alternative to Incarceration Centers, drug offenders received education and treatment. Women drug offenders were allowed to keep their children with them during the period of drug treatment. "A three-year longitudinal study of AIP by the Justice Education Center, Inc. completed in 1996, found that program participants were less likely to commit crimes than offenders who had been in prison" (Critical Choices, 2001, p. 8). Texas Governor, Rick Perry, signed a bill in 2003 that mandated probation and treatment instead of incarceration for first time drug offenders caught with less than a gram of most drugs. (National Governors Association Center for Best Practices, 2003) A similar bill was passed in Pennsylvania in 2004.

For three decades, New York had some of toughest drug laws in the nation. New York's Rockefeller Drug Law statutes, enacted in 1973, established mandatory prison sentences of fifteen years to life in prison for certain drug offenses. "Generally, the statutes require judges to impose a sentence of 15-years to life for anyone convicted of selling two ounces, or possessing four ounces of 'narcotic drug'(typically cocaine or heroin)"(Wilson, 2000, p. 1). This was the same punishment given to someone convicted of murder in New York. In 2003, about 38 percent of New York's prison population was drug offenders and 45 percent of women prisoners were convicted of drug offenses. In 2004, after a decade of intense legislative debate and public criticism, New York enacted a new law to reduce the sentencing guideline from fifteen-years to life to 8 to 20 years. It was not a significant change, but it was an indication that the state policy-makers in New York and other get tough states are re-examining their drug policy strategies.

3. 6 Crimes of Illicit Drugs:
Role of the U.S. Supreme Court

From the beginning of drug prohibition in the early twentieth century, the U.S. Supreme Court has been playing an important role through its interpretation of the constitutionality of different drug law enforcement strategies. During the last one hundred years of drug prohibition, the U.S. Supreme Court has made a series of landmark drug decisions. Most of these decisions are in favor of drug prohibitions and the criminalization of addiction and illicit drug use. Since the beginning of the modern drug war in the 1970s, the issues of mandatory drug testing, no-knock drug raid policy, the denial of federal benefits to illicit drug users, the use of drug sniffing dogs during traffic stops, the use of surveillance technology to control drug trafficking, mandatory sentencing for drug offenses and many other policy issues raised a host of constitutional questions. Concerns were raised as to whether those drug law enforcement strategies are in violation of the constitution, particularly the First, Fourth, Fifth, and the Eighth Amendments of the Bill of Rights. Except in a few cases during the last three decades, the U.S. Supreme Court found that those drug policy enforcement strategies are not in violation of the Bill of Rights.

Similar to members of Congress, the majority of the Justices of the U.S. Supreme Court during the last three decades of the drug war have consistently acted on the basis of the harm principle and the utilitarian notion of common good—"the best interest of the state" (Husak & Peele, 1998). The majority of the Justices share the view that illicit drugs are socially harmful and morally unjustifiable. The issues of the constitutional violation of individual rights have largely been interpreted in the context of the government's overriding responsibility of protecting citizens from the harmful effects of illicit drugs. "Acceptance of drug menace was unanimous among Supreme Court Justices. Even those Justices who might have been thought most likely to resist anti-drug measures— such as Marshall and Brennan—were inclined to base their reservations on grounds that seem more procedural than substantive" (Husak & Peele, 1998, p. 20).

The enactment of the Harrison Narcotic Act in 1915 was immediately followed by a number of Supreme Court cases: *United States v. Jim Fuey Moi* in 1916, *United States v. Doremus in 1919, United States v. Web et al.* in 1919, *Whipple v. Martinson* in 1921, *United States v. Behrman* in 1922, and *Linder v. United States* in 1925. In the *United States v. Jim Fuey Moi,* the Court ruled in favor of the Act as a revenue measure, but opposed "broad police power under the Act" (Cohen, 2004, p. 97). In *United States v. Doremus,* the Court ruled that the regulation of narcotic prescription under the Harrison Act was not unconstitutional. In the *Behrman* decision, the Court similarly ruled that the regulation, under the Harrison Act, of medical prescription of narcotics for addiction maintenance was not unconstitutional. In *Linder v. United States,* the Court, for the first time, recognized addiction as a disease and ruled in favor of prescribing narcotics on medical grounds.

From the 1970s, when drug policy began to expand primarily as a policy of criminalization, and hence a policy for behavioral change for those who use and deal with illicit drugs, the U.S. Supreme Court began to hear more cases about the possible governmental infringement on individual rights, freedom, and privacy. In *Oliver v. United States* in 1984, the U.S. Supreme Court ruled that a police officer can enter and search an open field for illicit drugs and drug plants without a warrant even if a "No Trespassing" sign is posted. The Court held that the government's intrusion into an open field is not one of those "unreasonable searches" proscribed by the Fourth Amendment.

In 1998, an Illinois state trooper stopped a man named Roy Caballes for speeding. After the police dispatcher was informed, a member of the Illinois State Police Drug Interdiction Team arrived at the scene and allowed his drug-sniffing dog to walk around the car. The officers searched the trunk and found about $250,000 worth of marijuana. Roy Caballes was convicted on federal drug charges, sentenced to 12 years in prison, and fined $256,136. After an appeal, the Illinois Supreme Court, on the ground of improper search and seizure, vacated the verdict of the lower court. But the U.S. Supreme Court challenged the judgment of the Illinois Supreme Court and ruled that police officers could use drug-sniffing dogs to search for drugs in cars stopped for traffic violations. In delivering the opinion of the Court in this landmark decision in 2005, Justice Stevens said: "A dog sniff conducted during a concededly lawful traffic stop that reveals no information other than the location of a substance that no individual has any right to possess does not violate the Fourth Amendment" (Legal Information Institute, 2005, p. 3).

In *Michigan v. Sitz et al* in 1990, the Supreme Court ruled that setting checkpoints and road blocks to search for intoxicated motorists was not "unreasonable searches." But in *Indianapolis v. Edmond* in 2000, the Court ruled that setting check points and roadblocks with the expressed intention of imposing criminal penalties was in violation of the Fourth Amendment. In 1991, an agent of the Department of Interior, by using a thermal imager, discovered the production of marijuana in the home of an Oregon man, named Danny Kyllo. Kyllo was indicted on federal drug charges, and the Ninth Circuit Court did not find any violation of the Fourth Amendment by law enforcement for using the thermal imager. The U.S. Supreme Court, in *Kyllo v. United States* in 2001, ruled that the use of a thermal imager to search a private home from afar without issuing a warrant is a violation of the Fourth Amendment. However, in *Maryland v. Pringle* in 2003, the Supreme Court opined that drug arrests could be based on improbable cause. That means that it will not be a violation of the Fourth Amendment if a police officer arrests someone who is found near drugs. In the Maryland case, a Baltimore County police officer stopped a car for speeding. The officer found some cash and a quantity of cocaine in the car, but all three passengers of the car denied any knowledge and ownership of the drug.

One of the significant policy strategies for demand reduction is drug testing. The Drug-Free Act of 1988 made drug testing mandatory for some types of federal and state employees. Drug testing can also be legally required for students, athletes, prisoners, welfare recipients, and residents living in public housing.

The legally acceptable method of drug testing is the urine analysis. This policy has brought a number of cases in the Supreme Court on the ground of the possible violation of the Fourth Amendment. In *Skinner v. Railway Labor Executive's Association* in 1989, *Treasury Employees v. Von Raab* in 1989, and *Veronica School District v. Wayne Action* in 1995, the U.S. Supreme Court ruled that drug testing through urine samples taken in a non-invasive manner does not violate the Fourth Amendment. In *Board of Education of Pottawatomie County v. Earls et al* in 2001, the Tenth Circuit Court ruled that the Board of Education's policy of drug testing of those students who participate in extracurricular activities was in violation of the Fourth amendment. The U.S. Supreme Court however, vacated the judgment of the Tenth Circuit and ruled in 2002 that the Board's policy is not in violation of the constitution. Justice Thomas in delivering the Court's opinion said: "Because this policy serves the School Districts' important interests in detecting and preventing drug use among its students, we hold that it is constitutional" (Legal Information Institute, 2002, p. 1). In 2002, the Supreme Court gave another ruling that now affects millions of Americans who live in public housing. The Court ruled that governmental policies to evict illicit drug users from public housing are not in violation of the Fourth Amendment.

Another landmark decision that came from the U.S. Supreme Court recently is about medical marijuana. In 1996, California voters enacted proposition 215 to legalize medical marijuana. There are ten more states—Alaska, Arizona, Colorado, Hawaii, Maine, Maryland, Nevada, Oregon, Vermont, and Washington—where medical marijuana is legal. In 2002, a California woman named Angel Raich filed a suit against the then Attorney General John Ashcroft and the Justice Department to prevent the DEA from destroying her sources of medical marijuana. The Ninth Circuit Court in 2002 gave a judgment that the federal Controlled Substance Act was in conflict with the state's Proposition 215 and issued an injunction to prevent the DEA from raiding the medpot clubs in California. In June 2005, the U.S. Supreme Court vacated the judgment of the Ninth Circuit Court, and ruled that the federal government, under the Controlled Substance Act, can arrest the users and producers of medical marijuana, and also the doctors who prescribe medical marijuana even in the states where state laws legalized the use and the production of medical marijuana. The Court based its ruling primarily on the power of Congress to regulate interstate commerce. The Court held the view that even if medical marijuana is used and produced within the states, it would have substantial impact on interstate commerce.

3.7 Criminalization, Legalization, and Harm Reduction: Future of National Drug Policy Debates

The recent legislations passed by Congress, the national policy strategies developed by ONDCP, different drug-related rulings of the U.S. Supreme Court, and recent drug policy developments in the states suggest that the nation is certainly searching for a more balanced approach to fight the drug war. In this search, however, one does not see the end of the era of criminalization, and the beginning of a new age of drug legalization in America. Legalization offers two alternatives: the first is the complete legalization of the production, manufacturing, trafficking, and use of all drugs. The second is the decriminalization of illicit drugs. Legalization ignores the harm principle and the issues of drugs and morality. The perspective of harm reduction, on the other hand, suggests a strategy not for incarceration but for the reduction of the effects of drugs. This strategy, widely used in some countries of Europe, includes drug education, drug treatments and counseling, needle exchange programs, methadone maintenance, and many other kinds of social intervention strategies (Inciardi & Harrison, 2000).

The harm reduction perspective proposes that drugs are physically harmful, but it ignores the issues of drug-crime connections in particular and the issues of drugs and morality in general. The advocates of harm reduction are in favor of illicit drug use and the decriminalization of drugs. Both the perspectives of legalization and harm reduction also ignore the magnitude of the global production and trafficking of illicit drugs and their impacts on drug use, global organized crime, global human trafficking, and global terrorism. In America, the search for a more balanced approach will continue, but it is very unlikely that the perspectives of legalization and harm reduction will bring any major departure from the existing drug policy paradigm of criminalization. As one recent DEA document reveals: "Legalization of drugs will lead to increased levels of addiction. Legalization has been tried before, it failed miserably. Europe's more liberal drug policies are not the right model for America. Illegal drugs are illegal because they are harmful" (United States Drug Enforcement Administration, 2003, pp. 2-3).

CHAPTER 4

POLICY-MAKING IN JUVENILE JUSTICE: GROWTH, CHANGE, AND CONTINUTY

The tradition of a separate system of justice for the juveniles is one of the unique characteristics of crime and justice in America. America's juvenile justice system is a complex network of institutions of court, police, and corrections specially created and trained for dealing with juvenile delinquency. The system also includes numerous federal and state laws and statutes, departments and agencies, commissions and task forces, and programs and initiatives created to control and prevent juvenile crime. With the progress of change and modernization, juvenile delinquency has increased in all societies of the world, including the United States. The social and economic transformations, particularly in the institutions of family, marriage, kinship, and parenting that came in the wake of industrialization and modernization vastly impacted the lives of children. In response to many challenges brought into the lives of juveniles by modernization, America's innovation has been the creation of a separate system of juvenile justice based on the doctrine of *parens patriae* and the enlightened correctional philosophy of rehabilitation. This chapter will examine the nature and extent of juvenile delinquency in America, the role of different federal and state policy actors in juvenile justice, and the policy debates and disputes about the shifting boundaries between adult and juvenile justice systems, on the one hand, and the philosophies of rehabilitation and punishment for juveniles on the other.

4.1 Juveniles within the Juvenile Justice System

The U.S. Census Bureau's projection is that by 2010, the U.S population will increase to about 309 million, and by 2020 to about 336 million. The U.S. juvenile population, ages 5-19, was about 22 percent of the total population in the year 2000. The Census Bureau projected that by 2050, juvenile population, ages 5-19, will remain around 19-20 percent of the total U.S. population. In the year 2000, the total number of juveniles' ages 10-19 was about 41 million, and juveniles ages 10-17 were about 33 million. The overall growth rate for juveniles under 18 of all races between 1999 and 2015 is projected to remain around 8-9 percent. However, between the same period, Asian and Hispanic juveniles will grow much faster than White and Black juveniles. Asian and Hispanic juveniles will grow at a rate of 74 percent and 59 percent, respectively. White and Black juveniles will grow at a rate of 3 percent and 19 percent, respectively.These profiles and developments will have important impacts on juvenile justice policymaking in the first decade of the 21st century.

In between 1945 and 1995—for half a century—juvenile offenses in all categories, including violent crimes, property crimes, drug law violations, and public order crimes, have consistently increased. It is only from the late 1990s that juvenile crime, particularly violent juvenile crime, is showing a slightly declining trend. In 1940, the rate of delinquency (ages 10-17) cases handled by the U.S. juvenile courts was about 10.5 per 1,000 population. The rate of court cases handled increased to 16.1 in 1950, 20.1 in 1960, 32.3 in 1970, 38.3 in 1980, and 47.0 in 1989. In 1950, there were about 37,000 training schools and 3,900 hundred detention homes for juvenile delinquents in the United States. In 1970, the total number of schools for juvenile delinquents increased to about 66,000, and total number of juvenile detention homes increased to about 10,000 (Kurian, 1994, pp. 163, 410).

Juvenile crime and delinquency emerged as a major challenge for crime policymakers particularly from the middle of the 1970s. Violent juvenile crime reached an alarming rate of growth in the 1980s—a phenomenon described as the coming of a new generation of "super-predators" and a potential "time bomb" for the 21st century. Between the 1960s and 1970s, the juvenile homicide rate nearly doubled. In 1976, the homicide offending rate for White juveniles ages 14-17 was 10.9 per 100,000 population. In 1994, it increased to 24.8 per 100,000 population. In 1976, the homicides rate for Black juveniles ages 14-17 was 80.3 per 100,000 population. In 1994, it increased to 235.1 per 100,000 population (see Table 16). In 2002, homicide rate for White juveniles of the same age group was 9.2 and the rate for Black juveniles was 54.5. Between 1976 and 2002, juveniles ages 14-17 comprised about 10.6 percent of the total homicide offenders. In 2004, juvenile's ages 13-19 committed 2,035 murders of which males committed 1,890 and females committed 144 murders. Out of 2,035 murders in 2004, White juveniles committed 855 murders, Black juveniles committed 1,079 murders, and juveniles of other races committed 56 murders (Federal Bureau of Investigation, 2004).

During the decades of the 1980s and 1990s, juvenile offenses for possession of illegal weapons, illicit drug abuse, property crimes, and public order violations also rapidly increased. In 1974, juveniles accounted for 16 percent of those arrested for possession of illegal weapons. It increased to 23 percent in 1993. Between 1985 and 1993, adult arrests for possession of illegal weapons grew by 33 percent, but juvenile arrests for illegal weapons increased by more than 100 percent (Bureau of Justice Statistics, 1995). Between 1980 and 1999, 62 percent of White juveniles, 76 percent of Black juveniles, and 71 percent of Asian and Pacific Islander juveniles used firearms in the commission of crimes (Office of Juvenile Justice and Delinquency Prevention, 2001). In 1976, juveniles ages 14-17 used guns in 1,067 cases of homicides. In 1993, the number of guns used increased to 3,531. In 2002, the number of homicides committed with guns was 1,018 (Bureau of Justice Statistics, 2004).

Table 16: Juvenile Male Homicide Offending Rates, 1976-2000
Age 14-17 (per 100,000 Population)

Year	White Male	Black Male	Year	White Male	Black Male
1976	10.9	80.3	1989	16.7	135.0
1977	11.2	73.8	1990	22.0	194.0
1978	11.0	70.1	1991	22.8	213.6
1979	13.5	78.4	1992	23.3	208.5
1980	13.9	83.5	1993	22.8	253.0
1981	11.6	82.6	1994	24.8	235.1
1982	11.6	69.0	1995	22.0	178.6
1983	11.0	57.3	1998	14.1	80.2
1984	10.0	52.6	1999	10.5	68.3
1985	10.4	68.9	2000	8.0	63.2
1986	13.0	79.8	2001	8.2	60.8
1988	14.6	125.1	2002	9.2	54.5

Source: Bureau of Justice Statistics (2004). Homicide Trends in the United States

During the decades of the 1980s and 1990s, illicit drug use by juveniles also considerably increased. The 2002 Monitoring the Future Survey found that 24.5 percent of 8th graders, 44.6 percent of 10th graders, and 53 percent of 12th graders used an illicit drug in their lifetime. The Survey also found that in 2002, 11.7 percent of 8th graders, 20.8 percent of 10th graders, and 25.4 percent of 12th graders used an illicit drug in the past month. The problem of juvenile drug abuse is related in different ways to juvenile violent crime, and juvenile gangs, sex, and prostitution. According to the National Youth Gang Survey, more than 24,500 gangs and 772,500 gang members exist in more than 3,330 cities across the United States. The gang members surveyed indicated that about 95 percent of their activities are within one or more high schools in their jurisdictions (Office of Juvenile Justice and Delinquency Prevention, 2002; 2004). Although more than ninety percent of juvenile offenses in all categories are committed by juvenile males, juvenile females are also participating in high proportions, particularly in gangs, drugs, and juvenile prostitution (Office of Juvenile Justice and Delinquency Prevention, 1998; 2004; 2006).

The nature and extent of juvenile crime can be understood also by looking at the rate and trends in juvenile arrests, court processing of juvenile cases, and the number of juveniles in correctional institutions (Office of Juvenile Justice and Delinquency Prevention, 2005). In 2003, there were 137,658 juveniles arrested for drug law violations by state and local law enforcement agencies. This represented about 11.7 percent of the total arrestees for drug violations in 2003 (Office of National Drug Control Policy, 2005). Between 1994 and 2003, according to the UCR 2004, the country's law enforcement agencies arrested over 1.9 million juveniles for drug law violations. During the same period, the juvenile proportion of arrests for drug abuse remained unchanged. In 1994, the juveniles accounted for 11.8 percent of arrests for drug law violations. Ten years later, in 2004, juveniles still accounted for 11.6 percent of all arrests for drug law violations (Federal Bureau of Investigation, 2004). In 2004, about 10.7 percent of those arrested for murder, and 16.3 percent of those arrested for forcible rape were juveniles. In 2004, Juveniles accounted for about 27.5 percent of all property crimes, 26.5 percent of all motor vehicles theft, 28.6 percent of all burglaries, 50 percent of all arsons, and 23 percent of all robberies (Federal Bureau of Investigation, 2004).

Between 1980 and 2001, juvenile arrests for all categories of crimes did not show any significant decline. In 1980, there were about 7,500 juvenile arrests per 100,000 population for all crimes. In 2001, the total number of juvenile arrests for all crimes still remained about 6,890 per 100,000 population. In 2003, the juvenile arrest rate for violent crime index and property crime index offenses showed a declining trend, but "between 1980 and 2003, juvenile arrests for simple assault increased 269% for females and 102% for males. During the same period juvenile arrest rate for drug abuse violations increased 51% for females and 52% for males" (Office of Juvenile Justice and Delinquency Prevention, 2005, p. 1).

Between 1960 and 1994, delinquency caseloads in juvenile courts increased 280 percent. In 1960, juvenile courts handled about 400,000 cases. In 1980, the number of caseloads increased to about 1,000,000. In 1994, the total caseloads in juvenile courts increased to about 1,500,000 (Office of Juvenile Justice and Delinquency Prevention, 1997). More than 50 percent of juvenile cases are at present formally processed. Between 1987 and 1996, the number of formally processed juvenile cases increased 78 percent. In 1987, about 575,000 cases were formally processed. In 1996, the total number of cases formally processed by juvenile courts increased to about 1,000,000 (Office of Juvenile Delinquency and Prevention, 1999). Between 1989 and 1998, the number of juvenile cases waved to criminal court increased 51 percent (Office of Juvenile Justice and Delinquency Prevention, 2001). Another trend is that more female juveniles are entering into the formal justice system. Between 1990 and 1999, the number of cases involving female delinquents increased 59 percent—from 250,100 cases in 1990 to 398,600 cases in 1999 (Office of Juvenile Justice and Delinquency Prevention, 2003). One of the Bureau of Justice Statistics (1999) report on women offenders found that "Juveniles accounted for about 28% of female violent offenders nearly identical to the juvenile percentage (26%) found among violent offenders" (p, 3).

As more juveniles were formally processed, the numbers of juveniles in corrections and residential facilities, both public and private, have also rapidly increased in the 1990s. In 1999, 134,000 juveniles were held in 2, 939 juvenile facilities in the United States. Between 1991 and 1999, juvenile delinquents committed to juvenile facilities grew by 51 percent. The national custody rate for juveniles in 1997 was 368 juveniles per 100,000 population but the state custody rate varies from 96 (Vermont and Hawaii) to 704 (District of Columbia). In 1999, about 35 percent of juveniles in juvenile facilities were person offenders, and minorities accounted for 70 percent of the juveniles held in custody for violent crime index offenses (Office of Juvenile Justice and Delinquency Prevention, 1999). Non-Hispanic black juveniles accounted for 55 percent of juveniles held for robbery and 65 percent of juveniles held for drug trafficking (Office of Juvenile Justice and Delinquency Prevention, 2004). The custody rate for Black juveniles was highest in the nation in 1999. About seventy percent of the juveniles in custody in 1999 were in locked rather than staff-secure facilities.

As a result of formal court processing and the growth of state transfer statutes, thousands of juveniles are now held in adult jails and prisons. In 2000, nationwide adult jails held about 7,600 juveniles younger than 18 years of age. The number of jail inmates younger than age 18 held as adults increased 50 percent between 1994 and 1996. Juveniles held as adults in state adult prisons are mostly minority males and person offenders. About 60 percent of the juveniles sent to adult state prisons committed person offenses (homicide, sexual assault, robbery, and assault). The one-day count of state prisoners younger than 18 years of age increased 135 percent between 1985 and 1997. It fell 28 percent by 2000, for an overall increase of 70 percent (Office of Juvenile Justice and Delinquency Prevention, 2004). These facts and figures about the nature and extent of juvenile crime and corrections suggest the need for understanding the nature of policy-making in juvenile justice. The nature and expansion of a separate system of justice for juveniles, the nature of organizing the juvenile court, the process of adjudication within the juvenile court, the nature of juvenile sentencing and corrections, and juvenile crime control and prevention strategies—all depend on policymaking in juvenile justice.

4.2 Evolution of Juvenile Justice:
Historical, Philosophical and Legal Roots

Although systematic federal policy-making in juvenile justice in America did not begin until the 1970s, the roots for a separate system of juvenile justice were established more than hundred years ago through the creation of juvenile court in Illinois in 1899. Within a decade after 1899, the juvenile court movement spread throughout the country, and by the 1930s separate juvenile courts were established in most of the states. At that time, there were no major federal agencies and initiatives for policy-making in juvenile justice, no effective system of gathering information about juvenile crime and corrections, and no judicial review of the functioning of juvenile courts. But still a system of juvenile justice was slowly evolving throughout the twentieth century as one of the major innovations in American criminal justice.

Colonial Juvenile Justice
In America

The judicial system is one of the first institutions set up in the American colonies in the late seventeenth and eighteenth centuries. In the thirteen different colonies, there were thirteen different judicial systems. There, were, however, many similarities. All colonial judicial systems were largely based on the English Common Law, and there was no separation of powers between the executive and the judiciary. The colonial governors and the members of the legislative councils used to sit in the courts along with the judges and justices. The judicial system was responsible not only for crime and justice but also for domestic peace and tranquility. The judges and justices used to render verdicts, the county sheriffs used to enforce the laws, and the constables used to carry out the punishment. According to one historical source, at the time of the American Revolution, colonial Virginia had more than sixty county courts where judges were appointed from local business and landed elites (Perry, 2001).

In the American colonies of the seventeenth and eighteenth centuries, juvenile delinquency was a problem of considerable concern. Juvenile delinquency came to be a problem of particular concern from the beginning of settlement in the New World (Senna, 1994). The New World was a world of new opportunities. But it was also a world of crisis in the functions and reconstruction of family. The New World of unbounded opportunities brought many youths who were socially and economically marginal and disadvantaged in the hierarchical society of feudal Europe. In the Colony of Virginia, "youths were sent over by 'spirits', who were agents of merchants or ship owners. The spirits attempted to persuade young people to immigrate to America. They often promised that the New World would bring tremendous wealth and happiness to the youthful immigrants" (Krisberg, 2004, p. 21). In the socially fragile societies of the new colonies, many of them were forced to turn into crime. One historical account finds that in the early nineteenth century, the city of Boston was flooded with juvenile thieves who caused a great concern for the whole Commonwealth of Massachusetts (The Encyclopedia of American Crime, 2001). Juvenile property theft was also widespread in the Colony of New York in the eighteenth century (Greenberg, 1976).

The colonial judicial systems made no difference between adult and juvenile criminals, adult and juvenile punishments, adult and juvenile prisons, and adult and juvenile justice systems. There were judicial discretions in colonial systems in terms of gender and social ranks and status, but not in terms of age. According to the English Common Law of the colonies, juvenile offenders from the age of seven were legally accountable for their actions and could receive the same penalties as adults. In Colonial Virginia, juvenile offenders of 7 and 8 years old were prosecuted as adults and received adult punishments. The theft of twelve pence or one shilling, according to the English Common Law, was punishable by death. The usual punishment for a felony conviction was death by hanging. "Children convicted of crime might be taken out to the whipping post after receiving a stern tongue-lashing from the justices" (Perry, 2001, p. 3).

The General Laws of the Massachusetts Colonies, described as "Body of Liberties of 1641," imposed death penalty for rebellious juveniles, and for juveniles 16 years of age and older for cursing a natural parent. This law, however, was repealed in 1672. Until the establishment of the Commonwealth of Massachusetts in 1780, juvenile murder, rape, unwed pregnancy, and arson were punishable by death (Burns, 1999). The American colonies made many innovations in representative government, bicameral legislature, decentralized judiciary, law enforcement, and jury system, but they made no significant innovations in juvenile justice. William Penn's "Great Law" enacted by the first legislature of Pennsylvania in 1682, contained ideas for the humanization and rationalization of prison and punishment, but it made no significant departure from the colonial model of juvenile justice.

Philosophical Roots

The creation of a separate juvenile court in Illinois in 1899, and hence the birth of a new institution of juvenile justice, was not an event of historical accident. The Illinois Juvenile Court Act emerged in the wake of the convergence of at least four major historical streams of thought about the modernization of crime and justice in general, and the concerns for juveniles within the system in particular. Ideas that set the context of the Juvenile Court Act of 1899, the ideology that contributed to the spread of juvenile court movement in the early twentieth century, and the many institutions that remain central to contemporary juvenile justice have evolved from those different streams of thought that have been growing over a long period of time.

The first stream of thought was philosophical in nature. It was a thought to understand the competing roles of family and the state. It was to understand the justifications on the part of the "king" or the state to intervene into the affairs of the juveniles. From the beginning of the breakdown of feudal societies in Europe, and the emergence of modern urban-industrial societies and nation-states in the late eighteenth and early nineteenth centuries, the institution of family has been rapidly changing. From that time, a philosophical notion began to grow that the state must act as the guardian of the children who are abused, neglected, and abandoned by their families. The state has the right to be concerned about the welfare of its children. This philosophical notion is the doctrine of *parens patriae* (in Latin, meaning Parent of the Country) came from English Common Law and the feudal notion of *"royal prerogative."* The Illinois Juvenile Court Act of 1899 was based on this doctrine of *parens patriae.* This doctrine provides the philosophical and legal justifications on the part of the government to send juvenile offenders in corrections, rehabilitation centers, mental health institutions, and Boot Camps. It is because of this doctrine that the government can enforce regulations to control juvenile behavior through such measures as compulsory school attendance, compulsory school drug testing, and juvenile curfew.

The Legal Traditions

The second historical trend that contributed to the growth of modern juvenile justice is the growth of laws and legal bodies related to crime and justice in general and juvenile crime in particular. Long before the rise of the doctrine of *parens patriae* in the English Common Law, the Code of Hammurabi in 1700 B.C. established the rights of the "king" to administer justice for common good. The Code of Hammurabi, as mentioned in Chapter I, established the notions of legal uniformity, codification of laws, victim-offender reconciliation, and victim's restitution. Section 185-186 of the Code of Hammurabi dealt with the issues of juvenile delinquency and juvenile justice. For Hammurabi, the first and foremost delinquency on the part of a son is to refuse to choose the profession of his father. Although the Code of Hammurabi prescribed severe punishment for juvenile delinquency and said that "If a son has struck his father, his hands shall be cut off," there were also provisions of foster homes for delinquent children.

In the Roman Law of the Twelve Tables in 450 B.C., there was a clear recognition that juveniles do not have a clear sense of responsibility and that the state has collective responsibility for the welfare of juveniles. The Twelve Tables regarded children as the property of their fathers, but if a father is convicted of crime, the children cease to be under his power. Even at that ancient time, there were conceptions of guardianship and mentoring which were described by Roman Law as tutoring for disadvantaged youths on state expenses. Section XX of the Twelve Tables states: "It is agreeable to the law that the person under the age of puberty should be under tutelage, so that persons of tender years may be under the government of another." These concepts of the Twelve Table pre-dated the modern notion of rehabilitation of delinquent juveniles. Roman Law, later codified by Byzantine Emperor Justinian I in 529 AD, is one of the two main legal systems that govern modern societies, particularly those of western civilization (the other is the English Common Law).

The English Common Law did not make a difference between juvenile and adult crimes, and juvenile and adult justice systems, but a series of institutional innovations in modern juvenile justice came from the English Common Law. The English Common Law is a body of laws evolved over a long period of time in England based on judicial precedents and common wisdom of people about right and wrong. British King Henry II in 1154 codified the English Common Law. The doctrine of *"doli incapax defence,"* the presumption of incapacity to commit a felony, was developed by the English Common Law. This doctrine, for the first time introduced the relevance of chronological age in juvenile justice. Children under the age of seven, in Common Law, are incapable of committing a felony crime. The Common Law further suggests that this presumption of innocence can be extended to children between seven and thirteen if it can be established that they did not have sufficient knowledge and experience to know the difference between right and wrong, and the consequences of their actions. The Common Law doctrine of the presumption of incapacity is the source of contemporary notions about criminal responsibility and juvenile court jurisdictions.

Modern parental responsibility laws, unfit parental laws, and the "contribution to the delinquency of a minor" clause came from the English Common Law. In English Common Law, parents are responsible for the behavior of their children. Parents have the obligations to direct and control the behavior of their children. In contemporary juvenile justice, this Common Law issue of parental responsibility is a matter of considerable attention to policy-makers. The modern concept of probation is also an extension of the English Common Law practice of the conditional suspension of punishment. It was on the basis of this notion that John Augustus (1785-1859), a Boston Shoemaker, led a movement for probation in the 1840s, and the Commonwealth of Massachusetts formally made it a law in 1878.

In addition to controlling juvenile delinquency and punishing the juvenile offenders, it is also a great concern in modern juvenile justice to protect the rights of juveniles and juvenile offenders. The legal heritage of the notion of the limits of power and the need for protecting the rights of the citizens goes back to the Magna Carta promulgated by King John of England in 1215 in response to a possible rebellion by his Barons. Clause 39 of the Magna Carta states: "No freeman shall be arrested or imprisoned, or disposed, or outlawed or exiled or in any way victimized, neither will we attack him or send anyone to attack him, except by the lawful judgment of his peers or by the law of the land." In the Magna Carta, King John proclaimed: "To none will we sell, will we deny, or delay right or justice." The Magna Carta since then remained as the principle source of the legal foundation of the concept of "rights of the citizen" in English Common Law.

The Magna Carta is the foundation not just of English Common Law, but also the American Bill of Rights which became the first constitutional document for modern criminal justice. Although it did not create a separate system of juvenile justice in America, the Bill of Rights established the legal framework of modern crime and justice more than hundred years before the Illinois Juvenile Court Act of 1899. All the Bill Rights clauses such as the freedom of speech, freedom of religion, right to trial by jury, and protection against unreasonable search and seizures, and cruel and unusual punishment are equally applicable to adult and juvenile justice systems.

Institutional Innovations Before the
Illinois Juvenile Court Act of 1899

The third historical trend was related to institutional innovations for juvenile corrections. In the nineteenth century, juvenile delinquency became a major concern particularly in big cities like New York, Boston, and Chicago. Increased use of child industrial labor, the growth of urbanization, the influx new immigrants, the rise of illegitimate births, and the deaths of hundreds of thousands of soldiers from the Civil War—all contributed to the rise of juvenile delinquency in the nineteenth century. Some have described the new trend as the emergence of a "dangerous class" (Bremner, 1970). The major concern for policy-making for the juveniles in the nineteenth century was to create not a separate system of juvenile justice, but separate institutions for juvenile corrections. Throughout the nineteenth century, separate institutions for juvenile corrections were built in different cities. These institutions were the precursors of many of the core institutions and ideas of modern juvenile justice.

An Act of Boston City Council created the first state institution for juvenile correction—the Boston House of Reformation—in 1826. Throughout the nineteenth century, state supported juvenile reform schools were established in Massachusetts, New York, Illinois, Maryland, Ohio, Michigan, Connecticut, Maine, Pennsylvania, Rhode Island, and Wisconsin (Bremner, 1970). Along with state supported institutions, there also grew institutions for juvenile corrections on the basis of the support of civil society organizations and philanthropic societies in different cities in the nineteenth century. One of the widely known was the House of Refuse established first in New York by the New York Society for Reformation of Juvenile Delinquents in 1825. The House of Refuge movement quickly spread in different states and cities in the early nineteenth century. House of Refuge was established in Philadelphia in 1828, Maryland in 1830, and Pennsylvania in 1850 (renamed as Pennsylvania Reform School in 1876).

The Enlightenment, Growth of Science, and Modern Juvenile Justice

The fourth stream of thought was about the application of science in solving juvenile delinquency. The evolution of modern juvenile justice came as a result of differentiation in the process of the evolution of modern criminal justice. One of the major intellectual contexts for the evolution of modern criminal justice was the philosophy of Enlightenment and the growth of science and scientific mentality in the eighteenth and nineteenth centuries. The core of the philosophy of Enlightenment was the theme that humans can create a good society with the application of science, reason, and rationality. Enlightened discussions on the problem of juveniles began in America in the middle of the nineteenth century in response to the trend of institutionalization of juveniles in the Houses of Refuge and other juvenile reformatories. A vigorous movement for a new style of policy-making for juveniles started during the era of Progressivism in the late nineteenth century. One group of progressive reformers, particularly women and social work reformers, known as "Child Savers" at that time, began to push for more rehabilitative measures to address the problem of juvenile delinquency. The Child Saver Movement galvanized a sense that the problem of juvenile delinquency was a national issue, and it must be in the agenda for policy-making by the federal government. The Juvenile Court Act of 1899 was the by-product of the Child Saver Movement. While the Child Saver advocates pushed for new policy directions in juvenile justice, another group of progressive reformers pushed for more scientific understanding of the problem of juvenile delinquency. Women groups, academic scholars, and social reformers who led the Progressive Movement believed in the philosophy of the Enlightenment. They had faith that through the application of social science, particularly sociological knowledge and research, many social problems, including the rising problem of juvenile delinquency, could be solved (Vidich & Lyman, 1985). Progressive activists brought science and scientific mentality into the core of policy-making for juvenile justice in general. Many philosophical ideas, legal doctrines, institutional developments, and scientific perceptions about juvenile delinquency and juvenile justice evolved a long time before the Illinois Juvenile Court Act of 1899. It was these different historical trends that set the stage for the growth of a separate system of juvenile justice in America from the beginning of the twentieth century.

4.3 Federal Policy Evolution in Juvenile Justice, 1900-1970

Federal involvement in policy-making for juvenile justice began at the beginning of the twentieth century as a part of national concern for the welfare of American children in general. Before the 1970s, there were no major institutions for federal policy-making in juvenile justice, and no major enactments were made by Congress. There was no national system of juvenile justice, but there were different systems of juvenile justice in different states centering primarily on the activities of juvenile courts. In 1904, two women social workers, named Lillian Wald and Florence Kelley, along with a group of Progressive activists, started a national movement, described as National Child Labor Committee, for the welfare of American Children. In 1912, the federal government, in response to that movement, created the Children's Bureau by an Act of Congress. It was the first federal enactment for the welfare of children in America. President Roosevelt saw the creation of the Bureau as a major step for research-based policy-making for juvenile welfare and juvenile justice. President Taft signed the Children's Bureau Act in 1912 (Lindenmeyer, 1977). One of the major functions of the Children's Bureau in the first four decades was to provide and synthesize research-based studies on the problems of children for federal policy-makers. The Children's Bureau currently is one of the oldest federal organizations. It is now one of the four Bureaus within the Office of the Administration for Children and Families, Department of Health and Human Services. The Children's Bureau is now responsible mainly for providing technical assistance to state and local government programs on children and family welfare. The Bureau currently has ten National Resource Centers including the National Resource Center for Special Needs Adoption.

The second most important federal policy innovation about the welfare of children before the 1970s was the decennial White House Conference on Children and Youth. The First Conference, convened by President Roosevelt, was held in 1909 on the problem of neglected and disadvantaged youth, and it was instrumental in the passing of the Children's Bureau Act of 1912. The 1950 White House Conference on Children and Youth, convened by President Eisenhower, particularly deliberated on the federal role in developing a national system of juvenile justice. After the 1950 Conference, President Eisenhower set up a Council of National Organization on Children and Youth. Within the Council, a division titled The National Committee for Children and Youth was created, through an Executive Order, to work as a federal clearinghouse and consultative agency for improving child welfare services of state and local organizations. After the 1970 White House Conference on Children and Youth, a federal policy was introduced for the creation of Committee on Children and Youth in all the states. The decennial White House Conferences played a significant role in creating a national agenda for policy-making on issues of children and disadvantaged youths, including juvenile justice.

On the recommendations of the National Committee for Children and Youth, and the President Kennedy's Committee on Juvenile Delinquency and Youth Crime, the Congress enacted the first juvenile crime control legislation titled as Juvenile Delinquency and Youth Offenses Control Act in 1961 (PL 87-274). In its signing ceremony on September 23, 1961, President Kennedy said: "The Nature of our country depends upon our younger people who will occupy position of responsibility and leadership in the coming days. Yet for 11 years, juvenile delinquency has been increasing. No city or state in our country has been immune." Through the Juvenile Delinquency and Youth Offenses Control Act of 1961, the federal government, for the first time, made a formal commitment to work with state and local agencies to control and prevent juvenile crime and to improve the nation's juvenile justice system. The Secretary of the Department of Health, Education, and Welfare was authorized to administer the Act in consultation with the National Committee for Children and Youth chaired by the Attorney General. The Act authorized 10 million dollars for three years. "Under this Act, the Department of Health, Education, and Welfare (HEW) provided funds to state, local, and private non-profit agencies to conduct demonstration projects on improved methods of preventing and controlling juvenile crime" (Raley, 1995, p. 12).

One of the major turning points in the growth of federal policy-making in juvenile justice, as mentioned in chapter 2, was the creation of the Commission on Law Enforcement and Administration by President Johnson in 1965. The President's Commission included a separate Task Force for the reorganization of juvenile justice on the basis of the "systems approach" recommended by the Hoover Commission on Law Observance and Enforcement in 1929. The Commission's Task Force on Juvenile Delinquency made six recommendations: 1) decriminalization of status offenses, 2) diversion of youth from the court system to alternative treatment programs, 3) protection of juvenile rights through the due process law, 4) deinstitutionalization, 5) diversification of services, and 6) decentralization of control (Raley, 1995). On the basis of these recommendations of the President's Commission, Congress passed the Juvenile Delinquency Prevention and Control Act of 1968 (PL 90-351) as a part of the Omnibus Crime Control and Safe Street Act of 1968. The Juvenile Delinquency Prevention and Control Act of 1968 mandated the modernization of the nation's juvenile justice system in light of the recommendations of the President's Commission, and attempted to prevent juvenile delinquency through community-based programs and approaches.

To summarize, in the first decade of the 1900, the federal government did not have any significant commitment and involvement in policy-making for juvenile justice. Federal commitment, however, began to grow from the second decade of the 1900s. The Hoover Commission of 1929 and the President's Commission of 1965 greatly emphasized the need for federal involvement in the modernization of the nation's juvenile justice system. The enactment of the Juvenile Delinquency and Youth Offenses Act of 1961 and the Juvenile Delinquency Prevention and Control Act of 1968 set the stage for greater involvement of the federal government in policy-making for juvenile justice in the three subsequent decades of the twentieth century.

4.4 Federal Policy Evolution in Juvenile Justice, 1970-2006

From the beginning of the 1970s, federal policy-making in juvenile justice began as an integral part of the growth of federal government's aggressive involvement in crime and justice in general. From the 1970s, the process of federalization in crime and justice began to be more prominent in the areas of the prevention of juvenile delinquency and the modernization of juvenile justice. A consensus emerged among policy makers at the beginning of the 1970s that the federal role in juvenile justice must expand not just in providing funds and technical assistance to the states, but also in reforming the juvenile justice system as a whole. During the last three decades, a series of new enactments were made, a number of federal organizations were created, and hundreds of programs for preventing juvenile crimes were developed by the federal government. At the beginning of the twenty-first century, the federal government remained deeply entrenched into the nation's policy-making for juvenile justice. The following section will describe federal policy developments for juvenile justice in five major sectors: federal institutional developments for juvenile justice, federal policy developments for a national system of juvenile justice, federal policy initiatives for juvenile justice process improvement, federal juvenile justice grants and programs, and the role of Congress in policy-making for juvenile justice in general.

Federal Juvenile Justice Policy Institutions

In addition to Congress and the U.S. Supreme Court, there are three major federal institutions responsible for policy-making in juvenile justice. These are the Office of Juvenile Justice and Delinquency Prevention (OJJDP) located in the Department of Justice, the Coordinating Council on Juvenile Justice and Delinquency Prevention located at the Executive Office of the President, and the National Institute for Juvenile Justice and Delinquency Prevention (NIJJDP) located within the Department of Justice. The basic authority for the federal government's involvement and policy-making in juvenile justice is derived from the

Juvenile Justice and Delinquency Prevention Act of 1974 signed into law by President Ford. The Juvenile Justice and Delinquency Prevention Act of 1974, by creating the above federal institutions, established the foundation of a unified national system of juvenile justice in America.

OJJDP originally was a part of Law Enforcement Assistance and Administration (LEAA). The OJJDP currently is one of the major components of the Office of Justice Programs of the Department of Justice. The OJJDP is the federal government's central agency for policy-making and policy implementations in juvenile justice. An administrator appointed by the President directs the OJJDP, and at present it includes four divisions: Child Protection Division, Demonstration Program Division, State Relations and Assistance Division, and Office of Policy Development. The OJJDP's major responsibilities include the administration of federal funds and grants for juvenile justice improvement programs in state and local agencies, development of innovative federal intervention and demonstration programs, coordination of all federal juvenile justice activities, and the organization of scientific research on delinquency prevention policy and justice system improvement. The OJJDP also oversees state compliance to federal juvenile justice statutes and programs. Under a mandate by the Congress, the OJJDP every year sends an Annual Report of its activities to Congress and the President.

In 1975, OJJDP's total budget appropriation was $25 million. In 1980, it increased to $100 million. During the 1980s, there was a move to eliminate OJJDP, and its budget was reduced. In 1990, OJJDP's budget declined to $77 million. "For about 10 years, the administration requested no funding for OJJDP's juvenile justice programs, but the Congress restored appropriations each year" (Ekstrand, 1996, p. 6). From the beginning of the Clinton presidency, however, OJJDP began to expand and revitalize. In 1995, the OJJDP's budget was increased to $162 million (Ekstrand, 1996).

The Coordinating Council on Juvenile Justice and Delinquency Prevention, created by the Act of 1974, is an independent policy-making body within the Executive Office of the President. The Council is chaired by the Attorney General, and other ex-officio members include the Secretaries of the federal Departments of Health and Human Services, Labor, Education, Housing and Urban Development, the Administrator of OJJDP, the Director of ONDCP, Chief Executive Officer of the Corporation For National Community Services, and the Assistant Secretary for Immigration and Customs Enforcement of the Department of Homeland Security. The Council's meeting, which is open to public, also includes nine juvenile justice practitioners and judges from outside the federal government. The Council makes annual recommendations to the Congress for congressional policy-making in juvenile justice. Some of the major national juvenile justice policy innovations came from the Coordinating Council on Juvenile Justice and Delinquency Prevention such as the Weed and Seed Program, Ida B. Wells Community Initiative, research on youth violence, youth justice in the Indian Reservations, and federal assistance for school drop-out prevention programs.

In 1996, the Council, under the leadership of Attorney General Janet Reno, developed a national comprehensive strategy for reforms in juvenile justice, titled "Combating Violence and Delinquency: The National Juvenile Justice Action Plan." This Plan, based on the findings of a decade of research on juvenile delinquency, included eight objectives. They are 1) appropriate sanctions and treatment for delinquent juveniles, 2) prosecution of serious and violent offenders, 3) reduction of youth involvement with guns, drugs, and gangs, 4) extension of opportunities for children and youth through comprehensive neighborhood revitalization plans, 5) breaking the cycle of violence by addressing youth victimization, abuse, and neglect, 6) mobilization of community involvements, 7) innovative research and evaluation, and 8) an aggressive public information program through the involvement of the media. This 1996 Plan of Action of the Coordinating Council and the 1993 OJJDP report on Comprehensive Strategy for Serious and Violent and Chronic Juvenile Offenders today constitute the major federal policy framework for juvenile justice.

The National Institute for Juvenile Justice and Delinquency Prevention (NIJJDP), created by the Juvenile Justice and Delinquency Prevention Act of 1974 is also an important part of the whole federal structure of policy-making in juvenile justice. The primary objective of NIJJDP is to conduct research and evaluation on issues and problems related to juvenile justice. NIJJDP, supported by an advisory committee, works closely with the National Institute of Justice. Some of the major research programs supported by NIJJDP include research on the causes and correlates of delinquency, National Youth Gang Center, national juvenile court data archive, hate crime and juvenile victims and offenders, juvenile family court training, restorative justice, community-based juvenile aftercare, and innovations for the reduction of disproportionate minority confinement. The Juvenile Justice Amendments Act of 1977 (PL 95-115) authorized NIJJDP to help state and local governments in policy-making for juvenile justice in light of federal programs and initiatives.

Federal Policy Developments for a National System of Juvenile Justice

During the last thirty years, a number of federal policy programs were developed to create a national system of juvenile justice as a part of the broader national system of criminal justice. The creation of a national system of juvenile justice was the primary goal of the Juvenile Justice and Delinquency Prevention Act of 1974 (see Table 17). The Act of 1974 required the development in each state of a separate agency responsible for comprehensive planning in juvenile delinquency prevention, and in administering juvenile justice. By the middle of the 1980s, separate departments or agencies of juvenile justice were created in almost all the fifty states. Most of the states have some forms of agencies for juvenile justice before the 1970s. In compliance with the Act of 1974, those agencies were reorganized and some states have upgraded them to cabinet level agencies. Each state also is mandated to have a designated juvenile justice specialist as OJJDP representative. The names and nomenclatures of these state agencies are different, but they all comply with the provisions of the Act of 1974. The state juvenile justice agencies carry different titles such as California Youth Authority in California; the Department of Juvenile Justice in Florida, Maryland, New York, North Carolina, and Virginia; Texas Youth Commission in Texas; Department of Children and Family Services in Illinois; Division of Youth Services in Ohio; and Commission on Crime and Delinquency in Pennsylvania. To comply with the JJDP Act of 1974, each state has also created a separate juvenile justice state advisory body or commission, appointed by the Governor such as the Illinois Juvenile Justice Commission, State Commission on Juvenile Justice in California, Juvenile Justice Commission in New Jersey, and the Juvenile Justice and Delinquency Prevention Advisory Committee in Virginia.

Table 17: Juvenile Justice and Delinquency Prevention Act of 1974: Key Legislative Developments and Amendments, 1974-2002

Years	Legislative Developments
1974 PL 93-415	Created Formula Grants Program Established the Core Separation Requirements Deinstitutionalization of Status Offenders Requirement (DSO) Created the Office of Juvenile Justice and Delinquency Prevention (OJJDP)
1977 PL 95-115	Expanded the DSO Requirements Public Access of Juvenile Record Made Unlawful Emphasized Prevention and Treatment
1980 PL 96-509	Established Jail Removal Requirement New Focus on Violent Juvenile Offenders
1988 PL 100-279	Created the Disproportionately Minority Conviction Statute Treatment for Juveniles in Gangs and Drugs
1992 PL 102-586	Amended DSO, Jail Removal, and Separation Requirements Created Programs to Address Gender Bias in Juvenile Justice Created the Graduated Sanction Provision Created the State Challenge Activities Program Treatment For Juvenile Sex Offenders Introduced Boot Camp Program Introduced Mentoring Grants Program
2002 PL 107-273	Created the Prevention Block Grant Statute Expanded Research, Evaluation and Statistical analysis Expanded Title V Revised the JAIBG Program Expanded the Disproportionately Minority Conviction Requirements Required Linkages between juvenile justice and child welfare Required the OJJDP to Develop Juvenile Mental Health Care Standards

Source: OJJDP. www.ojjdp.ncjrs.org

The federal juvenile justice institutions, the state juvenile justice departments and agencies, and the state juvenile justice advisory bodies, created by the JJDP Act of 1974, comprise the major sectors of the nation's juvenile justice system. The national system is an interconnected structure of federal and state agencies, and an expanding network of juvenile justice research and information. Before the 1970s, there was no national system, but a set of disconnected state juvenile courts and juvenile justice programs. As a result of different legislations enacted between 1974 and 2006 and a number of federal grants and intervention programs administered by the OJJDP, Coordinating Council on Juvenile Justice and Delinquency Prevention and the National Institute for Juvenile Justice and Delinquency Prevention, the nature and performance of the national juvenile justice system is now vastly different from what it was in the 1960s. The 2002 Amendment of the JJDP Act of 1974 has particularly focused on the need for systemic improvements through more emphasis on information gathering and dissemination, training and technical assistance, and evidence-based policy-making.

A number of federally managed information gathering programs provide juvenile justice data and information. Some of the major programs include the Uniform Crime Reports, National Incidence-Based Reporting System, National Monitoring Survey, Federal Justice Statistics Program, National Clearing House on Child Abuse and Neglect Information, Bureau of Justice Statistics, National Criminal Justice Reference Services, National Clearinghouse on Families and Youth, National Child Care Information Center, Criminal Justice Record Improvement Program, National Criminal History Improvement Program, and Global Justice Information Sharing Initiative. A vast amount of juvenile justice system information is also available from the Juvenile Justice Clearinghouse (JJC) established by OJJDP in 1979. The JJC is a component of the National Criminal Justice Reference Services (NCJRS). Out of more than 150,000 publications of the NCJRS, more than 40,000 are related to juvenile justice. The JJC currently offers more than 300 publications on juvenile justice policy. More than 5,000 juvenile justice professionals are subscribers of OJJDP's informative E-Mail Service—JUVJUST (Office of Juvenile Justice and Delinquency Prevention, 2005). OJJDP has also funded the development of the National Juvenile Court Data Archive.

Juvenile Justice Process Improvement: Federal Policy Initiatives

Juvenile justice, internally, is a process of juvenile law enforcement, court-case processing, diversion and prosecution, adjudication, and sentencing and corrections. The laws that govern these processes, however, depend on policy-making by legislatures who make the laws and the judges and justices who interpret them. Juvenile justice is primarily within the jurisdictions of the states. The federal government is merely a policy-maker, facilitator, and a trendsetter. The federal government does not have juvenile courts and juvenile correction centers.

In the federal system, juvenile arrests are less than 2 percent of the total arrests. In the state system, juveniles constitute about 18-20 percent of the total arrests.

Since the enactment of the JJDP Act of 1974, the federal government, however, has become involved in policy-making that not only created, in an institutional sense, a national system of juvenile justice, but also deeply affected and impacted the nature and functioning of juvenile justice as a whole. In each step of the amendment of the JJDP Act of 1974, made between 1977 and 2002, new legislations have been added to improve the law enforcement, judicial and delinquency prevention functions of the nation's juvenile justice system.

One of the federal statutes that remained in force for state juvenile justice systems since the enactment of the JJDP Act of 1974 includes a set of core requirements for the protection of juveniles, and the states receiving federal juvenile justice grants are required to comply with the core requirements. There are four areas of core requirements: 1) deinstitutionalization of status offenders (DSO); 2) separation of juveniles from adult offenders; 3) adult jail and lockup removal; and 4) disproportionately minority conviction (DMC). "If a state, despite its good faith efforts, in any year fails to demonstrate compliance with any of the four core requirements, its formula grant for the subsequent fiscal year is reduced by 20 percent for each requirement for which noncompliance occurs" (Office of Juvenile Justice and Delinquency Prevention, 2004, p. 1).

The DSO statute makes its legally mandatory for states not to send juvenile status offenders to secure juvenile detention and correctional facilities. Through the Amendment of the JJDP Act in 1977, Congress further expanded the DSO statute to include dependent and neglected youths. Through the DSO statute, Congress required the states to create alternative placements for status offenders. However, in the JJDP Act Amendments in 1980, Congress made a provision that status offenders who violate valid court orders could be placed in secure facilities (Holden & Kapler,1995). The separation mandate of the OJJDP Act required the states to completely separate—without any sight or sound contact— the juveniles in secure facilities from incarcerated adults. The jail and lockup mandate established the same general rule for juveniles in jails and detention centers. The DMC mandate is that states are required to address the issue of minority conviction through the identification of the extent of the problem, assessment of why DMC exists, what can be done to reduce DMC, how DMC intervention programs are working, and what strategies are there to monitor the progress of DMC compliance. In the 2002 Amendment of the JJDP Act, the DMC requirement is extended to cover not only minority juveniles who are confined but also minorities who come into contact with the juvenile justice system. Each state is required to report its progress in DMC in its comprehensive three-year JJDP Plan.

Federal Juvenile Justice Grants And Programs

The federal government's another policy direction for improvements in national juvenile justice includes a set of federal grants administered by the OJJDP.

These are Community Prevention Grants Program (Title V of the JJDP Act), Formula Grants Program (Title II of the JJDP Act), State Challenge Activities Grant Program, Juvenile Accountability Block Grant Program, Tribal Youth Program (see, Table 18). Each of these grant programs is a bundle of policy directives broadly mandated by Congress and administered by OJJDP.

Table 18: Federal Policies for Improvement in Juvenile Justice: The Grants Programs

Grant Titles	Major Policy Objectives
Formula Grants Program Title II	To improve state juvenile justice systems; to conduct and expand research and evaluation; and to develop delinquency prevention and reduction programs
Community Prevention Grants Program Title V	To provide state and local governments incentives to develop, demonstrate and evaluate delinquency prevention programs with community involvement
State Challenge Activities Program	To provide state incentives to participate in one or more of ten challenge activities: 1) provide basic system services to juveniles including health, mental health, and educational services; 2) develop programs for juvenile access to counsel; 3) develop community-based alternatives to incarceration; 4) develop programs to keep violent juveniles in secure facilities; 5) develop gender-specific juvenile justice programs; 6) establish a state ombudsman office for youth and families; 7) create innovative programs to deinstitutionalize the status offenders; 8) create program alternatives to school suspension and expulsion; 9) develop juvenile re-entry programs; and 10) develop a state agency for programs on children with emotional and behavioral problems
Juvenile Accountability Block Program	To provide state and local governments incentives for programs aimed to encourage youth responsibility such as victim-offender mediation, family group conferencing, neighborhood reparative boards, and juvenile gun court
Tribal Youth Program	To develop programs for improving the juvenile justice system for the American-Indian tribes and Alaskan native youth

Source: OJJDP

These grants are federal mechanisms to direct change and improvements in state juvenile justice systems. The states receiving these grants are required to comply not only with the core requirements of the OJJDP Act, but also to implement the policies specific to each grant program. The JJDP Act of 2002 consolidated all these programs into a single Prevention Block Grant.

The OJJDP funds also a number of policy programs outside this cluster of grants. Some of the major OJJDP policy initiatives taken in recent years include Youth Gang Survey Program, Drug-Free Community Support Program, Missing and Exploited Children Program, Safe Start Program, Internet Crimes Against Children Program, Commercial Sexual Exploitation of Children Program, Juvenile Faith-Based Correction Initiative, Serious and Violent Offender Reentry Initiative, and Census of juveniles in Residential Placement (Office of Juvenile Justice and Delinquency Prevention, 2004). On the basis of research and evaluation of hundreds of policy strategies developed and demonstrated during the last two decades, the OJJDP has developed a Model Policy Guide for juvenile justice. This evidence-based policy model, as described in Table 19, includes prevention programs, programs on immediate sanctions, programs on intermediate sanctions, residential programs, and reentry programs. This is not a legal document but a model for policy development by state policy-makers in juvenile justice.

Table 19: OJJDP Model Policy Guide: Some Major Policy Strategies

Program Types	Specific Policy Strategies
Prevention	Academic skill enhancement, After School Program; Alternative School, Cognitive Behavioral Treatment, Community Policing, Drug and Alcohol Therapy, Family Therapy, Gang Prevention, Mentoring; Leadership Training, Parent Training, and Truancy Prevention
Immediate Sanctions	Teen Youth Court, Restorative Justice, Conflict Resolution Training, Interpersonal Skill Enhancement Training, and Cognitive Behavioral Treatment
Intermediate Sanctions	After School Recreation, Cognitive Behavioral Training, Drug Court, Gun Court, Home Confinement, Probation Services, and Restorative Justice
Residential Programs	Cognitive Behavioral Therapy, Correctional Facility, Day Treatment, Group Home, and Residential Treatment Centers
Reentry	After care, Cognitive Behavioral Therapy, Day Treatment, Reentry Court, and Vocational Training

Source: OJJDO Model Policy Guide

Federal Policy-Making in Juvenile Justice: The Role of the Congress

The OJJDP Act of 1974 and its various subsequent amendments and reauthorizations constitute the federal government's core policy instrument for juvenile justice. The nation's juvenile justice, however, is also impacted by a number of other federal Acts and Statutes, particularly by those enacted for policy-making in crime and justice in general. There is hardly any crime legislation enacted by Congress that did not influence policy-making in juvenile justice (see Table 20).

The Comprehensive Crime Control Act of 1984 created the Office of Justice Programs that now includes the OJJDP. The Act of 1984, overhauled the federal sentencing guidelines, introduced mandatory sentencing, and made a provision for maximum penalty for career offenders. The Act, however, mandated that age be taken as an important factor in creating mandatory sentencing guidelines. The Comprehensive Crime Control Act of 1990 introduced the Crime-Victim Bill of Rights and provision for treatment of juvenile offenders who are victims of abuse and neglect.

**Table 20: Major Comprehensive Crime Bills and
Juvenile Justice Related Statutes, 1984-2004**

Major Crime Enactments	Major Provisions and Policies
Crime Control Act of 1984 PL 98-473	Federal sentencing system overhauled Office of Justice program created Crime Victims Bill of Rights introduced
Crime Control Act of 1990 PL 1001-647	Drug-Free School Zone Treatments for victims of child abuse Mandatory reporting of suspected abuse cases Televised testimony by juveniles
Violent Crime Control and Law Enforcement Act of 1994 PL 103-322	Prosecution of violent juveniles as adults Criminalization of street gang participation Lawful public access to juvenile record Community-Oriented policing
21st Century Department of Justice Reauthorization Pl 107-278	Juvenile offenders reentry program Restorative justice program Child abuse training for judicial personnel Juvenile justice system improvement
Advancing Justice Through DNA Act of 2003	Access to DNA profile of juvenile offenders FBI access to state juvenile DNA profiles Juveniles DNA in the FBI's CODIS system National Forensic Science Commission Post-conviction testing of DNA samples

Source: Compiled by the Author

The Violent Crime Control and Law Enforcement Act of 1994 introduced laws for prosecuting serious and violent juvenile offenders as adults, criminalized street gang participation, and made it legal for juvenile courts to release juvenile criminal records to FBI and other agencies. The 21st Century Department of Justice Reauthorization Act of 2002 created the juvenile reentry program, made provisions for restorative justice, and authorized more funds for juvenile justice system improvement. The Advancing Justice through DNA Technology Act of 2003 made the first federal statute to add DNA profile of juvenile offenders, even those who are not convicted, to federal and state DNA databanks. The FBI's DNA databank, Combined DNA Index System (CODIS), can obtain juvenile DNA from state and local law enforcement agencies.

4.5 State Juvenile Justice Policy, 1970-2006

Before the federal government mandated the creation of separate organizations for juvenile justice in the states in compliance with the JJDP Act of 1974, each state has an executive agency or some form of arrangements within the executive branch for juvenile justice. The California's Division of Juvenile Justice, for example, was created in 1943 as a reform school for juveniles. The Texas Youth Development Council that later became Texas Youth Council, was established in 1949. Maryland established four reform schools between 1850 and 1882. The Maryland Juvenile Services Administration became a part of the Maryland Department of Health in the 1960s. The Maryland Juvenile Services Administration became a cabinet level agency in 1989. North Carolina established a juvenile reform school in 1909 and a Department of Youth Development that was renamed as Department of Juvenile Justice and Delinquency Prevention in 1971. After the JJDP Act, however, it became mandatory for the states to reorganize and revitalize their old structures of juvenile justice. Today, each state has a separate policy regime for juvenile justice that includes the state executive agency for juvenile justice, and state juvenile justice advisory bodies and commissions. There are also state-wide organizations such as the National Governors Association, National Conference of State Legislatures, and the National Governors Association Center for Best Practices that make recommendations for juvenile justice policy.

The process and the functions of juvenile justice in the states widely vary. In twelve states including Delaware, Florida, Kentucky, Maine, Maryland, North Carolina, South Carolina, and Vermont, the juvenile justice system is centralized at the state level where a state executive agency is responsible for over-all policy-making in juvenile justice. In eighteen states including California, Michigan, New York, Pennsylvania, and Texas, juvenile justice is decentralized with power in the hands of local governments and local juvenile courts. In twenty-one states including Connecticut Georgia, Massachusetts, New Jersey, and Virginia, juvenile justice is administered through a combination of state and local control. The lowest age for original jurisdiction in 2005 was age six in North Carolina, age seven in Maryland, Massachusetts, and New York, age eight in Arizona, and age ten in Kansas, Pennsylvania, South Dakota, and Texas. There is no specific lowest age limit for juvenile court jurisdiction in thirty states. The oldest age limit for juvenile court jurisdiction is age seventeen in thirty-seven states, age sixteen in ten states, and age fifteen in three states—Connecticut, New York, and North Carolina (National Center for Juvenile Justice, 2006). The states also vary the way they administer juvenile detentions, length of commitment, placement, and release decisions.

Impact of Federal Programs

Although diversity exists in juvenile justice administration and management in the states, there are also similarities in the way they perceive and pursue different policy issues and options relevant to improving juvenile justice. One of the reasons for similarities is the requirement for the states to comply with federal juvenile justice enactments and statutes The states receiving the federal juvenile justice grants—the Title II Formula Grants, Title V Community Prevention Grants, the Challenge Grants, and JABG Grants—are required by law not only to comply with the core requirements of the JJDP Act of 1974, but also to spend the federal dollars in the development, implementation, and monitoring of policies broadly defined and designated by those Grant Programs. These Grant Programs, in fact, provide important models for state policy-making in juvenile justice.

The states receiving Formula Grants from the OJJDP largely comply with the core requirements. The OJJDP's 2002 Annual Report found that the majority of participants in the Formula Grants Program were in full or near full compliance with the Core Requirements. In 2002, out of 54 U.S. states and territories, 51 were in full or near full compliance to the DSO requirement, 53 were for Separation requirement, 42 for jail and lockup removal, and 52 for disproportionate minority conviction statute. During FY 2002, the states received more than $75 million under the OJJDP's Formula Grant. Since the statute requires that two-thirds of Formula Grants is allocated to local governments and private agencies, many of them were also brought into local policy-making for delinquency prevention through the Formula Grants (Office of Juvenile Justice and Delinquency Prevention, 2004).

Title V Community Prevention Grants Program, established by the Congress in 1992 amendments of the JJDP Act, requires states to develop community-based intervention policies and programs for delinquency prevention. From 1994 to 2002, all the states and the U.S. territories received the Title V grants. Between 1994 and 2002, the nine highest recipients of Title V grants were Alabama ($31,903,000), California ($29,245,000), Connecticut ($21,337,000), Texas ($17,274,000), New York ($13,412,000), Florida ($11,337,000), Illinois ($9,863,000), Pennsylvania ($9,483,000), and Ohio ($9,397,000). It is estimated that more than 1,500 communities who received Title V grants have "launched efforts to reduce the risk factors in a young person's life associated with juvenile delinquency and enhanced the protective factors that support healthy personal and social development" (Office of Juvenile Justice and Delinquency Prevention, 2005, p. iii).

The 1992 amendments to the JJDP Act also created the State Challenge Grants Program for improvement in state juvenile justice systems. From the middle of the 1980s, when violent juvenile crime began to rise, many raised concerns about the role and effectiveness of juvenile court in addressing the problem of serious and violent juvenile offenders. Others raised concerns about the lack of due process protection and adequate services for juvenile offenders. The State Challenge Activities Program was created by Congress to address some of these systemic problems in juvenile justice (Office of Juvenile Justice and Delinquency Prevention, 2000). During the last ten years, states receiving the Challenge Activities Grants developed a number of innovative policies and programs. Out of the ten activity areas, most of the states have chosen and developed policies for improvement in basic system services, community-based alternatives, gender specific programs, alternatives to school suspension and expulsion, and aftercare service improvement. Since 1995, a total of $10 million was available every year for this program. In 2002, the OJJDP awarded nearly $8 million, and in 2003 nearly $8.8 million to the states for policy-making under this program. In 2003, seventeen states selected system improvement, twenty two states selected community-based alternatives, gender-specific policies, and alternatives to school suspension, and twenty six states selected aftercare service improvement as their policy priorities under the State Challenge Activities Program (Office of Juvenile Justice and Delinquency Prevention, 2004). Through the State Challenge Activities Program, considerable understanding has been gained that policy-making for improvement in juvenile justice needs to emphasize systems approach, holistic perspective, inter-agency cooperation, legislative reforms, top-down and bottom-up commitment, and the use of research-based knowledge (Office of Juvenile Justice Delinquency Prevention, 2000).

In addition to the State Challenge Activities Grants Program, the states are also developing programs funded by the Juvenile Accountability Incentive Block Grant (JAIBG) created by an Act of the Congress in 1998. The JAIBG is renamed as Juvenile Accountability Block Grant (JABG) by the 2002 Reauthorization of the JJDP Act. The JABG program is designed "to promote greater accountability in the juvenile justice system and held communities to become more effective in holding juvenile offenders accountable" (Office of Juvenile Justice and Delinquency Prevention, 2003, p. 4). The JABG is the largest federal program for improvement in state juvenile justice systems. Congress appropriated $250 million for JABG program in 1998, and subsequent appropriations from 1999 to 2002 remained at approximately the same level. In 2002, all 50 states including the District of Columbia and six U.S. territories were awarded $215 million under the JABG Program. In 2004, the JABG program awarded a total of $350 million to the states.

The states receiving JABG grants are required to develop legislations and programs, and spend funds in varying proportions in all of the 16 purpose areas mandated by the program. Each state receiving JABG grants is also required to set up a local JABG Advisory Board to be responsible for developing a coordinated enforcement plan. Unless there is a waiver, the states are required to allocate no less than 75 percent of the JABG grants to local government agencies and private non-profit organizations interested in developing accountability-based intervention programs. In order to be eligible for JABG grants, the Chief Executive Officer of each state must also certify to the OJJDP for program developments in the area of graduated sanctions (increased penalties for repeat offenders), prosecution of juveniles as adults, juvenile record keeping, and parental responsibility (Office of Juvenile Justice and Delinquency Prevention, 2003).

The JABG Grants Program has generated a considerable number of new policy initiatives and legislations by the states in recent years in such areas as juvenile gun court, juvenile drug court, youth court, interagency information sharing, graduated sanctions, restorative justice, diversion programs, and automated juvenile record keeping (see Table 21). The drug court for court-ordered drug treatment services as an alternative to incarceration was first established in Miami in 1989. By 1997, 300 hundred-drug courts were established in different states. In 2003, it is estimated that there were more than 1000 drug courts in the nation, and many of them were established under the JABG program. One of the innovative accountability-based sanctions, came out of different JABG projects, is the Balanced and Restorative Justice (BAR) approach—an approach that shifts the burden of justice and accountability directly to juvenile offenders. The JABG program, for example, has funded more than 80 projects in California. Some of the major projects include the Alameda County Youth Court, Berkeley Youth Court, Fremont Youth Diversion Program, Fresno County Juvenile Drug Court, Los Angeles Gang Intervention Program, Oakland Youth Court, San Mateo County Victim Impact Awareness, and Riverside Youth Court. The California's collaborative justice model, based on balanced and restorative justice approach, came out of projects funded by the JABG program (Office of Juvenile Justice and Delinquency Prevention, 2005).

Table 21: Juvenile Accountability Block Grants Program (Purpose Areas)

Purpose Area 1	Graduated Sanctions
Purpose Area 2	Corrections/Detentions
Purpose Area 3	Court Staffing and Pretrial Services
Purpose Area 4	Prosecutor (Staffing)
Purpose Area 5	Prosecutor (Funding)
Purpose Area 6	Training for Law Enforcement and Court Personnel
Purpose Area 7	Juvenile Gun Courts
Purpose Area 8	Juvenile Drug Courts
Purpose Area 9	Juvenile Record System Improvement
Purpose Area 10	Interagency Information Sharing
Purpose area 11	Accountability-Based Recidivism Program
Purpose Area 12	Risk and Needs Assessment for Juvenile Offenders
Purpose Area 13	Accountability-Based School Safety Programs
Purpose Area 14	Restorative Justice
Purpose Area 15	Juvenile Courts and Probation
Purpose Area 16	Detention/Correction Personnel

Source: OJJDP

A 21-month follow-up and evaluation study of JABG programs in Pennsylvania, conducted by the National Center for Juvenile Justice found that "most local JAIBG-funded efforts have aimed at promoting juvenile accountability within a broader and balanced and restorative justice framework" (Griffin, 2001, p. iii). The study further added that "Front-end diversion programs, particularly community service programs, have been the most common choices, followed in order by specialized/enhanced probation programs, victims programs, and school-related initiative" (Griffin, 2001, p. iii). The main projects of the JABG program in the Commonwealth of Virginia, developed by the Virginia Department of Juvenile Justice, for example, include alternatives to detention, mental health needs of juvenile offenders, and aftercare needs of juveniles coming out of secure placements. Similar programs in different purpose areas have been undertaken in all the states awarded by JABG grants (Office of Juvenile Justice and Delinquency Prevention, 2003; 2005).

State Legislative Developments
In Juvenile Justice

Since juvenile justice is primarily a state responsibility, it receives considerable attention from state policy-makers. In addition to federal Acts and statutes, state policy-making in juvenile justice is shaped by the economics of crime control. Juvenile justice occupies about 23-25 percent of state expenditure for corrections (Bureau of Justice Statistics, 2004). A number of major juvenile justice legislations have been enacted by the states during the last three decades. Some of these legislations are related to organizational improvement, and some are for reforming the process of juvenile justice. Some were directly related to federal Acts and statutes, and some have evolved out of the economic and political realities of the states.

State Juvenile Transfer Laws

During the decades of the 1980s and 1990s, almost all the states have made enactments to transfer serious and violent juvenile offenders to criminal courts and adult prisons. Serious and violent juvenile offenders were treated in adult courts as early as the 1920s, but the state lawmakers in recent decades "enacted new and expanded transfer mechanisms on an almost annual basis" (Butts & Mitchell, 2000, p.178). The Department of Justice estimates that "more than 100,000 juveniles are tried as adults every year, about 5,000 are sent to adult prison" (Butts, 2004, p. 1). There are various mechanisms through which juveniles are transferred to adult courts. These mechanisms fall into three general categories: judicial waiver, concurrent jurisdiction, and statutory exclusion, and many states use a combination of these mechanisms of transfer. As of 2004 legislative session, 45 states used discretionary judicial waiver where juvenile judges are not legally compelled but may waive jurisdictional authority to criminal court as long as the due process rights of the juveniles are respected, and the principle of the "best interest of the child and the public" is applied. Under a mandatory judicial waiver policy, a juvenile judge is legally compelled to transfer juveniles to adult courts based on a probable cause. As of 2004, 15 states used the mandatory judicial waiver provision. The statutory exclusion, used in 29 states, is a provision under which state laws exclude certain juvenile offenders from juvenile court jurisdiction. In 2004, 38 states used a combination of statutory exclusion and mandatory judicial waiver provisions.

Another dominant trend is the increased role given to state prosecutors for presumptive judicial waiver. Sixteen states including California, Illinois, New Jersey, and Pennsylvania used presumptive waiver provision in 2004. The provision of presumptive judicial waiver shifts the transfer decision to juveniles to prove that rehabilitative measures are suitable for them. Through the provision of presumptive judicial waiver—which relies less on juvenile judges and more on prosecutorial rebuttals—some states have transferred more juveniles to adult courts in the 1990s. Florida, which is one of the first states to adopt the presumptive judicial waiver, sent thousands of juveniles to adult courts. In Florida, the number of cases waived to criminal court every year in the late 1990s rose to more than 6,500. Many states have also introduced statutes of minimum age for transfer to criminal court. In twenty-three states, there is no minimum age requirement for transfer. In two states, Kansas and Vermont, juveniles as old as age ten could be transferred to adult court. In three states—Colorado, Missouri, and Montana—the minimum age for transfer is age twelve, and in six states (Illinois, Mississippi, New Hampshire, New York, North Carolina, and Wyoming) the minimum age for transfer is age thirteen.

State Sentencing Laws

From the beginning of the 1980s, the state policy-makers began to move away from offender-based sanctions to offense-based sanctions for more punishment and incapacitation rather than rehabilitation. "This trend had resulted in dramatic shifts in judicial disposition/sentencing practices in three areas: (1) imposition of 'blended sentences,' 2) imposition of mandatory minimum sentences, and 3) extension of juvenile court jurisdiction for dispositional purposes beyond the age of majority" (Torbet & Szymanski,1998, p. 1). The 1980 Amendments of the JJDP Act that added a new focus on violent juvenile offenders, the federal Sentencing Reform Act of 1984, the 1992 Amendments of the JJDP Act that created the statute of graduated sanctions, and the Violent Crime Control and Law Enforcement Act of 1994 that made provisions for treating and punishing violent juvenile offenders as adults largely impacted the state's sentencing reform policies in the 1980s and1990s.

Blended sentencing is a strategy to combine criminal sentencing with juvenile dispositions. There are two categories of blended sentencing: juvenile blended sentencing and criminal blended sentencing. Under juvenile blended sentencing laws, juvenile judges can impose criminal sanctions for certain types of violent crimes. Under this law, judges are authorized to send juveniles receiving blended sentencing to adult corrections. The criminal blended sentencing, on the other hand, is a strategy that authorizes criminal court judges to impose juvenile sanctions on transferred juveniles. The juveniles receiving criminal blended sentencing usually stay in adult corrections, but judges can conditionally send them to juvenile custody. As of the end of 2004 legislative sessions, 32 states have enacted blended sentencing laws. Juvenile blended sentencing laws have been enacted in 15 states, and criminal blended sentencing laws have been enacted in 17 states. Some states have also developed laws for inclusive blended sentencing in which both juvenile and adult sanctions are imposed (Griffin, 2003).

In addition to blended sentencing, many states in the 1980s and 1990s have also enacted legislations for mandatory sentencing guidelines for juveniles following a general trend in the nation to move more towards determinate and structured sentencing and truth-in-sentencing polices. Some states required juvenile judges to follow the mandatory sentencing guidelines such as Arizona, Utah, and Wyoming. Others required mandatory sentencing only for juveniles transferred to adult criminal courts. Eighteen states, including California, Florida, New York, North Carolina, and Virginia have enacted mandatory sentencing guidelines for juveniles (Butts & Mitchell, 2000). In order to make blended sentencing and mandatory sentencing more effective, and juvenile sentencing longer, many states have enacted laws to extend the juvenile court jurisdiction. As of the end of 2002 legislation, the upper age limit for juvenile jurisdiction was age nineteen in 2 states (Mississippi and North Dakota), age twenty in 34 states including Massachusetts, Michigan, New York, Pennsylvania, Texas, and Virginia, age twenty one in one state (Florida), age twenty two in one state (Kansas), and age twenty four in 4 states (California, Montana, Oregon, and Wisconsin).

Juvenile Records: Confidentiality and Information Sharing

One of the philosophical elements in traditional juvenile justice is the confidentiality of juvenile court records. This is based on the assumption that juveniles are still not matured, and that the opening of juvenile court records may lead to further stigmatization. "Almost all juvenile court proceedings and records were confidential as recently as the 1960s. Confidentiality was an integral part of the traditional juvenile justice model, based upon the theory that publicly designating a juvenile as a law breaker would stigmatize a young person" (Butts, 2005, p. 6). Most of the states in the 1980s and 1990s have moved away from this philosophy and enacted legislations to make juvenile court hearings open to public, to provide more public access to juvenile court records, share juvenile records among different federal and state law enforcement agencies, and to limit the destruction of juvenile records, particularly those related to violent and habitual juvenile offenders. In addition to juvenile records, many states made laws for public access to juvenile photographs and fingerprints. A consensus emerged among state policy-makers that public access to juvenile records may work as deterrence, and sharing juvenile records among different law enforcement agencies and departments dealing with child welfare services may have a positive impact on reducing juvenile crime and strengthening the system of juvenile justice.

Juvenile code of North Carolina, that became effective from July 1999, for example, stated that certain designated agencies can share juvenile court records and information such as mental health facilities, local health departments, the district attorney's office, the office of juvenile justice, and the office of Guardian ad Litem Services of the Administrative Office of the Court. The juveniles, the parents of the juveniles or their representatives and custodians, prosecutors, and court counselors may have access to juvenile records without an order of the court. In the Commonwealth of Virginia, the Governor's Commission on Juvenile Justice Reform in 1996 recommended to make all juvenile court proceedings and juvenile crimes and traffic offenses open to public. The Commission also recommended the collection of fingerprints and photographs from all juveniles charged with a delinquent act, and blood samples for DNA analysis from all juveniles charged with felony crimes. Florida made an enactment that, in addition to various law enforcement agencies, licensed professional organizations, licensed community organizations, and school administrators may share juvenile records. According to a Florida statute, if a juvenile is on probation or committed for a felony, his or her classroom teacher must be immediately notified. Florida also has a statute that the Department of Juvenile Justice may not destroy records of juvenile crimes and delinquent acts for a period of 25 years after a youth's final referral to the Department.

4.6 Juvenile Justice and the U.S. Supreme Court

The U.S. Supreme Court in *Re Gault* made one of the earliest constitutional decisions about juvenile justice in 1967. Since then, the U. S. Supreme Court has rendered a number of decisions that have significantly shaped the nature and directions of juvenile justice. Many of these decisions suggest that the U.S. Supreme Court does not see juvenile court as an extra-constitutional arrangement for dealing with juvenile crime and delinquency. The Supreme Court believes that both adults and juveniles are protected by the U.S. constitution. The constitution does not provide any special treatment for juveniles. The constitution and the Bill of Rights are equally applicable to adults and juveniles. The Supreme Court also believes that juvenile justice is primarily a matter of state statutory laws. The states can send juveniles to adult courts, develop new programs to control delinquency, and devise new detention methods and sentencing structures for juveniles as long as the process of juvenile policy-making and adjudications do not violate the Bill of Rights and other constitutional provisions.

In *Re Gault* in 1967, the Supreme Court ruled that juveniles, like adults, are equally protected by the due process clause of the Fourteenth Amendment. "Neither the Fourteenth Amendment nor the Bill of Rights is for adults alone" (*Re Gault*, 387 U.S. 1, 1967). The due process rights include: 1) right to have a timely and adequate written notice of charges, 2) right to have a counsel, 3) right to have sworn testimony of the witness available for cross-examination, 4) privilege against self-incrimination, 5) right to have a written transcript of the trial proceedings, and 6) right to appellate review. The *Re Gault* case started in 1964, when a fifteen-year-old Arizona juvenile, Gerald Francis Gault, was sentenced to six years in prison for making some obscene phone-calls to neighbors. In the whole process of his arraignment and trial, his parents were not notified, he was not given the privilege to have a counsel to represent him, his parents and complainant were not present in the trial, and the trial was not recorded. After the Arizona Supreme Court turned down a habeas corpus appeal, the case came to the U.S. Supreme Court. The U.S. Supreme Court, in one of its most elaborate opinions, ruled that due process rights are equally applicable to all processes related to juvenile arrests, arraignment, and trials and proceedings in juvenile courts. In delivering the majority opinion in *Re Gault*, Justice Fortes said: "Due process law is the primary and indispensable foundation of individual freedom. It is the basic and essential term in the social compact which defines the rights of the individual and delimits the power which the state may exercise." Justice Fortes further added that juvenile courts, since their inception in 1899, have been denying juvenile the due process rights on the basis of the doctrine of parens patriae and the philosophy of rehabilitation. These "highest motives and enlightened impulses led to a peculiar system for juveniles, unknown to our law in any comparable context. The constitutional and theoretical basis for this peculiar system is—to say the least—debatable." For the last forty years, the *Re Gault* decision remained central to almost all juvenile justice decisions delivered by the U.S. Supreme Court (Legal Information Institute, 1967).

The U.S. Supreme Court ruled on a number cases in recent years on juvenile search and seizures, arrests and intake processing, jails and detentions, juvenile transfer to adult courts, dispositions and hearings, mandatory sentencing, and juvenile court records and proceedings. The Supreme Court's position in all these areas is derived from *Re Gault*. In *New Jersey v. T.L.O* in 1985, the Supreme Court ruled that the Fourth Amendment's prohibition of unreasonable searches and seizures applies to searches of juveniles both by law enforcement officers and public school officials. In *Yarborough v. Alvarado* in 2004, the Supreme Court ruled that juveniles are equally entitled to Miranda rights (*Miranda v. Arizona,* 1966). Michael Alvarado, a 17-year old juvenile was sentenced to 15 years-to-life for his role in a second-degree murder and robbery by a state court in Santa Fe Springs, California, in 1985. The sentencing was based largely on Alvarado's admission of participation in the crime in his interview with a Los Angeles detective. The case was appealed to the State Court of Appeals on the ground that Alvarado did not receive the Miranda warning in his interview with the detective. The State Court of Appeals affirmed the lower court decision and ruled that Alvarado was not in custody for Miranda purpose. On appeal, the Federal Appeal Court of the Ninth Circuit reversed the decision because of the violation of an established law—*Miranda v. Arizona*. The Ninth Circuit Court argued that, because of his age and inexperience, Alvarado's interview turned into a custodial interview, and it required Miranda warning. The U.S. Supreme Court upheld the decision of the Ninth Circuit Court. In delivering the majority opinion, Justice Kennedy said: "*Miranda* itself held that preinterrogation warnings are required in the context of custodial interrogation" because a sense of compulsion is inherent in custodial surroundings (Legal Information Institute, 2004).

One of the earliest cases on juvenile transfer to adult court decided by the U.S. Supreme Court was *Kent v. United States* in 1966—a year before the *Re Gault* decision. In 1961, a 16-year old juvenile Morris Kent was arrested and brought into juvenile court in the District of Columbia. Morris Kent was on probation since he was 14 for several housebreaking and purse-snatching crimes. The juvenile Court of the District of Columbia decided to waive the jurisdiction for this case to adult criminal court. The district criminal court tried the case and sentenced Kent, for six counts of housebreaking and robbery, to 30 to 90 years in prison. He was not found guilty on two counts of rape by reason of insanity. Kent's counsel appealed the case to the United States Court of the District of Columbia challenging the ground of the legality and constitutionality of Kent's transfer from juvenile jurisdiction to adult criminal court. After the United States Court of Appeals of the District of Columbia affirmed, the case came to the U.S. Supreme Court. The Supreme Court made a ruling that Kent's transfer from juvenile jurisdiction to adult court was invalid. The Supreme Court found the transfer invalid not because it brought adult punishments for Kent but because in the process of his transferring to adult court, the due process rights of the Fourteenth Amendment were violated. The Supreme Court said that state statutes create the "exclusive jurisdiction" of a juvenile court. In transferring juveniles from the exclusive jurisdiction of a juvenile court, extreme cautions must be taken to protect their due process rights. In *Breed v. Jones,* the U.S. Supreme Court in 1975 made a related ruling that a juvenile once determined by a juvenile court as a delinquent cannot be tried as an adult, and to do so would be a violation of the double jeopardy clause of the Fifth Amendment. In delivering the majority opinion in *Breed v. Jones,* Chief Justice Burger said that the "prosecution of respondent as an adult, after Juvenile Court proceedings which resulted in a finding that respondent had violated a criminal statute and a subsequent finding that he was unfit for treatment as a juvenile, violated the Fifth and Fourteenth Amendments to the United States Constitution."

The U.S. Court of Appeal of the Second Circuit delivered the same type of opinion in case of *Murray v. Owen* in 1972 with respect to juvenile placement in adult correctional facilities. The New York Family Court sent Murray, a 15-year old adjudicated juvenile for first degree robbery and first degree rape, to Elmira —a medium security adult facility. On appeal, the New York Supreme Court dismissed the rape charge but affirmed the decision to keep Murray in an adult correctional institution. The U.S. Court of Appeals of the Second Circuit upheld the New York Supreme Court decision, and ruled that "it is reasonable for states to shunt 'criminally mature' 15-year-old out of training schools and into adult correctional facilities since failure to do so could have adverse effects on younger children as well as the objective and proper functioning of training school" (Hemmens, Steiner, & Mueller, 2004, p. 91). In the process of adjudication, the juvenile courts are also needed to apply the "reasonable doubt" standards applied in adult courts. In *re Winship* in 1970, the U.S. Supreme Court ruled that "proof beyond a shade of reasonable doubt" standard is an essential part of due process and fair treatment. The due process clause of the Fourteenth Amendment, as ruled by the Supreme Court in *McKeiver v. Pennsylvania* in 1971, however, does not require jury trials in juvenile courts. But the Fifth Amendment's Double Jeopardy clause, as ruled by the Supreme Court in *Breed v. Jones in 1975,* is applied to juvenile adjudication.

Concerning public access to juvenile court trials, proceedings, and records, the Supreme Court is largely in favor of an open court and lifting the traditional notion of confidentiality. This is clearly evidenced in the Supreme Court opinions given in *Smith Broadcasting Corporation v. Cohn* in 1975, *Oklahoma Publishing Company v. District Court* in 1977, and *Smith v. Daily Mail* in 1979.

In delivering the majority opinion in *Smith v. Daily Mail,* Chief Justice William Rehnquist said that the historically important characteristic of confidentiality in juvenile court proceedings, especially shielding the process from the public and media to reduce juvenile stigmatization, have "largely changed" (Shepherd, 2000, p. 1).

The U.S. Supreme Court has also made some landmark decisions about juvenile mandatory sentencing, juvenile sentencing for life without parole, and juvenile capital punishment. In *Harmelin v. Michigan* in 1991, the Supreme Court did not find any violation of the Eighth Amendment clause of "cruel and unusual punishment." Ronald Harmelin was sentenced to life in prison without the possibility of parole, under a Michigan mandatory minimum statute, for the possession of 650 grams of cocaine. The issue in this case was whether a mandatory sentencing statute, that does not consider mitigating circumstance, is a violation of the Eighth Amendment's protection against cruel and unusual punishment. The U.S. Supreme Court in this case ruled that the concept of "mitigating factors" has no "support in the Eighth Amendment." In delivering the majority opinion, Justice Scalia said that "mandatory penalties may be cruel, but they are not unusual in the constitutional sense, having been employed in various forms throughout the nation's history. Harmeiln's sentence cannot be considered unconstitutionally disproportional." A similar ruling came from the Supreme Court in the case of *Rummel v. Estelle* in 1980. Under a Texas recidivist statute, Rummel received a sentencing of life in prison without the possibility of parole. The Supreme Court held that it did not constitute a violation of the Eighth and Fourteenth Amendments. With respect to mandatory life in prison for juveniles, the U.S. Supreme Court position is that the gravity of the offense is more important than offender culpability and individual mitigating circumstances. "Challenges of sentences of life without parole have met limited success in state courts and almost no success in Federal court in cases involving juvenile offenders" (Walsh, 2000, p. 3).

The Supreme Court's other landmark decision made recently is about juvenile capital punishment. In *Thompson v. Oklahoma* in 1988, the Supreme Court ruled that execution of a juvenile who is 15 or younger is a violation of the Eighth Amendment. In *Stanford v. Kentucky* and *Wilkins v. Missouri* in 1989, the Supreme Court made a ruling that execution of a juvenile age sixteen or seventeen is not a violation of the Eighth Amendment. In *Ring v. Arizona* in 2002, the Supreme Court ruled that jurors, and not judges, should make death penalty decisions. In *Atkins v. Virginia* in 2002, the Supreme Court decided that the execution of a severely retarded person is a violation of the Eighth Amendment. In *Roper v Simmons,* in 2005, the Supreme Court, reversing its 1989 decision on *Stanford v Kentucky,* made a ruling that the execution of a juvenile under eighteen is a violation of the Eighth Amendment. "The Eighth and Fourteenth Amendments forbid imposition of the death penalty on offenders who were under the age of 18 when their crimes were committed .... Reject ion of the imposition of the death penalty on juvenile offenders under 18 is required by the Eighth Amendment" (Legal Information Institute, 2005, p. 1).

4.7 The Future of Juvenile Justice: The Search for a Balance

Juvenile justice has significantly changed from the days of the Progressive Era and the establishment of juvenile court in Illinois in 1899. Currently, there are two groups of critics of the evolution of policy-making in juvenile justice. One group, the traditionalists, argue that juvenile justice has significantly moved away from its core philosophy of informal, rehabilitative, and exclusive system for juveniles. The juvenile justice policies of applying the due process, juvenile transfer to adult courts, mandatory sentencing, blended sentencing, and public access to juvenile hearings and court records and proceedings have dismantled the border between juvenile justice and adult justice "brick by brick" (Butts & Mitchell, 2000). The other group, the abolitionists, argues that juvenile justice as a separate system should be eliminated because the traditional model is grossly inadequate and inappropriate to deal with the challenges of juvenile crime in modern times. The last three decades of juvenile justice policy growth and change, however, suggest that neither the traditionalists nor the abolitionists are close to the realities of policy-making.

The traditionalist perspective is limited because its advocates underestimate the significance of formal institutions in juvenile justice and the application of the Bill of Rights and the constitutional principles of due process so that juvenile offenders do not become the victims of arbitrary judicial opinions, discrete systems of justice, and diverse statutory standards. The traditional notion of juvenile justice has probably permanently changed. Today, there is a national juvenile justice system with an interconnected group of federal, state, and local policy-makers, and an interrelated set of laws, statutes, and programs. The system is hugely complex, and highly differentiated, but tightly integrated through a complex array of federal statutes and programs. And the system is bound to function within the framework of the constitution. The abolitionists, who claim that juvenile justice is becoming increasingly ineffective and it has outlived its utility, on the other hand, seem to underestimate grossly the policy achievements made during the last three decades to preserve the core and the soul of juvenile justice.

Currently, a search for a balance between formal and informal justice, formal and informal control, and punishment and rehabilitation is a dominant policy issue in juvenile justice. From the late 1990s, there is growing a realization among both federal and state policy-makers that get-tough policy strategies of the 1980s and 1990s are not without limitations. Although violent juvenile crime began to decline from the middle of the 1990s, partly as a result of get-tough strategies, policy-makers since then began to think of recasting the whole system of juvenile justice in the context of the renewed understanding of the larger issues and challenges in the 21st century. In this renewed understanding, there is no assumption to go back to the old rehabilitative model of the 1970s. There is a consensus that the traditional system of juvenile justice—a system that was local, isolated, discrete, court-centered, and offender-based—is incompatible to face the challenges of modern society. There is needed a new system which is competent, collaborative, open, proactive, balanced, accountability-based, and tough but caring and compassionate. Today's policy-makers are more informed by natural science understanding of juvenile brains and brain chemistry, psychological understanding of juvenile developmental needs and processes, and social science understanding of the impact of poverty and the media, and the influence of the changing nature of family, marriage, and divorce on juvenile crime and delinquency. So, there is growing now a new search for a balance in juvenile justice—a new search for "reinventing juvenile justice."

In this new search, the get-tough policies are not being entirely thrown out. They are being recast and reexamined within a new set of policy models. Some of the new policy models include "systemic change," "systemic accountability," "graduated sanctions," "balanced and restorative justice," "offender accountability," "community involvement," "comprehensive approach," and "public safety and community protection." Many of these policy models came out of federal initiatives, particularly the Title V Community Prevention Grants Program, State Challenge Grants Program, Juvenile Accountability Grants Program, OJJDP Model Policy Guide, the 21st Century Department of Justice Appropriations Reauthorization Act of 2002, Keeping Children and Families Safe Act of 2003, and the recommendations of the 2003 White House Task Force on Disadvantaged Youth.

One of the important evidences of this changing trend in state policy-making is slow but steady decline in the number of juveniles transferred to adult courts. In the nation, the number of juvenile cases waived to criminal court reached its peak in 1994 with 12,100 cases. "This represented a 45% increase over the number of cases waived in 1990 (8,300). Since 1994, however, the number of cases waived to criminal court declined 38% to 7,500 cases, representing less than 1% of formally processed caseload" (Office of Juvenile Justice and Delinquency Prevention, 2003, p. 1). In 1998-1999, Florida transferred 4,211 juveniles to adult courts. In 2003-2004, the number of juveniles transferred came down to 2,284. Since 1998-1999, the number of juveniles transferred in criminal courts in Florida declined by nearly 46 percent. In 2004, California arrested 206,201 juveniles. Out of those arrested, 78.4 percent were referred to probation, and 19.4 percent were counseled and released. Out of 206,201 arrested juveniles, 252 (0.3 percent) were remanded to adult court. Out of 1,049 juveniles convicted in adult court in 2004, 23.8 percent received prison sentence, 29.1 percent received probation with jail, and 8.1 percent received jail time. The total juvenile arrest in California in 2004 was 15,000 less than total juvenile arrestees in 2003 (Office of the Attorney General of California, 2005).

More states today are sending juveniles to probation, diversion, and residential placements. More juvenile drug offenders are receiving treatments instead of mandatory sentences. More serious and violent juvenile offenders are receiving mental health treatments. The 2002 Juvenile Justice State Legislation Report of the National Conference of State Legislatures summarized this trend in the following words: "State lawmakers passed measures that will result in treating serious and violent juvenile offenders like adult offenders and also continued to craft policies that provide treatment for juvenile delinquents with substance abuse and mental health problems (National Conference of State Legislatures,

2003, p. 1). The 2004 Report observes the same trend: "Juvenile Justice was addressed by state lawmakers in 2004 with measures that supervise juveniles in the community and provide treatment to address alcohol, drug, and mental health problems. Other laws address delinquency prevention, safe schools, due process and punishment for juveniles" (National Conference of State Legislatures, 2005, p. 1).

The balance in juvenile justice will not be achieved once and for all, but policy search and innovations for balanced strategies seem to have started. In addition to state initiatives, Congress is demanding the development and funding of more prevention programs. The nation's juvenile justice system is not weakening; it is emerging with new goals and directions, and new tools and technologies for policy-making. And the U.S. Supreme Court is not entirely against a separate system of juvenile justice. In many recent cases, federal circuit courts and the U.S. Supreme Court ruled in favor of the doctrine of *parens patriae* (*Addington v. Texas,* 1979), preventive detention (*Schall v. Martin,* 1984), and juvenile rights for treatments in juvenile custody and corrections (*Morales v. Turman,* Fifth Circuit, 1974).

CHAPTER 5

SEX CRIMES: LAWS AND POLICY DEVELOPMENTS

The last three decades in America have been the decades of increasing expansion of legal and moral boundaries of tolerance for a wide variety of behaviors related to sex, body, and intimacy. There is now a high degree of legal protections and moral tolerance for cohabitation, same-sex unions, unwed motherhood, teen pregnancy, inter-racial marriage, no-fault divorce, surrogate mothering, reproductive rights, and adult pornography. The philosophical demand for freedom in the domain of intimacy, that started with the rise of the Renaissance and the advent of the Age of Enlightenment, began to get its foremost expression in American culture from the beginning of the 1970s, particularly in the context of the expansion of open society, the rise of women's revolution, the discovery of new biology, and the growth of service economy "Profound shifts in the cultural meaning of sexuality inform and follow from these developments" (Cohen, 2002, p. 2). However, from around the same time in the 1970s, there also began in America a new era of law and policy-making for the control and regulation of sex and intimacy. This chapter will examine this new trend of policy-making in sex crimes in America. The chapter will discuss the nature and the extent of sex crimes, growth of federal and state sex crimes statutes, the nature of judicial policy-making related to sex and intimacy, and the models of policy-making in sex crimes in general in America.

5.1 Sex Crimes and Policy-Making: Some Historical Notes

Human sexual behavior is one of the areas that probably have the longest history of criminalization. The wide varieties of sexual behavior defined as crimes today have existed in almost all ages and civilizations, although their nature and expressions varied from time to time and culture to culture. The diversity in human sexual behavior has also been a subject of intellectual curiosity in all ages. Herodotus, a Greek historian in the fifth century, who is regarded by many as the father of modern anthropology, theorized that people in warmer climates are more likely to be engaged in sexual deviance than those who live in colder climates (Levinson & Ember, 1995).

The evolutionary anthropologists, such as Johann Jakob Bachofen, Lewis Henry Morgan, E. B. Taylor, John Lubbock, and John McLennan, have argued that human sexual behavior has evolved from an unregulated promiscuous stage to a more regulated formal structure of monogamy with the gradual evolution of human societies, particularly the rise of settled agricultural civilizations about ten thousand years ago. The discovery of agriculture led to the growth of settled villages, cities, governments, and laws, and they, in turn, led to the growth of the institutions of monogamy marriage and family. From that historical time, there began an era of policy-making for the regulation of human sexual behavior. The history of modern policy-making in sex crimes, in one sense, is less than fifty years old. Its origin, however, can be traced back to the time of the evolution of governments, laws, polities, cities, and the institution of monogamy in earlier agricultural civilizations.

Almost all major legal historical documents, such as the Code of Hammurabi in 1700 B.C, Laws of Manu in India in 1200 B.C., Draco's Law in 621 B.C., The Chinese Book of Punishment in 536 B.C., and the Twelve Tables of the Roman Empire in 450 B.C., came in the context of the expansion of agricultural civilizations and the institution of monogamy marriage and family. Policy-making in sex crimes in ancient times began through these legal historical documents. As the Code of Hammurabi stated: "If a man violates the wife (betrothed or child-wife) of another man, he shall be put to death, but the wife is blameless" (Code 130). Code 154 of Hammurabi stated: "If a man is guilty of incest with his daughter, he shall be exiled." And "If one be guilty of incest with his mother, both shall be burned" (Code 157).

Most of the major forms of sexual behavior defined as crimes today were morally condemned and forbidden by the Holy Texts of all great world religions. Adultery, incest, rape, and bestiality were punishable by death in the Old and the New Testaments, various Hebrew Texts, and the Quran (Kirsch, 1997; Weems, 1995). The Old Testament (Chapter 18 of Leviticus) had forbidden sex with stepmother, stepsister, and with neighbor's wife. Verse 15 of Leviticus states: "If a man has sexual relations with animal, he must be put to death, and you must kill the animal." Verse 20 of Leviticus reads: "The man who lies with his father's wife has uncovered the father's nakedness; both of them shall be put to death, their blood is upon them." The prophets of the Old Testament punished women "with rape, beatings, exposure of their body parts, and mutilation of their bodies" as metaphors for the prophetic message for moral control on sex. (Weems, 1995, p. 2).

The diversities in human sexual behavior and expressions remained seemingly unchanged since ancient times (Foucault, 1990). There are rapes and incest today as they were in ancient times. Prostitution is probably more pervasive today than it was in ancient times. In ancient Greece, homosexuality and violence against women were as common as they are in modern societies. At the same time, however, the boundaries of what is right and wrong, moral and immoral, and legal and illegal in sexual behavior that were created by the ancient laws, and particularly by the Judeo-Christian thought and religion more than three thousand years ago, have also remained largely intact and pervasive. Throughout the whole medieval period in Europe, the Catholic Church became the major institution that further strengthened those boundaries of law and morality in sexual behavior. The Code of the Roman Emperor Justinian in 529 AD described sodomy as a capital crime. In 1300, homosexuals were burnt alive in England (Boswell, 1994). Fornication was regarded as heresy by the fourteenth and fifteenth centuries' canonical laws (Naphy, 2002). The Catholic Church regarded adultery as a grievous sin. "Virtually all restrictions that now apply to sexual behavior in Western societies stem from moral convictions enshrined in medieval canonical laws" (Brundage, 1987, p. 587).

The ideas and moralities about sexual behavior in colonial America in the seventeenth century came from the same source of the Judeo-Christian tradition and the medieval canonical laws. In the American colonies, the biblical ideas and moralities about sexual behavior were first codified in Puritan jurisprudence of the Massachusetts Bay Colony in the early seventeenth century. The sex crimes that were punishable by death in the Bible—adultery, incest, bestiality, and sodomy—were also punishable by death in the Puritan jurisprudence (Horowitz, 2002; McClendon, 1990; Onishi, 1999). The Puritans "left a legacy of statutes designed to protect their communities from sacrilege. In a famous 1656 example, a Captain Kemble, was convicted of 'lewd and unseemly' behavior when he kissed his wife in public after returning from three years at sea" (Finer, 2004, p. 1).

5.2 Criminalization of Sexual Behavior: The Major Policy Perspectives

Policy-making in sex crimes, like all other domains of policy-making is based on certain explicit and implicit assumptions. These assumptions are historically grounded and morally and philosophically contingent. These assumptions, however, vary across time and age (Holmes & Holmes, 2002). The Biblical assumptions were dominant in Puritan jurisprudence in the seventeenth and eighteen centuries, but they are no longer dominant in the context of modernity. Most of the states, for example, have recently repealed their sodomy statutes. There are laws against adultery and fornications in most of the states, but they are rarely applied. There are four major set of assumptions or perspectives that form the basis of contemporary policy-making in sex crimes: 1) moral perspective 2) rights perspective 3) power perspective, and 4) scientific perspective.

Moral Perspective

The notion of morality is inseparable from crime and deviance. All forms of crimes and deviance are seen as violations of society's collective moral standards. But some crimes are seen as morally more reprehensible than others. There is not, for example, a huge moral cry for increased use of marijuana by high school students, or increased property crimes in inner cities, or the increasing growth of identity theft. But many sex crimes such as rape, violent rape and murder of young women, molestation of young children, forcible sodomy, date rape, gang rape, and trafficking of women and children for sexual exploitation are seen as morally evil and unjustifiable. The more compelling question, however, is not whether sex crime policies are based on moral grounds. The compelling question is about the grounds of moral justifications.

There are three major theories about the grounds of morality: religion, utilitarianism, and normative theory. The religious justification of morality is based on the teachings of the sacred Texts. In America, open justification of policies on religious grounds is a violation of the First Amendment, although America is one of the most religious countries of all industrialized nations. The PEW Global Attitudes Project of 2002, conducted by the PEW Research Center, showed that 59 percent of Americans, as opposed to 30 percent of Canadians, 33 percent of British, 27 percent of Italians, 21 percent of Germans, and 11 percent of French, considered religion as one of the very important factors in their lives (PEW Research Center, 2002). However, the views of the majority of the Americans today on sexual behavior are significantly different from those of the Old and the New Testaments. There is a high degree of moral tolerance and legal protections in America for such behaviors as adultery, fornication, seduction, abortion, adult pornography, adult entertainment, divorce, cohabitation, unwed motherhood, and same-sex union. According to a Gallup Poll survey conducted in 2003 (N=1,005 adults national wide), a majority of the Americans believe that divorce (66 percent), sex between unmarried men and women (58 percent) and having a baby outside of marriage (51 percent) are morally acceptable. About 44 percent of the respondents answered that homosexual behavior is also morally acceptable. In a study conducted by the Monitoring the Future Survey, about 80 percent of the high school seniors said that they believe that having a child out of wedlock is not a "violation of a basic principle of human morality" (Whitehead & Popenoe, 1999, p. 6). Most sex-offender policies are morally contingent, but they are not openly justified on religious grounds. The religious notion of morality is prominent only on the issue of policy-making for the legalization of same-sex marriage. About 45 percent of Americans believe that same-sex marriage is not a violation of morality, but the issue of redefining the biblical definition of marriage is highly unlikely to be on the agenda of policy-making in the near future (PEW Research Center, 2002).

The utilitarian theory of morality is based on the notion that a policy or a law that can bring collective good is morally justified. The justification of a policy is based on its long-range consequences for the good of the community at large. Most of the major federal sex crime enactments—the Jeanne Clery Act of 1990, Jacob Wetterling Act of 1994 (Title XVII of the Violent Crime Control and Law Enforcement Act of 1994), Pam Lychner Act of 1996, and Megan's Law of 1996—are based primarily on this utilitarian notion of morality. Each of these legislations came in the wake of major national outcry for Congress to do something for a more collective sense of security of citizens in their homes, schools, and communities. These sex crime episodes, as discussed in Chapter 1, raised a collective moral uproar in the nation, and policy-makers responded to them by developing new laws and enactments. As a result of the Jeanne Clery Act and its subsequent amendments, we now have a national database on campus sex crimes. As a result of the Wetterling Act of 1994 and the Megan's Law of 1996, the names and addresses of more than half a million sex offenders are now in the sex offender registries of all the states. These sex crime policies carry a sense of "collective intrinsic good", and, hence, they are justified on utilitarian grounds.

The normative ground of morality, on the other hand, centers not on the consequences of a particularly policy, but on the kind of acts and actions of individuals that it seeks to control and constrain. It is based on the assumption that certain human acts and actions are intrinsically "good" or intrinsically "bad." As a human person living in a community of people, our actions ought to be rational and reasonable. Some ethical theorists argue that rational and reasonable actions are timeless and invariant; others argue that reason and rationality are relevant to time and space. A number of sex crime laws and policies can be seen from this normative perspective such as laws against date rape, spousal rape, child pornography, sexual harassment, stalking, obscene phone calls, and indecent exposure to minors. Laws and statutes regarding these behaviors suggest that we should have a certain sense of reason and rationality about what is intrinsically "bad" in sexual acts and behavior.

Rights Perspective

One of the major justifications for policy-making in crime and justice is that the government has an obligation to protect the fundamental rights of its citizens. As the Founding Fathers in the American Declaration of Independence said: "We hold these truths to be self-evident, that all men are created equal, that they are endowed by their Creator with certain unalienable Rights, that among these rights are life, liberty, and the pursuit of happiness." The legitimate authority of a government to govern the behavior of its citizens is born out of "social contract." The Declaration of Independence states again: "That to secure these rights, governments are instituted among men, deriving their powers from the consent of the governed."

The rights of the body are some of the most fundamental rights of a human person. Most of the violent sex crimes, such as rape, incest, object penetration, forced sodomy, child molestation are violations of the rights of the body. If the car of a seventeen year old is stolen, it is not a serious violation of her right to life. But if she is raped, her right to life and body are seriously violated. Analysis of many recent sex crime laws and statutes will show that this notion of protecting the rights of the victims has been a major justification in policy-making. It is because of this victim's perspective in policy-making that "consent" has become one of the central notions in sex crimes. A series of recently enacted federal and state laws and statutes have increased punishment for sex crimes involving children or mentally retarded individuals because of their relative inability to consent to sexual relations. In the United States, the average age of consent for heterosexual relations is age sixteen. In some states, such as California, Delaware, Florida, Idaho, Montana, North Dakota, Oregon, Tennessee, Utah, Virginia, Washington, and Wisconsin, the legal age of consent is age eighteen. The marital rape, date rape, acquaintance rape, and rape shield statutes are also based on this notion of protecting the rights of the victims.

Power Perspective

The power perspective in sex crime laws and policy comes from the contribution of feminism. The root cause of sex crimes, according to feminists, particularly the radical feminists, is the men's inner sense of power and domination over women—a sense that goes back to the evolution of patriarchal civilizations. The rise of patriarchal civilizations has relegated women to a subordinate status in economic and social hierarchy. The legal institutions of patriarchal societies not only seek to preserve but also continuously recreate the subordinate status of women, and hence, the proliferation of sex crimes. Feminists claim that the laws and statutes to reduce sex crimes must be based on the understanding of this phenomenon of men's power and domination. The feminist perspective came to policy-making related to sex crimes primarily through the recent growth and expansion of feminist jurisprudence. "In the past decade, feminist legal theory has become a formidable presence in many of America's top legal schools" (Weiss & Young, 1996, p. 2). The core assumption of the feminist jurisprudence is that laws must be addressed to remove the unequal structures of male domination of women. Laws must act to restore women's rights to their body and women's reproductive autonomy. Laws must also protect women from the expanding culture of the commodification of sex and the objectification of the body (Naffine, 1998; Smith, 1993). Law, in feminist jurisprudence, is seen as an instrument of change and transformations.

The expansion of feminist jurisprudence and the growing presence of feminist jurists in the American court in the last three decades have made significant impacts on many recent sex crime laws and statutes in such areas as rape shield laws, domestic violence, child sexual abuse, sexual battery, sexual harassment, prostitution, stalking, and sex trafficking (Daly & Maher, 1998). Catharine Mackinnon, a feminist professor of law at Michigan School of Law, "spearheaded the first major court victory of radical feminist jurisprudence. In 1986, in *Meritor Savings Bank v. Vinson,* the United States Supreme Court adopted her theory that women should be able to sue an employer for sexual harassment based on hostile work environment" (Weiss & young, 1996, p. 6). In recent years, many states have enacted new laws to facilitate the prosecution of rape cases. Almost all the states have enacted rape shield laws that made information about the prior sexual history of the rape victims inadmissible in the court. Most states have also changed the requirement of the "reasonable resistance" clause from rape prosecutions. Many states have enacted laws that shifted the burden of proving "consent" to defendant and made rape a civil rights offense. The Violence against Women Act of 1994, passed as a part of the Violent Crime Control and Law Enforcement Act of 1994, defined rape and violence against women as hate crimes based on gender bias. Hate crimes are both federal crimes and civil rights violations (Weiss & Young, 1996). Battered Women Syndrome is now an accepted defense in the court for women who kill their spouses and commit other domestic violence acts. Many of these developments in policy-making for sex crimes came through the active engagement of feminists both inside and outside American courts.

Scientific Perspective

Sex crimes touch the very core of the bodies and the minds of the victims. Sex crimes are not mere invasions of privacy and violations of the social codes of decency. Since the birth of the Freudian School of Psychoanalysis in the early twentieth century, a number of scientific specialties such as psychology, psychiatry, behavioral pediatrics, behavioral neurology, criminology, and sociology have been studying the impact of sexual abuse and violence on the minds and personalities of the victims. There is now a large volume of empirical research that demonstrates that sexual abuse leaves permanent marks on the minds and mentalities of the victims. Strong correlations have been found between sexual abuse, particularly childhood sexual abuse, and a variety of psychosomatic abnormalities including eating disorder; sleep disorder, post-traumatic-stress disorder syndrome, separation anxiety, substance abuse disorder, depression, anxiety disorder, and sexual disorder (Ackard & Neumark-Sztainer, 2002; Faravelli, Giugni, Salvatori, & Ricca, 2004; Mullen & Fleming, 1998). A Ten–Year Research Update on the impact of childhood sexual abuse done in 2003, where the author has conducted a review of most of the literatures on child sexual abuse published after 1989, showed that childhood sexual victimization "results in adult psychopathology. Specific disorders included major depressive disorder (MDD), borderline personality, summarization, substance abuse, posttraumatic stress disorder, and bulimia nervosa" (Putnam, 2003). The existing research also confirms that children with the history of childhood sexual victimization "were more likely to exhibit sexualized behaviors" (Putnam, 2003).

Another study on the impact of childhood rape on alcohol use in adult women, done by researchers from the Medical University of South Carolina and National Crime Victims Research and Treatment Center, concluded that: "A history of childhood rape doubled the number of alcohol abuse symptoms that women experiences in adulthood. Path analysis and cross-validation results demonstrated significant pathways connecting childhood rape to PTSD symptoms and PTSD symptoms to alcohol use" (Epstein, Sanders, Kilpatrick, & Resnick, 1998, p. 223). The victims of childhood sexual abuse are more likely to have problems in their adult love and attachment relations. "Sexual abuse severity and attachment have significant but distinct effects on long term outcomes; abuse characteristics predict classic PTSD symptoms and attachment insecurity predict distress, depression, and personality disorders above and beyond any effects of abuse severity" (Alexander, Anderson, Brand, Schaffer, Grelling, & Kretz, 1998, p. 45). Studies on female juvenile prostitutes (Finkelhor & Ormrod, 2004) find that a higher percentage of them experienced childhood sexual victimization. A study conducted by the Bureau of Justice Statistics (1999) on prior abuse reported by inmates and probationers in federal and state correctional institutions found that "A third of women in State prison, a sixth in federal prison, and a quarter in jail said they had been raped before their sentences" (p. 1).

Many studies have found that suicidal ideation among older women can be traced back to their childhood sexual victimization. "Women who reported abuse histories were more likely to report suicidal ideation at the time of the hospitalization and a history of multiple suicide attempts" (Talbot, Duberstein, Cox, Denning, & Conwell, 2004, p. 536). Researchers have also found that women who are the victims of sexual abuse are more likely to abuse their partners. The battered women who kill or seriously injure their partners are more likely to be those who experienced spousal and sexual abuse in the past (O'Keefe, 1998). Many stricter laws and statutes to control sex crimes are justified on the basis of these and many other scientific theories and research studies. The American courts are also increasingly accepting the scientific hypothesis of repressed memory syndrome and the notion of psychopathic personality disorder related to sexual crimes and abuse.

5.3 Sex Crimes in America: Nature, Types, and Trends

Sex Crimes: Types and Characteristics

The major governmental sources and surveys on sex crimes data include the Uniform Crime Reports (UCR), National Crime Victimization Survey (NCVS), National Incidence-Based Reporting System (NIBRS), and the National Corrections Reporting Program (NCRP). Sex crimes data are also collected by many advocacy organizations such as the National Sexual Violence Resource Center (NSVRC), National Violence against Women Survey, and the National College of Women's Victimization Survey. The NCVS and NIBRS, however, collect and codify more reliable and comprehensive data on sex crimes. The UCR collects sex crimes data, on an annual basis, primarily on forcible rape and attempted rape that are reported to law enforcement. The UCR defines rape as "the carnal knowledge of a female forcibly and against her will." The cases that are not reported to law enforcement are not included in the UCR report.

The NCVS includes both reported and unreported sexual offenses collected every six months from a nationally representative sample of American households. The NCVS system has an extended definition of rape and other sexual assaults. It defines rape as "forced sexual intercourse including both psychological coercion as well as psychical force. Forced sexual intercourse means vaginal, anal, or oral penetration by the offender." The NCVS system includes same-sex rape and object penetrations within its definition of rape—the data that are not available from the UCR system. The NCVS also generates data on date rape, acquaintance rape, and other unwanted sexual acts.

The NIBRS collects data in terms of two major offense categories: Group A Offenses and Group B Offenses. Sex crimes are reported as Group A Offenses, and they include forcible sex offenses (forcible rape, forcible sodomy, sexual assault with an object, and forcible fondling), non-forcible sex offenses (incest, statutory rape), prostitution offenses (prostitution, assisting or promoting prostitution), and offenses related to pornography and obscene materials. The NIBRS not only has expanded definitions of rape and sexual assaults but also has an expanded list of sexual crimes including statutory rape, oral or anal forcible sodomy, forcible fondling, child molestation, and indecent exposures. The NIBRS provides a more refined understanding of the nature and the extent of sex crimes by collecting sex crimes data in terms of gender, race, age, victim-offender relationship, and the time and place of occurrence of sex crime incidents.

The Uniform Crime Reports collects sex crimes data in terms of two major categories: forcible rape and sex offenses that include sodomy, statutory rape, and offenses against chastity, decency, and morals. The National Crime Victimization Survey collects sex crimes data also in terms of two major categories: rape and sexual assault. The National Incidence Based Reporting System divides sex crimes data into six major categories: forcible rape, statutory rape, forcible sodomy, forcible fondling including indecent liberties and child molestation, incest, and sexual assault. In addition to these national statistical surveys, there are also sex crimes categories defined and described by different state statutes. On the basis of these sources, a three-fold typology of sex crimes can be developed: sex crime acts, behavior, and expressions. Certain sexual acts such as rape, incest, adultery, and bestiality, as mentioned before, are forbidden from the time of the New Testament. But what is happening today is that law is increasingly defining a wide range of sexual acts, behavior, and sexual expressions as crimes (see Table 22).

Although sex crime acts, behaviors, and expressions are wide-ranging, sex crimes have some general characteristics. Sex crime is predominantly a male crime. About 90-95 percent of the sex crime offenders are males. According to the National Judicial Reporting Program, 98 percent of the felons convicted for rape and 97 percent of felons convicted of sexual assault in state courts in 2002 were males (Bureau of Justice Statistics, 2005). The victims of sex crimes are mostly female, particularly female children and adolescents. The sex offenders usually know the victims, particularly those who are children. In about 80 percent of the rape cases, the victim knows the offender (Tjaden & Thoennes, 2000). Sex crime is usually not a group phenomenon. About 90 percent of rape and sexual victimizations involve a single offender (Bureau of Justice Statistics,

1997). In 2002, of all the felons convicted of rape in state courts, 63 percent were Whites and 33 percent were Blacks. Of all the felons convicted of sexual assault in the same year in the state courts, 71 percent were Whites and 25 percent were Blacks (Bureau of Justice Statistics, 2005). The average age of those convicted for sexual assault offenses in state courts in 2002 was thirty four.

Table 22 : Major Categories and Types of Sex Crimes

Sex Crime Categories	Major Sex Crime Types
Sex Crime Acts	Rape, Male Rape, Forcible Sodomy, Conspiracy to Commit Forcible Sodomy, Attempt to Commit Forcible Sodomy, Marital Rape, Date Rape, Acquaintance Rape, Child Rape, Object Rape of a Child, Sodomy on a Child, Child Molestation, Forcible Fondling, Incest, Bestiality, Object Sexual Penetration, Adultery, and Prostitution
Sex Crime Behaviors	Sexual Harassment, Stalking, Indecent Exposure, Exhibitionism, Fornication, Custodial Sexual Relations, Custodial Sexual Misconduct, Marital Sexual Assault, Spousal Violence, Lewdness Involving a Child, Enticing a Child Over the Internet, Attempt to Rape a Child, Conspiracy to Rape a Child, Attempt to Commit Object Rape, Conspiracy to Commit Object Rape, Solicitation to Commit Object Rape, Aggravated Kidnapping, Attempt or Conspiracy to Aggravated Kidnapping, Participation in Child Sex Tourism, Participation in Global Trafficking of Children and Women, Financing of Global Sex Tourism and Trafficking, Commercial Sexual Exploitation of Women, and Commercial Sexual Exploitation of Children at Home and Abroad
Sex Crime Expressions	Production and Sale of Child Pornography, Possession of Child Pornography, Financing of Child Pornography, Internet Child Pornography, Videotaping and Filming Minors for Sexual Purposes, Indecent Liberties, and Obscene Phone Calls

Source: Compiled by the Author

Sex offender treatment research shows that juvenile sex offenders are more responsive to treatments than adult sex offenders. Sex offenders have a high rate of recidivism. The rate of recidivism is particularly high among the rapists and child molesters. Based on the nature of their crimes, their violence associated with the commission of crimes, and their likelihood of recidivism, sex offenders in most states are grouped into three categories: violent sex offenders, sexual predators or psychopaths or super-predators, and non-violent sexual offenders. Sex offender punishments and treatments depend on how the state statutes define the nature of the sex offenders and classify the nature of sex offenses (Shahidullah & Green, 2007).

Sex Crimes: Prevalence, and Trends

According to the National Crime Victimization Survey, about 50 percent of all violent crimes are not reported to law enforcement, and of all violent crimes, rape and sexual assaults are less likely to be reported (Shahidullah & Green, 2007). From 1992 to 2000, on an average only 31 percent of rape and sexual assaults were reported to law enforcement (Bureau of Justice Statistics, 2003). Reporting of sexual offenses increased by about 6 percent between 1992 and 2000, but on an average about seventy percent of cases remain unreported. The National Crime Victimization Survey estimated that in 2004, U.S. residents age 12 and over experienced about 5.2 million violent crimes including rape and sexual assault. The average annual number of rape and sexual assault victims in 2003-2004 was 204,370 thousand (rape, 65,510; attempted rape, 43,440, and sexual assault, 95,420). During the same period, annual victimization rate for rape and sexual assault was 0.9 per 1,000 households (Bureau of Justice Statistics, 2005).

Juveniles comprise the majority of the victims of sexual offenses. In his analysis of NIBRS data on reported sexual offenses in 12 states covering the years 1991 through 1996, Snyder (2000) finds that about 67 percent of all victims of sexual assault were juveniles under the age of 18, and 34 percent of all victims of sexual assaults were juveniles under the age of 12. One of every seven victims was under the age of 6. Another report that analyzed the National Violence against Women Survey (NVAW) data collected in 1995-1996 presented similar findings. The report found that "Many American women are raped at an early age. Thus, more than half (54 percent) of the female rape victims identified by the survey were younger than age 18 when they experienced their first attempted or completed rape" (Tjaden & Thoennes, 2000, p. iii-iv). The same report also observed that "Women who reported that they were raped before age 18 were twice as likely to report being raped as an adult" (Tjaden & Thoennes, 2000, p. iv).

Another study by the Centers for Disease Control and Prevention and the National Center for Injury Prevention and Control that analyzed the data provided by the National Violence against Women Survey in 2004, estimated that about 5.3 million women become the victims of intimate partner violence in the United States every year. "The cost of intimate partner rape, physical assault, and stalking exceeds $5.8 billion each year, nearly $4.1 billion of which is for direct medical and mental health care services" (Centers for Disease Control and the National Center for Injury Prevention and Control, 2004, p. 1). The same study also estimated that in the United States "nearly 7.8 million women have been raped by an intimate partner at some point in their lives, and an estimated 201,394 women are raped by an intimate partner each year" (Centers For Disease Control and the National Center for Injury Prevention and Control, 2004, p. 1). It is also estimated that intimate partners kill about 30 percent of female murder victims and 4 percent of male murder victims each year (Bureau of Justice Statistics, 2000).

Sexual assaults take place at homes, schools, colleges, work, and a variety of custodial organizations such as day care centers, nursing homes, and prisons. About 70 percent of sexual assaults reported to law enforcement take place in the homes of the victims or the offenders. Snyder's (2000) analysis of NIBRS data reveal that 83.3 percent of rape, 81.5 percent of forcible sodomy, and 82.4 percent of forcible fondling, where victims were ages 6 to 11, occurred within a residence. For juveniles ages 12 to 17, 68.7 percent of forcible rape, 72.7 percent of forcible sodomy, and 68.8 percent of forcible fondling occurred within a residence. Juvenile sexual offending, particularly the victimization of female juveniles ages 6 to 17, are more likely to have occurred within a residence (Snyder, 2000, p. 6).

In recent years, sexual assaults prevalent in custodial organizations, particularly in prisons, have raised serious policy concerns. A report of the United States Office of Inspector General (2005) found that in many federal prisons, managed by the Bureau of Prisons, correction officers, prison guards, prison psychologists, case managers, and maintenance workers sexually abuse the inmates, and abuse is not limited by gender. Between 2000 and 2004, the Office of the Inspector General "presented 163 sexual abuse cases for prosecution. Sixty five of these cases, or 40 percent, resulted in prosecution" (United States Office of the Inspector General, 2005, p. 9). The report noted that most sexual abuses cases in federal prisons are not prosecuted. The federal prosecutors are "less interested in prosecuting sexual abuse cases" reported in federal prisons, "regardless of the strength of the evidence, because the crimes are not felonies" (United States Office of the Inspector General, 2005, p. 1).

In 2005, the Bureau of Justice Statistics conducted a survey of 2,730 correctional facilities to study the prevalence of prison sexual abuse. The survey found that in 2004, the correctional authorities received 8,210 allegations of sexual abuse in the nation. Of these allegations, 42 percent of the cases involved staff sexual misconduct, 37 percent of the cases were inmate-on-inmate nonconsensual sexual acts, 11 percent were about sexual harassment, and 10 percent of the cases involved abusive sexual conduct (Bureau of Justice Statistics, 2005, p. 1) According to this survey, in state prisons 69 percent of victims of staff sexual abuse were males, and 67 percent of perpetrators were females.

The nation's federal prisons house less than 2 percent of convicted sex offenders. In 2004, the number of total inmates sentenced in federal prisons was 169,370. Out of these inmates, only 1.1 percent of inmates were sentenced for sex offenses as opposed to 53.3 percent of inmates sentenced for drug offenses. However, there is a trend growing since the middle of the 1990s for increased federal involvement in prosecuting sex offense cases. Between 2000 and 2004, sex offense cases and defendants in federal courts both "jumped 24 percent to 1,638 cases and 1,709 defendants. Defendants charged with sexual abuse rose 11 percent, and sexual abuse cases increased 10 percent" (Newsletter of the Federal Court, 2005, p. 4).

5.4 Sex Crimes: Nature and Evolution of Federal Laws and Policy

Federal Sex Crime Policies 1870-1970

There are no reliable sources of the extent and prevalence of sex crimes in America in the nineteenth century. The Uniform Crime Reports introduced sexual assault (mainly rape) as one of its eight categories for collecting crime data only in the 1930s. A more systematic and elaborate collection of sex crime data did not begin until the introduction of the National Crime Victimization Survey and the National Incidence-Based Reporting System by the Department of Justice about two decades ago. However, the social historians, on the basis of court records, have informed that sex crimes were widespread in America in the nineteenth century. Throughout the nineteenth century, "child victims had always featured in American courts; in New York city in the years 1790 to 1876, with the exception of a spike in the 1820s, between one-third and one-half of females in rape cases were younger than nineteen years of age (Robertson, 2005, p. 1). In the late nineteenth century, prostitution rapidly spread in New York, Chicago, Los Angeles, and other big cities as new immigrants from Russia, Austria, Hungary, and other East European countries began to arrive in large numbers. The rising rate of sexual crimes in the late nineteenth century was also accompanied by the emergence of various strands of movements for sexual freedom and sexual liberty. Many reformist groups began to advocate for free love and the attainment of sexual pleasure outside the institution of marriage (Horowitz, 2000). It was at that time of the first wave of sexual revolution in the late nineteenth century that the issue of sexual morality for the first time became an agenda for policy-making in sex crimes by the federal government.

The Comstock Law of 1873
Criminalization of Obscenity

From the beginning of the Republic, the issues of morality were prominent in political and social discourses of the American elites. The founding fathers wanted to create not only a good government but also a good society based on law, justice, and morality. Up to the end of the nineteenth century, many enactments were made to set the trajectories of law and justice but not of morality. The Comstock Law passed by Congress in 1873 was the first systematic attempt of the federal government for the legislation of morality. The Comstock Law made birth control and the use of contraception a federal crime. The law criminalized the possession, exhibition, publication, advertisement, selling, mailing, and writing, printing, or drawing of obscene pictures, books, and materials. The law was passed in the context of a movement against birth control and obscenity led in the 1860s by a man named Anthony Comstock of New York. About twenty-four states enacted their own versions of the Comstock Law in the 1870s and 1880s. Some of the most restrictive states included Connecticut and Massachusetts dominated by Puritan ideology. Under the law, married couples could be arrested and sentenced to prison for a year for using contraceptive devices. The authors of many classics censored under Comstock Law include Victor Hugo, Oscar Wilde, D. H. Lawrence, William Faulkner, John Steinbeck, and Ernest Hemingway. The Comstock Law dominated the minds and morality of American people until it was challenged by the U.S. Circuit Court of Appeals in New York in 1936. The U.S. Circuit of Appeals in the case of *United States v. One Package* in 1936 made a decision that "Laws prohibiting Americans from importing contraceptive devices or items causing 'unlawful abortion' did not apply to physicians who used the items to protect the health of patients." The ruling of the U.S. Circuit of Appeals decriminalized the use and the supply of contraceptives. The Anti-Comstock Movement led by Margaret Sanger, who opened up the first birth control clinic in New York, contributed to the decriminalization of birth control in the 1920s.

The Mann Act of 1910: Criminalization of Prostitution

The social and economic transformations and the growth of urbanization in the late nineteenth century brought a series of social problems. Prostitution began to grow from the beginning of the nineteenth century, but it became particularly widespread in the late nineteenth century (Anbinder, 2001). "Sex, or 'red-light', districts were well known before 1850 and later. New York's Five Points and the Tenderloin, San Francisco's Barbary Coast, New Orleans's Basin Street and Stormville, Chicago's Levee, and even the Alley in Boise, Idaho, were nationally known for the promiscuous sexuality they promoted" (Gilfoyle, 1991, p. 1). By the late nineteenth century, "prostitution was a multimillion-dollar business, with organized networks of madams, landlords, doctors, and municipal officials" (Gilfoyle, 1991, p. 1). In 1910, in a report on Importation and Harboring of Women for Immoral Purposes, the U.S. Immigration Commission noted: "The importation of women for immoral purposes has brought into the country evils even worse than those of prostitution. Immigration and prostitution were perceived by many during the progressive years as contiguous pieces of social pathology" (Connelly,1980, p. 48).The moral advocates of the Progressive Movement wanted federal interventions to address the problem of prostitution. In 1910, Congress passed the Mann Act to criminalize prostitution. "The Common Law tradition never implicated the owners of houses of prostitution. Indeed, until the twentieth century, no statutory definition of prostitution existed in most American communities" (Gilfoyle, 1991, p. 1).

The Mann Act made it a federal crime to transport women from one state to another for the purpose of engagement in commercial sex. James Robert Mann of Chicago, a House Republican (1897-1922), proposed the Mann Act. He was also the architect of the Mann-Elkins Act of 1910 that gave more federal power to the Interstate Commerce Commission. In 1917, the Supreme Court, through its ruling in the case of *Caminetti v. United States*, extended the scope of the Mann Act by criminalizing the transportation of women even for non-commercial sex. Until the middle of the 1980s, someone traveling with a woman other than his wife and falling in romantic relationships could be convicted for violation of the Mann Act. The Mann Act "resulted in 1,537 convictions by 1916. By the 1920s, the era of the brothel and open prostitution had ended and significant changes emerged over the next four decades" (Gilfoyle, 1991, p. 2).

The 1969 President's Commission on Obscenity and Pornography

The moral discourse on sex and sex crimes that began in the late nineteenth century, the discourses that led to the enactment of the Comstock Law and the Mann Act, began to be widen in the 1930s and 1940s in the context of rising organized gangs and prostitutions, and escalated sexual crimes against children. However, in the subsequent decades of the 1950s and 1960s, the moral climate of policy-making in sex crimes was greatly impacted by Alfred Kinsey's report on *Sexual Behavior in the Human Male* published (with W. B. Pomeroy and C. E. Martin) in 1948. Based on his survey of thousands of white middle class college educated Americans, Kinsey reported that fornication, adultery, sodomy, and bisexuality are widespread in America. Human sexuality, the report concluded, is much more complex, varied, and diverse than it is commonly understood. The Kinsey's Report brought a formidable challenge to the traditional notion of sexual morality, justified sexual openness, and thus laid the foundation for the sexual revolution that spread and engulfed America in the 1970s. The U.S. Supreme Court in *Roth v. United States* in 1957 made a landmark decision that the First Amendment protects sexual materials that have literary value and "redeeming social importance."

It was in this context that the "deeply concerned" Congress allocated $2 million and authorized President Lyndon B. Johnson in 1969 to set up a Commission to study the impact of obscenity and pornography on sex crimes, and recommend measures to congress to control and contain the spread of obscenity (Edwards, 1992). The President's Commission was the first systematic effort by the federal government to formulate sex crime policies on the basis of scientific research. After a year of intensive research and surveys, the eighteen-member President Commission concluded that there are no strong correlations between pornography and sex crimes. The Commission recommended legislations to restrict the exposure of pornographic materials to children, but not to adults. The Commission found that "it is inappropriate to adjust the level of adult communication to that considered suitable for children" (Edwards, 1992, p. 2). Policy-making for sex crimes in the decade of the 1960s ended with the publication of the report by the President's Commission on Obscenity and Pornography. However, the President's Commission did not settle but it rather intensified the moral storms that began after the publication of the Kinsey's Report. In October 1970, after two weeks of its publication, the "Senate voted 60-5 (with 35 abstentions) to reject the findings and recommendations of the Commission on Obscenity and Pornography" (Edwards, 1992, p. 2).

Federal Sex Crime Policies: 1970-2006

In the 1970s, there were no significant developments in policy-making for sex crimes by the federal government, except another landmark Supreme Court decision on the protection of obscenity. In 1973, in *Miller vs. California*, the U.S. Supreme Court ruled that the First Amendment protects all obscene materials, unless they are distributed to minors. In *Miller*, the Court abandoned the *Roth* test of obscenity on the basis of the doctrine of "redeeming social importance." The 1970s, however, was the beginning of a culture war in America's search for liberty and morality in sex, law, and politics. The spread of Sexual Revolution, Women's Revolution, Gay Movement, and Counter Culture brought a new sense of moral crusade in federal policy-making, and it started from the beginning of the Nixon Presidency in 1969. President Nixon quickly rejected the findings of the President's Commission on Obscenity and Pornography. President Nixon was quoted as saying: "So long as I am in the White House, there will be no relaxation of the national effort to control and eliminate smut from our national life" (as quoted in Edwards, 1992, p. 2).

The 1985 Meese Commission on Obscenity and Pornography

During the presidencies of Gerald Ford and Jimmy Carter, from 1974 to 1981, crime in general was not high on the agenda for policy-making. The Nixon's War on Crime metaphor reemerged, as mentioned in Chapter 3, after Ronald Reagan came to power in 1981. President Reagan, under the chairmanship of Attorney General Edwin Meese, set up a new eleven-member Commission in 1985 to reexamine the problem of obscenity and pornography, and on that basis to recommend measures to the Attorney General to control their use and publications. After a year of research and interviews, the Meese Commission concluded, in contrast to the previous President's Commission, that there are positive correlations between sexual crimes and exposure to obscene and pornographic materials. Those who are exposed to sexually violent materials are more likely to be engaged in sexual crimes and violence. After the publication of the Meese Commission Report, legal restrictions began to be imposed on the sale and the distribution of obscene and pornographic materials by the Department of Justice. "Groups such as the Mississippi-based National Federation for Decency advocated picketing and consumer boycotts, claiming that they had stopped some 5,000 chain stores from selling magazines such as *Playboy* and *Penthouse*" (Edwards, 1992, p. 4). Under threats of legal actions by the Department of Justice, "the 7-Eleven chain stopped selling adult magazines in 7500 of its stores" (Edwards, 1992, p. 4).

President Reagan signed five major crimes Bills related to drug abuse and sentencing reforms, but they did not include any significant legislation on sex crimes. In fact, except for the President Commission and the Meese Commission on Obscenity and Pornography, federal activities related to sex crime legislations did not begin until the beginning of the 1990s. The Omnibus Crime Control and the Safe Street Act of 1968 signed by President Johnson, The Omnibus Crime Control Act of 1970 signed by President Nixon, and the Comprehensive Crime Control Act of 1984 signed by President Reagan created a series of federal statutes on crime and justice, but they did not include any significant sex crime legislations. In fact, after the Mann Act of 1910, almost eighty years have passed without any major sex crime enactment by Congress, although during that time sex crimes in the nation escalated and the issues of sexual morality remained dominant in public discourses. Almost all of today's major federal sex crime legislations were enacted between 1990 and 2005 (see Table 23). The following section will discuss some of these legislations in terms of six broader sets of laws and sex crime policies. These are 1) sex offender registration and community notification policy, 2) campus sex crime notification policy, 3) child sexual abuse laws and policy, 4) laws and policy on domestic violence, stalking, and sexual harassment, 5) sex crimes in American prisons, and 6) sex and obscenity in the Media.

Sex Offender Registration and Community Notification Policy

In 1947, the state of California made a significant sex crime policy innovation. The state enacted a law to require sex offenders to register with local law enforcement agencies. In the 1950s and 1960s, five other states (Alabama, Arizona, Florida, Nevada, and Ohio) enacted laws for sex offender registration policy. The sex offender registration law has now become one of the major federal policy strategies for the control and containment of sex crimes in America. Many countries including Canada, United Kingdom, and Australia are now adopting this American innovation in sex offender registration policy. All twenty-six countries belonging to the European Union have adopted a common European Union Sex Offender Program following the American model. Congress made four major enactments related to sex offender registration and notification policy: Jacob Wetterling Act of 1994, Megan's Law of 1996, Pam Lychner Sexual Offender Tracking and Identification Act of 1996, and the Children Safety Act of 2005.

The Jacob Wetterling Act of 1994, enacted as a part of the Violent Crime Control and Law Enforcement Act of 1994 signed by President Clinton, established the basic provisions for the current sex offender registration and notification policy. The Wetterling Act includes five major sets of guidelines related to the creation of an interconnected system of national sex offender registration. The first set of guidelines is about the creation in each state of a statewide and centralized sex offender registration and notification system. The core objective of the Act is to help develop, in each state, a central repository system, or an agency, for keeping and organizing information on all state sex offenders information that can be readily available, shared, and exchanged both locally and nationally.

Secondly, the Act mandates that the states follow the registration classification provided by the Act either by developing new state statutes or through new law enforcement rules and procedures. Under the Wetterling Act, states must notify their sex offenders about their registration obligation, collect registration information before a sex offender is released, and send registration information to state registration agency within 3 days after the release of a sex offender. The Act made a provision of mandatory registration for at least ten years for all child molesters and violent sex offenders, and a provision of registration for life for highly dangerous sex offenders described as sexual predators. The sentencing court assisted by a panel of experts was made responsible to make the determination of whether a sex offender is a violent sexual predator. The predator determination can be made at the time of sentencing, during the prison time, or at the time of the release of a sex offender. The Act does not require registration and notification for juvenile sex offenders, unless they are treated as adults.

Table 23: Major Federal Sex Crime Legislations 1990-2005

Major Federal Legislations 1990 -1999	Major Federal Legislations 2000-2005
Jacob Wetterling Crimes Against Children and Sexually Violent Offenders Registration Act of 1994 PL 103-322	Children's Internet Protection Act of 2000 (CIPA) PL 106-141
The Violence Against Women Act of 1994 PL 103-322	Victims of Trafficking and Violence Protection Act of 2000 PL 106-386
Sex Crimes Against Children Act of 1995 PL 104-71	Aimee's Law of 2000 PL 106-386
Megan' s Law of 1996 PL 104-145	Federal Campus Sex Crimes Act of 2000 PL 106-386
Pam Lychner Act of 1996 PL 104-236	Sex Tourism Prohibition Improvement Act of 2002 PL 107-525
The Communications Decency Act of 1996 (CDA) PL 104-104	Child Obscenity and Pornography Prevention Act of 2002 PL 107-526
Child Pornography Prevention Act of 1996 (CPPA) PL 104-208	Prison Rape Elimination Act of 2003 PL 108-79
Child Online Protection Act of 1998 (COPA) PL 105-775	PROTECT Act of 2003 PL 108-21
Protection of Children From Sexual Predators Act of 1998 PL 105-314	Broadcast Decency Enforcement Act of 2005 PL 109-235

Source: Compiled by the Author

The third set of guidelines is about sex offender information verification. The Act required each state to establish a sex offender address verification system consistent with the provisions of the Act. According to the Act, the addresses of the violent sex offenders must be verified annually, and those of violent sexual predators every ninety days through the mailing of address verification cards. A registrant is legally obligated to give an address change to local law enforcement within 10 days of moving, and local law enforcement is legally obligated to notify immediately the state registration agency of that change. Most states maintain addresses of sex offenders in terms of name, address, photograph, birth date, and social security number. The fourth set of guidelines is about the state's responsibility of sex offender information notification. The Act required all states to develop a system of notification of sex offender information to their law enforcement agencies. The Act authorized the states to decide the methods of notification.

Finally, under the Wetterling Act, states are also required to develop mechanisms for collaboration both within a state and among different states to share and exchange sex offender registration information. The states are required to develop programs for effective distribution and dissemination of information about sex offenders both locally and nationally. The Act gave three to five years time, from its initial period of enrollment in 1994, for the states to implement its statutory guidelines without losing 10 percent of the Federal Byrne Grant given for criminal justice system improvement.

Megan's Law, enacted in 1996, amended some of the notification provisions of the Wetterling Act. The Wetterling Act made a general provision that sex offender registration information be treated as private data to be selectively used by law enforcement agencies. The states, under the Wetterling Act, were not required to release registration information to the public. Megan's Law eliminated the privacy provision of the Wetterling Act, and it created the provision of mandatory community notification. Under Megan's Law, states are required, for the necessity of public safety, to release sex offender registration information to the public. States, of course, are given the authority to make determination about the nature and methods of information disclosure.

The Pam Lychner Sexual Offender Tracking and Identification Act of 1996 further extended the roles and obligations of the federal, state, and local governments with respect to sex offender registration and notification policy. One of the key provisions of the Lychner Act is that it authorized the Attorney General to set up a nationally centralized database—a sex offender registry—within the Federal Bureau of Investigation to facilitate the tracking of movements of all categories of sex offenders. Under the Wetterling Act, states were generally required to transmit their sex offender conviction records and fingerprints to the FBI. The Lychner Act "imposes a number of requirements to make sure States are communicating with the FBI about sex offenders living in their jurisdictions" (Sorkin, 1998, p. 38). The FBI, under the Lychner Act, also is required to communicate with the states, and disclose sex offender registration information to federal, state, and local agencies for employment related background checks, law enforcement purposes, and general public safety.

The second most important provision of the Lychner Act is that it required sex offenders, residing in a state that lacks a "minimally sufficient" registration and notification system, to register directly with the FBI in order to be included in the national registry system. In other words, the Act required the FBI to handle the sex offender registration problems of the states that do not have minimally sufficient registration programs. The Wetterling Act required the states to register only the violent sexual predators for life. The Lychner Act amended this provision and required states to register sex offenders for life who have two or more convictions, and who have been convicted of aggravated sexual abuse. The Act mandated for the inclusion of victim's rights advocates and representatives from law enforcement agencies to the panel of experts charged with the responsibility to determine offender classifications. The lifetime registration of aggravated sex offenders, repeat sex offenders, and violent sexual predators became a new requirement for states under the Lychner Act. The Lychner Act created mandatory penalties for offenders who knowingly fail to register. For repeat sex offenders who knowingly fail to register, the Act made a provision for imprisonment for up to 10 years and a fine not to exceed more than $100,000.

Another significant amendment made by the Lychner Act is related to sex offender information verification guidelines. Under the Wetterling Act, sex offenders were required to verify their addresses by sending out the address verification card mailed to them by local law enforcement or state agencies. Under the Lychner Act, the offenders are required to include also their photographs and fingerprints with address verification cards. According to the Lychner Act, sex offenders, residing in a state that does not have a minimally sufficient registration program, are required to notify their change of address information to the FBI within three days. The Act gave three years, from the time of its enactment in 1996, for the states to implement its new statutory guidelines.

In 1997, Congress enacted an amended version of the Wetterling Act of 1994—Jacob Wetterling Crimes against Children and Sexually Violent Offenders Registration Improvements Act of 1997. One of the major policy directions came from the amended Wetterling Act of 1977 is the new classification of a group of sexual offenders as sexual predators. Sexual predators are defined as violent and high-risk repeat sex offenders who have the characteristics of psychopathic personalities. The Act required that the determination of whether a sex offender is in the category of a violent sexual predator be made by a court with the advice of a board composed of mental health and behavioral science experts, representatives from law enforcement agencies, and victim rights advocates.

Almost all federal sex offender legislations enacted after the Wetterling Act of 1994 made new provisions and amendments to improve and strengthen the sex offender registration system. One of the recent legislations that brought far more stringent laws is Children Safety Act of 2005. Title I of the Children Safety Act is the Sex Offender Registration and Notification Act of 2005. One of the major purposes of the new law was to establish a comprehensive national system of sex offender registration by developing a national website titled as Dru Sjodin National Sex Offender Website. The Act instructed and authorized the Attorney Generally to create and maintain a National Sex Offender Registry (NSOR) that can be electronically accessed by the public and all law enforcement and concerned agencies from anywhere in the country. The new law extended the registration policy to include all federally recognized Indian Tribes and the American territories in Guam, American Samoa, the Commonwealth of Puerto Rico, and the United States Virgin Islands.

The Children Safety Act of 2005 specified and broadened the definition of sex offenses against a minor and included in this category child kidnapping (unless committed by a parent), solicitation to engage in sexual conduct, use of a minor in a sexual performance, solicitation to practice juvenile prostitution, and possession, production and distribution of child pornography. Some of the new requirements of the Act include mandatory registration for juvenile sex offenders, for sex offenders who committed their crimes in foreign countries, and persons convicted of possession, production, and distribution of child pornography. One of the new laws included in the Act is that a sex offender is required to register before the completion of his or her sentencing. A sex offender sentenced to life is required to register no later than five days after the sentencing. The Children Safety Act made an amendment to the Wetterling Act and made a provision for mandatory lifetime registration for persons convicted of felony sex offenses and 20 years for non-felony sex offenses. The Act required a DNA sample, vehicle information, employment information, and school and college information to be included in the list of required information for sex offender registration.

Under the Wetterling Act, sex offender registration verification remained a responsibility of local and state agencies. The Children Safety Act of 2005 made it a legal responsibility also of the sex offenders. The Act required that sex offenders physically verify and update their registration information once every six months. The failure by sex offenders to comply with registration requirements or giving false information for registration were made felonies punishable by a maximum term of prison that is greater than one year. The Children Safety Act created the Jessica Lunsford Address Verification Program that requires law enforcement agencies to verify registration information of felony sex offenders monthly, and that of misdemeanor sex offenders once every three months. The Act also introduced a new notification program titled as "Megan Nicole Kanka and Alexander Nicole Zapp Community Program." Under this Program, local and state law enforcement agencies are required to notify electronically the FBI, school authorities, housing authorities, employment agencies, social service entities, child welfare agencies, and voluntary organizations dealing with children within five days of changes in a sex offender's registration information.

The Children Safety Act provided more responsibilities to the federal government for the organization and maintenance of the national sex offender registration system. The Act authorized the Attorney General to establish a federal sex offender management assistance program, creation of demonstration projects to study the effective use of electronic devices for sex offender management, and a bonus payment system for prompt and effective compliance by the states The Act gave two years, from the time of its enactment in 2005, for states to implement their statutory guidelines without losing 10 percent of the federal Byrne Grant and Local Government Law Enforcement Block Grant.

In compliance with the Lychner Act, the Department of Justice formally announced the activation of a National Sex Offender Registry (NSOR) website in July, 2005. The FBI's Crimes against Children unit is responsible for developing and coordinating the NSOR system. Currently the NSOR website gives real-time access to sex offender registration information to the public from about

41 states. In addition, there is a major federal program named as Center for Sex Offender Management (CSOM) program located at the Department of Justice. The Office of Justice Program of the Department of Justice, National Institute of Corrections, and the State Justice Institute created the CSOM in 1997. The federal executive branch does not have a separate agency for policy-making with respect sex offenders like that of the OJJDP for juvenile justice and the DEA for combating drug crimes. The CSOM was created on the basis of the perspective of comprehensive management of sex offenders when they return to communities after serving their prison times. The CSOM provides grants and technical assistance to state and local governments for community-based innovative sex offender management programs and strategies. From 1999 to 2005, under the Department of Justice's Comprehensive Approach to Sex Offender Management (CASOM) Discretionary Grant, $17.5 million have been awarded to different state and local agencies for developing innovative programs on sex offender management.

Federal Campus Sex Crime Notification Policy

The Bureau of Justice Statistics report on The Sexual Victimization of College Women (Fisher, Cullen, & Turner, 2000), on the basis of interviews of 4.446 college women attending a 2 or 4-year college or university, found that 15.5 percent of college women were sexually victimized in any given academic year. Of those who were sexually victimized, 7.7 percent experienced the use or threat of physical force. The same study also reveals non-violent sexual victimization such as stalking, and visual and verbal harassment. "Unwanted or uninvited sexual contacts were widespread, with more than one-third of the sample reporting these incidents" (Fisher, Cullen & Turner, 2000, p. 17). The study found that about 13.1 percent of college women were stalked in any given year, and 80 percent of them knew their stalkers. The majority of the stalkers, about 42.5 percent, were boyfriends or ex-boyfriends. A considerable number of college women also experienced visual and verbal sexual victimization. "About 6 percent of female students had been shown pornographic pictures, almost 5 percent had someone expose their sexual organs to them, and 2.4 percent were observed naked without their consent. About half of the respondents were subjected to sexist remarks" (Fisher, Cullen, & Turner, 2000, p. 30). It is estimated that colleges with 10,000 women students are likely to experience 350 incidents of rape in a given academic year (Fisher, Cullen, & Turner 2000).

The United States Department of Education reported that between 2002 and 2004, 69 students on campus and 64 students in the Residence Halls of Harvard University were forcibly raped and sexually assaulted. In the same period, 16 students at Massachusetts Institute of Technology, 25 students at Yale, 40 students at Princeton, 60 students at Stanford, 59 students at Berkeley, and 42 students at Duke were forcibly raped and sexually assaulted in their Residence Halls and on campuses (Office of Post Secondary Education Website, 2004). It is estimated that about 65-70 percent of violent campus crimes, particularly violent sex offenses, are not reported to law enforcement.

In 2002, there were approximately 16 million students enrolled in 4,200 institutions of higher education in the United States. Before 1990, there was no major federal policy specifically related to campus crime. From the beginning of the 1990s, however, a federal policy has been in force in all U.S. public and private institutions of higher education. During the last fifteen years, the Federal Campus Crime Statistics and Notification Policy has evolved on the basis of three major congressional enactments: Jeanne Clery Disclosure of Campus Security and Campus Statistics Act of 1990, The Campus Sexual Assault Victim's Bill of Rights of 1992, and the Campus Sex Crime Prevention Act of 2000.

The Jeanne Clery Act made two requirements: public disclosure of campus security policies and public disclosure of campus crime statistics. The Act required all participating public and private campuses to develop and publicly notify their policies related to: 1) security consideration used in the maintenance of campus facilities, 2) collaborations with state and local law enforcement agencies, 3) professional counseling of campus crime victims to disclose voluntarily crime information, 4) campus programs to inform current and prospective students and employees about campus crime and security information, 5) security information at off-campus student organizations and housing facilities, 6) education programs to promote the awareness of rape, acquaintance rape and other forcible and non-forcible sex offenses, 7) the availability of campus counseling and mental health services for sex crime victims, and 8) institutional disciplinary policies to address campus sex offenses. With respect to crime statistics, the Act required that all participating institutions collect their annual campus crime statistics and send them to the U.S. Department of Education. All institutions are required to disclose their last three years of campus crime statistics to the public. Almost all public and private institutions of higher education in the nation today largely comply with the Jeanne Clery Act. Most campuses collect their sex crime statistics in terms of forcible (forcible rape, forcible sodomy, sexual assault with object, and forcible fondling) and non-forcible (incest and rape) sex offences.

The Campus Sexual Assault Victim's Bill of Rights was enacted as part of the Higher Education Amendment Act of 1992 signed into law by President George Bush. The Act requires that all public and private institutions of higher education, participating in federal student aid programs, extend certain basic rights to the victims of campus sex crimes. One of the major provisions of the Act is that a school must notify its sex crime victims of their options to report campus sex crimes to proper law enforcement authorities. The schools that are in violation of this provision can be fined up to $27,500, or lose eligibility to participate in federal student grants program. The Act made it a right for campus sex assault victims to be able to report their victimizations to proper law enforcement authorities. The Act also made it a requirement for all participating schools to develop an annual security report to include information on campus assault investigation procedures, campus procedures for taking disciplinary actions in sex assault cases, campus sex assault awareness program, and campus program on sex assault prevention.

The Campus Sex Crimes Prevention Act of 2000 (CSCPA) was enacted by the Congress for the tracking of convicted sex offenders enrolled in the institutions of higher education. The CSCPA made several amendments to the Jeanne Clery Act of 1990 and the Wetterling Act of 1994. Under the CSCPA, each institution of higher education is required to establish its own sex offender registry, following the registration guidelines of the Wetterling Act, for sex offenders who are enrolled as students or are working as employees. Each campus is required by this Act to: 1) notify the state with jurisdiction where the campus is located and where the sex offenders are studying and working; and 2) notify the campus community about the registered sex offenders on campus. The CSCPA made it mandatory for all campuses to notify how information about registered sex offenders may be obtained from local and state agencies. The U.S. Department of Education was made responsible to prepare guidelines related to these laws. The Act does not prohibit educational institutions to disclose publicly information about their registered sex offenders.

In addition, the Act also made states responsible to collect information about registered sex offenders from all campuses of higher education located within their respective jurisdictions, and to make that information promptly available for local, state and federal law enforcement agencies. The Act authorized the Attorney General and the Department of Justice to prepare guidelines for implementation of the new laws by the states. Congress mandated that the states comply with the CSCPA within two years, from the initial period of enrollment in October 2000, or otherwise they will lose 10 percent of their federal Byrne Grants.

Federal Child Sex Abuse Laws and Policy

Federal policy on sex offender registration and notification is a policy for sex offender tracking primarily for the purpose of law enforcement. The purpose of community notification is for the public to make responsible decisions with respect to living in communities with sex offenders. From the beginning of the 1990s, Congress also began to address seriously the issues related to sexual behavior such as child sexual abuse, violence against women, intimate partner violence, and children and women trafficking. One of the issues that have consistently remained as a major policy concern since the1990s is about the control and containment of child sexual abuse. Almost all federal sex crime legislations have addressed the problem of child sexual abuse. There are, however, six major Acts that define and describe the present federal policy on child sexual abuse. These Acts are: The Crime Control Act of 1990, The Violent Crime Control and Law Enforcement Act of 1994, Sex Crimes Against Children Act of 1995, Protection of Children From Sexual Predators Act of 1998, PROTECT ACT (Prosecuting Remedies and Tools Against the Exploitation of Children Today Act) of 2003, and the Children Safety and Violent Crime Reduction Act of 2005.

The Crime Control Act of 1990, signed into law by George Bush, is the first federal enactment that made significant policy innovations in criminalizing child abuse. The Act defined child abuse broadly to include "physical or mental injury, sexual abuse or exploitation, or negligent treatment of children." The Act is the first federal law to codify a definition of child sexual abuse. Child sexual abuse, according to the Crime Control Act of 1990, includes enticement or coercion of a child to engage in explicit sexual activities, child rape and molestation, enticement of children to engage in prostitution, and child incest. The Act criminalized explicit sexual conduct with children including genital-genital, oral-genital, anal-genital, or oral-anal contact; sexual touching either directly or through clothing; child sexual humiliation; child sexual harassment; and child sexual degradation and exploitation by means of creating, using or possession of child pornography.

Two of the major policy innovations of the Act of 1990 are related to professional responsibility for reporting suspected child abuse cases, and the creation of a legally enforceable method of child abuse investigation. After the enactment of the Crime Control Act of 1990, it became legally mandatory for all categories of professionals including physicians, psychologists, social workers, teachers, child care workers, child care administrators, law enforcement employees, juvenile detention or rehabilitation employees, foster parents, ambulance drivers, and others who deal with children and child care management to report to concerned child welfare agencies or social services agencies any suspicion about child abuse. The Act made a policy directive that all child abuse cases must be reported to concerned federal or state agencies for immediate investigation and reporting to law enforcement. Under the Act, a failure to report suspected child abuse cases to concerned agencies or authorities became a Class B misdemeanor. The Act made new provisions for childcare employee background checks, and professional training on child abuse and neglect.

The Violent Crime Control and Law Enforcement Act of 1994 established a new federal mechanism to deal with child sexual abuse. The Act created the Morgan P. Hardeman Task Force on Missing and Exploited Children. The Task force was given the authority to mobilize and combine all available federal resources including the FBI, U.S. Secret Service, Bureau of Alcohol, Tobacco, and Firearms, U.S. Customs, U.S. Postal Inspection, U.S. Marshall Services, and Drug Enforcement Administration to assist state and local government agencies to deal effectively with cases of missing and exploited children. Title I of the Violent Crime Control Act of 1994 created new federal initiatives to develop child abuse training programs for judicial personnel and practitioners, expand court-appointed special advocate programs for abused and exploited children, and improve the methods of televised testimony in child sexual abuse cases. The Act authorized the spending, over a period of five years (1996-2000), of $8 million for the program of child abuse training for judicial personnel, $38 million for court-appointed special advocate program, and more than $4 million for the televised testimony program.

Through the enactment of the Sexual Crimes against Children Prevention Act of 1995, Congress made a renewed appeal to the nation that child pornography and child sexual abuse are destructive forces and that they must be controlled and contained to save the American families. Through this Act, Congress instructed the United States Sentencing Commission to increase the base offense level of penalties at least by two levels for the creation, possession and trafficking of child pornography, and the use of the Internet for advertising child pornography. The new law increased the penalties for the creation and possession of child pornography from 5 to 6 years to 6 to 7 years in prison for first time offenders. The penalties for trafficking in child pornography for first time offenders were increased from 1 to 2 years to 2 to 3 years in prison. For offenses related to the use of the Internet in creating and advertising child pornography and transportation of children with the intent to engage in criminal sexual activity, Congress instructed the Sentencing Commission to increase the base level penalties at least three times. The Sexual Crimes against Children Prevention Act of 1995 put more responsibilities on the United States Sentencing Commission to study the evolving nature of child sexual abuse in the nation. Through this Act, Congress instructed the Sentencing Commission to send yearly reports to Congress on sentencing guidelines for child sexual crimes and exploitations, the nature of judicial compliance to those guidelines, and the impact of increased penalties and treatments on sex offender recidivism.

From the beginning of the 1990s, with the expansion of information technology, sex crimes, particularly child sex crimes began to take a new shape through the use of the Internet. The Internet from the 1990s began to be increasingly used for advertising and trafficking in child pornography, global sex tourism, and enticement of children for prostitution and other illicit sexual activities. In 1998, Congress enacted the Protection of Children from Sexual Predators Act to express its "zero tolerance" for Internet production and trafficking in child pornography. "The Sexual Predator Act was a bipartisan effort to once again address these issues, and its enactment occurred after more than a year of hearings and debates in the Congress, during which testimony was given by law enforcement officers and others on matters relating to Internet crime and safety online" (United States Sentencing Commission, 2000, p. 5). The Sexual Predator Act, created two new sex crimes: 1) transmission of identity information of minors for illicit sexual activity and 2) distribution of obscene materials to minors. Title I of the Act amends the Federal criminal code to prohibit the transmission of names, mailing addresses, social security numbers, telephone numbers, and Internet addresses of minors under the age of 16 with the intent to entice, encourage, or solicit any person to engage in sexual activity. Title II of the Act made the production, possession, and the distribution or attempt for the production, possession, and distribution of child pornography, through the Internet and interstate or foreign commerce, a federal crime. Before the 1998 Act, the possession of three or more child pornographic materials was considered to be a crime. Under the 1998 Act, the possession of even one visual depiction of a minor engaging in sexual activity became a federal crime.

Through the Sexual Predator Act, the Congress instructed the United States Sentencing Commission to impose enhanced prison sentences for crimes related to child pornography and child sexual exploitation. Title III of the Act doubles the term of imprisonment for abusive sexual conduct with a minor below the age of 12, and for sex offenders with a prior conviction. Title IV made a provision for life imprisonment for crimes relating to coercion or enticement of children below the age of 14 to travel interstate or foreign commerce for illicit sexual activity. Title VI made it legally mandatory for electronic communication service companies and Internet service providers to report suspected violations of the above laws immediately to law enforcement agencies and the Department of Justice. Title IX of the Act instructed the Attorney General to conduct studies, in collaboration with the National Research Council and the National Academy of Sciences, on the problem of child pornography in the Internet, and the ways of developing legal and technological interventions to control the use and expansion child pornography through the Internet.

During the 1990s, most sex crime legislations enacted by Congress were focused on sex offender registration and notification policy. For Congress, the dominant perspective at that time was "problem-solving" through the involvement of communities (Travis, 1997). From the late 1990s, Congress began to focus more on the "rule-enforcing approach" and the concept of "just deserts" (Travis, 1997). The Sexual Predator Act of 1998 was the first sex crime legislation that began to bring mandatory tougher penalties for sex crimes.

In 2000, Congress enacted the Aimee's Law for making the states more responsible for incarcerating violent sexual predators for longer times. Aimee's Law is named after Aimee Willard, a student of George Mason University who was raped and murdered by a sex offender released from prison in Nevada. Aimee's Law was enacted as a part of the Victims of Trafficking and Violence Protection Act of 2000. Aimee's Law amended Title 18 of the United States Code and made a provision for mandatory life imprisonment for violent repeat sex offenders who commit sex offenses against children. The Act required the states to keep violent sex offenders in prison for longer terms, and made provisions for holding the states that would fail to do so financially accountable. Aimee's Act made a law that the states that do not adopt the federal truth-in-sentencing guidelines for violent sex offenders, and the states where the average length of imprisonment for violent sex offenders is less than 10 percent of that of national average, will lose a part of their share of federal law enforcement assistance grants. Under the Act, if a sex offender released from a state commits sex offenses again in another state, the federal government will compensate the second state the costs of prosecution and incarceration of that sex offender. But the state that initially released the sex offender will lose a part of its share of federal law enforcement assistance grants. The Act directed the Attorney General to create a data bank in the Department of Justice by collecting information on annual convictions for rape, murder, and sex offenses against minors below the age of 14 from all states. The Attorney General was also instructed to submit a yearly report to the Congress on the nature and degree of compliance to Aimee's Law by the states.

From 2000 to 2005, five major sex crime incidents again shocked the nation. Alexander Nicole Zapp of Bridgewater, Massachusetts was brutally murdered by a repeat sex offender in 2002. In 2003, Dru Sjodin, a 22-year old University of North Dakota student was sexually assaulted and murdered by Alfonso Rodriguz—a registered sex offender from Minnesota. In 2004, Carlie Jane Brucia, a Florida girl was kidnapped, raped, and murdered by a man named Joseph Smith. In Florida again in 2005, Jessica Lunsford was abducted, raped, and buried alive by John Couey—a man with a long criminal history. After a month in the same year of 2005, Sarah Michelle Lunde, a thirteen-year-old Florida girl, was raped, strangled, murdered, and thrown into a fishpond by David Onstott—a sex offender who failed to register. These incidents horrified the nation, and Congress responded by enacting two tough sex crime legislation—the PROTECT Act of 2003 and the Children Safety Act of 2005. The PROTECT Act (Prosecutorial Remedies and Other Tools to End the Exploitation of Children Today Act) imposed a mandatory sentencing of life in prison for repeat and violent sex offenders, and removed the statutes of limitations for child abduction and child sexual abuse cases. The Children Safety Act of 2005 made new provisions for an expanded system of national sex offender registration and notification policy. But more importantly, the Act created new mandatory sentencing provisions for violent sex offences against the minors.

Title III "Prevention and Deterrence of Crimes against Children, and Title IV "Protection against Sexual Exploitation of Children" of the Children Safety Act of 2005 made new federal guidelines (see Table 24) for mandatory minimum penalties for sex offenders. The new guidelines provided mandatory life in prison or the death penalty for a sex crime resulting in the death of a minor under the age of eighteen. The guidelines imposed a mandatory minimum of 30 years or life in prison for kidnapping, aggravated sexual abuse, and sexual abuse that result in serious bodily injury. Title V of the Act, the "Foster Child Protection Act of 2005," requires sex offenders to submit to searches as a condition of supervised release or probation. Under the Act, law enforcement officers, when a reasonable suspicion exists, can search a registered sex offender and his property, house, residence, vehicle, computers, and electronic devices with or without a warrant. The Act made civil commitment mandatory for violent federal sex offenders who had been certified to have incurable psychopathological problems and disorders.

Domestic Violence,
Stalking, and Sexual Harassment

In the United States, according to data from the Office of Justice Statistics, "almost 700,000 incidents of domestic violence are documented each year. FBI data further show that in the last 25 years almost 57,000 individuals have been killed in domestic violence situations" (Office of Justice Program, 2002, p. 1). Domestic violence is primarily violence against women. About 75-80 percent of victims of domestic violence are women. It is also not merely violence between married couples. For law enforcement, domestic violence now includes a wide range of behavior such as intimate partner violence, spousal rape, acquaintance rape, date rape, stalking, and sexual harassment (Bureau of Justice Statistics, 2003). And these behaviors fall within the broader definition of sex crimes. Before the 1960s, the federal government did not have any significant policy involvements in matters of domestic violence. Traditionally, law enforcement agencies and the court and prosecutors, under the doctrine of family privacy, largely ignored domestic violence cases and issues. From the beginning of the 1970s, domestic violence began to be increasingly addressed by law enforcement, and from that time there began a new process of criminalization of domestic violence.

Table 24: Mandatory Minimum Penalties for Sex Offenses: Children Safety Act of 2005

Nature of Sex Offenses	Mandatory Minimum Penalties
Violent sex offenses that result in death of a minor under the age of 18	Sentenced to death or life in prison
Violent sex offenses that result in death of minor under the age of 12	Sentenced to death or life in prison
Kidnapping, aggravated sexual abuse, and sexual abuse that result in serious body injury	Life in prison, but not less than 30 years of imprisonment
Use of dangerous weapons in child sexual abuse	Life in prison, but not less than 15 years of imprisonment
Attempted or conspiracy to attempt crimes against children	Life in prison, but not less than 10 years of imprisonment
Sexual contact with children	10 to 25 years of imprisonment
Child pornography and child sex trafficking	Life in prison, but not less than 25 years of imprisonment
To direct harmful materials to children through the Internet; Use of misleading domain names to deceive minors in the Internet	10 to 30 years of imprisonment
Production of sexually explicit depiction of children	Life in prison, but not less than 25 years of imprisonment; mandatory life for repeat offenders
Coercion and enticement of children by sex offenders	10 to 30 years of imprisonment
Sexual crimes related to child prostitution	Life in prison, but not less than 30 years of imprisonment

Source: Children Safety Act of 2005: Report of the Committee on the Judiciary, U.S. House of Representative. Washington DC: U.S. Government Printing Office

The women's revolution and the growth of feminist movements particularly contributed to the development of a series of legal reforms on domestic violence in the1970s. These include the development of laws on mandatory arrests, arrests without warrant, protective and restraining orders, and community-based treatment for abusive spouses and partners (Fagan, 1996). These legal developments came mostly from the states. "By 1980, 47 states had passed domestic violence legislation mandating changes in protection orders, enabling warrantless arrests for misdemeanor assaults, and recognizing a history of abuse and threat as a part of legal defense" (Fagan 1996, p. 6).

Federal laws on domestic violence also began to slowly evolve from that time. Between 1976 and 1981, the federal government's Law Enforcement Assistance Administration funded 23 programs for domestic violence services "including shelters, special prosecution units, treatment programs for wife beaters, mediation units, and civil legal interventions" (Fagan 1996, p. 5). Between 1994 and 2005, Congress has enacted three major legislations focusing particularly on laws and issues related to domestic violence. These legislations are: the Violent Crime Control and Law Enforcement Act of 1994 (Title IV—Violence against Women), the Victims of Trafficking and Violence Protection Act of 2000, and the Violence against Women and Department of Justice Reauthorization Act of 2005 (VAWA). These legislations developed four policy approaches for the control and containment of domestic violence: 1) deterrence of domestic violence through increased penalties, 2) improvement in criminal justice system capacity to respond effectively to and prosecute domestic violence cases, 3) improvement in victim assistance programs, and 4) research on domestic violence.

The Violence against Women Act of 1994 is the first comprehensive federal legislation on domestic violence. In the crime bills enacted before 1994—the Omnibus Crime Control and Safe Street Act of 1968, Comprehensive Crime Control Act of 1984, and The Comprehensive Crime Control Act of 1990—the issues of domestic violence did not receive serious policy attentions. "The Violence Against Women Act, the first federal legislation to comprehensively address violence uniquely targeted at women and their children, represents key turning points in our nation's response to sexual violence, domestic violence, and stalking" (Roe, 2004, p. 1). The Act, passed with bipartisan support, "contained a combination of new federal penalties and a myriad of grant programs to support both state and local criminal justice and victim services responses to violence against women" (Roe, 2004, p. 2). The major policy directives and guidelines of the Act are contained in six major subtitles: A) Safe Street for Women, B) Safe Homes For Women, and C) Civil Rights for Women, D) Equal Justice For Women, E) Violence against Women Act Improvement, F) National Stalker and Domestic Violence Reduction, and G) Protection of Battered Immigrant Women and Children. Each of these Subtitles again contains a number of Chapters with legislative directions on four policy tracks: new laws for punishment and deterrence, improvement in criminal justice system, victim's assistance programs, and research on domestic violence.

The Act imposed increased penalties for interstate domestic violence and interstate stalking, and authorized the Department of Justice to provide funds to state and local governments to implement mandatory arrests policy for domestic violence and protective order violations. It introduced a new law that the protection order issued by one state must be accorded "full faith and credit" by the court of another state For the violation of the provisions of interstate domestic violence laws and interstate protective order laws, the Act imposed a penalty of life imprisonment if such violations result in a death of the victim. The Act imposed 20 years of imprisonment if such violations cause life-threatening bodily injury to the victim, and 10 years of imprisonment if such violations cause serious bodily injury because of the use of dangerous weapons. The United States

Sentencing Commission was instructed to prepare the new penalty guidelines. The Act amended the federal criminal code and made a provision for restitution for the victims of domestic abuse and sexual abuse offenses. The new law made it legally mandatory for defendants to pay to the victim, through appropriate court mechanisms, the full amount of losses incurred by the victim because of medical expenses, lost income, attorney's fees, and other costs as determined by the court. A provision was made for the suspension of federal benefits if the defendants fail to comply with the restitution laws. The Act also amended the Federal Rules of Evidence 412 and enacted a federal version of the "rape shield laws." The Amended Federal Rules of Evidence 412 made information about a victim's past sexual behavior and a victim's sexual predisposition inadmissible in federal criminal and civil trials for rape cases.

One of the major policy goals of the Act of 1994 was to improve the institutional and organizational capacities of the criminal justice system to respond effectively to problems of domestic violence. In order to accomplish this goal, the Act made provisions for a series of federal grants for state and local governments. Some of the important grants were related to 1) introduction of National Domestic Violence Hotline, 2) encouragement of mandatory arrests policies, 3) effective law enforcement and prosecution strategies to combat domestic violence, 4) community-based domestic violence prevention programs, 5) youth education on domestic violence, 6) education and training of family court judges and court personnel, 7) improvement of federal, state, and local databanks on stalking and domestic violence, 8) improvement of safety for women in public transportation and public parks, and 9) rape prevention and education.

Another significant policy innovation made by the Violence against Women Act of 1994 is related to victim assistance programs. The Act made provision for grants to: 1) develop, expand, and strengthen sexual assault and domestic violence victim services programs, 2) develop and improve delivery of victim services to racially and culturally diverse groups of women, 3) provide domestic violence court advocates, 4) create programs for increased reporting of domestic violence, and 5) formulate strategies to reduce attrition rates for cases related to violence against women and crimes of sexual violence. Through the Act, Congress authorized $205 million, over a period of five years from 1996 to 2000, for the development of programs to assist victims of domestic violence and sexual assault.

Through the Violence against Women Act of 1994, Congress also for the first time required the Department of Justice, Department of Health and Human Services, and the Department of Education to provide grants for research on sexual assault and domestic violence. The Act instructed the Department of Justice to develop, in collaboration with the National Academy of Sciences and the National Research Council, a research agenda to increase knowledge and understanding of the causes of domestic violence and rape and sexual assault behavior, and the ways to prevent them. The Attorney General was authorized to convene a panel of national experts to develop a national research agenda on domestic violence. The Act required the Attorney General to fund studies also for the improvement of state databases on sexual and domestic violence, and to report annually to the Congress on those developments.

Violence against Women Act of 1994 created for the first time a central federal organization to be responsible for policy-making on domestic violence. This federal organization is the Office of Violence against Women (OVAW) created within the Department of Justice in 1995. Since its inception, the OVAW's discretionary grants have substantially grown. Between 1996 and 2000, according to the data provided by the Office of Justice Statistics, OVAW's "discretionary grant awards increased about 940 percent—from just over $12 million in fiscal year 1996, the first full year of funding, to about $125 million in fiscal year 2000" (United States General Accounting Office, 2002, p. 2). Some of the major grant programs administered by the OVAW include S-T-0-P Violence against Women Formula Grants, Grants to Encourage Arrest Policies and Enforcement of Protection Orders, Legal Assistance for Victims Grants Program, Grants to Reduce Violent Crimes against Women on Campus, Grants to State Sexual Assault and Domestic Violence Coalition Program, Transitional Housing Assistance Grants Program, and Supervised Visitation and Safe Exchange Grants Program.

The Department of Justice has also established in 2002 a National Advisory Committee on Violence against Women as a national forum to deliberate on policy issues related to domestic and sexual violence. This National Advisory Committee meets annually, and its members include judges, attorneys, law enforcement officers, representatives from women groups, representatives from victim advocacy groups, policy experts, and researchers from the academia.

Six years after passage of the first Violence against Women Act of 1994, Congress enacted the second Violence against Women Act in 2000 as a part (Division B) of the Victims of Trafficking and Violence Protection Act of 2000 signed into law by President Clinton. The Act of 2000 increased and created new penalties for offenses related to sexual and domestic violence, put more emphasis on rape and sexual assault prevention, provided more grants for women in underserved groups and areas, set up new national resource centers, and made increased appropriations for further improvement in the ability of the criminal justice system to deal with sexual and domestic violence cases. The Act of 2000 created new crimes and new penalties by making amendments to the interstate domestic violence, interstate violation of protection orders, and national stalker and domestic violence reduction provisions of the Act of 1994. The new law in the Act of 2000 made it a felony crime to travel in interstate and foreign commerce "with the intent to kill, injure, harass, or intimidate a spouse or intimate partner." The Act also made it a felony crime for a person "who causes a spouse or intimate partner to travel in interstate or foreign commerce ... by force, coercion, duress, or fraud." What is unique about the Act of 2000 is that it made stalking, harassment, intimidation, and attempt to use force, coercions, mails or any other interstate or foreign commerce facility to cause violence against the spouse, or intimate partner federal felony crimes punishable by imprisonment. Under the Act, not just violent acts, but also certain forms of behavior related to spousal and intimate partner relations came to be defined as crimes.

One of the important policy directions that came through the Act of 2000 was related to work place violence against women. New laws were enacted, through amendments in the Internal Revenue Code, to give tax incentives to employers to implement safety and education programs to address problems related to sexual assault and violence against women in work place, and to provide unemployment compensation for victims of domestic violence. The Family and Medical Leave Act of 1993 was amended to make it eligible for persons, working in both federal and non-federal agencies, to take a leave of absence for reasons related to domestic violence and sexual assault victimization. The Act made it easier for alien battered spouses to prosecute their abusers, and stay in the United States with their children.

The Act of 2000 brought a series of amendments to include more federal energy and resources for the prevention of rape, date rape, and sexual assault violations. Subtitle F of Title III of the Act of 2000 instructed the Attorney General for rescheduling and reclassifying certain date-rape drugs. The Act instructed to transfer flunitrazepam from Schedule IV to Schedule I, and add ketamine hydrochloride (KH) to Schedule III, and Gamma Hydroxy Butyric (GHB) to Schedule I of the Controlled Substance Act. Under the Controlled Substance Act, any person convicted for the possession of GHB or KH receives at least three years of imprisonment.

Title II of the Act of 2000 made more provisions to strengthen rape prevention and education program enacted under the 1994 Act. The Act of 2000 made it mandatory for the Attorney General to spend most of the rape prevention and education grants through local and state rape crisis centers and sexual assault coalitions. The Act authorized the spending of $600 million, for a period of five years from 2001 to 2005, to further expand and strengthen the nation's rape and sexual assault prevention education. The Attorney General was also instructed to create a National Resource Center for Sexual Assault, as a central resource library within the federal government, to provide technical assistance and policy guidance to local and state agencies. The Act mandated that related grants be equally given to rural areas and Indian territories to prevent rape and sexual assault among the elderly and women in disadvantaged groups. In addition, the Act made reauthorization of S-T-O-P grants, grants to increase mandatory arrests for domestic violence and protective order violations, grants for National Domestic Violence Hotline, grants for increased use of televised testimony in child rape and sexual abuse cases, grants to include stalker and domestic violence data into state crime information database, grants to schools to teach about domestic violence and sexual assaults, grants for training of judges, prosecutors and law enforcement, and grants for improvement in forensic training for sexual assault examination.

In the area of research, the Act of 2000 amended the Act of 1994, and directed the Secretary of the Department of Health and Human Services and the Attorney General of the Department of Justice to establish a multi-agency task force for organizing and coordinating research on domestic violence. The Act authorized the Secretary and the Attorney General to establish three research centers. The first is on the advancement of basic understanding of the causes of domestic violence and sexual assault behavior, the second is to develop institutional mechanisms for researchers and practitioners to collaborate, and the third is on the ways to integrate research into policy-making for effective victim assistance and service delivery. The Act of 2000 authorized in total $3.2 billion for its different grants and development programs from FY 2001 through FY 2005 (Congressional Research Service, 2001). The Act also directed the National Institute of Justice to develop a coordinated national research agenda on domestic violence on the basis of the recommendations made in the report "Understanding Violence against Women" produced by the National Academy of Sciences in 1996.

In 2005, the Congress passed the Violence against Women and the Department of Justice Reauthorization Act, and it was signed into law by President Bush. The 2005 Act further increased penalties for interstate domestic violence and interstate violation of protective orders, and reauthorized most of the grant programs mandated by the Act of 2000. Title 1 of the 2005 Act "Enhancing Law Enforcement and Judicial Tools to Combat Violence against Women" extended the scope of technical assistance and training for a wide variety of domestic violence service providers including law enforcement, judges, prosecutors, court personnel, human and community service providers, educational institutions, and health care providers. Title I of the 2005 Act created a new S-T-O-P funding stream, described as Crystal Judson Domestic Violence Program, to develop in different states and localities trained domestic violence service providers who can closely work with law enforcement and the judicial system. Title I put more emphasis on providing grants to underserved groups and areas and enhancing culturally and linguistically specific services for the victims of domestic violence.

One of the new policy directions of the Act of 2005 is that the definition of domestic violence is extended to include dating violence, sexual assault, and stalking. Another new direction is more emphasis on the understanding of the nature of youth offending and youth victimization in domestic violence. Title II of the Act requested the Attorney General to provide more grants to schools and institutions of higher education to train school administrators, faculty, counselors, coaches, security personnel, and other staff on issues of youth victimization and youth offending in domestic violence, dating violence, sexual assault, and stalking. The Secretary of the Department of Health and Human Services and the Director of the Office of the Domestic Violence against Women were instructed to provide policy guidance to the nation's educational institutions on domestic violence. Title IV of the Act "Strengthening American Families by Preventing Violence" specifically instructed the Department of Health and Human Services and the Centers for Disease Control to examine and develop domestic violence prevention programs.

The Act of 2005 put more emphasis on the need for research on domestic violence. Title I of Act required the Comptroller to conduct a study and to send it to the Congress within a year, on the extent of domestic violence, dating violence, sexual assault, and stalking, and the nature of the availability to all victims of counseling and legal services. The Comptroller was also instructed to set up a database on domestic violence, dating violence, sexual assault, and stalking combining data from the Department of Justice and other academic research institutions. The Act authorized about $510 million for the Office of Justice Programs and about $63 millions for the Office of Violence against Women to implement its policies between the FY 2006 and FY 2009.

Sex Crimes in American Prisons:
Federal Law and Policy Initiatives

According to the Bureau of Justice Statistics report on Prisoners in 2004, there were about 170,535 inmates in federal prison. Approximately 1.2 million inmates were housed in states' prison at the end of 2004. In addition, there were about 713,990 persons under the custody of local jails. Between 1995 and 2005, the U.S. prison population increased annually on an average by 3.4 percent. It is estimated that during this period about 600,000 new inmates were added to the prison population. One of the currently growing trends is the increased number of females joining the prison population. Between June 2003 and June 2004, male prison population increased by 2 percent. During the same period, female prison population increased by 2.9 percent. The total female prison population in the nation reached about 103,310 by the middle of 2004 (Bureau of Justice Statistics, 2005). There are also a large number of youths serving time in adult prisons. According to the Bureau of Justice Statistics' Prison and Jail Inmates at Midyear 2005 report, about 6,759 inmates held in adult prisons in 2005 were under the age of 18. About 2,266 inmates in state prisons were under the age of 18 in 2005.

Sexual violence in American prisons is widespread. Although the federal government is collecting data on prison population since the 1920s, data on sex crimes in prisons are still in infancy. One of the Congressional documents (The Prison Rape Elimination Act of 2003, PL 108-79) noted that about 13 percent of the inmates in the United States are sexually assaulted every year. According to this estimate, about 1,000,000 million inmates were sexually assaulted in the past 20 years. The Department of Justice published its first report on sex crimes in prisons in 2005 titled as "Sexual Violence Reported by Correctional Authorities, 2004." This study, based on the survey of more than 1.7 million adult and juvenile inmates in 2,700 public and private correctional institutions, is probably one of the most reliable documents presently available on sex crimes in American prisons. The survey was conducted on four categories of sex crimes in custody: nonconsensual sexual acts, abusive sexual contacts, staff sexual misconduct, and staff sexual harassment. According to this survey, 8,210 allegations of sexual violence were reported nationwide in 2004. Out of 8,210 allegations, 42 percent involved staff sexual misconduct, 37 percent involved nonconsensual inmate-on-inmate rape and sexual assault, 11 percent were about staff sexual harassment, and 10 percent were related to abusive sexual contact. Out of these allegations, the correctional authorities substantiated about 2,100 incidents of sexual violence in 2004. In state-operated juvenile facilities, 69 percent of the victims were male, and 47 of the perpetrators were found to be females. The survey showed that male and female staffs are equally likely to be the perpetrators of staff sexual misconduct that includes intentional touching, completed and requested sexual acts under threat, rape, and indecent exposure (Bureau of Justice Statistics, 2005; Office of the Inspector General, 2005).

Research has shown that prison rape and sexual abuse have serious consequences. Juveniles, mentally ill inmates, and transgender inmates are more likely to be sexually victimized. Victims of prison sexual abuse are more likely to be exposed to HIV/AIDS infections, develop rape-trauma syndrome, manifest suicidal ideations, be unable to lead a normal work and family life after release, and show a higher rate of recidivism. In 1994, the U.S Supreme Court ruled, in *Farmer v. Brennan*, that deliberate indifference to the exposure of inmates to violent sexual environment in prisons is a violation of the cruel and unusual punishment clause of the Eighth Amendment of the Constitution.

In 1988, the United States signed the International Convention against Torture and Other Cruel and Inhuman or Degrading Treatment or Punishment of Prisoners. In 1994, President Clinton ratified this International Treaty. However, until recently, the issue of rape and sexual violence in American prisons did not appear very prominently in the federal crime policy agenda. The first comprehensive set of federal policy initiatives to address the issue of prison rape and sexual violence came through the enactment of the Prison Rape Elimination Act of 2003 (PL 108-79) signed into law by President Bush. The Act of 2003 has been supported by a broad array of policy advocacy groups and organizations including the American Psychological Association, Harvard Law School, Human Rights Watch, Justice Policy Institute, NAACP, National Mental Health Association, Prison Fellowship, The Sentencing Project, Southern Baptist Convention, and Stop Prison Rape Organization.

The Prison Elimination Act of 2003 was enacted with five major objectives: 1) to introduce a policy of zero-tolerance for prison rape and sexual violence in all federal, state, and local correctional institutions, 2) to develop national standards for the detection, prevention, reduction, and punishment of prison rape, 3) to increase accountability of correctional institutions and correctional staff with respect to the responsibility of dealing with prison rape issues, 4) to enhance the capacity of all correctional institutions and correctional staff for detection, prevention, reduction, and punishment of prison rape and sex abuse cases, and 5) to protect the Eighth Amendment right of all federal, state and local prison and jail inmates. According to the Act of 2003, prison rape means carnal knowledge, oral sodomy, sexual assault with an object, or sexual fondling of a person forcibly or through the use of fear and threat of physical violence, or against the will of a person who is incapable of giving consent because of his or her youth or mental incapacity.

The Act made it a statutory requirement for the Department of Justice to carry out, in each calendar year and submit it to the Congress, a comprehensive statistical review and analysis of the nature, extent, and effects of prison rape and sexual abuse. All federal, state, and local jails and prisons are required by the Act to participate in this annual study and to provide the necessary information to and access needed by the Department of Justice. The Department of Justice was authorized to set up a Review Panel on Prison Rape charged with the responsibility of collecting prison rape information through research, public hearings, and victim testimonies. For each fiscal year between 2004 and 2010, the Act appropriated $15 million for the Department of Justice to conduct this study. The Bureau of Justice Statistics' Report on Sexual Violence Reported by Correctional Authorities, 2004, published in 2005, came in response to this statutory requirement of the Act.

For the development of national standards to prevent and reduce prison rape, the Prison Rape Elimination Act created a National Prison Rape Reduction Commission. The members of this Commission, who are appointed by the President, were given a statutory responsibility to develop national standards on the basis of an objective study of all penological, physical, mental, medical, sociological, and economic aspects of prison rape and sexual abuse. In compliance with the Act, President Bush created the National Prison Rape Reduction Commission in June 2004, and Judge Walton of the United States District Court for the District of Columbia was appointed as its first Chairman. The Commission is required to submit its recommendations on national standards to the Congress and the Attorney General of the Department of Justice within two years of its creation. The Act required immediate adoption of the national standards by all federal, state, and local correctional institutions. The Department of Justice was given the responsibility to implement this program through grants and technical assistance and to report annually to Congress about its compliance by all correctional institutions.

For education and training of the prison staff and capacity enhancement of the correctional institutions to deal with prison rape issues, the Act also created a new National Clearinghouse within the National Institute of Corrections. The Act made a provision for an annual appropriation of $5 million for each fiscal year between 2004 and 2010 for the National Institute of Corrections to develop programs on prison rape training and education. The National Institute of Corrections is required by the Act to submit annually to Congress a report on the status of the programs and activities by the Department of Justice on prison rape prosecution, education, and prevention.

Sex and Obscenity in the Media: The Federal Policy Initiatives

The invention of radio, television, computer, satellite, Internet, and a variety of digital technologies in the twentieth century have brought unprecedented transformation in the way information can be produced, stored, and disseminated, and symbols and images can travel across time and space. The invention of satellite and digital communication technologies and the creation of the global information super highway through the World Wide Web have opened up remarkable opportunities for societal growth and productivity. But they have also opened up new opportunities for the global commercialization of human sex and the body. The emerging world of virtual sex and pornography is qualitatively different from the age-old institution of prostitution. Separate walls and separate zones do not protect the world of virtual sex. It travels across time and space without much regard for the age, mind, and the morality of its consumers. The birth of this new virtual world of sex and pornography has raised new debates about what is moral and immoral, and decent and indecent about sex, body, and profanity in the media. It has raised new concerns about the boundaries of control and freedom and the balance between the rights of privacy and standards of decency.

In 2004-2005, the Kaiser Family Foundation conducted a study on sexual themes, topics, and portrayals involving sex in 959 programs from 10 major television channels in America. These programs included the top 20 programs that are mostly viewed by teens between the ages of 12 and 17; these programs include "American Idol," "the Simpsons," "Desperate Housewives," "Extreme Makeover," "Family Guy," and "One Tree Hill." The study finds that out of 959 general audience programs "more than two of every three shows (70%) contained sexual content in the form of talk about sex and/or sexual behavior" (Kaiser Family Foundation, 2005, p. 20). The study noted that "data make clear that not only are sexual talk and behavior a common element across most television programming, but also that most shows including sexual messages devote a substantial attention to the topic" (Kaiser Family Foundation, 2005, p. 20). The Kiser Family Foundation has started this on-going series of studies in 1997-1998, and its researchers found that there is a consistent pattern of growth of sexual themes and behaviors on TV. "The percentage of programs that include sexual content has increased significantly from 56% in 1997-98 to 64% in 2001-02 to 70% in 2004-05. Similarly, the number of scenes within each program that involves sex has increased significantly from 3.2/hour in 1997-98 to 4.4/ hour in 2001-02 to 5.0/hour in 2004-05" (Kaiser Family Foundation, 2005, p. 22). Similar findings came from a Harvard study on sex and profanity in the media in 2004 (Harvard School of Public Health, 2004).

In recent years, there is also an alarming growth of sexual content and profanity in video games used mostly by teens. One study found that in mature rated video games, games that children can relatively easily buy, sexual content has increased 800 percent and profanity has increased 3,000 percent since 1990 (The Associated Press, 2005, p. 1). Sexual contents, talks, and themes are explicit in such video games as Grand Theft Auto: San Andreas, Grand Theft Auto: Vice City, Grand Theft Auto 3, The King of Fighters '99, The Simpsons Wrestling, Tiny Tank: Up Your Arsenal, and Lunar 2:Eternal Blue. Grand Theft Auto: San Andreas, that was sold 3.6 million copies within two months after its release in 2004, contained hidden links to explicit pornography. Many video games like F.E.A.R. and Stubbs the Zombie in Rebel without a Pulse contain explicit scenes of cannibalism. The Kids Risk Project of the Harvard School of Public Health recently conducted a study on the presence of sex and violence in video games. The study found that both teen rated and mature rated video games contain significant amounts of sex and violence. According to this study, "81%

of a random sample of Mature-rated video games included content that was not noted on the game box" (Harvard School of Public Health, 2006, p. 1). The Internet and the new digital technologies can play a far more invasive role in producing and disseminating sexual themes and images. New computer digital technologies have made it possible to produce and store explicit graphic images of sex and pornography in various forms such as videotape, films, compact disc, CD-Rom, and DVD. These devices can transmit images through Computer Bulletin Board System (BBS), USENET Newsgroups, Internet Chat Rooms, Web-Based Groups, and variety of other web-based technologies. In the cyberspace, these images can travel across time and space, and they can continue to travel forever. Once the images are in the cyberspace, they are irretrievable (National Center for Missing and Exploited Children, 2003). One of the reports from National Research Council, published in 2002, estimated that cybersex industry generates about $1 billion annually, and it is expected to grow to $5-7 billion by 2007. The Family Safe Media, a policy advocacy group, found that children between 12 and 17 formed the largest group of viewers of Internet porn in 2005 (Protectkids.Com). The PEW Internet and American Life Project found that in 2001, about 73 percent of youth ages between 12 and 17 used the Internet.

Researchers have found that childhood exposure to sex and sexual themes in the media and early initiation of sexual activities among adolescents are strongly correlated and that adolescents with early initiation of sexual activities are more likely to engage in deviant and violent sexual activities, develop STD's, and show lower academic performance. A study conducted by the RAND Corporation in 2004 found that "adolescents who viewed sexual content at baseline were more likely to initiate intercourse and progress to more advanced noncoital sexual activities during the subsequent year. Exposure to TV that included only talk about sex was associated with the same risks as exposure to TV that depicted sexual behavior"(Collins, 2004, p. 2). A number of recent studies on teen brains have found that TV programs and video games with contents of sex and violence have negative effects on the frontal cortex of adolescent brains—the region of the brain that is responsible for self control and emotional stability.

The debates about sexual morality in America that began in the late nineteenth century, as mentioned earlier, led to the enactment of the Comstock Law in 1873, and the Mann Act in 1910. The same debates, however, continued to engulf America throughout the twentieth century. The Sexual Revolution of the 1970s, the escalation of sex and violence in the 1980s, and the birth of the new media in the 1990s vastly widened the debates about the role of the federal government and the need for the criminalization of sex in the media. There is a general concern that federal control on sex in the media may lead to an infringement on the First Amendment right of free speech, but "there are a number of points of broad national agreement on issues relating to entertainment and the government's role in reducing offensive content" (Pew Research Center, 2005, p. 2). A study conducted by the PEW Research Center has found that majority of Americans "are very concerned over what children see or hear on TV (61%), in music lyrics (61%), video games (60%), and movies (56%). An even higher percentage (73%) expresses a great deal of concern over the internet. Fully 68% believe that children seeing so much sex and violence on TV gives them the wrong idea about what is acceptable in society" (PEW Research Center, 2005, p. 2). According to a survey conducted by the Digital Media Forum, a consortium of six public interest and consumer groups interested in media policy, a vast majority of Americans are in favor of installing filters in school computers to block access to pornography (ninety two percent) and hate speech (seventy nine percent) (Weiner, 2000).

After the Mann Act of 1910, the federal policy on the criminalization of sex in the media has evolved and expanded through the enactment of six major bills by Congress: The Communications Act of 1934, The Communications Decency Act (CDA) of 1996, The Child Pornography Prevention Act of 1996 (CPPA), The Child Online Protection Act of 1998 (COPA), The Children's Internet Protection Act of 2000 (CIPA), and the Broadcast Decency Enforcement Act of 2005. Systematic federal involvement in policy-making to regulate the growth and expansion of the media began particularly after the enactment of the Communications Act in 1934. Title 1 of the Communications Act of 1934 established the Federal Communications Commission (FCC) as an independent federal agency responsible for the regulation of the communication industries. For the last seventy-two years, particularly after the birth and expansion of the new media in the 1980s and 1990s, the FCC has remained as one of the most powerful federal organizations responsible for regulating interstate and international communications by radio, television, wire, satellite, cable networks, and cell phones. Communications in all fifty states, the District of Columbia, and in U.S. territories abroad are within the regulatory jurisdictions of the FCC. The FCC administration is composed of five Commissioners, headed by a Chairman, and they are appointed by the President and confirmed by the Senate for five-year terms. In 1934, the FCC was composed of three divisions: Broadcast, Telegraph, and Telephone. In the context of the growth of new communication technologies, the FCC today has vastly expanded and is composed of six Bureaus responsible for developing regulatory programs and ten Divisions responsible for providing support services. The creation of the FCC is one of the major legacies of the Communications Act of 1934. The present United States Code 464 of Title 18 that bars the use of obscene and indecent language by broadcasting stations came from Title III of the Communications Act of 1934.

From 1934 to 1995, for sixty one years, the regulations of obscenity and indecency in the media by the FCC were based generally on the obscenity provisions of Title III of the Communications Act of 1934. During this time, obscenity and indecency in the world of the new media vastly escalated, but Congress did not enact any major statutes to control the new media. The modern era of federal regulation of sex and indecency in the new media began through the enactment of the Communications Decency Act of 1996 (CDA) signed into law by President Clinton. The CDA was passed as Title V of the Telecommunications Act of 1996. It was a landmark legislation enacted by Congress to deregulate the growth and functions of modern communication technologies. But it was also one of the most comprehensive federal legislations enacted to regulate and criminalize sex and indecency in the new media—the cable television and the Internet.

The CDA of 1996 amended the Communications Act of 1934 and enacted new provisions to criminalize: 1) the use of telecommunications device for indecent and obscene communications with the intent to abuse, threaten and harass another person, particularly minors under the age of 18; 2) the use of computer services to send, display and depict, to any person under the age of 18, comments, solicitations, and communications that are obscene according to contemporary standards of decency; 3) the display of obscene and explicit adult video service programming on cable television without installing a system of rating and blocking technologies; 4) the use of the Internet for the trafficking of obscene materials and the coercion and enticement of minors to engage in prostitution and other illicit sexual activities; and 5) the posting of indecent and "patently offensive" materials in web pages, newsgroups, Internet chat rooms, and online discussion lists. The CDA required the broadcast television, cable, satellite, syndication, and other video programming distributors to develop, for parental knowledge and notification, a rating system for programs that include sexual content and indecent materials. Under the Act, they were also required to develop and install blocking technologies for programs with sexual themes and contents. The Act made it mandatory for multi-channel video programming distributors to block or scramble adult programming for non-subscribers. The cable operators were allowed by the Act to refuse to transmit public access programs that contain obscenity, indecency, and nudity.

The CDA of 1996 criminalized the use of indecent and offensive materials on the Internet as a whole. From 1996, the Congress, however, began to focus more on the prohibition of obscene and indecent materials that are harmful particularly to minors. In 1996, the Congress enacted the Child Pornography Prevention Act of 1996 (CPPA). The CPPA made new laws that prohibited the depiction not only of actual children engaged in sexually explicit activities but also computer-generated images of children engaged in the creation of virtual pornography. The Act made it illegal to advertise, promote, describe, and distribute materials on the Internet that generate even an impression of minors engaged in explicit sexual activity. The rationale behind the banning of virtual pornography on the part of Congress was that it contributes to the promotion of real child pornography and child sexual exploitation. Virtual pornography is equally harmful to minors and presents the same danger to the well being of children as real child pornography. The CPPA sets a new mandatory prison term of at least 15 years for the production and distribution of child pornography. The Act sets a mandatory term of 5 years for possession offenses and life in prison for repeat offenders convicted of sexual abuse of a minor. The PROTECT ACT of 2003 (PL 108-21) imposed further restrictions on the production and dissemination of virtual pornography through the Internet.

Two years after the Child Pornography Protection Act of 1996, Congress enacted the Child Online Protection Act of 1998 (COPA). The preamble of the COPA describes "the protection of the physical and psychological well-being of minors by shielding them from materials that are harmful to minors is a compelling governmental interest." Congress found that the existing industry efforts "have not provided a national solution to the problem of minors accessing harmful materials on the World Wide Web." COPA makes it a federal crime for anyone to communicate and solicit through the World Wide Web, knowingly, intentionally, and with commercial purposes, materials that are harmful to minors under the age of 17. The materials "harmful to minors" include "any communication, picture, image, graphic image file, article, recording, writing, or other matter of any kind that is obscene" according to the contemporary community standards of decency. The obscene materials include among others "an actual or simulated sexual act or sexual contact, an actual or simulated normal or perverted sexual act, or a lewd exhibition of the genitals or post-pubescent female breasts." The Act described obscene materials as those devoid of any "serious literary, artistic, political, or scientific value for minors." COPA imposed criminal and civil penalties up to $50,000 per day and a prison term of 6 months, or both for violations. According to the Act, each day of violation shall constitute a separate violation.

COPA established a temporary 19-member Commission on Child Protection to study the ways and means of reducing harmful Internet materials. The Commission was charged with the responsibility to identify innovative filtering and blocking technologies that can reduce and restrict Internet materials that are harmful to minors. The Commission was entrusted with the task of submitting its detailed report on the nature and cost of the new blocking technologies to Congress within one year from the date of the enactment of COPA. The Act also required all commercial Internet service providers to notify parents and customers about the commercial availability of technologies that can block obscene materials on the Internet.

In 2000, Congress enacted a new legislation with the aim of controlling the access of harmful Internet materials to minors. This was the Children's Internet Protection Act of 2000 (CIPA) signed into law by President Clinton. The CIPA required that all elementary and secondary schools and public libraries of the nation, that receive federal finding, develop an Internet safety policy. One of the core requirements of the CIPA is that all schools and public libraries install filtering software in their computers in order to block access of obscene and harmful materials to minors (below 16), restrict unauthorized access to hacking and other unlawful online activities to minors, and ensure the safety and security of the minors when using electronic mails, chat rooms, and other forms of electronic communications. The schools and libraries, under the Act, were also required to monitor regularly the online activities of minors in their computers and maintain an open Internet safety policy through public notice and hearing. The Federal Telecommunications Act of 1996 made a provision that the nation's elementary and secondary schools and public libraries, in order for them to be able to keep abreast with the growth of information technology, are given federal assistance to use telecommunication services and computer and internet services at discounted rates. The FCC described the schools and libraries that receive the discounted rates—rates that range from 20% to 90%—as universal service providers. The CIPA made a provision that schools and public libraries that fail to comply with the CIPA requirements will lose the discounted rates (Federal Communications Commission, 2004).

In order to address the problem of indecent materials and vulgar language in the media in a more serious way, Congress enacted the Broadcast Decency Enforcement Act in 2005 (Pickler, 2006). The new law authorized the FCC to increase the fines for and even revoke the licenses of broadcasting companies that harbor and transmit the use of obscene and indecent language and materials. The new law increased the maximum fine from $25,000 to $500,000 for each violation of the FCC rules by broadcasting companies, and from $10,000 to $500,000 for each violation by individuals. The Congressional Budget Office estimated that under the new law, FCC revenues will increase from less than $500,000 in 2005 to about $10 million in 2015.

Different enactments made by Congress during the last three decades have created a number of new federal obscenity and child sexual exploitation statutes (see Table 25). These enactments and statutes include four major policy directions: 1) V-Chip Policy Initiative for TV broadcasting and manufacturing industries, 2) installation of filtering and blocking technologies for computer and Internet service providers, 3) a La Carte Program for cable industries, and 4) the introduction of family-friendly tier programming for television broadcasters. The FCC has statutory authority, under the CDA of 1996, the CPPA of 1996, the COPA of 1998, and the CIPA of 2000 to enforce the V-Chip and internet filtering and blocking policy strategies. The La Carte Program and family-friendly programming initiatives are enforced by FCC rules and mandates.

Under the Communications Decency Act of 1996, the broadcasting industries were asked by the FCC to voluntarily develop a rating system for their programs that contain sexual, obscene, and violent contents. The National Association of Broadcasters, National Cable Television Association, and the Motion Picture Association of America established the system. The rating system includes six tiers: 1) TV-Y (All Children), 2) TV-7 (Directed to Older Children), 3) TV-G (General Audience), 4) TV PG (Parental Guidance Suggested), 5) TV-14 (Parents Strongly Cautioned), and 6) TV–MA (Mature Audience Only). Under the CDA of 1996, the FCC developed a policy that required all television sets with picture screen 13 inches or larger to be equipped with a feature—V-chip—that can control programs based on the rating system. It is required by the FCC that all television sets 13 inches or larger manufactured after January 2000 contain the V-Chip technology.

The federal policy initiative to control the computer and Internet service providers through the installation of filtering technologies, under the guidelines of the CPPA and COPA, raised a number of First Amendment's Free Speech issues. However, the CIPA laws that require the schools and public libraries to install Internet filtering technologies in their computers to restrict children from access to adult materials are largely in force and widely applied.

From the late 1990s, the FCC has worked with TV and cable industries to include more family friendly programs in their broadcast schedules. Currently, the cable subscribers are required to buy a package of programs where all pro-

grams are not family-friendly. When they subscribe a package, the cable subscribers currently do not have the choice to unbundle a package and subscribe
the programs they specially want. The FCC has a policy proposal for cable service providers to develop a new model of programming—a La Carte Model—
based on the principle of consumer choice. Under the La Carte Model, the consumers will have the choice to subscribe to a package of programs of their own
choosing. The La Carte Model is now being widely debated within the television
broadcast industries, satellite operators, and cable programming networks. Although the FCC did not make any formal ruling on this policy initiative, several
major cable companies such as Comcast and Time Warner have already taken
up measures to implement the La Carte Model.

Table 25: Major Federal Obscenity and Child Exploitation Statutes

Federal Codes	Federal Statutes/Federal Crimes
18 U.S.C. #1460	Selling of obscene materials on federal property
18 U.S.C. #1461	Mailing obscene materials
18 U.S.C. #1462	Importing or transporting obscene materials
18 U.S.C. #1465	Transporting obscene materials for distribution/sale
18 U.S.C. #1466	Engaging in the business of selling obscene materials
18 U.S.C. #1468	Distributing obscene materials by cable television
18 U.S.C. #1470	Transferring obscene materials to minors
18 U.S.C. #2241	Producing and distributing child pornography
18 U.S.C. #2422	Coercing and enticing of minors for prostitution
18 U.S.C. #2423	Transporting minors across state lines for prostitution
47 U.S.C. #223	Displaying child pornography through the Internet
47 U.S.C. #231	Using child pornography for commercial goals

Source: National Law Center for Children and Families, 2004

5.5 Sex Crimes: Growth of State Laws and Policy

Rape and sexual assault comprise about 11 percent of the crimes committed by
all inmates sentenced for violent crimes in state prisons (Bureau of Justice Statistics, 2005, p. 9). However, the number of inmates sentenced for sex offences
vary from state to state. In 2002, Montana had the highest percentage of inmates
incarcerated (33 percent) for sexual offenses, followed by Vermont (29 percent),
New Hampshire (27 percent), and Massachusetts (26 percent). In the same year,
New Jersey and the District of Columbia had the lowest percentage (7 percent)
of inmates incarcerated for sexual offenses (see Table 26). Since the definition
of sex crime is broadening, more sex crimes today are being reported to law
enforcement, more sex crimes are being prosecuted in federal and state courts,
and more sex offenders are being sentenced to prison for longer terms. Felony
sex offences are more likely than other violent and non-violent felony cases to
result in convictions. More than 50 percent of felony sex offences in state courts
result in a prison sentence. Although the incidence of rape has been declining

since the 1970s (Bureau of Justice Statistics, 2005), the rate of victimization by a variety of other sex crimes in recent years has increased.

From around the same time in the 1980s and 1990s, when sex crimes began to appear at the top of federal policy-making in crime and justice, the state policy-makers began to embark on a series of reforms in sex crime laws and statutes. The state policy-makers from that time began to reexamine the traditional definitions of sex crimes based on the Common Law. They began to reform and redefine them in the light of a growing series of federal statutes, on the one hand, and the evolving societal demands for decency, on the other.

Table 26: High Rates of Incarceration of Sex Offenders in Some Selected States, 2000

States	Number of Incarcerated Sex Offenders	Percentage of total incarcerated offenders
Alaska	496	24%
California	22,720	15%
Colorado	3,391	22%
Hawaii	634	18%
Iowa	1,228	17%
Kansas	2,002	23%
Massachusetts	2,769	26%
Michigan	9,756	21%
Minnesota	1,164	20%
Montana	465	33%
New Hampshire	633	27%
New Mexico	910	18%
North Carolina	5,101	16%
Ohio	9,100	19%
Pennsylvania	6,931	19%
South Dakota	550	22%
Tennessee	3,036	18%
Texas	25,398	17%
Vermont	362	29%
Virginia	5,400	18%
Washington	3,117	22%
West Virginia	518	17%
Wisconsin	4,000	19%
Wyoming	257	18%

Source: Colorado Department of Corrections. (2000)

The rapid increase in violent sex crimes, the growing societal concern to protect the children from the emerging vices of the movement of sexual revolution, and the birth of the new information age that created a virtual world of sex and intimacy brought sex crimes at the top of the agenda for state policy-making in crime and justice from the beginning of the 1990s. In the context of the brutal rape and murder of Alexander Zapp of Massachusetts, Dru Sjodin of North Dakota, and Carlie Brucia and Jessica Lunsford of Florida within a period of four years from 2002-2005, the state policy-makers from the beginning of the 21st century have begun to wage a new "war on sex crimes" (Abner, 2006). While the get-tough approach is currently being reexamined by the states in the context of the war on drugs and juvenile justice, the view that there is a great need to be tough with sex crimes is now widely shared by state policy-makers. Sex offender tracking, according to the National Conference of State Legislatures, was one of the top ten issues for policy deliberations by state policy makers in 2006.

In January 2006, Governor Pataki of New York, for example, unveiled a new policy to get- tough on sex crimes that would require the civil confinement of violent and dangerous sex offenders for life, sex offender notification through the Internet, longer and mandatory sentences for sex crimes, and the abolition of the statute of limitations for rape and other sex crimes. In California, Governor Arnold Schwarzenegger proposed new legislations to increase punishments for sex crimes and require the wearing of electronic monitoring devices by violent sex offenders for the rest of their lives. In South Carolina, Governor Mark Sanford proposed a new bill to impose the death penalty for twice convicted sex offenders. Similar get tough legislations have been recently proposed by most state policy-makers. The following section will examine these policy developments in terms of two broad categories: 1) policy developments related to substantive and procedural reforms in state sex crime laws and statutes, and 2) policy developments related to state sex offender registration, treatment, and management strategies.

State Sex Crime Laws:
Substantive and Procedural Reforms

During the last two decades, most of the states enacted legislations for substantive and procedural reforms in sex crimes including such areas as statutory rape, rape shield laws, date rape, mandatory HIV testing for sex offenders, mandatory collection of DNA samples from both adult and juvenile sex offenders, marital rape and intimate partner violence, incest, and child prostitution. Most states have also enacted legislations to criminalize new forms of sexual acts and behavior such as child molestation, forcible touching, child pornography on the Internet, and cyber stalking.

State Statutory Rape Law Reforms

One of the earliest attempts for reforms in sex crimes by the states was related to statutory rape. From the middle of the 1980s, the state legislatures began to debate the notion of consent and the age in which a person is competent to consent for sexual acts and contact. The sexual acts and contacts that violate the states' age-of-consent law are described as statutory rape. In sex crimes in general, according to the American Penal Law, consent is a vital component. A sexual act without consent is criminal sexual conduct. Lack of consent, according to the New York States' Penal Law, for example, occurs when sexual relations are based on expressed or implied use of threats and physical force and when the victim is in fear of being physically harmed. The lack of consent also occurs when a person is legally incapable of consenting to sexual acts and contact, when a person is emotionally and mentally incapable to understand what sexual acts and contacts mean and involve, and when a person in custody is forced to enter into sexual acts and contact. Almost all the states in recent years have revisited their consent statutes, particularly with respect to the lack of consent based on age. Most of the states have increased the upper limit of the age of consent for sexual acts and contact, and it ranges from 14 to 18 years. Some states also define the minimum age limit below which a person cannot legally consent to engage in sexual activities. A number of states also codify the age ranges beyond which the persons involved cannot consent for sexual activities. As one of the consent statutes of the Commonwealth of Pennsylvania describes: "A person commits a felony of the first degree when he or she engages in deviate sexual intercourse with a complainant who is less than 13 years of age; or who is less than 16 years of age and the person is four or more years older than the complainant and the complainant and the person are not married to each other." There is a general assumption that the rising rate of teen pregnancy in America is related to statutory rape. Most of the states are in favor of enforcing their new statutory rape laws to reduce teen pregnancy and, hence, the dependency of young mothers on state welfare.

State Rape Shield Laws

English Common Law defines rape as an act of "penetration of a woman forcibly and against her will." The contemporary definition of rape, as defined by different state penal codes, is much wider and includes not just a man's forcible sexual penetration of a woman but also women's infliction of forced sexual acts on men. Forced homosexual sodomy, forced heterosexual sodomy, forced oral and anal sexual contact, forcible touching and fondling, object penetration, and a number of other sexual acts and contacts are generally described by the state laws as violent sexual assaults. One of the general principles used in rape prosecutions, according to the English Common Law, is the doctrine of *utmost resistance*. The doctrine of *utmost resistance* implies that a man is not guilty of rape unless his victim can prove that she used utmost resistance but was overpowered. This doctrine was based on the assumption that women are generally ashamed of consenting to sexual intercourse, and women who do not have a general reputation for chastity are more likely to be sexually victimized.

Under English Common Law, sexual histories and reputations of rape victims were admissible in court. It was legal and justified to cross-examine rape victims about their past sexual histories and activities. Through a series of legislations in the 1980s and 1990s, states have substantially reformed these Common Law notions of rape and rape prosecutions (Anderson, 2002). One of the important policy developments and legal reforms was the enactment of rape shield laws. All fifty states have rape shield laws—the laws that are aimed primarily to protect the rights and the credibility of the victims of rape and sexual assaults irrespective of their past marital and sexual histories (see Table 27).

Under the rape shield laws, the sexual manners and behaviors of the rape victims are inadmissible in the court of law. The rape victims may not be cross-examined to reveal information about their past and present sexual activities. The California Rape Shield Statute, for example, maintains that opinion evidence, reputation evidence, and evidence of specific instances of the complaining witness' sexual conduct to prove consent are inadmissible in rape prosecutions. The Florida Statute describes that specific instances of prior consensual sexual activity between victims and any person other than the accused are inadmissible.

Table 27: Rape Shield Statutes of Some Selected States

States	What is Generally Inadmissible
Alabama ARE, R412	Any evidence related to past sexual behavior of the complaining witness
California Code 782, 1103	Opinion evidence and reputation evidence of the victim to prove consent
Florida Statute 794.022	Specific instances of prior consensual sexual activity
Georgia OCGA 24-23	Evidence relating to the past sexual behavior of the complaining witness
Maryland 3-319	Reputation and opinion evidence of a victim's chastity
Massachusetts Statute 233, 21-B	Reputation evidence and specific instances of a victim's sexual conduct
New York CLS CPL 60-42	Evidence of a victim's sexual conduct
North Carolina Statute 8C-1 Rule 412	Sexual behavior of the complainant
Ohio ORC 2907.02 (D)	Specific instance of victim's sexual activity, opinion, and reputation evidence
Pennsylvania PA CS 3104	Evidence of specific instances of the victim's past sexual conduct
Texas Rules of Evidence 412	Reputation or opinion evidence of the past sexual behavior of a victim
Virginia 18.2-67.7	General reputation or opinion evidence of the victim's prior sexual conduct

Source: American Prosecutor Research Institute, 2003

Under Common Law, wives are treated as properties of their husbands, and, hence, husbands are never to be found guilty of rape even if force is used in the sexual act. According to Common Law, marital rape is an impossible notion. However, in the United States, instances are not few and far between when women are forced, chocked, dragged, beaten, and then brutally raped by their husbands. Research shows that in the United States about 10-14 percent of married women are forcibly raped by their husbands (Bureau of Justice Statistics, 2002; 2003). By the middle 1990s, all fifty states and the District of Columbia enacted spousal rape laws that deny this notion of complete immunity for husbands given under the Common Law—the notion described as "spousal exemption" or "marriage defense." In 17 states including Colorado, Florida, Georgia, Indiana, Massachusetts, New Jersey, North Carolina, Oregon, and Texas, spousal rape statutes do not give any exemption to husbands for forcible rape and sodomy. In other thirty three states, some general exemptions are given if wives are mentally or physically impaired to consent to sex. In Connecticut, Iowa, Minnesota, and West Virginia such exemptions are given also to those who live together (National Online Resource Center for Violence against Women, 2004).

State Date Rape and Marital Rape Laws

In addition to spousal rape, all fifty states in the 1990s also enacted laws to criminalize date rape, acquaintance rape, gang rape, and male rape. Laws against drug-induced date rape and sexual assaults have been enacted in all fifty states and in the District of Columbia. From the middle of the 1990s, date rape began to increase in the United States and drugs, such as Rohypnol, GHB, and Ketamine, commonly described as club drugs, induced many of them. "Rohypnol is one of the drugs most commonly implicated in drug-facilitated rape" (Office of National Drug Control Policy, 2003, p. 2). According to the DEA, 7,100 cases of GHB use in date rape cases were reported to law enforcement in 45 states between 1990 and 2000 (Dubun & Hutt, 2001). In 1996, Congress enacted the Drug-Induced Rape Prevention Act of 1996. The Act required the DEA to study the need for rescheduling Rohypnol, and it imposed "a penalty of up to 20 years in prison and a fine for the importation and distribution of I gram or more of Rohypnol. Simple possession is punishable by 3 years in prison and a fine" of $30,000 (Office of National Drug Control Policy, 2003, p. 3). Rohypnol, however, still remains in Schedule IV of the federal Controlled Substance Act, but GHB has been placed in Schedule I. In 1999, Congress passed a new legislation on drug-induced date rape—the Hillory J. Farias and Samantha Reid Date Rape Drug Prohibition Act—and it was signed into law by President Clinton in 2000. The Act of 2000 directs the Attorney General to place GHB in Schedule I. Ketamine still remains in Schedule III of the Controlled Substance Act.

By 2001, Rohypnol, however, was already classified as a Schedule 1 drug by eleven states including Florida, Idaho, Minnesota, Michigan, New Hampshire, New Mexico, North Dakota, Oklahoma, and Pennsylvania (Office of National Drug Control Policy, 2003). GHB has been reclassified as a Schedule I drug by forty states. In addition to the rescheduling of the club drugs, many states, such as Georgia, Iowa, Maryland, Missouri, Ohio, Oklahoma, Vermont, Virginia, and Wyoming, enacted legislations to impose increased mandatory sentencing for their production, sale, possession, and use particularly, for rape and sexual assault purposes (National Conference of State Legislatures, 2001).

Rohypnol and GHB induced rape is considered as a second-degree rape where the victim is made unconscious and incapable of consent for sex, and it can carry a penalty of life in prison in many states. In Michigan, for example, four boys—Daniel, Erick, Joshua, Nicholas—were convicted in 2000 for raping and killing their high school freshman friend, Samantha Reid, by slipping GHB into her drinks. Joshua was given 7-15 years in prison, Nicholas and Daniel received 5-15 years in prison, and Erick was sentenced to 3-5 years in prison. Samantha Reid's death resulted in Congress's enactment of the Samantha Reid Date Rape Drug Prohibition Act in 2000.

State Reform of the Statutes of Limitations

The Common Law concept of rape also includes a doctrine of what is known as *fresh complaint rule*. The doctrine of *fresh complaint rule* implies that if a genuine sexual attack had occurred, the victim, irrespective of her age and knowledge about the context in which the crime had occurred, would immediately raise a "hue and cry." It is this *fresh complaint rule* doctrine that led to the development of the notion of the statute of limitations in rape and sexual assault cases under the American penal code. In the 1980s and 1990s, all fifty states and the District of Columbia revised their statutes of limitations for rape and sexual assaults cases (see Table 28).

The PROTECT Act of 2003, as mentioned, earlier, has eliminated the statutes of limitations for federal child abduction and child sexual abuse cases. The general trend in the states is also for the elimination or the lengthening of the statutes of limitations for rape and sexual assault cases. In six states—Alabama, Delaware, Idaho, Mississippi, North Carolina and Virginia—there are no statutes of limitations for rape cases. In a number of states, class A felonies, including rape and sexual assaults irrespective of the age of the victim, have no time limit for prosecution (National Conference of State legislatures, 2006). The rapid use of DNA technology in crime investigation, particularly sex crimes investigation, in recent years has made the notion of the statute of limitations obsolete. The DNA samples, collected from the rape victims—samples that are seemingly indestructible—can be used for rape prosecution long after the crime had occurred. In all fifty states, law requires the collection of DNA samples from all sexual offenders. These DNA samples are then kept and stored both in the DNA laboratories of the states and the FBI's CODIS system. These samples can be analyzed, examined, and shared by law enforcements of different states to solve the cold cases of rape and sexual assaults irrespective of the time when they had occurred. It is in this context of the new DNA technology in criminal justice, that most of the states in recent years have revisited their statutes of limitations for the reporting of rape and sexual assault cases. "Availability of DNA in sexual assault cases also has altered statutes of limitations. Some states extend and others eliminate the statutes of limitations on specified crimes if identity of the perpetrator is established by DNA" (National Conference of State Legislatures, 2006).

State Child Pornography Laws

Since the beginning of federal involvement in combating obscenity and child pornography in the Internet from the middle of the 1990s, and the growth of such federal enactments as the Communications Decency Act of 1996, Child Pornography Prevention Act of 1996, Child Online Protection Act of 1998, and the Children's Internet Protection Act of 2000, many states have also been developing and strengthening their Internet obscenity and child pornography laws (National Conference of State Legislatures, 2006).

Table 28:   Statutes of Limitations for Rape and Sexual Assaults in Some Selected States, 2006 (If DNA Involved)

State	Statute of Limitations
Alabama	No period of limitation for the offense of rape
California	Prosecution within 10 years; permits the prosecution of certain sex offenses within I year if the identity is established by DNA
Florida	No time limit for prosecuting capital and Class A felonies; prosecution for sexual assault within 1 one year if DNA is available
Georgia	Prosecution within 15 years; no time limit if DNA is available
Minnesota	Within 9 years if the victim is minor; no time limit if DNA is available
New Jersey	No time limit for prosecuting rape and sexual assault cases
New York	No time limit for prosecuting rape and sexual assault cases
North Carolina	No time limit for prosecuting rape and sexual assault cases
North Dakota	Prosecution of sexual offense within 20 years
Texas	Prosecution within 7 years; no time limit if DNA is available
Virginia	No time limit for prosecuting rape and sexual assault cases
Washington	Prosecution within 10 years if the rape is reported within 1 year of its commission

Source: National Conference of State Legislatures on Statute of Limitations, 2003 and 2006

During the last five years, a number of states have enacted new legislations, following those of the federal government, to control the activities of Internet Service Providers (ISP), require public schools and libraries to install blocking technologies in their computers with Internet services, and to impose increased sentences for violations of child pornography and obscenity laws. As Governor

Bob Riley of Alabama, in signing a child pornography legislation in March 2006, said: "all crimes are an assault on our society, but crimes against children are an attack on the very soul of our society. Among the very worst crimes is child pornography because child pornography is nothing more than a visual depiction of a child being sexually exploited" (Office of the Governor of Alabama, 2006, p. 1). "By 2005, 38 states had enacted 'electronic luring' statutes, which outlaw the online solicitation of children for sexual acts" (Midwest office of the Council of State Governments, 2006, p. 3).

In 2002, Pennsylvania enacted a law to make Internet Service Providers responsible for what children see on the Internet. The law required Internet Service Providers that provides Internet services within the states to shut down the sites that contain Internet child pornography and obscene materials harmful to minors within five days after the Office of the Attorney General notifies them. The law imposed a fine of $5,000 for the first offense of violation, $20,000 for the second offense of violation, and $30,000 for the third offense of violation. South Dakota passed a similar legislation in 2002. In 2001, South Carolina made a law that required the state's computer technicians to report to state law enforcement agencies if they find sites of child pornography in the course of their regular computer work. Arkansas, Illinois, Missouri, New York, Texas, South Carolina and Utah have enacted similar legislations (National Conference of State Legislatures, 2002).

In compliance with the federal Children's Internet Protection Act of 2000, twenty-one states, as of January 2006, have enacted laws to require their public schools and libraries to install filtering software in their computers to prevent children from accessing to obscene and harmful materials. Out of these twenty-one states, California, Delaware, Maryland, Michigan, Minnesota, New York, Ohio, and Pennsylvania require only their public libraries to install Internet filtering technology. New Hampshire, Oklahoma, South Dakota, South Carolina, and Texas require only their public schools to install the filtering technology. Arizona, Arkansas, Colorado, Kentucky, Missouri, Utah, and Virginia are in full compliance with the CIPA (National Conference of State Legislatures, 2006). In 2006, The Commonwealth of Virginia enacted a law under which all public schools of the Commonwealth are required to teach their students about online safety. The law directs the Commonwealth Department of Education to develop guidelines for schools to integrate Internet safety in their instructional curriculum (Helderman, 2006).

Reforms in State Sex Offender Registration Laws

State legislative activities related to sex crimes from the middle of the 1990s began to be focused, in addition to executing reforms in many substantive areas, mostly on the problem of sex offender registration, notification, and management. This came in the context of the federal enactments of the Jacob Wetterling Act of 1994, Megan's Law in 1996, Pam Lychner Sexual Offender Tracking and Identification Act of 1996, Children Safety Act of 2005, and the Adam Walsh Child Protection and Safety Act of 2006. All fifty states and the District of Columbia complied with the guidelines of these five major federal legislations related to sex offender registration and notification. According to the Bureau of Justice Statistics, as of July 2005, all fifty states and the District of Columbia had centralized sex offender registries, and they all had policies to send their registration data to the FBI's National Sex Offender Registry (NSOR). Although specific laws related to sex offender classification, the nature and types of reportable offenses, time and duration of registration, registration verification procedures, community notification of sex offenders, sex offender tracking strategies, and the penalties for the violation of sex offender registration laws somewhat vary from state to state, all fifty states closely follow the federal standards and guidelines.

In 2001, according to the data from the Bureau of Justice Statistics, there were about 386,000 registered sex offenders in 49 states including the District of Columbia. According to the data from the Center for Missing and Exploited Children, as of mid-year 2006, the total number of registered sex offenders in the U.S. reached 566,782. In 2006, California has the highest number of registered sex offenders (106,376) followed by Texas (44,789), Florida (37,217), and New York (22,486). There were 16 states that had more than 10,000 registered sex offenders, and 14 states that had registered sex offenders between 5,001 and 10,000.

Some of the general trends in the development of state sex offender registration and notification laws include mandatory registration for all categories of offenders convicted of sex offenses, lengthening of the time of registration requirement, community notification of sex offenders through the Internet, mandatory registration for juvenile sex offenders convicted as adults, GPS tracking of sex offenders, and increased inter-agency and inter-state sharing of sex offender registration information. In recent years, most of the states have reformed and strengthened their registration laws. In all fifty states, both violent and non-violent sexual offenders are required to register. The Sex Offender Code of Virginia, for example, maintains that those who are convicted of rape, abduction for immoral purpose, forcible sodomy, aggravated sexual battery, sexual battery with a minor, carnal knowledge of minors between 13-15, and sexual object penetration must register. Registration in Virginia is also mandatory for those who are convicted of taking indecent liberties with minor, crime against nature (sodomy), adultery, fornication, marital sexual assault, prostitution, possession of child pornography, sale and distribution of child pornography, and peeping. In New York, from 2002, sex offenders convicted of misdemeanor sex offenses are required to register. In California, a person convicted of even annoying a child with sexual intent must register. Under a California statute, a person convicted of oral copulation or lewd and lascivious act or conduct must register. The Georgia statute put it broadly and said that any conduct that is a sexual offense against a minor requires registration. In Pennsylvania, registration requires also for those who are convicted of unlawful contact or communication with a minor, first-degree misdemeanor indecent assault, and involuntary deviant sexual intercourse. What these examples of different state statutory requirements suggest is that registration as a form of punishment and deterrence is applied today not only for violent sexual acts but also for a wide variety of sexual conduct and behavior.

In recent years, most states have enacted laws to require registration for juvenile sex offenders. In some states, juvenile sex offenders treated as adults and sentenced in adult courts must register. In others states, even adjudicated delinquent sex offenders are required to register. In North Carolina, for example, "A juvenile transferred to Superior Court pursuant to G.S. 7A-608 who is convicted of a sexually violent offense or an offense against a minor must register in accordance with this law just as an adult convicted of the same offense must register" (North Carolina Department of Justice, 2001, p. 6). The South Carolina registration law requires that juvenile sex offenders, not only those who were treated as adults but also those who were sentenced by juvenile courts, must register. Similar laws that require registration for juvenile sex offenders exist in other states. In California, convicted and adjudicated juvenile sex offenders must register for life.

The length and the duration of registration in most states depend on sex offense categories. The general trend is towards the lengthening of the requirement of registration for violent sex offenders. In most states, as in California, Florida, Georgia, Maryland, New Jersey, New York, North Carolina, Pennsylvania, Texas, Virginia, Vermont, and Washington, violent sex offenders and sexual predators are required to remain registered for life. In Florida, both non-violent and violent sex offenders (sexual predators) are required to remain registered for life. However, a sex offender in Florida who can remain free from sex offenses for 20 years after serving time for his or her first sex offense conviction, or someone who was less than 18 year of old at the time of the first offense and remained free of sex offenses for 10 years may petition to the criminal division of the circuit court for exemptions from life-time registration requirement. California's sex offender registration statute is even broader, and it describes that "Every offender required to register must do so for the rest of his or her life while residing in, or, if he or she has no residence, while located within California, or while attending school or working in California." In California, sexual predators must verify their addresses and update their information every three months. In Texas, lifetime registration is required even for those who are convicted of possession and promotion of child pornography and indecent exposure. According to the Sex Offender Registration Act (SORA) of New York, violent sex offenders and sexual predators must remain registered for life, and non-violent sex offenders are required to remain registered for at least 20 years.

State Sex Offender Notification Laws

All fifty states and the District of Columbia, as of 2006, have not only established centralized sex offender registration systems but also, in compliance with the Federal Megan's Law of 1996, centralized Internet community notification systems. All fifty states have sex offender registry websites. In most states, community notification systems are a part of the main state sex offender registry (Carpenter, 2006). In some states, there are separate websites for community notification. In Texas, for example, the sex offender website is within the Criminal Record Service of the Texas Department of Public Service, and community notification is a part of the sex offender registration website. In California, on the other hand, there is a separate Megan's Law Home Page located at the California Department of Justice. In Florida, the notification web page is titled Sex Offenders and Predators: A Course of Public Safety. The Commonwealth of Virginia describes it as the Sex Offender and Crimes against Minor Home Page. In addition to community notification websites with access for public to search for sex offenders, many states have laws for their law enforcement to notify electronically information about sex offenders to agencies and organizations dealing with children. In Virginia, for example, the Central Criminal Records Exchange of the Virginia Department of Police is authorized by law to send electronic notification of sex offender information to elementary and secondary schools, institutions of higher education, trade or professional institutions, child care providers, child services agencies, foster homes, and certified nursing facilities. In Texas, the Crime Record Service of the Texas Department of Public Safety is authorized to notify others about violent sex offenders, if needed, even in the form of a postcard.

The state Internet notification systems are generally similar in nature and procedures. In all notification websites, information can be accessed in terms of a sex offender's first and last name, date of birth, gender, race, home address, county or city of residence, and zip code. In some states, information is given also on sex offenses and offense categories. In the sex offender registration and notification website of South Carolina, for example, the public can search the names of sex offenders in terms of their specific nature of convictions. The New Jersey website contains seven search categories: geographic search, individual search, advanced search, vehicle search, statistics, recently published sex offenders, and the listing of fugitives. In advanced search, one can get information even about the physical characteristics of a specific sex offender. Through the geographic search category, or the neighborhood search category as it is described in the website of Florida, one can receive information about the sex offenders living within 1-5 miles radius of the address and zip code entered. The Texas website maintains a program called Sex Offender Mapping Utility that helps to find the location of sex offenders in different cities and counties of the state. The Texas site even provides tutorial lessons for the public to perform quick and advanced searches for sex offender information. North Carolina's Criminal Information and Identification Section of the Bureau of Investigation provides "free public access to automated date from the statewide registry, including a photograph provided by the registering sheriff via the Internet" (North Carolina Department of Justice, 2007, p. 1).

Records from different states show that public access to state sex offender notification websites have been rapidly growing. The New Jersey website shows that, as of 2006, more than 5.5 million searches have been requested. Data from a North Carolina website reveal that between February and July of 2006—in a period of six months—more than 1.6 million people searched the notification registry. All states, however, made it a crime to misuse or misrepresent the sex offender registration and notification information given to public. As the New Jersey Sex Offender Internet Registry notes: "Megan's Law, the Internet registry law expressly prohibits the use of registry information for the purpose of applying for, obtaining, or denying health insurance, insurance, loans, credit, education, scholarships or fellowships, benefits privileges or services provided by any business establishment ... or housing or accommodation."

State Sex Offender Tracking Laws

According to the Center for Missing and Exploited Children, out of 560,000 current registered sex offenders in 2006, about 100,000 are missing from law enforcement tracking. The federal Pam Lychner Sexual Offender Tracking and Identification Act of 1996 made it mandatory for the states to develop programs to deal effectively with the problem of fugitive sex offender and sex offender tracking. Hundreds of thousands of sex offenders, including many described as sexual predators, are not registered, and they desperately try to avoid registration moving from place to place, state to state, and even from country to country. All states recently have reformed their timeline of requirements for registration and strategies for sex offender tracking. In Florida, a sex offender is legally required to register within 48 hours of entering a county and changing an address. In California, sex offenders are required to update their registration information every year. The violent sex offenders and sexual predators are required to report changes in registration information every 3 months. In Georgia, North Carolina, Pennsylvania and many other states, sex offenders are required to register within ten days of release from a penal institution. In the Commonwealth of Virginia, a sex offender must register upon conviction, and within 72 hours after his or her release from a correctional center. In South Carolina, a convicted sex offender must register within 24 hours of release from a prison. In all fifty states, violation of registration is a crime. In California, Florida, Georgia, New York, North Carolina, Pennsylvania, South Carolina and many other states, violation of registration is a felony crime. California maintains a separate program of Sex Offender Tracking within the Department of Justice. The federal Adam Walsh Act of 2006 requires "that sex offender registration occurs before an offender is released from imprisonment or within three days of non-imprisonment sentence. Changes in registry information must be reported in that time period as well" (National Conference of State Legislatures, 2007, p. 1)

Several states, including Florida, Louisiana, Massachusetts, Missouri, Ohio, Oklahoma, North Carolina, South Carolina, and Tennessee have enacted legislations to use the technology of global positioning system (GPS) for sex offender tracking. "People on the tracking system must wear the electronic waterproof ankle bands at all times and stay within a certain distance from their separate GPS transmitters, which can be carried on belts, in purses or set down on desks and tables when at work or home" (National Conference of State Legislatures, 2005, p. 9). As of January 2006, thirteen states had laws requiring the use of the GPS system for sex offender tracking. Through the GPS system, law enforcement can develop a density map of sex offenders showing the places and people they regularly meet and visit. Many states, such as Texas and Minnesota, are now using the GPS system and considering new legislations to make it mandatory for use by law enforcement in tracking sex offenders. Michigan and Oklahoma require their sex offenders to pay for the GPS monitoring that costs about $4,000 a year. The Jessica Lunsford Bill, introduced in the Congress (HR 1505-109th Congress) in 2005, has proposed to make GPS tracking of sex offenders a federal law.

State Sex Offender Sentencing Reforms

From the late 1990s, most of the states have also been reforming their sentencing guidelines for sex crimes. This came partly in response to various related federal enactments such as the Aimee's Law of 2000 and the PROTECT Act of 2003, partly in response to increased public outcry for more control on violent sex offenders, and partly in response to the general perspective that sex crimes are morally more abominable than drugs and other crimes. The federal Aimee's Law, also described as "No Second Chance for Murderers, Rapists, or Child Molesters Act," put more responsibility on the states to reduce sex offender recidivism by pitting more sex offenders behind bars for longer times. The Act made a provision, as mentioned earlier, to decrease federal law enforcement funds for the states whose sex offenders commit similar crimes in other states. In 2006, at least fourteen governors have signed bills that extended sex offender prison sentences, improved sex offender registration and notification systems, imposed sex offender residency restrictions, mandated the use of GPS tracking of sex offenders (Koch, 2006).

As of July 2005, thirty six states, including California, Colorado, Florida, Minnesota, Utah, and Washington have enacted laws for mandatory life imprisonment and mandatory enhanced sentences for repeat and violent sex offenders (see Table 29). One of the significant policy developments in this area in the states recently came through the enactment of Jessica Lunsford Act, commonly described as Jessica's law, in Florida in 2005. The Jessica Lunsford Act made a provision of mandatory sentencing of 25 years to life in prison for first-time sex offenders and the molesters of children below the age of 12. The Act also requires life-time electronic monitoring of sexual predators. Under the Jessica Lunsford Act, those who are designated by the court as sexual predators are required to verify their registration twice a year, and it is third-degree felony to harbor or conceal a sexual predator.

Alabama, Arizona, Arkansas, Georgia, Indiana, Iowa, Nevada, Oklahoma, Oregon, Virginia, and Wisconsin have laws similar to those of the Jessica Lunsford Act. In 2005, Michigan, following the Jessica Act, made a law that says that violent sex offenders can even be forced to wear GPS electronic devices for life. Following the Jessica's Law, "Iowa mandates life sentence for certain sex crimes against children. Indiana authorized a life sentence for certain repeat sex offenders. Minnesota mandated life without parole for certain violent sex crimes" (National Conference of State Legislatures, 2005, p. 1). In 2006, Wisconsin and Kansas enacted laws similar to Jessica's Law. In Georgia, the mandatory sentencing of 25 years in prison statute is applicable also for teen sex offenders, ages 13 through 15, who are tried as adults for forced rape, molestation, and sodomy of children. "Jessica's case helped spark the passage in 2005 of more than 100 new sex offender measures around the country— the most ever in a given year, and twice as many as in 2004. Several Midwestern states enacted laws in 2005 and 2006 similar to Florida" (Midwest Office of the Council of State Governments, 2006, p.1). In 2006, a Virginia man was sentenced to 150 years in prison for child sexual exploitation and operating child pornography websites (The Associated Press, 2006, 1).

Table 29: Sentencing Guidelines for Repeat and Violent Sex Offenders in Some Selected States

State	Life Sentences	Penalties for Repeat Offenders
AL	Longer sentences for repeat offenders, Penal Code 13A-5-9	Enhanced sentences for repeat sex offenders
AR	Mandatory life without parole for violent sexual assault ARS 13:1423	Enhanced sentences for repeat sex offenders
CA	Mandatory life imprisonment for certain sex offenses Penal Code, 667-61	5 year enhancement for each prior conviction; fine up to $20,000
CO	Mandatory life in prison for habitual offenders CRS 18-13-801	Mandatory life in prison for repeat sex offenders
CT	Mandatory life in prison for persistent and dangerous sex offenders CT General Stat. 53a-40	Mandatory life for repeat sex offenders
FL	Mandatory imprisonment of 25 years to life for dangerous sexual felony offender FL Stat. 794-0115	Mandatory increased prison term for repeat sex offenders
MN	Mandatory life for violent sex offenders, MN Stat. 609-109	Mandatory increased sentences for repeat sex offenders
WY	Mandatory life without parole for repeat sex offenders WY 6-2-306	Mandatory increased sentences for repeat sex offenders

Sources: Center for Prosecution of Child Abuse, and American Prosecutor Research Institute 2005

Several states in recent years have also enacted laws to restrict the mobility of their sex offenders released to the community. Many states have enacted laws, and many cities have created ordinances, to bar sex offenders living near places where children gather—schools, playgrounds, churches, amusement parks, gyms, community swimming pools, movie theaters, and school bus stops. The state of New York enacted a law in 2005 that bars a sex offender to be employed as an ice-cream truck driver. In Illinois, a state law bars "sex offenders from being employed for holiday events that include contact with children who are not related to the offender, such as in passing out Halloween candy or playing Santa Clause or the Easter Bunny" (National Conference of State Legislatures, 2005, p. 2).

State Sex Offender Civil Commitment Statutes

One of the battles the states are fighting in the war on sex crimes is aimed to reduce the rate of sex offender recidivism. In 2003, the Bureau of Justice Statistics has completed a major study on sex offender recidivism. The study has analyzed data on 9,691 sex offenders, including 4,295 child molesters, released from prison in 15 states in 1994. One of the findings of the study is that compared "to non-sex offenders released from prison, released sex offenders were 4 times more likely to be rearrested for a sex crime" (Bureau of Justice Statistics, 2003, p. 1). The same study also found that the "more prior arrests they had, the greater the likelihood of being rearrested for another sex crime after leaving prison" (Bureau of Justice Statistics, 2003, p. 1). The rate of recidivism is higher particularly among the rapists, child molesters, and other violent sex offenders. Jessica Lunsford, Sarah Lunde, Carlie Brucia were raped and killed by convicted sex offenders. It is this possibility of violent sex offenders to commit a violent sex crime again that has given birth to the policy of civil commitment (Levenson, 2004). The policy of civil commitment allows states to confine violent sex offenders in state managed and state funded mental institutions as long as offenders are judicially and professional determined to be of high-risk nature for public safety.

As of 2006, seventeen states—Arizona, California, Florida, Illinois, Iowa, Kansa, Massachusetts, Minnesota, Missouri, New Jersey, Nevada, North Dakota, South Carolina, Texas, Virginia, Washington, and Wisconsin—have made laws for civil commitment of sex offenders. Most of the other states are presently considering similar laws for civil commitment of violent sex offenders. To be considered for civil commitment, most states "require that the offender suffers from mental abnormality or personality disorder that makes it likely the offender will commit future acts of sexual violence" (The Council of State Governments, 2005, p. 1). The court, in consultation with a team of medical and psychiatric experts, usually makes the decision whether a sex offender is of high-risk nature. In the state of Washington, for example, a civil commitment trial is held before a judge or a jury empanelled by the court.

However, the nature of civil commitment and mental health care available for sex offenders varies from state to state. In most states with civil commitment laws, violent sex offenders are placed in locked and secure residential facilities, and they can choose not to participate in mental health treatment programs. In some states, participation in mental health treatment programs is judicially mandated (see Table 30). Texas has developed an innovative approach to civil commitment. In Texas, the sex offenders referred to civil commitment live in the community, but they are legally mandated to participate in outpatient sex offender treatment programs. Under the Washington State statute, violent juvenile sex offenders can also be confined to civil commitment. Since the enactment of the statute in 1990, 31 juveniles have been sent for civil commitment in the state Washington. In the Commonwealth of Virginia, sex offenders who receive civil commitment are confined in secure facilities and receive inpatient mental health treatment.

Sex offender Castration as a Policy Alternative

Formal psychiatric treatment for incarcerated sex offenders has long been a policy to combat sex offender recidivism. As of 2000, thirty four states had formal psychiatric treatment methods available for their sex offenders. Alabama, California, Delaware, Florida, Mississippi, New Mexico, and Oregon do not have any formal treatment options available for their incarcerated sex offenders (Colorado Department of Corrections, 2000).

The most commonly used method for sex offender treatment is cognitive behavior therapy. The state programs are "unanimous in using cognitive-behavior group therapy, with relapse prevention as the focus of treatment. Twenty states—almost 50% of the programs—offer more intensive forms of this approach through therapeutic communities or residential programs" (Colorado Department of Corrections, 2000, p. 5). The general duration of the treatment in twenty eight states is over 1 year. North Dakota, Arizona, and Massachusetts provide treatments for over 5 years.

As an alternative to traditional cognitive behavior therapy, some state legislatures have recently approached the problem of sexual predators and repeat child molesters in terms of castration. In 1996, California became the first state to legalize chemical castration. In 1997, a mandatory chemical castration law was passed in Florida. As of 2006, nine states—California, Florida, Georgia, Louisiana, Montana, Oregon, Texas, Virginia, and Wisconsin—have enacted laws for chemical castration. Options for surgical castration—removal of the testes—are available in California, Florida, and Texas. The Florida statute mandates that repeat sex offenders are given court-ordered weekly injections of hormones and antiandrogenes drugs, such as Depo-Provera and Depo-Lupron that reduce sex drives. Under the Florida statute, chemical castration can be a part of sentencing given to sex offenders. Mandatory court-ordered chemical castration is also a part of the castration law in Montana. In Montana, a judge can legally require a repeat violent sex offender to undergo chemical castration. In Texas, both chemical and surgical castrations are voluntary, and juvenile sex offenders are not allowed for castrations. The Texas statute describes that castrations are legally allowed when the offender is a repeat child molester, and it is recommended through psychiatric evaluations and prescribed in addition to other offender treatments. The California law mandates chemical castration even for a first-time sex offender if the victim is below 12 years of age.

Table 30: Civil Commitment Statutes of Some Selected States, 2005

State	Commitment Eligibility	Commitment By Jury Trial	Treatment
CA	Repeat violent sex offenses	Yes Unanimous	Confinement in secure facilities; inpatient treatment
FL	Convicted or found guilty by reason of insanity	Yes Unanimous	Confinement in secure facilities; inpatient treatment
KS	Convicted or found guilty by reason of insanity	Yes Unanimous	Confinement in secure facilities; voluntary treatment program
MN	Convicted of violent and harmful sexual and violent	NO	Less restrictive programs
NJ	Convicted or found guilty by reason of insanity; adjudicated delinquents included	NO	Confinement in secure facilities; inpatient treatment
SC	Convicted or found guilty by reason of insanity; adjudicated delinquents included	Yes Unanimous	Confinement in secure facilities; inpatient treatment
TX	Repeat violent sex offenders	Yes Unanimous	Outpatient treatment and supervision
VA	Convicted or incompetent to stand trail	Yes Unanimous	Secure facilities; inpatient treatment

Sources: Center for Prosecution of Child Abuse, and American Prosecutor Research Institute, 2005

5.6 Sex Crimes and Judicial Policy-Making

Judicial policy-making in sex crimes began in the early part of the twentieth century particularly in the context of the issues raised by the Federal Comstock Law of 1873 and the Mann Act of 1910. The Comstock Law that criminalized the use and the distribution of information about birth control was one of the issues that were highly debatable in the 1940s and 1950s. The Comstock's idea of contraception as contraband was highly contentious until the Supreme Court ruled against the law in 1965. In compliance with the Comstock Law, the state of Connecticut enacted a statute in 1879 that criminalized the use and prescription of birth control and even an advice on contraception. Estelle T. Griswold, the Director of the Planned Parenthood League of Connecticut took the case to court. The Supreme Court in *Griswold v. Connecticut* ruled (7-2 decision) that the Connecticut statute was an infringement on the constitutionally protected rights of married couples. Following the *Griswold* decision in 1965, Congress in

1971, after almost one hundred years, repealed the Comstock Law. In 1972 again, in *Eisenstadt v. Baird*, the Supreme Court ruled that not just married but also unmarried women have the right to have access to contraceptive information. In 1973, the Supreme Court in its landmark decision on *Roe v. Wade* legalized abortion in America. In 1977, the Supreme Court, through its ruling in *Carey v. Population Services International* in New York, extended the constitutional protection of right to privacy with respect to contraceptive information and reproductive rights to minors under sixteen.

Unlike the Comstock Law, the Mann Act, described also as White Slave Traffic Act, of 1910, was not that much controversial until the1960s. In a number of cases, the Supreme Court ruled in favor of the Mann Act. In *Hoke v. United States* in 1913, the Supreme Court ruled that the Congress has the legitimate constitutional authority to regulate interstate travel for the purpose of prostitution and other immoral sexual activities. In *Caminetti v. United States* in 1917, the Supreme Court, as mentioned before, upholds the Mann Act not only in relations to commercial prostitution but also non-commercial sexual activities. In 1932, in *Gebardi v.United States*, the Supreme Court held that the Mann Act applies even when the interstate travel of women for the purpose of engagement in prostitution and other immoral activities was consensual. In *Cleveland v. United States* in 1946, the Court ruled that a person could be prosecuted under the Mann Act even when he is married to the woman if the marriage is polygamous. Between the Mann Act of 1910 and the Jacob Wetterling Act of 1994, for more than eighty years, Congress did not pass any major sex crime legislations. During the same period, the judicial policy-making in sex crimes, except in cases related to the Comstock Law and the Mann Act, therefore, remained limited. Sex crimes cases began to reach to federal courts in large numbers as Congress began to enact a large number of sex crime legislations from the middle of the 1990s.

Federal Court and Challenges to Rape Shield laws

The Supreme Court has not yet heard and ruled on cases related to rape shield laws. But numerous cases have gone to state supreme courts and federal appeal courts challenging the validity of rape shield laws. In many cases, jurors made decisions without any knowledge about the history of sexual relations and activities of both the accuser and the accused. There are cases where rape shield laws have protected the accused because the prosecutors could not present any past evidence. There are also cases where the accused has been wrongly convicted because the defense could not present any past evidence. Many superior state and federal court judges have recently ruled against the rape shield laws. One of the recent notable cases is of Oliver Jovanovic, who was a doctoral student in microbiology at the University of Columbia at the time of the incidence in April 1998. Oliver was accused of kidnapping and sexually abusing a 22-year Barnard College student, Jamie Rzucek, he had met through the Internet chat room. After they met, Oliver and Jamie had dated several times, and they had several email exchanges about their mutual sexual preferences and fantasies. In the Supreme Court of New York, Justice William Wetzel strictly applied the New York's rape shield laws, and the defense was not allowed to present any evidence about the email exchanges Oliver had with the accuser. Oliver, who had no prior criminal record, was sentenced to 15 years in prison. The Oliver's case raised new controversies about the validity of rape shield laws. In 1999, after serving 20 months in prison, Oliver was freed, and the case was dismissed by the Appellate Division of the Supreme Court of New York on the grounds that the trial court judge "improperly hampered defendant's ability to present a defense" through the misapplication of rape shield laws.

In Connecticut, the evidence or information about the sexual past of both the accused and the accuser is admissible in the court if that is of "material" interest to the case in question. The Supreme Court of Connecticut, in a 5-0 ruling, made that decision in 2004 related to a rape case involving prostitution. Many states in recent years, in the context of a number of court cases like those of New York and Connecticut, have revised their rape shield laws, and made provisions for the admissibility of information about the sexual past of both the accuser and the accused under certain circumstances. The rape shield statute of Kentucky, for example, makes an exception when evidence is related to semen or injury. This exception is applied when a defendant in a rape case claims that he is not the rapist. The Kentucky statute also has a provision for the admissibility of past sexual behavior if that is relevant to establish the claim of a defendant that relations were consensual. In Massachusetts, the Supreme Judicial Court allows information about the complainant's past sexual conduct if that is relevant to establish his or her bias or motive to lie. In the recent case of Kobe Bryant, the Colorado Supreme Court is also seen to have made an exception to the state's rape shield statute. Kobe Bryant was accused of raping a 19-year old hotel employee in 2003. The defendant's argument was that sex was consensual. The Colorado Supreme Court ruled in 2004 in favor of admitting detailed information about the past sexual conduct of the accuser.

Federal Court and Challenges to
State Sodomy Statutes

One of the recent landmark decisions of the U.S. Supreme Court concerns the constitutionality of the states' sodomy laws. Before the 1970s, sodomy, described also as crimes against nature, was a punishable crime in most states. Sodomy is still punishable with 15 years of prison in Michigan, 10 years in North Carolina, Mississippi, and Oklahoma, and 5 years in Idaho, Louisiana, South Carolina, and Virginia. During the last three decades, however, twenty seven states and the District of Columbia repealed their sodomy laws through legislative actions. In ten states including Arkansas, Georgia, Kentucky, Maryland, Massachusetts, Minnesota, Montana, New York, Pennsylvania, and Tennessee, sodomy laws were struck down by the state superior courts.

The Supreme Court decided to hear about the states' sodomy laws first in case of *Bowers v. Hardwick* in 1986. In 1982, Michael Hardwick, a person of gay orientation in Georgia, was charged with the violation of Georgia's sodomy laws. Hardwick brought the case to the Federal district court and asserted that Georgia's sodomy laws are in violation of the federal constitution and the constitutionally protected right of privacy. The Federal district court ruled in favor of the defendant, Hardwick, relying on the decision made in the case of *Doe v. Commonwealth Attorney's of the City of Richmond* in 1975. The state of Georgia appealed the decision to the 11th Federal Circuit Court of Appeals. The 11th Circuit Court in 1985 ruled in favor of the defendant and remanded the case for retrial. The 11th Circuit Court argued that the defendant's "homosexual activity is a private and intimate association that is beyond the reach of state regulation by reason of the Ninth Amendment and the Due process Clause of the Fourteenth Amendment." The State of Georgia appealed the 11th Circuit Court's decision in the U.S. Supreme Court. In *Hardwick v. Bowers* in 1986, the U.S. Supreme Court ruled (5-4 decision) against the decision of the 11th Circuit, and argued that the federal constitution does not confer the fundamental right on individuals to engage in homosexual activities. The *Hardwick* ruling basically suggested that the Georgia's sodomy laws are not in violation of the federal constitution (Legal Information Institute, 1986).

However, in 2003, the U.S. Supreme Court in its decision on *Lawrence et al v. Texas* made a ruling that brought fundamental challenges to all state sodomy statutes (Legal Information Institute, 2003). In September 1998, the Harris country officers in Houston, Texas entered the apartment of John Lawrence responding to a call about weapons disturbance. After entering the apartment, the officers found Lawrence and another man named Tyron Garner engaged in homosexual activities. Lawrence and Garner were immediately arrested by the police officers. They were later found guilty, and each fined $200 for engagement in deviant sexual intercourse in violation of the Texas sodomy laws. Lawrence and Garner appealed the decision of the trial court to the Texas Court of Appeals of the 14th District claiming that the Texas sodomy laws were in violation of the equal protection clauses of the state and federal constitutions. A three-judge panel of the Texas Court of Appeals ruled that the convictions of Lawrence and Garner were discriminatory on the basis of sex and it violated the Equal Rights Amendment of the Texas Constitution. However, in 2001, a full Panel of seven judges of the Texas Court of Appeals reviewed the case and ruled that the state's "homosexual conduct" law was "facially" constitutional. The judges uphold the view that the Texas sodomy statute "advances the state interest of preserving public morality."

Lawrence and Gardner brought the case to the U.S. Supreme Court after the Texas Court of Criminal Appeals declined to review it. The U.S. Supreme Court, in 6-3 decision, in June 2003, made the landmark ruling that the Texas homosexual conduct statute was unconstitutional. Justice Anthony Kennedy, in writing the majority opinion, argued that the "Texas statute making it a crime for two persons of the same sex to engage in certain intimate sexual conduct violates the Due Process Clause" of the Fourteenth Amendment. Justice Kennedy further added that the "liberty protected by the Constitution allows homosexual persons the right to choose to enter upon relationships in the confines of their homes and their own private lives and still retain their dignity as freepersons." The majority opinion in *Lawrence et al v. Texas* recognized that the rationale given in *Bowers v. Hardwick in* 1986 that upheld the Georgia sodomy statute "does not withstand careful analysis. *Bowers* was not correct when it was decided, is not correct today, and is hereby overruled." The *Lawrence* decision of 2003 has brought significant challenges to states' sodomy laws and such issues as same-sex marriage and adoption of children by gay parents (Legal Information Institute, 2003).

Challenges to the CDA and Child Internet Pornography Statutes

As states' sodomy laws have been challenged in the court on the ground of the constitutionally protected right to privacy, most of the federal decency laws and Internet child pornography statutes have been challenged on the grounds of the constitutionally protected right to free speech. The federal Communications Decency Act of 1996, Child Pornography Protection Act of 1996, Child Online Protection Act of 1998, and Child Internet Protection Act of 2000—all have been challenged in federal courts on the claim that they are in violation of the First Amendment provision of free speech. The First Amendment to the U.S. Constitution states that "Congress shall make no law respecting an establishment of religion, or prohibiting the free exercise thereof; or abridging the freedom of speech, or of the press; or the right of the people peaceably to assemble, and to petition the government for a redress of grievances." With respect to free speech, the principle that is at the core is to protect the right to free speech to "foster the market place of ideas."

The Communications Decency Act, as described earlier, made a provision to criminalize the use of the Internet to post, transmit and communicate materials "harmful to minors." The Act criminalized the "knowing" transmission of materials to minors, under the age of 18 that will be judged obscene and indecent according to contemporary community standards. In *Reno, Attorney General of the United States et al. v. American Civil Liberties Union et al.* in 1997 (*Reno v. ACLU*), the Supreme Court ruled, (7-2 decision), against the above provisions of the Communications Decency Act. The Supreme Court recognized that the Congress has a compelling interest in the protection of minors from being exposed to "indecent" and "patently offensive" materials on the Internet. But according to the Court, the CDA has not provided any precise definitions of these terms, and there has remained a great scope for vagueness and conflicting interpretations. "The vagueness of such a content-based regulation, coupled with its increased deterrent effect as a criminal statute" the Supreme Court argued, "raise special first Amendment concerns because of its obvious chilling effects on free speech." The CDA is a "content-based blanket restriction on speech." The Court even went to the extent of saying that the breadth of the CDA "is wholly unprecedented" (Legal Information Institute, 1997).

In *Reno v. ACLU*, the Supreme Court's decision was based on previous decisions on the issue of obscenity made by the Court particularly in *Roth v. Unit-*

ed States in 1957 and in *Miller v. California* in 1972. In *Roth v. United States,* the Supreme Court argued, as mentioned before, that obscenity is not protected by the First Amendment right to free speech. The First Amendment does not protect the materials that appeal to "prurient interest" according to contemporary community standards, and those that are without any "redeeming social importance." The Court ruled that "Obscenity is not within the area of constitutionally protected freedom of speech or press either (1) under the First Amendment, as to the Federal Government, or (2) under the Due Process Clause of the Fourteenth Amendment as to States" (Legal Information Institute, 1957). But in *Roth*, the Supreme Court recognized that sex "is a great and mysterious motive force in human life, [and] has indisputably been a subject of absorbing interest to mankind through the ages. It is one of the vital problems of human interests and public concerns" (Legal Information Institute, 1957).

In *Miller v. California* in 1972, the Supreme Court reaffirmed the *Roth* decision and established the key standards of obscenity—the standards that the federal and state governments must use to regulate obscenity without any infringement on the First Amendment right to free speech. The basic guidelines, according to the Supreme Court, are: 1) whether "the average person applying contemporary community standards" finds something that appeals to prurient interest in sex; 2) whether the work describes and depicts sexual conduct in a patently offensive way, and is in violation of related state laws, and 3) whether the work, taken as a whole, lacks any serious literary, artistic, political or scientific value. These three guidelines established in *Miller v. California have* remained at the core of many of the Supreme Court's subsequent decisions on obscenity and indecency in the media and the Internet. The CDA was found to be in violation of the First Amendment precisely because, as argued in *Reno v. ACLU,* the Congress did not use these guidelines in defining obscenity on the Internet.

After the Communications Decency Act, Congress enacted the Child Pornography Protection Act in 1996 (CPPA), Child Online Protection Act in 1998 (COPA), and Child Internet Protection Act in 2000 (CIPA). All three legislations were challenged in the Court, and both CPPA and COPA were found to be in violation of the First Amendment by the U.S Supreme Court. The CPPA prohibited child pornography on the Internet by using not only actual images of children but also images generated by computers described as "virtual pornography." A group of artists, publishers, adult entertainment associations, and the Free Speech Coalition immediately challenged the CPPA and filed a suit in the United States District Court of the Northern District of California claiming that the legislation was "overboard and vague." The District Court disagreed and granted judgment in favor of the CPPA. The plaintiffs appealed the decision to the United States Court of Appeals for the Ninth Circuit. The Ninth Circuit Court of Appeals reversed the lower court decision on the basis of the reasoning that the "Government could not prohibit speech because of its tendency to persuade viewers to commit illegal acts." The Ninth Circuit's decision was appealed by the U.S Department of Justice to the U.S. Supreme Court. The U.S Supreme Court in this case—*Ashcroft v. The Free Speech Coalition*— ruled in

2002 that the "CPPA is inconsistent with *Miller.* It extends to images that are not obscene under the *Miller* Standard." CPPA is also in violation of the First Amendment right to free speech. In writing the majority opinion, Justice Kennedy said that the CPPA abridges "the freedom to engage in a substantial amount of lawful speech. For this reason, it is overboard and unconstitutional."

The Children Online Protection Act of 1988 (COPA) was directed mainly to restrict commercially available materials on the World Wide Web that are harmful to minors under 17 years of age. Like the CPPA, the COPA was also immediately challenged in the court by the American Civil Liberties Union (ACLU) on behalf of Internet site operators, Internet content providers, American Book Seller Foundation for Free Expressions, Electronic Privacy Information Center and other groups. The ACLU filed a motion in the United States District Court of the Eastern District of Pennsylvania for immediate injunction to stop the enforcement of the legislation on the claim that it was in violation of the First and Fifth Amendments. The District Court, in February 1999, issued a preliminary injunction pending a final decision on the constitutionality of the COPA. The Department of Justice appealed the injunction decision to the United States Court of Appeals for the Third Circuit. The Third Circuit Court of Appeals unanimously ruled in favor of the District Court injunction against the COPA in June 2000. The Circuit Court said: "We will affirm the District Court's grant of preliminary injunction because we are confident that ACLU's attack on COPA's constitutionality is likely to succeed on the merits" (United States Court of Appeals for the Third Circuit, 2000, p. 4). The Third Circuit Court also argued that the Court's contemporary "community standards jurisprudence" is not applicable to the new technology of the Internet and the World Wide Web that does not have any definite geographical boundary. The jurors of different counties and communities may have different community standards to measure what is harmful for minors. The World Wide Web is "not geographically constrained. Web publishers are without any means to limit access to their sites based on the geographic location of particular interest users."

The Department of Justice appealed the Third Circuit decision to the U.S. Supreme Court in 2001. In 2002, in *Ashcroft v. ACLU,* the Supreme Court made a decision focusing narrowly on the question of whether COPA's use of "community standards" of *Miller* to identify materials harmful to minors violated the First Amendment. The Supreme Court reversed the decision of the Third Circuit and ruled that "this aspect of COPA does not render the statute facially unconstitutional." "It is sufficient to note," the majority opinion of the Court said, "that community standards need not be defined by reference to a precise geographic area." In 2004, the Supreme Court, in a 5-4 decision, however, again ruled in connection with the COPA. In this ruling, the Supreme Court asked for the exploration of new technologies to control the access of children to harmful materials on the Internet.

The Supreme Court's preference for a technological solution, rather than a censorship, to limit the access of minors to harmful materials became more evident through its ruling in favor of the Children's Internet Protection Act of 2000 (CIPA). The CIPA required all schools and public libraries receiving federal assistance under the E-rate program to install Internet filtering software in their computers to control the access of children to harmful materials. In a 6-3 decision, the Supreme Court in 2003, in *United States et al. v. American Library Association, Inc., et al.*, said that the CIPA was not in violation of the First Amendment. Chief Justice Rehnquist, in writing the majority opinion, said, "CIPA does not induce libraries to violate the Constitution, and is a valid exercise of Congress's spending power" (Legal Information Institute, 2003, p. 2). Justice Rehnquist further added that "Government has broad discretion to make content-based judgments in deciding what private speech to make available to the public" (Legal Information Institute, 2003, p. 1).

Sex Offender Registration, Notification, and Civil Commitment Laws: Constitutional Challenges

The federal and state sex offender registration, notification, and civil commitment laws have also been challenged on constitutional grounds. The issues of long-term and life-time sex offender registration, sex offender community notification through the Web, mandatory sentencing guidelines for sex offenders, developing separate registration system for violent sex offenders, sex offender residency restrictions, mandatory collection of DNA samples from sex offenders, public access to juvenile sex offender information, application of the "three-strikes" law to sex offender registration, involuntary civil confinement of sex offenders—all have raised crucial constitutional questions, and they have been challenged in state and federal courts (Carpenter, 2006). Questions have been raised and debated whether these laws are in violation of the Constitution's *ex post facto clause*, and the First Amendment's right to privacy, due process clause of the Fourteenth Amendment, and cruel and unusual punishment clause of the Eighth Amendment.

In 2003, the U.S. Supreme Court, for the first time, reviewed and ruled on two cases arising out of the Jacob Wetterling Act of 1994 and Megan's Law of 1996. These two cases are: 1) *Smith et al. v. John Doe* of Alaska and 2) *Connecticut Department of Public Safety et al. v. John Doe*. The state of Alaska enacted the sex offender registration law in 1994 and both the sex offender registration and notification laws of the state are retroactive. Delbert Smith and Bruce Botelho—two men and the wife of one of them—challenged the retroactive nature of Alaska's Megan's Law. Smith and Botelho were released from prison in Alaska in 1990 after serving time for aggravated sexual assault charges. Immediately after their release, Smith and Botelho also completed their court-ordered rehabilitation programs. But after Megan's Law was enacted in Alaska, the Alaskan Department of Public Safety required them to include their names and addresses in the Alaskan Sex Offender Registry. After the initial registration, they filed a suit in the United States District Court for the District of Alaska on the claim that the Alaskan Megan's Law statute was in violation of the Constitution's *ex post facto clause* of Article 1 and the due process clause of the Fourteenth Amendment. The District court gave a summary judgment for petitioners, and the case was appealed by the state of Alaska to the Ninth Circuit. The Ninth Circuit Court ruled that Alaska's Megan's Law was in violation of the Constitution's *ex post facto clause* and the First Amendment right to privacy. The judges in the Ninth Circuit Court argued that even though the legislatures intended to make Megan's Law a civil regulatory scheme, "the effects of the Act were punitive despite the legislature's intent." The Ninth Circuit's decision was appealed to the U.S. Supreme Court in 2002.

The Supreme Court reversed the Ninth Circuit Court's decision and ruled in a 6-3 decision in 2003 that Alaska's Megan's Law was not in violation of the Constitution's *ex post facto clause*—a clause that forbids retroactive punishment. The Supreme Court was concerned primarily with the question whether the intent of the legislation was to develop a civil regulatory system to address a particular kind of crime, and whether it violated the Constitution's *ex post facto clause*. Having examined primarily the text and the structure of the statute, the Court found that the intent of Alaska's legislatures in enacting Megan's Law was to protect the public from the danger posed by high-risk sex offenders. The protection of the public was the "primary governmental interest." The intent of "Alaska legislature was to create a civil, nonpunitive regime" (Legal Information Institute 2003, p. 9). Even though some of the procedures to implement the registration and notification laws are a part of Alaska's criminal code, the Supreme Court said: "The partial codification of the State's criminal procedure code is not sufficient to support a conclusion that the legislative intent was punitive" (Legal Information Institute, 2003, p. 7).

One of the arguments of the respondents in this case was that the sex offender notification system is a way of public shaming comparable to punishments in colonial days. The Supreme Court argued that in Megan's Law stigma results "not from public display for ridicule and shaming but from the dissemination of accurate information about a criminal record, most of which is already public." The majority opinion added: "Our system does not treat dissemination of truthful information in furtherance of a legitimate governmental objective as punishment. The fact that Alaska posts the information on the Internet does not alter our conclusion." The Court recognized the need and the utility of widespread dissemination of sex offender information for the success of a valid regulatory scheme. The people of Alaska interested in receiving information about sex offenders in their communities are required to search the Alaska Department of Public Safety's website."The Internet makes the document search more efficient, cost effective, and convenient for Alaska citizenry" (Legal Information Institute, p. 12). The U.S. Supreme Court disagreed with the finding of the Ninth Circuit Court that the Alaska's Megan's Law is a retributive measure and it is parallel to probation and supervised release. "This argument has some force, but after due consideration, we reject it." In conclusion, the Court said: "The Act is nonpunitive, and its retroactive application does not violate the *Ex Post Facto Clause*" (Legal Information Institute, 2003, p. 18).

While the key issue in *Smith et al. v. John Doe* of Alaska was about the violation of the Constitution's *ex post facto clause* of Article I, the Connecticut case—*Connecticut Department of Public Safety et al. v. John Doe*— was based on the issue of whether the Connecticut Megan's Law is in violation of the "liberty clause" and the due process clause of the Fourteenth Amendment. A sex offender in Connecticut filed a suit with the United States District Court on the claim that Connecticut's Internet notification of sex offender information deprived him of a liberty interest by describing him as a dangerous sex offender without any hearing. He claimed that the inclusion of his name in the Internet notification system of sex offenders violated the due process clause of the Fourteenth Amendment. The District Court gave a summary judgment in support of the respondent's claim on due process clause. The Court of Appeals of the Second Circuit in 2001 affirmed the lower court's decision. The Court of Appeals reasoned that the state of Connecticut violated the "liberty interest" of the respondent by describing and stigmatizing him as a dangerous sex-offender without a hearing to that end. The Due process clause, the Second Circuit court added, "entitles class members to a hearing to determine whether or not they are particularly likely to be currently dangerous before being labeled as such by their inclusion in public dissemination registry" (Legal Information Institute, 2003, p. 2).

In 2003, the U.S. Supreme Court in a 9-0 decision reversed the Second Circuit Court decision and gave a ruling that the Connecticut Megan's Law was not in violation either of the liberty clause or the due process clause of the Fourteenth Amendment. The Court examined primarily the issue of whether the Connecticut Megan's Law statute was defective from the point of view, not of procedural due process, but of the substantive rule of law. The majority opinion delivered by Chief Justice Rehnquist said that the Second Circuit Court decision must be reversed because "due process does not require the opportunity to prove a fact that is not material to the State's statutory scheme." Connecticut Megan's Law requires that sex offender registry decisions be based on prior convictions and not on the "fact of current dangerousness." About the issue of whether the statute was in violation of the liberty interest of the respondent due to its stigmatizing effects, the Court noted that "mere injury to reputation even if defamatory, does not constitute the deprivation of a liberty interest" (Legal Information Institute, 2003, p. 2).

Through these two major rulings, the Supreme Court has addressed some of the key challenges raised by state sex offender registration and notification laws. There are still many issues related to sex offender residency requirements, mandatory sentencing, and mandatory collection of DNA samples from sex offenders, GPS tracking of sex offenders and other substantive and procedural laws that are still being challenged in state and federal courts. The Iowa Supreme Court, for example, in *State v. Seering* in 2005, ruled that Iowa's sex offender residency restriction laws are not in violation of the due process clause of the Fourteenth Amendment and prohibition against cruel and unusual punishment of the Eighth Amendment. In 2006, the Arizona Supreme Court rejected a defendant's claim (*Arizona v. Berger*) that his 200-year prison sentence for the possession of child pornography was in violation of the Eighth Amendment's prohibition of cruel and unusual punishment.

The states' civil commitment statutes equally have raised many constitutional questions, and they are being challenged in state and federal courts. In

1997, the U.S. Supreme Court, in *Kansas v. Hendricks*, made a ruling on the constitutionality of civil commitment. The Kansas civil commitment statute requires that sexual offenders who are convicted of violent sex crimes or those who committed violent sex crimes but found to be not guilty by reason of insanity are placed, with a unanimous jury trial, in secured confinement after their release from prison. A Kansas man, named Leroy Hendricks, was repeatedly convicted of child molestations and taking indecent liberties with minors since 1957. Before he was to be released from prison in 1994 serving a 10-year prison term for taking indecent liberties with minors, a unanimous jury found him mentally abnormal, and a Kansas court sent him for civil commitment in 1995. Hendricks appealed the lower court decision to the Supreme Court of Kansas on the claim that the Kansas Act is in violation of the constitution's due process clause, double jeopardy, and *ex post facto* clause.

The Supreme Court of Kansas reversed the lower court decision and invalidated Kansas' Sexually Violent Predator Act on the grounds that "the preeminent condition of "mental abnormality" did not satisfy what is perceived to be the 'substantive' due process requirement and that involuntary civil commitment must be predicated on a 'mental illness' finding" (Legal Information Institute, 1997, p. 1). But on appeal, the U.S. Supreme Court reversed the decision of the Kansas Supreme Court and ruled that the Kansas Act was not in violation of the due process clause. The majority opinion noted that the "Act's definition of 'mental abnormality' satisfies 'substantive' due process requirements. An individual's constitutionally protected liberty interest in avoiding physical restraint may be overridden even in civil context." The majority opinion further added: "The Act does not violate the Constitution's double jeopardy prohibition or its ban on *ex post facto* lawmaking. The Act does not establish criminal proceedings, and involuntary confinement is not punishment" (Legal Information Institute, 1997, pp. 1-2). In 2002, the U.S. Supreme Court made another ruling about the constitutional validity of Kansas Sexually Violent Predator Act. The Court in *Kansas v. Crane* extended the definition of the concept of mental abnormality and argued that for the Act to remain within the due process clause, the state must prove that one is suffering not just from mental abnormality but also from an inability to control his or her behavior. There "must be a 'lack- of –control' determination." In recent years, a number of similar cases related to state sex offender registration, notification, and civil commitment statutes have been litigated in state and federal courts. Since these statutes are still evolving, and since Congress and the state legislatures are expected to expand their get-tough approach to sex crimes, the state and federal courts will remain more involved in policy-making for sex crimes in future.

CHAPTER 6

CYBER CRIMES: LAWS AND POLICY DEVELOPMENTS

With the invention of new technology, societies and civilizations at every stage of history reached to a new threshold of power and possibilities for transformations. The invention of fire and the use of iron in ancient times, the invention of cool for energy and the use of wind power for sailing on seas in the early middle ages, the invention of gun powder and the printing press in the late middle ages in the sixteenth century, the invention of electricity and the steam engine in the beginning of industrialization in the nineteenth century—all brought societies and civilizations to a new threshold for transformations. With the birth of the computer and the spread of information revolution, modern post-industrial societies have reached a new threshold for change and transformations. At every stage of societal evolution, technology expanded the means and scope of material production and created new structures and forms of law, government, culture, education, art, literature, and philosophy. The birth of the steam engine and the rise of industrialization brought opportunities for the discovery of new lands, new markets, and new forces of production. With industrialization, came new towns and cities, cultures and creativities, and new forms of law, government, and governance. New technology and industrialization at every stage of societal evolution also brought new deviance, crimes, and criminality.

The major concerns for policy-makers in crime and justice in America in the second half of 20th century were mostly about organized crimes, drug crimes, sex crimes, street gangs, street violence, gun violence, juvenile crimes, and the rise of transnational criminal groups. The arrival of the information age and the expansion of digital revolution from the 1990s, however, brought an entirely unique set of crimes and criminality—described as cyber crimes (Wall, 2007). One of major policy concerns in crime and justice today is the control and containment of cyber crimes. Drug crimes, street gangs, gun violence, and sex crimes cost life, time, and money, but they do not challenge the very core of societal growth, security, and governance as do cyber crimes. The computer and the Internet are at the core of organizing modern post-industrial global information societies. The growth and organizing of almost all aspects of modern societies are centered on the use of computer and the Internet. The criminal use of the computer and the Internet can bring an unprecedented degree of harm and destructions not just in the progress but also in the very continuity and survival of modern post-industrial societies. This chapter will describe the nature and extent of cyber crime in America, the development of federal and state cyber crime laws and statutes, and the judicial response to control and govern the cyber space and cyber criminals.

6.1 Cyber Crime: Nature and Types

Cyber crime includes a variety of activities deliberately performed for the damage and destruction of digital information. The organization, storage, and sharing of information are the most critical functions in today's digital economy, e-governance, and the virtual world of the Internet. Like capital, information is the critical property that needs to be securely stored, efficiently organized, and effectively delivered on demand. The use and organization of information have always been central to societal organizations. The development of global colonial economies, the conduct of transnational war, and the functioning of large empires in the past were dependent on information use and organization. But what is qualitatively different today is that information is stored, organized, and transmitted primarily through the means of digital technology—the computer and the Internet. A new virtual cyber space has emerged, and it is the core of the new information society. Governmental organizations, defense systems, business organizations, agriculture, power supply, water supply, public health, education, communication systems, telecommunications, postal services, shipping, and other vital sectors of the American economy and society are crucially dependent on the use of the computer and the Internet. "Cyber space is their nervous system—the control system of our country. Cyber space is composed of hundreds of thousands of interconnected computers, servers, routers, switches, and fiber optic cables that allow our critical infrastructures to work" (The White House, 2003: vii).

Cyber space is a boundless digitalized virtual territory. As the use of the computer and the Internet expands, both locally and globally, the boundaries of cyber space are becoming increasingly larger and complex. In 1998, Congress made a special law—Government Paperwork Elimination Act of 1998—for the expansion of e-governance in all vital sectors of the American government. The Act mandated all governmental organizations to acquire information technology "for electronic submission, maintenance, or disclosure of information as a substitute for paper and for the use and acceptance of electronic signatures." The Act particularly stated that "electronic records and their related electronic signatures are not to be denied legal effect, validity or enforceability merely because they are in electronic form, and encourages Federal government use of a range of electronic signatures alternatives" (Office of Management and Budget, 2006, p. 1).

The United States Department of Commerce's report (2004), *Nation Online: Entering the Broadband Age,* found that about 61.8 percent of American households used computers in 2003 and 87.6 percent of those households used computers to access the Internet. The report, based on a survey of 57,000 households, observed that in between 2001 and 2003, "the number of households with Internet connections grew by 6.9 million. However, the percentage of households with high-speed Internet or broadband connections more than doubled, increasing from 9.1 to 19.9 percent of all U.S. households, or by 12 million households" (United States Department of Commerce, 2004, p. 5). These trends of growth suggest the emergence of a new broadband age in America. About 31.9 percent of Americans "access the Internet on a regular basis. Ninety percent of these frequent users have Internet access in their homes" (United States Department of Commerce, 2004, p. 8).

As more households acquire computers and broadband Internet connections, more individuals become engaged in online activities of different kinds. The above survey also found that in between 2001 and 2003, Internet users above the age of 15 were online about 88 percent for email and instant messages, 76.5 percent for searching product and service information, 66.5 percent for getting news, weather, and sports information, 52.1 percent for purchasing products and services, 41.6 percent for health services information, 35.7 percent for governmental services information, 27.8 percent for banking online, and 18.7 percent for searching a job. During the same period, the number of Americans engaging in e-commerce grew 8 percent and online banking 10.4 percent. The use of the Internet is equally common among male (59.2 percent) and female (59.2 percent) and rural (57.2 percent) and urban areas (59.2 percent). Use is higher among those who are educated, employed and married with children. In terms of race and ethnicity, the survey found that 65.1 percent of Internet users in 2003 were Whites, 45.6 percent were Blacks, 63.1 percent were Asian Americans and Pacific Islanders, and 37.2 percent were Hispanic Americans (United States Department of Commerce, 2004). The United States Department of Commerce's 2002 report on the growth of cyber economy in America—*A Nation Online: How Americans are Expanding Their Use of the Internet*—found that 143 million of Americans were using the Internet by 2001, and that was an increase of about 26 million users in 13 months. The report estimated that the "rate of growth of Internet use in the United States is currently two million new Internet users per month" (United States Department of Commerce, 2002, p. 1).

E-commerce and e-governance are also rapidly progressing in the countries of the European Union and in Canada, Australia, Japan, China, Russia, India, Malaysia, Taiwan, Hong Kong, Brazil, Argentina, and other economically advanced countries of Asia, Africa, and Latin America. Even in the poorest countries of the world today, Internet users are rapidly growing. These rapid expansions of the use of the computer and the Internet have given birth to a new domain of criminality—cyber crime—and have led to new concerns for the use and security of the cyber space. Cyber crime is the deliberate damage, manipulation, piracy, and obstruction of information stored and available in the cyber space.

The Council of Europe Convention on cyber crime of 2001, which was one of the major and earliest global initiatives for policy-making in cyber crime, developed a seven-fold typology (see Table 31) and defined cyber crime (Articles 2-8) as "Illegal access, Illegal interception, Data Interference, System Interference, Misuse of Devices, Internet forgery, and Internet Fraud" (International Telecommunication Union. 2005, p. 5). Forty-two countries, including the United States, have ratified the Council of Europe Convention on Cyber Crime of 2001. One of the major goals of the Convention was to reach a common definition about the substantive nature of cyber crime and develop a common set of procedural laws for investigating cyber crimes and prosecuting cyber criminals.

The countries that ratified the European Convention of 2001 have their own specific definitions and typologies of cyber crime, but they broadly fall within the seven-fold typology framework suggested by the Convention. The U.S. federal codes on computer intrusions, for example, describe that "knowingly accessing a computer without authorization", knowingly accessing a computer "with the intent to defraud," accessing a nonpublic computer of a federal department or agency intentionally without authorization, knowingly causing "the transmission of a program, information, code or command, and as a result of such conduct, intentionally" causing the damage are punishable cyber crimes.

Two of the basic categories of cyber crime are use of the computer as a target and use of the computer as a tool. Both are defined as substantive cyber crime offenses. In the first category, a cyber crime is committed when a computer system is targeted through unauthorized use and the use of illicit computer programs and software for the damage, destruction, deletion, or suppression of data, or software programs, or its functioning devices. "Illegal access or unauthorized access to data is a basic cyber crime" (International Telecommunication Union, 2005, p. 11). One of the earliest examples of a cyber crime of this kind in the United States is when a Massachusetts juvenile intentionally and without authorization entered into and disabled the computer system of the Worcester Airport operated by NYNEX and kept the Airport cut off from the Federal Aviation Authority (FAA) for hours on March 10, 1997. Another major cyber crime episode of this kind came in 2000 from a Canadian young man described by the FBI as "Mafia boy." Mafia boy unleashed major cyber attacks, described as distributed denial-of-service (DDoS) attacks, on CNN, Yahoo, eBay, Amazon, Dell Computer, and other major websites. The DDoS attacks flooded the victim computer systems with a massive amount of data and email messages that eventually collapsed the websites.

Table 31: Cyber Crime: Nature and Types

Crime Types	Nature of Criminal Activities and Offenses
Illegal Access	Unauthorized access to data; illegal access to computer systems and networks defined as "hacking"; mere illegal access is an offense even though data are not accessed and the content of the data is not understood, deliberate access to a computer system to acquire data by checking passwords, and unauthorized access to observe and download information
Illegal Interception	Electromagnetic emissions to or within a computer system through email or file transfer; monitoring, surveillance, and listening to the content of the transmission of computer data either through direct access to a computer system or through the use of electronic eavesdropping, or tapping devices
Data Interference	Damaging, deletion, deterioration, alteration, and suppression of computer data; damage or deletion of a small amount of data, or a complete database, or computer programs; alteration of data through obscene word or website defacements; and spreading of computer virus—a specific type of malicious code—that replicates itself and invades other programs and computer systems
System Interference	Hindering the functioning of a computer system by inputting, transmitting, damaging, deleting, altering and suppressing computer data, crashing the computer system of critical infrastructures, such as transportation, telecommunications, energy, and defense
Misuse of Devices	Possession, production, sale, and distribution of computer viruses and other malicious programs with the intent to damage, delete, alter, and suppress computer data
Internet Forgery	Unauthorized creation or alteration of stored computer data for fraud and deceptions; assumption of false identity; and identity theft.
Internet Fraud	Manipulation of computer data or a computer system to obtain money or property, or to cause property loss, manipulation of computer data or giving false Internet information to effect an illegal transfer of property

Source: International Telecommunication Union. (2005)

In 2000, another computer science student from the Philippines unleashed a virus, named as "I love You" on the World Wide Web and it brought major damage and disruptions in Asia, Europe and the United States. I love Bug email affected and shut off the computers of the White House, both Houses of Congress, the Pentagon, and the FBI. It also affected the computer systems of the U.K. House of Commons, Danish Parliament, Federal Government of Switzerland, and Dow Jones News Wires of many Asian countries. The DDoS attacks and Net Jam, where a global system of computer network is a target for attacks, constitute high crimes. A group of hackers from Brazil, nicknamed "Crime Boy's" in the same year of 2000, defaced the websites and disrupted the functioning of the computer network systems of NASA's Jet Propulsion Laboratory, U.S. Army's Reserve Officer Training Corps Command, and the U.S. Bureau of Land Management's National Training Center (Verton, 2000).

In the second category, a cyber crime is committed when computers or the World Wide Web and the Internet are used as tools and vehicles to commit such crimes as auction fraud, investment fraud, online banking fraud (phishing), business fraud, check fraud, identity theft, credit card fraud, online gambling, telemarketing schemes, and tax scams. Cyber crime also includes the use of the Internet for the production, possession, sale, and distribution of hate crime materials and materials harmful to minors. Anonymous threat to, harassment of, and abuse of any person, groups or organizations through the Internet or the posting of annoying emails and websites—described as cyberstalking, cyber extortion, and cyber terrorism—are also criminal offenses. In 1994, the United States saw one of the first major cyber crimes of this kind committed by a Los Angeles man in his mid-thirties named Kevin Mitnick. He used the computer system of the University of Southern California, and engaged in a massive computer fraud where he stole 20,000 credit card numbers, and broke into the database of the Department of the Motor Vehicle of the state of California. For his criminal activities, Mitnick used computer systems both as targets and tools. He altered and corrupted system's software and then used them to commit fraud and deception. In 2000, another hacker stole about 28,000 credit card numbers by entering the e-commerce websites in the United States, Canada, United Kingdom, Japan and Thailand. The U.S. Internal Revenue Service regularly deals with a number of tax scams, dubbed as Dirty Dozen, that provide false tax information over the Internet.

Cyber crime is a unique form of crime. It is not a street crime with bloods and bullets, and it is not committed with knives and guns. The weapons of cyber crime are computer commands, codes, and software that are deliberately designed to damage, delete, destroy, and suppress computer data and information. These commands, codes, and software made with malicious intent are described as malware. There are different types of malware made with different software codes aimed to perform different roles and functions. Some of the major types of malware include spyware, adware, Trojan horse, worms, and viruses. Cyber crime is commonly seen as a virus attack. Computer virus is a particular code or a set of commands that are designed to delete and suppress information and damage and destroy the hard disk. A computer virus is not a natural but a man-made virus, but it has some of the same characteristics of a biological virus. After invading into the body of a computer, it can mutate and multiply in millions and thus can damage and destroy both its physiology—the intricate system of internal software connections and functions, and its anatomy—the hard disk. The computer scientists and computer security specialists have discovered different types of computer viruses used in cyber crime—boot sector viruses, companion viruses, email viruses, logic bombs, macro viruses, and cross-site scripting viruses (see Table 32).

Table 32: The Weapons of Cyber Crime:
Some Selected Malicious Software

Software	Malicious Roles and Functions.
Spyware	Spy on emails and Internet information; steal data and information; transfer information from host computers; and monitor and relay information covertly without the knowledge of the owners and users of computers.
Trojan Horse	Erase and delete information from the hard disk; and open a backdoor for computer hackers to steal passwords, email addresses, and other information.
Worm	A program that travels from computer to computer without the help of file in the host computer; can scan the security programs of a host computer; can read the email addresses of a host computer and automatically travel to those addresses and computers.
Virus	Spreads through email attachments; replicate in millions, like a biological virus, in the body of an infected computer system; written in scripting languages for Microsoft programs; capable of infecting millions of computers in the global information network; some of the common forms of viruses are: boot sector viruses, email viruses, companion viruses, logic bombs and time bombs, macro viruses, and cross-site scripting viruses.
Bundling	A program that covertly attach a virus to materials that are legitimately downloaded in a computer.
Keyloging	A program secretly sends all information keyed in a computer automatically to the author; passes information from the host computer without the knowledge of the user.
Zombie	A program that transfers all controls and commands of an infected host computer from the user to the attacker. Zombies are bot-loaded computers that can recognize commands only from the attackers; zombies are placed by sending an executive command code to the attacked computers through email attachments or through a Trojan.

Sources: wikipedia.org/wiki/Computervirus, and McAffe. (2005). McAfee Virtual Criminology Report. McAffe, Inc. CA: Santa Clara

There is a variety of strategies and processes through which the cyber criminals target computers and computer networks for attacks and then use those
host computers as tools for stealing information, fraud, money laundering, and
even to threat the organizations and companies owning those affected computers
for ransom (cyber terrorism). One of the emerging strategies is described as a
bot (short of robot). A bot is a computer that has already been affected by a virus, and it takes commands, most often through Internet chat rooms, only from
the attackers. A new trend is growing among many cyber criminals and in the
market of cyber crime to buy bot networks—a collection of infected computers— and then to systematically retrieve, steal, and sale stolen information.

6.2 Cyber Crime: Characteristics, Offender types, and Prevalence

Cyber crime is fundamentally a different type of crime. The growth and evolution of cyber crime is intimately connected with the rise of information technology, the growth of the cyber space through the world-wide-wave, the expansion
of service economy, and the spread of globalization. It is a crime that centers on
the misuse and abuse of information. It is a crime that centers on the abusive
control, and illegal occupation and dominance of the cyber space. One of the
major characteristics of cyber crime is that it is global and borderless in nature.
Traditional crimes such as homicide, arson, sex crimes, and property crimes are
local and space-bound. In traditional crimes, the offenders are mostly known to
families and communities they live. Cyber crime is elusive in nature, and it may
originate from any unknown place of the world where there is even no law for
defining and prosecuting cyber crime. The Filipino student who spread the "I
love Virus" went unpunished because the Philippines did not have a statute to
prosecute cyber crimes in 2000. The FBI's 2005 Computer Crime Survey found
that computer intrusion attacks in the U.S. in 2005 came from 36 countries.

    The second most important characteristic is that cyber crime is predomi-
nantly economic in nature. Cyber crime began in the 1990s by some isolated
individuals and juveniles, described sometimes as script kiddies or cyber punks,
who were led mostly by a curiosity and a sense of psychological empowerment
to be able to move and control the computer and the Internet. From the beginning of 2000, cyber crime, however, is increasingly becoming an act of "rational
choice" by organized hackers and gangs with planned and deliberate economic
motivations. The script kiddies and cyber punks did not have much knowledge
of the technology, and any sense of criminality. The contemporary hackers and
cyber gangs are more trained and educated in computer technology, and they
have deliberate intent to engage in cyber crime to make economic gains. From
the victim's point of view, cyber crime is largely a form of economic victimization. When the computer networks of banks and business organizations are attacked, or the communication system is halted and disrupted, billions of dollars
are lost in terms of lost time, service deliveries, and business transactions. The
private individuals lose millions of dollars every year because of stolen credit
cards, social security numbers, and numerous forms of online business frauds

and deceptions. The 2005 FBI Computer Crime Survey, based on information from 2,060 private and public sector organizations in four States (Iowa, Nebraska, New York, and Texas), estimated that cyber crime costs about $67.2 billion to U.S. private and public sector organizations every year, or 7.6 million per hour (United States Department of Justice 2005, p. 10).

Another characteristic of cyber crime is that its scope is more invasive, and its ability to cause damage and destruction is enormous. The I Love You virus affected about 40 million computers around the world in 2000. In 2004, the U.S Secret Service, through an investigation described as Operation Firewall, arrested 28 cyber crime gangsters from eight States and six foreign countries (Bulgaria, Belarus, Poland, Sweden, the Netherlands, and Ukraine) on charges of computer fraud and identity theft. The investigation found that the gangsters stolen about 1.7 million credit cards numbers and sold them to different countries (TechWeb News, 2004). In 2005, a jury convicted a California man, a former Program Manager of Silicon Valley-based debt Collection Company, for corrupting information of more than 50,000 debtor accounts. In May 2005, a North Carolina man illegally accessed the American College of Physician database that includes information about 80,000 physicians. In 2005, a San Diego man charged with hacking for illegally entering and damaging the computer system network of the University of Southern California that has a database containing personal information of about 275,000 student applicants from 1997 to 2005 (United States Department of Justice, 2006). In New York, in 2005, law enforcement agencies arrested a large group of drug traffickers who were selling prescription drugs such as Valium, Codeine, and Morphine over the Internet (Office of New York State Attorney General, 2005). These and many other cases point to the very invasive and economically damaging nature of cyber crime (United States Department of Justice, 2006). In a recent IBM survey of 600 healthcares, financial, retail, and manufacturing industries, 57 percent of firms responded that cyber crime was more damaging than conventional crimes. About 74 percent of chief information officers said that cyber attacks originating from inside the industries was a significant risk, and 84 percent "reckon technically sophisticated criminal groups are replacing lone hackers as their principal adversaries" (Leyden, 2006, p. 1).

In terms of offender characteristics, the cyber criminals are mostly male and relatively young, educated, mobile, and technically literate. In 2003, The United States Sentencing Commission made a study of 116 cyber crime cases that received convictions and sentencing in fiscal years 2001 and 2002. The study found that cyber criminals were well educated (66 percent had completed at least some college education), and mostly motivated by economic reasons (48 percent). About 65 percent of offenses originated from the offender's current or former work place. These findings were consistent with those made in a similar study conducted by the United States Sentencing Commission in 1996 (United States Sentencing Commission, 2003).

Systematic studies on the growth and prevalence of cyber crime are still in their infancies. The major federal crime surveys—the Uniform Crime Reports, National Crime Victimization Survey, and the National Incidence-Based Reporting System—have not yet included cyber crime in their list of crime categories for surveys. In 2004, the National Crime Victimization Survey added questions only about identity theft. Some of the reliable data on cyber crime in the U.S. are currently collected by the National Computer Security Survey (NCSS) sponsored by the Bureau of Justice Statistics, Internet Crime Complaint Center (IC3) of the FBI, National Cyber Security Division (NCSD) of the U.S. Department of Homeland Security, United States Sentencing Commission, U.S. Department of Commerce, Federal Trade Commission, CERT (Computer Emergency and Response Team) Coordinating Center of the Software Engineering Institute at the Carnegie Mellon University of Pittsburgh, Computer Security Institute of San Francisco, and many private sector computer software and security industries such as Microsoft, McAfee, and Oracle.

The FBI's Internet Crime Complaint Center (IC3) compiles information on complaints received through the IC3 website and cases referred to law enforcement and regulatory agencies for investigation. The IC3's 2005 Annual Report stated that from January 2005 to December 2005, the IC3 website "received 231,493 complaint submissions. This is an 11.6% increase over 2004 when 207, 449 complaints were received" (Internet Crime Complaint Center, 2005, p. 3). In 2001, IC3 received about 40,000 complaints. In 2005, within a period of four years, the number of complaints increased to 231, 493. In 2001, the IC3 referred about 15,000 cases to law enforcement and regulatory agencies for investigation. In 2005, the number of referred cases jumped to about 95,000.

The reported complaints included both non-fraudulent cases such as computer intrusions, spam, unsolicited emails, and child pornography; and fraudulent cases such as action fraud (62.7 percent), non-delivery (15.7 percent), and credit/debit card fraud (6.8 percent). "The vast majority of cases was fraudulent in nature and involved a financial loss on the part of the complainant. The total dollar loss from all referred cases of fraud was $183.12 million with a median dollar loss of $424.00 per complaint. This is up from $68 million in total reported loses in 2004" (Internet Crime Complaint Center, 2005, p. 3). Among the perpetrators, 75.4 percent were male and half were the residents of seven States (California, New York, Florida, Texas, Illinois, Pennsylvania, and Ohio). California had the highest number of perpetrators in 2005 (15.2 percent) followed by New York (9.9 percent), Florida (8.4 percent), and Texas (6.9 percent). Two of the most common methods of fraudulent contact included email (73.2 percent), and web page (16.5 percent).

In 2001, the Bureau of Justice Statistics, in collaboration with the U.S. Census Bureau, conducted a survey on cyber crime against businesses. Out of 198 business organizations responded, 75 percent said that they were victims of at least one form of cyber attack in 2001. The rate of victimization was higher in companies with more than 1,000 employees. They detected more denial of service attack (52 percent), more virus attack on their computer systems (49.5 percent), and a higher percentage of Internet fraud (70.6 percent), embezzlement (75 percent), and theft of proprietary information (70 percent). Most of the companies (56.5 percent) reported that the attackers were not their employees. The survey found that cyber crime cost 147 companies, out of 198 companies who responded, a total of $61.0 million in 2001. The survey also observed that between 2000 and 2001, cyber crime incidents in the respondent companies increased about 25 percent (Bureau of Justice Statistics, 2004).

A survey conducted by the Federal Trade Commission (2003) found that about 10 million consumers and businesses were victims of identity theft in the preceding 12 months, costing an estimated $48 billion of losses to business, and additional $5 billion to consumers. On the basis of the data collected by the National Crime Victimization Survey in 2004, the Bureau of Justice Statistics compiled a similar report in 2006 on identity theft in the United States. The report found that in 2004, at least one member of 3.6 million U.S. households "had been the victim of identity theft during the previous 6 months. Households headed by persons age 18-24 and those in the highest income bracket ($75,000 or more) were the most likely to experience identity theft" (Bureau of Justice Statistics, 2006, p. 1). The estimated loss reported by the households victimized by identity theft was about $3.2 billion. Identity theft included a number of strategies such as unauthorized use of existing credit cards (48.4 percent), unauthorized use of existing bank accounts (25 percent), and misuse of personal information (15 percent). "The most common type of identity theft was unauthorized use of credit cards, experienced by 1.7 million (1.5 %) households" (Bureau of Justice Statistics, 2006, p. 2).

One of the common types of cyber crime is the spread of fraud and deception through unsolicited commercial emails, described as "spam." In 2003, the Federal Trade Commission conducted a study of 1,000 spams randomly chosen from FTC's three spam databases containing about 11,000 spams. The study examined seven types of spams: investment and business opportunities, adult information, non-delivery of product and services, healthcare products, computer and Internet services, leisure and travel services, and educational benefits and opportunities. The study showed that about 55 percent of the spams were related to business and investment fraud and adult information. About 17 percent of pornographic offers in the spams contained "adult imagery," and over 40 percent of these pornographic spam messages contained false statements in their "From" or "Subject" lines, making it more likely that recipients would open the messages without knowing that pornographic images will appear (Federal Trade Commission, 2003). One of the studies by McAffe on cyber crime and spams (2005) estimated that in 2004, each spammer sent out "as many as 200 million messages a day" (p. 15).

In addition to the federal government, CERT Coordinating Center of the Carnegie Mellon Software Engineering Institute conducts annual studies on the nature and prevalence of cyber crimes. The Center's 2004 study is based on a survey of 500 respondents drawn from the subscribers of the online CSO magazine (a computer security magazine for security executives both in public and private sectors that has more than 80,000 circulation), and from members of the U.S. Secret Service's Electronic Crime Task Force. The analysis of the data showed that 43 percent of "respondents report an increase in e-crime and intrusion versus the previous year and 70% report that at least one e-crime or intrusion was committed against their organization" (CERT Coordinating Center,

2004, p. 6) The respondents said that their organizations experienced different types of cyber crimes and they include virus attacks (77 percent), denial of service attacks (44 percent), unsolicited email (38 percent), unauthorized access by an insider (36 percent), phishing (31 percent), unauthorized access by an outsider (27 percent), fraud (22 percent), and theft of intellectual property (20 percent). According to the respondents "e-crime cost their organizations approximately $666 million in 2003" (CERT Coordinating Center, 2004, p. 6).

The private sector computer and security industries and research organizations also regularly collect cyber crime data. The McAfee's Virtual Criminology report published in 2005 presents a much broader picture of the growth of cyber crime all over the world. The study came up with some significant observations about the new trends of growth in cyber crime. Cyber crime is increasingly becoming an organized crime with the emergence of many transnational cyber gangs who are global, mobile, and technically literate. "The most interesting development may be the ability of these more advanced criminal groups to plan and execute long-term attack strategies" with more advanced software techniques and technologies (McAffe, 2005, p. 10). It is consistent with the recent confirmation by Microsoft that "well organized mobsters have established control on a global billion-dollar crime network using keystroke loggers, IRC bots and rootkits" (Naraine, 2006, p. 1). Since its creation and use of MSRT (Malicious Software Removal tool) in 2005, "Microsoft has removed 16 million instances of malicious software from 5.7 million unique Windows machines. Of the 5.7 million infected Windows machines, about 62 percent was found with a Trojan or bot" (Naraine, 2006, pp. 1-3).

The darkest side of cyber crime is in the realm of online sex and sexual activities. The hidden and dark alleys of the cyber space are rapidly proliferating online cyber sex, cyber prostitution, child pornography, global sex tours, and global trafficking of women and children for sexual slavery and exploitation. The pedophiles and prostitutes today are roaming cyber space in ways unprecedented and unseen in any period of human history. According to a survey, done by the Family PC Magazine, 66 percent of youth ages 12-17 spend 1-5 hours each week surfing the web, and 79 percent spend 1-5 hours emailing (Office of Juvenile Justice and Delinquency Prevention, 2002). About "30 million children use the Internet every year to research homework assignments and learn about the world [in which] they live" (Office of Juvenile Justice and Delinquency Prevention, 2002, p. 1). There are thousands of websites containing adult and child pornographic materials harmful to minors. Millions of youths are also becoming the victims of online child sexual molestation, child pornography, child enticement, child prostitution, and child sex tourism. The FBI's Innocent Images Project—an undertaking that investigates online pedophiles, child enticement, and child pornography—recently noted that between 1996 and 2006, a 2025 percent increase occurred in cases related to online child sexual crimes opened by the Innocent Images Project (Federal Bureau of Investigation, 2006).

Information technology brought unprecedented opportunities for business and economic growth, global expansion of communications, effective governance, and the spread of democracy, equality, and justice for all. But the rise of cyber crime is eroding public trust in information technology's ability to deliver these promises and to help develop a society based on a strong economic foundation and a strong moral fabric. In 2004, the PEW Internet and American Life Project conducted a telephone survey on public attitudes on information technology. In the survey, 29 percent of email users said, "They have reduced their overall use of email because of spam. 63% of email users said that the influx of spam made them less trusting of email in general. 77% of emailers said the flood of spam made the act of being online unpleasant and annoying" (PEW Internet & American Life Project, 2004, p. 1).

6.3 Federal Policy Policy-Making in Cyber Crime

The challenges of cyber crime are economic, social, and moral. Cyber crime can damage and destroy cyber space, steal identities, invade privacies, and corrupt businesses. What is more challenging is that cyber crime can bring massive destruction to critical infrastructures dependent on, but physically outside the boundary of, cyberspace. Vulnerable infrastructures are those such as governmental installations, power plants, electrical lines, oil pipelines, water supply lines, ports, aviation, nuclear power stations, and defense and security installations. Cyber criminals also pose serious threats to the global political system. Cyber criminals, in alliance with other transnational organized criminal groups and global terrorist organizations, may participate in the illegal trade and proliferation of chemical, biological, and nuclear materials and weapons (Sussmann, 1999). The securing of cyber space through the control of cyber crimes has emerged as one of the major crime policy challenges in the United States and in all other industrialized countries of the world. The 2003 White House report on *National Strategy to Secure Cyber Space* recognized that the " primary concern is the threat of organized cyber attacks capable of causing debilitating disruption in our nation's critical infrastructures, economy, or national security" (The White House, 2003, p. 6).

Cyber Crime Policy, 1970-1990

Cyber crime has been in the federal crime policy agenda in America since the late 1970s. The Department of Justice began to mobilize knowledge and experts for developing new laws on cyber crime from the middle of the 1970s. One of the first policy-makers in the U.S. to raise the issue of cyber crime in federal policy-agenda was Senator Abe Ribicoff. As a Chair of the then Senate Government Operations Committee, he commissioned a staff study on computer crime in 1977. "This staff study addressed several problems associated with computer programs, and recommended that legislation should be considered that would prohibit unauthorized use of computer" (Schjolberg, 2004, p. 1). Senator Ribicoff introduced a Bill (S.1776) in Congress in 1977. "This Bill was the first proposal for Federal computer crime legislation in the U.S. that would specifically prohibit misuse of computers" (Schjolberg, 2004, p. 2). Congress did not adopt the Bill, but "this pioneer proposal became the model legislation in state computer crime legislation in the United States and created awareness all around the world" (Schjolberg, 2004, p. 2).

The first U.S. law related to computer crime was made by Congress in 1984 through the enactment of the Computer Fraud and Abuse Act of 1984 (CFAA). The Act for the first time made it a federal crime to have unauthorized access to "federal interest computers" with the deliberate knowledge and intent to obtain federal government information on defense and foreign relations, cause damage and destructions to federal computer systems, prevent the authorized use of federal computers, and engage in password fraud and trafficking. The Act also criminalized unauthorized access and intentional denial-of-service attacks to computers of federal financial institutions such as the Federal Reserve Bank, Federal Home Loan Bank System, the institutions of the Farm Credit System, National Credit Union Administration, branches and agencies of Foreign Banks, and the computers of brokers and dealers registered with the Securities and Exchange Commission. The Act imposed both fines and a prison term of 1-10 years for its violation. A student named Robert Morris of Cornell University was the first person convicted under the 1984 Act for spreading a computer virus. The Act authorized the United States Secret Service as a federal agency to be mainly responsible for computer crime investigation while working in collaboration with the Attorney General, Secretary of the Treasury, and other agencies. The Computer Fraud and Abuse Act of 1984 "played a major role in prohibiting and sanctioning cyber attacks. Congress has continued to amend the CFAA over the last several years to increase its effectiveness as the threat and technology have evolved" (National Research Council, 2003, p. 37).

Another significant computer crime bill that was enacted by Congress in the 1980s was the Electronic Communications Privacy Act of 1986 (ECPA). The federal criminal codes related to Electronic Communications Interception (18 U.S.C 2510) and Electronic Communications and Transactional Record Access (18 U.S.C. 2701) originated from the Electronic Communication Act of 1986. The ECPA was enacted as a result of increasing concerns about the erosion of privacy in the wake of the information revolution. It was essentially an amendment to the Title III of the Omnibus Crime Control and Safe Street Act of 1968. Title III of the 1968 Crime Control Act made it a federal crime to spy on and wire tap telephone conversions. The ECPA extended the wire tapping statute to cover not just telephone conversations but also electronic and computer communications such as email and computer network communication systems. The ECPA also criminalized the wiretapping of cellular and cordless communication devices that used digitalized communication networks. The Act criminalized spying on electronic communications both when they are in transit (Title I) and when they are stored in computer networks (Title II). Title III of the ECPA prohibited the use of trap and trace devices to intercept electronic communications both in transit and stored. Since the ECPA was intended to limit government's intrusion into privacy, and not necessarily to control cyber crimes, the Act remained controversial with respect to achieving a balance between the role of law enforcement and the constitutional right to privacy of the citizens. The USA PATRIOT Act of 2001 has substantially amended the core provisions of the ECPA of 1986.

Cyber Crime Policy, 1990-2000

The information revolution that started with the use of computers, primarily by industries in the 1980s, reached a new stage of expansion with the widespread use of personal computers and the Internet since the 1990s. In 1984, about 8.2 percent of U.S. households had computers. In 2000, U.S. households using computers rose to 56.5 percent. In 1997, about 18.6 percent of U.S. households had Internet connections. In 2000, U.S. households with Internet connections rose to about 41.5 percent. Between 1999 and 2000, within a period of one year, individuals using the Internet from any location increased 47.1 percent in the United States. During the same period, the use of the Internet spread more rapidly in other countries such as Sweden (58.1 percent), Denmark (53.6 percent), the Netherlands (53.3 percent), Finland (51.1percent), and Austria (47.9 percent) (United States Department of Commerce, 2002). This rapid growth in the use of personal computers and the Internet, both locally and globally, led to the rapid growth of computer crimes in the 1990s. The CERT Coordinating Center reported in 2003 that "from 1991 through 1994, there was a 498% increase in the number of computer intrusions, and a 702% rise in the number of sites affected" (United States Department of Justice, 2003, p. 1).

Congress enacted four major cyber crime legislations in the 1990s. These include the National Information Infrastructure (NII) Protection Act of 1996, Child Pornography Prevention Act of 1996 (CPPA), Child Online Protection Act of 1998 (COPA), and Identity Theft and Assumptions Deterrence Act of 1998. From the beginning of the 1990s, a new sense was dawning in the minds of the policy-makers that computer crime needs to be addressed not just in the context of the use and abuse of the new technology but also in the context of the evolving nature of the information revolution. A new concept of national information infrastructure, commonly known as cyber space or the information super-highway, thus began to shape policy-making in cyber crime from the early 1990s. In the United States, Vice-President Al-Gore during the Clinton administration aggressively pushed forward this vision of the emerging world of information super-highway (United States Department of Justice, 1999). The National Information Infrastructure Protection Act of 1996 was enacted on the basis of this emerging perspective of information super-highway or cyber space. It is a realm of both physical and virtual realities. Physically, it is a highly interconnected system of computers, fiber optic cables, satellite connections, wireless technologies and audio and video linkages (Congressional Research Service, 2000). Virtually, the national and global information infrastructure is an unseen, borderless, and continuously moving and evolving information system. This virtual world is the world of cyber space. Cyber crimes are targeted both at the physical and virtual realms of the information infrastructure. The NII Protection

Act of 1996 was enacted to have more controls on cyber crimes committed on both domains of information infrastructure.

The NII Protection Act made a series of amendments to the Computer Fraud and Abuse of Act of 1984 (CFAA). The CFAA, for example, criminalized the trespassing of "federal interest computer." The NII Protection Act of 1996 changed the concept of "federal interest computer and inserted a new concept of "protected computers." The Act criminalized the trespassing of all "protected computers" that include computers used in interstate or foreign commerce or communications; computers used in running critical physical infrastructures such as power lines, defense installations, and communication systems; and computers used by both governmental and non-governmental agencies. This amendment broadened federal power to prosecute cyber crime of all kinds and in all places. The NII Protection Act criminalized intrusions into "government and financial institution computers, even if they are not used in interstate communication" (United States Department of Justice, 1996, p. 14). The NII Protection Act made stealing of classified information related to national defense and foreign relations via computers and the Internet a high crime punishable by life imprisonment. The act imposed "harshest penalties for those who obtain classified information that could be used to injure the United States or assist a foreign state" (United States Department of Justice, 1996, p. 11).

Another new provision of the NII Act was related to the notion of "obtaining information." According to the CFAA of 1984, "obtaining information" meant the physical removal of data from its original location in a computer or a computer network system. The NII Act amended this definition of obtaining information, and criminalized even the mere observation of data in protected computers. What this means is that the 1996 Act made a new law to treat an intangible piece of information as valuable as a tangible piece. The new law "would ensure that the theft of intangible information by the unauthorized use of a computer is prohibited in the same way theft and physical items are protected" (United States Department of Justice, 1996, p. 11).The offense, under the new law, "is the abuse of a computer to obtain information" (United States Department of Justice, 1996, p. 11). The law made obtaining information of high value a felony offense. "The crime becomes a felony if the offense was committed for the purpose of commercial advantage of private financial gain" (United States Department of Justice, 1996, p. 11). The 1996 Act asked for more precise definitions of the notion of "intent" behind unauthorized access to computer data, damage to a computer system, denial of service attacks, spreading computer viruses, and other forms of abuse to the computer and Internet. The Act defined intentional, unauthorized, and reckless damage and destruction of data and programs by both inside and outside users, as felony crimes. "In such cases, it is the intentional act of trespass that makes the conduct criminal" (United States Department of Justice, 1996, p. 15).

The NII Act broadened the definition of "damage" caused by cyber crimes. According to the CFAA of 1984, financial loss was the main criteria to estimate intrusive damage. The NII Act made provisions to define damage both in terms of tangible loss and intangible harms caused by computer crimes. Intangible harms may include physical injury, loss of time, loss of jobs, impact on medical treatment, and impact on public safety. "Thus, the definition of 'damage' is amended to be sufficiently broad to encompass the types of harm against which people should be protected" (United States Department of Justice, 1996, p.16). The Act introduced a civil penalty provision that now makes it possible to bring a civil suit against a cyber criminal to obtain compensatory damages, injunctive relief, or other equitable relief" (United States Department of Justice, 1996, p. 16).

Another important aspect of the NII Protection Act of 1996 is that it criminalized what is now known as cyber extortion or cyber terrorism. The Act provided law enforcement the power to prosecute even those who threaten to commit cyber crimes and computer intrusions. "This covers any interstate or international transmission of threats against computers, computer networks, and their data and programs whether the threats are received by email, telephone call, electronic mail, or through a computerized messaging service" (United States Department of Justice, 1996, p. 17). Cyber threats may include denial of service attacks, data corruption, data encryption, program distortions, and denial of access to authorized users. The NII Act brought a major organizational change in the federal role for combating cyber crime. The CFAA Act of 1984 made the U.S. Secret Service responsible for investigating cyber crimes. Under the NII Act, cyber crime investigation became a major responsibility of the Federal Bureau of Investigation.

The second major enactment made by the Congress related to cyber crime in the 1990s was the Identity Theft Assumption Deterrence Act of 1998. Identity theft is one of the major and fastest growing forms of cyber crime. Since the beginning of the expansion of the Internet revolution in the middle of the 1990s, identity theft has been rapidly growing with participation from both domestic and international groups of cyber criminals. As a form of cyber crime, identity theft is the use of computers and the Internet for stealing personal information contained in such documents as social security number, credit cards, bank accounts, and health records. Every year, Americans are losing millions of dollars for being victims of identity theft, and it has become a major threat to the effective functioning of e-governance and e-commerce.

One of the major innovations of the Identity Theft and Assumption Deterrence Act of 1988 was that it broadened the boundary of the definition of identity theft in the context of the evolving nature of the national information infrastructure. Identity theft in the form of stealing personal documents and their unauthorized use has been a criminal act long before the computer and the Internet revolution. The Act of 1998 amended the concept of "identity document" and replaced it with the concept of the "means of identification." Under the new law, identity theft does not need to include the stealing of actual identity documents such as credit cards or social security cards. Under the new law a person commits a federal crime if he or she steals, through the use of computers and the Internet, the identity information of an individual or a group of individuals. Unauthorized access, possession, use, and transfer of identity information are now federal criminal acts that may or may not involve the stealing or the possessing of any tangible identity documents. The Act of 1998, therefore, defines identity theft as to "knowingly transfer or use, without lawful authority, a means of identification of another person with the intent to commit, or to aid or abet, any unlawful activity that constitutes a violation of Federal Law, or that constitutes a felony under any applicable State or local law." The knowing production, transfer, sale, and distribution of any "document-making implement" or computer programs that can facilitate unauthorized access to the means of identification also fall within the definition of federal identity theft. One of the deterrent issues addressed by this new law is the behavior of identity take-over and assumption. Law-makers were greatly concerned that with the expansion of the information revolution, the behavior of identity take-over and assumption would greatly increase, and that, in turn, would greatly jeopardize the notion of privacy and an individual's reputation and credit rating. The law made provisions to take into account two kinds of harm in prosecuting identity theft: harm to reputation and inconvenience (United States Sentencing Commission, 1999, p. 4).

The Identity Theft and Assumption Deterrence Act of 1988 broadened the definition of a victim of identity theft. Under the old statutes on identity theft, an individual whose means of identification were stolen was generally not recognized as a victim. Victims were generally considered to be the organizations or financial institutions that suffered the economic loss because of identity fraud. Under the new law, an individual whose means of identification are stolen and who suffers economic loss, reputation damage, and inconvenience is a victim of identity theft. The United States Sentencing Commission, under a mandate from Congress, produced revised guidelines for sentencing identity theft offenses. The new guidelines treated all kinds of identity theft—from stealing credit cards to false identity assumption—in the same way, and increased "penalty levels for virtually every offense in which the misuse of an identification means is a part of the offense conduct" (United States Sentencing Commission, 1999, p. 6). Most of the provisions of the two other cyber crime enactments made by Congress in the 1990s—the Child Pornography Protection Act of 1996 (CPPA) and the Children Online Protection Act of 1998 (COPA)—were declared unconstitutional by the U.S. Supreme Court, and hence, those enactments remained mostly inactive.

Cyber Crime Policy, 2000-2006

From the beginning of the year 2000, the control and containment of cyber crime has remained one of the major federal policy concerns (Congressional Research Service, 2005). As the boundary of cyber space began to grow rapidly through the expansion of broadband Internet connections from the year 2000, cyber crime of different kinds also began to escalate from that time. "The proportion of U.S. households with computers reached 61.8 percent in 2003, and 87.6 percent of those households used their computers to access the Internet. As a result, 54.6 percent of U.S. households had Internet connections" (United States Department of Commerce, 2004, p. 5). Between 2001 and 2003, Internet connections through cable modem increased 90.9 percent and through DSL

181.8 percent (United States Department of Commerce, 2004, p. 6). With the growth of broadband Internet connections, e-commerce rapidly expanded. The U.S. Census Bureau estimated that retail e-commerce sales in the fourth quarter of 2004 were $938.5 billion (Congressional Research Service, 2005).

A report on National and State Trends in Fraud and Identity Theft published by the Federal Trade Commission (2005) noted that the "percentage of complaints about 'Electronic Fund Transfer' related identity theft more than doubled between 2002 and 2004" (Federal Trade Commission, 2005, p. 3) This was followed by rapid increases in Internet auction fraud, catalog sales fraud, foreign money laundering fraud, and lottery fraud. Between 2002 and 2004, Internet services and computer complaints increased 6 percent (from 25,705 complaints received in 2002 to 37,094 complaints received in 2004). The FBI's Internet Crime Complaint Center (IC3) noted that just in one year from 2004 to 2005, there was an 11.6 percent increase in overall cyber crime complaints received by the Center (from 207,449 complaints received in 2004 to 231,493 complaints received in 2005). The U.S. Department of Treasury recently noted "that cyber crime has now outgrown illegal drug sales in annual proceeds, netting an estimated $105 billion in 2004" (Cable News Network, 2005, p. 1).

Between 2000 and 2006, Congress has enacted six major cyber crime legislations. These include the Internet False Identification Prevention Act of 2000, Computer Crime Enforcement Act of 2000, Cyber Security Research and Development Act of 2002, Cyber Security Enhancement Act of 2002, CAN-Spam Act of 2003, and Identity Theft and Penalty Enhancement Act of 2004. Laws against cyber crime were also enacted by Congress through a number of other legislations such as the USA PATRIOT Act of 2001, the 21st Century Department of Justice Appropriation Reauthorization Act of 2002, E-Government Act of 2002, Federal Information Management Act of 2002, PROTECT Act of 2003, Fair and Accurate Credit Transactions Act of 2003, Intelligence Reform and Terrorism Protection Act of 2004, and Violence against Women and Department of Justice Reauthorization Act of 2005.

From 2000, particularly after the event of September 11, 2001, cyber crime began to be addressed by policy-makers broadly in the context of national security and the protection of critical infrastructures. The USA PATRIOT Act of 2001 amended the Computer Fraud and Abuse of Act of 1984 and the Electronic Communications Act of 1986, and it provided more authority to law enforcement to investigate cyber crimes (Congressional Research Service, 2002). The law "modifies the definition of 'pen registers' and 'trap and trace devices' to include devices that monitor addressing and routing information for Internet communications" (Congressional Research Service, 2005, p. 6). The new law made it mandatory for Internet service providers to disclose stored computer communications and IP addresses to law enforcement if they are related to issues of protecting national security and critical infrastructures or to death and personal injuries. The Act also required the Internet service providers to disclose the means and sources of payments used by Internet customers including numbers of credit cards and bank accounts (United States Department of Justice, 2006). The Act made a new provision that it is not just only the act of damaging a computer that is to be defined as a cyber crime. The "intention" of causing damage to protected computers is also a federal crime. "Section 814 of the Act restructures the statute to make it clear that an individual need only intend to damage the computer or the information on it, and not specific dollar amount of loss or other special harm" (United States Department of Justice, 2006, p. 8). The PATRIOT Act defined also the damage or the intention to damage computers of foreign countries that have an impact on interstate and foreign commerce as a federal crime. "Section 814 of the Act amends the definition of 'protected computers' to make clear that this term includes computers outside the United States so long as they effect 'interstate or foreign commerce or communication of the United States'... the United States can now use speedier domestic procedures to join international hacker investigation" (United States Department of Justice, 2006, p. 9). The Act increased penalties for the crime of damaging protected computers from a maximum of 10 years to maximum of 20 years in prison.

A much broader approach by Congress to control cyber crime came through the Cyber Security Enhancement Act of 2002. This landmark legislation was enacted as part (section 225) of the Homeland Security Act of 2002. One of the major provisions of the Act was that it authorized the Attorney General and allocated $125 million for the fiscal year of 2003 to establish a National Infrastructure Protection Center (NIPC). The main objective was to create a national coordinating agency for cyber threat assessments, and to investigate and prosecute criminals of cyber crimes, particularly those related to critical infrastructures. Secondly, the Act made a provision to create an Office of Science and Technology (OST) within the Office of Justice Programs of the Department of Justice. OST was created to provide technical assistance to federal, state, and local law enforcement agencies on emerging law enforcement technologies including computer forensic and correction technologies. Third, the Act required state and local law enforcement agencies to share cyber crime information with those of the federal government.

The Cyber Crime Security Enhancement Act of 2002 is particularly significant because it made a series of provisions for enhanced penalties for cyber crime. The Act authorized the United States Sentencing Commission to prepare new sentencing guidelines for computer crimes. In developing the guidelines, the Commission was instructed to take into account a number of factors such as the seriousness of cyber crime, the level of sophistication and planning involved in committing the offense, actual and potential loss resulting from the offense, commercial or economic motivations, malicious intent, harms caused to the privacy rights of individuals, harms done to critical infrastructures, the intent of harm to critical infrastructures, and threats posed to national security, public health, and public security in general. In 2003, the United States Sentencing Commission submitted a report to Congress on the revised sentencing guidelines. The new guidelines imposed expanded and upward sentencing for offenses that resulted in death and brought debilitating impact on critical infrastructures. Expanded sentencing was also imposed for extortion and cyber terrorism (United States Sentencing Commission, 2003).

In 2003, Congress enacted the CAN-SPAM Act of 2003 (Controlling the Assault on Non-Solicited Pornography and Marketing Act of 2003) in the context of the rising problem of a large volume of unsolicited emails. The CAN-SPAM Act was designed to create a set of national standards for commercial emails. The Act made it a federal crime to send commercial emails without a domain name, an opt-out mechanism, a valid subject line, header information, routing information, valid physical address of the mailer, and a label if the content includes explicit adult sexual information. The Act criminalized the unauthorized use of both federal and non-federal computers for commercial emails, deceptive emails, abusive emails, predatory emails, or emails with false identity assumption that impact on interstate or foreign commerce. The Federal Trade Commission was made responsible to develop guidelines, implement, and review the impacts of the Act, and the United States Sentencing Commission was instructed to develop appropriate sentencing guidelines for its violations.

In 2004, Congress passed the Identity Theft and Penalty Enhancement Act of 2004. The Act made a new offense category of aggravated identity theft and made new provisions for enhanced penalties. Under the new Act an aggravated identity theft occurs "when a person knowingly transfers, possesses, or uses, without lawful authority, a means of identification of another person" during the commission of any other felonies. The Act imposed a mandatory sentencing of two years in prison for aggravated identity theft in addition to sentencing for the commission of other felonies. The term of imprisonment is increased to five years for aggravated identity theft related to certain terrorism offenses (Congressional Research Service, 2005). The United States Sentencing Commission was authorized to develop appropriate sentencing guidelines for aggravated identity theft offenses.

In 2006, President Bush signed a new legislation—the Violence against Women and the Department of Justice Reauthorization Act of 2005. Section 113 of Title I of the Act made a new law against cyberstalking—a harassment of a person through the means of the Internet. It includes such activities as denial-of-service-attack, identity assumption, and construction of websites targeting the victim, posting of false profiles of a victim on the web, direct email threats, and the posting of a sexual image of a victim on the web. The growth of cyberstalking is one of the major cyber crime challenges for law enforcement. The cyber stalking law, passed as a part of the Violence against Women and the Department of Justice Reauthorization Act of 2005, amended the Communications Act of 1934 and made cyberstalking a federal crime.

Cyber Crime: The Presidential Initiatives

The various cyber crime legislations passed by Congress during the last fifteen years have created an array of cyber crime laws and statutes. Along with Congress, the Office of the President and various executive agencies of the federal government have also taken a number of cyber crime policy initiatives. Before the 1990s, there was hardly any institutional framework within the federal government for policy-making in cyber crime. Both President Clinton and President

G. W. Bush recognized the serious nature of cyber crime and the need to control its growth and escalation. Congress passed the National Information Infrastructure (NII) Protection act in 1996 as a result of the active involvement of President Clinton and Vice-President Al-Gore. "In 1997 and 1998, the NII policy debate was set by the Clinton administration, particularly by Vice-President Gore" (Congressional Research Service, 2000, p. 2). In 1998, in a Presidential Decision Directive (PDD 63), President Clinton outlined the guidelines of a national policy to protect America's critical infrastructures and to control cyber terrorism and cyber crime. In his Directive, he said: "I intend that the United States will take all necessary measures to swiftly eliminate any significant vulnerability to both physical and cyber attacks on our critical Infrastructures, including especially our cyber systems" (The White House, 1998, p. 1). PDD 63 created the Critical Infrastructure Assurance Office within the Department of Commerce, a National Infrastructure Protection Center (NIPC) within the FBI, and a national Infrastructure Assurance Council for public and private collaborations to fight the cyber crime. Under the PDD 63, National Infrastructure Protection and Computer Intrusion Centers (NIPCI) were also established in all FBI's field offices. In response to PDD 63, the White House announced its National Plan for Information System Protection in January 2000. "The national plan provided a vision and framework for the federal government to prevent, detect, respond to, and protect the nation's critical cyber-based infrastructure from attack and reduce existing vulnerabilities" (United States General Accounting Office, 2002, p.11). Some of the other cyber crime control initiatives taken by the Clinton administration included the creation of the CERT Coordinating Center at the Carnegie-Mellon University in Pittsburgh in 1998, the creation of cyber corps program in 1999, and the creation of an Internet Fraud Complaint Center within the FBI in collaboration with the National White Collar Crime Center in 2000 (renamed as Internet Crime Complaint Center—IC3 in 2003).

Cyber security remained at the top of policy agenda also for President Bush. Many new cyber crime policy initiatives expanded during the Bush administration. President Bush, through a Presidential Executive Order (Number 13231), in 2001 created a new office—he Critical Infrastructure Protection Board—to coordinate all federal cyber security programs and to advise the President on critical cyber security issues. The Board was given the task of recommending policies and coordinating programs related to cyber security. The Executive Order "also established 10 standing committees to support the board's work on a wide range of critical information infrastructure efforts" (United States General Accounting Office, 2002, p. 11). Under Executive Order 13231, a National Infrastructure Advisory Council (NIAC) for advising the President on public and private sector innovations in cyber security was also created (White House, 2001). In 2003, through another Executive Order (Number 13286), President Bush amended Executive Order 13231 and renamed his initiative "Critical Infrastructure Protection in the Information Age" (Federal Register, 2003).

The high priority given by the Bush administration in policy-making for cyber security is evidenced by the publication of a series of major studies and national policy directives on cyber security in recent years. Some of the major studies included the report on *National Strategy for Homeland Security* published in 2002, General Accounting Office's (GAO) report on *Critical Infrastructure Protection* published in 2002, the White House report on *The National Strategy for the Physical Protection of Critical Infrastructures* published in 2003, the White House report on *The National Strategy to Secure Cyberspace* published in 2003, the President's Information Technology Advisory Committee (PITAC) report on *Cyber Security: A Crisis of Prioritization* published in 2005, and the President's National Science and Technology Council report on *Federal Plan For Cyber Security and Information Assurance Research and Development* published in 2006.

An Office of Homeland Security was created within the White House in October 2000—a month after the attack of September 11, 2001. The White House presented the *Report on National Strategy for Homeland Security* in July 2002. In November 2002, President Bush signed a new Bill—Homeland Security Act of 2000—and established a new federal agency—Department of Homeland Security. The Department of Homeland Security is the lead federal agency to protect the nation's critical infrastructures from physical, chemical, biological, nuclear, and cyber attacks from home and abroad (United States Department of Homeland Security, 2003). As the report on *National Strategy for Homeland Security* noted: "Terrorists continue to employ conventional means of attack, while at the same time gaining expertise in less traditional means, such as cyber attacks. Our society presents an almost infinite array of potential targets that can be attacked through a variety of methods" (The White House, 2002, p. vii). In 2003, the White House came up with a national policy framework—*The National Strategy to Secure Cyber Space* —for the Department of Homeland Security and other federal agencies to remain focused on the possibilities and seriousness of catastrophic cyber attacks on the nation's critical infrastructures.

The National Security to Secure Cyber Space made cyber security a national priority, and identified it as an integral component of achieving homeland security. "This *National Strategy to Secure Cyber Space* is a part of our overall effort to protect the Nation" (The White House, 2003, p.vii). Its purpose "is to engage and empower Americans to secure the portions of cyber space that they own, operate, control, or with which they interact" (The White House, 2003, p. vii). The report included five areas of policy interventions: 1) the creation of a National Cyber Security Response Team through public and private collaborations; 2) creation of a National Cyberspace Security Threat and Vulnerability Reduction Program; 3) development of a National Cyberspace Security Awareness and Training Program; 4) Securing the Government's Cyberspace; and 5) National Security and International Cyberspace Security Cooperation (The White House, 2003). The Department of Homeland Security was entrusted with the task and responsibilities of implementing these policy guidelines in cooperation with other federal agencies and the private sector. Homeland Security was made the "primary federal point-of-contact for state and local governments, the private sector, and the American people on issues related to cyber security" (The White House, 2003, p. 54). The PITAC Report of 2005 and the President's National Science and Technology Council Report of 2006 equally voiced the same concern that cyber attack is a major threat to the nation's critical infrastructures, and they asked the federal government to invest more on cyber security research and technology (Congressional Research Service, 2002).

Cyber Crime Initiatives: The Federal Agencies

The federal cyber crime policy regime is a complex totality of various legislations enacted by Congress, and the Presidential Directives, Executive Orders, and Advisory Panels related to cyber crime and cyber security. It also includes the cyber security programs and organizational structures created within different federal departments and agencies. In response to federal enactments and related Presidential Directives and Executive Orders, almost all federal departments and agencies have created cyber security programs. The Department of Homeland Security, FBI, Department of Defense, and the Federal Trade Commission more directly approach the issues of cyber crime. Within the Department of Homeland Security, there is a National Cyber Security Division (NCSD), created in 2003, that is primarily responsible for implementing the missions of the President's 2003 National Strategy to Secure Cyberspace. The NCSD has recently established a number of programs in collaboration with other federal agencies, state and local governments, and private sector agencies such as the United States Computer Emergency Readiness Team (US-CERT), National Cyber Response Coordination Group, Center for Academic Excellence in Information Assurance Education, Chief Information Security Officers Forum, National Cyber Alert System, and CyberCop Portal. The US-CERT is particularly an important program for national cyber security. The NCSD created the US-CERT in 2003 to be responsible for the analysis of U.S. cyber vulnerabilities, dissemination of cyber threats warning information, and coordination of cyber incidence response activities.

Within the FBI, the important cyber security programs include the creation of the Internet Crime Compliant Center (IC3), InfraGard Program, National Innocent Images Initiative, Regional Computer Forensic Laboratory Initiative, and Anti-Piracy and Intellectual Property Rights Investigation Program. The IC3 is presently the main source of federal data on cyber crime. "For law enforcement and the regulatory agencies at the federal, state, and international level, IC3 provides a central referral mechanism or complaints involving Internet related crimes" (Federal Bureau of Investigation, 2006, p. 1). From 2001, the IC3 has produced five major survey studies on the nature, prevalence, and trends of cyber crime in the United States.

The FBI's Innocent Images—an online child pornography investigation program—was created in 1995, and presently 28 of FBI's 56 field offices have innocent images operations. The FBI's Innocent Images National Initiative Program found that between 1995 and 2005, there was a 2026 percent increase in cases opened by the Innocent Images Program, 856 percent increase in indictments, 2325 percent increase in arrests, and 1312 percent increase in convictions related to online child pornography (Federal Bureau of Investigation, 2003;

2006). The FBI's InfraGard Program, initiated in 1996, is a nationwide secret surveillance and investigation of online hackers and compute crimes. The FBI launched the Regional Computer Forensic Laboratory (RCFL) initiative in 1999 to develop the technical competence for investigating digital evidence by federal, state, and local law enforcement agencies. The RCFL Initiative in 2006 offered services to 3,500 law enforcement agencies in 13 States. "Each RCFL is equipped with a modern computer classroom where they train law enforcement personnel regarding handling sensitive electronic equipment that becomes evidence, computer investigation techniques, and computer forensics" (Schmitknecht, 2004, p. 180). The FBI's CART (Computer Analysis Response Team) Program that uses the Linux-based Software is an integral part of the RCFL Initiative. Since its inception, the RCFL Initiative has considerably expanded. As of 2003, there were about 200 FBI computer forensic examiners in all 56 FBI's filed offices.

Another major source of federal data on cyber crime, particularly those related to consumer fraud and identity theft, is the Consumer Sentinel Program operated by the Federal Trade Commission. This online program created in 1997, "provides hundreds of law enforcement agencies immediate access to Internet cons, telemarketing scams and other consumer fraud related complaints. Numerous public and private organizations contribute data to Sentinel" (Federal Trade Commission, 2004, p. 1). More than 90 federal and 1,000 state and local law agencies of the United States and also of Canada, Australia, and other countries have access to Sentinel data (Federal Trade Commission, 2004). In 1999, The Federal Trade Commission also established a Toll Free Hotline for reporting consumer fraud and identity theft. Because of this online reporting program, the Federal Trade Commission is now a major federal clearinghouse for information on identity theft and consumer fraud.

Within the Department of Defense, the Cyber Crime Center, established in 2001, is the major organization for research and training on cyber security. The Center, described as DC3, includes a Defense Cyber Crime Institute, Defense Computer Forensics Laboratory, and a Defense Cyber Investigations Training Academy. "DC3 was created as a DOD center of excellence to efficiently organize, equip, train, and employ scare resources to more effectively address the proliferation of computer crimes affecting the DOD" (United States Department of Defense, 2004, p. 1).

Cyber Crime and the U.S. Global Initiatives

Cyber space is a boundless and borderless invisible territory on which no single nation has the sovereign power. It belongs to all the nations of the world. Cyber crimes committed within a nation are investigated by its law enforcement and are defined and punished by its cyber crime laws and statutes. But cyber crimes are also transnational in nature. If a student from Ukraine hacks a computer system of the Citibank in New York, he or she is committing a transnational cyber crime. If an American hacker joins a Canadian cyber gang, and they launch a denial-service-attack to a computer system in Europe, their crimes are transnational. This transnational nature of cyber crimes poses a serious challenge to national law enforcements. During the last decade, there has emerged a consensus among the political and business leaders of the world nations that the control of cyber crime needs transnational cooperation, the development of a unified legal framework to define and investigate cyber crime, and specified punishment for transnational cyber criminals. Many international organizations such as the United Nations General Assembly, the United Nations Crime Congress, World Summit on the Information Society, Group of G-8, Organization of American States (OAS), Asia-Pacific Economic Cooperation (APEC), and Organization for Economic Cooperation and Development (OECD) in recent years have taken initiatives to develop a common international legal framework for defining, investigating, and prosecuting transnational cyber criminals.

The United States has actively participated in most of the international conventions on cyber crime. The U.S. Senate has ratified the Council of Europe Convention on Cyber Crime in 2006. The Convention has entered into force for the United States from January 2007 (United States Department of State, 2006). As of 2006, 43 countries including the United States have adopted the legal framework of the European Convention on Cyber Crime (Bureau of International Information Programs, 2006).

6.4 Cyber Crime: State Laws and Policy-Making

In addition to federal laws and initiatives, there has recently evolved also a large number of state statutes and programs for the control of cyber crime. Policy-making to control cyber crime has become a major concern for state policy-makers in recent years partly because of the last two decades of federal efforts in this area, and partly because of the rapid escalation of cyber crime and increased vulnerability of the state's critical infrastructures. In its 2006 Annual Report, the Federal Trade Commission noted that it received 674,354 computer crime complaints from the states between January 1 and December 31, 2006. Out of all complaints from the states, 36 percent were related to identity theft. Other top complaints are related to shop-at-home catalog sales, prizes, sweepstakes and lotteries, Internet services and computer complaints, and Internet auctions. The report shows that identity theft complaints per 100,000 population in 2006 was highest in Arizona, Nevada, California, Colorado, Florida, Georgia, New York, Texas, and Washington. The analysis of the report also shows that Internet and computer intrusion related complaints were more from the states that are urban and that have more people using the Internet such as California, Maryland, New Jersey, New York, and Virginia. The states with more diverse populations and new immigrants reported more computer fraud complaints (see Table 33).

As one of the first steps for policy-making on cyber crimes, almost all the states in recent years have established separate units and organizations within their respective criminal justice agencies. The State of Florida, for example, created the Florida Computer Crime Center (FC3) within the Florida Department of Law Enforcement in 1988. The Nevada Advisory Board for Technological Crime was created in 1999. The State of New York established the Office of Cyber Security and Critical Infrastructure Coordination (CSCIC) in 2002. The state of South Carolina created a Computer Crime Center within the Law Enforcement Division in 2002. The Office of the Illinois Attorney General has five different organizational units responsible for cyber crime investigation and prosecution: Internet Criminal Activity Unit, High-Tech Crimes Investigation Unit, Illinois Computer Crimes Institute, Regional Computer Crimes Enforcement Groups, and Illinois Internet Child Exploitation Task Force. The Office of the Attorney General of New Jersey has a separate Cyber Crime Bureau composed of a Cyber Crimes Unit and a High-Technology Crimes and Investigations Unit. New Jersey has also set up a Commission of High Technology Crime Investigation. In Arizona, the Office of the State Attorney General has a separate Technology Crime Division for investigating and prosecuting cyber crimes. There are similar specialized units for cyber crimes with both statutory and advisory authorities in other states.

Table 33: Cyber Crime Profiles of Some Selected States, 2006

States	ID Theft Complaints	Fraud Complaints	Internet/ Computer	Rank in ID Theft
Arizona	9,113	9,222	952 (10%)	Ist
California	41,396	49,070	5,324 (11%)	3rd
Colorado	4,395	7,657	723 (9%)	6th
Florida	17,780	25,902	2,601 (10%	5th
Illinois	10,080	13,908	1,354 (10%)	12th
Georgia	8,084	11,914	1,171 (10%	7th
Maryland	4,656	8,653	998 (12%)	11th
Michigan	6,784	11,665	1,164 (10%)	16th
Nevada	2,994	4,222	397 (9%)	2nd
New Jersey	6,394	11,284	1,320 (12%)	14th
New Mexico	1,621	2,406	222 (9%)	10th
New York	16,452	21,129	2,157 (11%)	8th
North Carolina	5,748	10,300	998 (10%)	20th
Oregon	2,815	5,583	564 (9%)	13th
Texas	26,006	25,425	2,328 (9%)	4th
Virginia	5,137	12,039	1,390 (12%)	15th
Washington	5,336	10,451	1,067 (10%)	9th

Source: Federal Trade Commission: Consumer Fraud and Identity Theft Complaint Data, 2006 Annual Report

Since cyber crime investigation and prosecution need new technical expertise for law enforcement and since there is a great need for education of the public about the rapid escalation of cyber crime, separate cyber crime units have been created in recent years also in many cities and local governments. Some of the examples of this effort are the High Technology Computer Crime Task Force (HTCCT) of Akron in Ohio, Internet Crimes Against Children Task Force of San Francisco, Phoenix Internet Crimes Against Children Task Force, High

Technology Analysis and Litigation Team of Los Angeles, Internet Crimes Against Children Task Force of Chicago, Internet Crimes Against Children Task Force of the Police Department of Boston, Tulsa Police Cyber Crime Unit of Oklahoma, Los Vegas Cyber Crime Task Force, and Austin Police High-Tech Crime Unit and Dallas Police Computer Crimes Squad of Texas.

There is now indeed growing an expanding network of federal, state, and local law enforcement organizations and policy programs dedicated to investigating and prosecuting cyber crimes. These organizations closely work particularly with the U.S. Homeland Security's Multi-State Information Sharing and Analysis Program for Cyber Security, the Electronic Crime Prevention Program of the National Institute of Justice, and the National White Collar Crime Center. One of the major goals of these national programs is the strengthening of the capacities of state and local governments to fight the cyber crime. The National Institute of Justice study (2001) on the role of state and local governments to fight cyber crime recommended some core areas for policy interventions such as public awareness, data gathering, training and technical assistance for law enforcement, management assistance, improvement in computer forensic investigation and technologies, establishment of specialized and dedicated computer crime investigation units and divisions, enhancement of research capabilities, and the creation of new cyber crime laws. The state's policy-making in cyber crime is focused in most of these areas.

Along with the creation of separate organizations dedicated to fight cyber crime, state policy-makers in recent years also enacted hundreds of cyber crime laws and statutes. All fifty states have enacted new statutes criminalizing all types of computer intrusions, computer trespassing, computer tampering, hacking, and fraudulent computer related activities. Since computer fraud is the main and fastest growing type of crime in the states, all fifty states enacted legislations on computer fraud. Computer fraud related statutes generally target such activities as identity theft, spam, business and investment fraud, auction fraud, internet child pornography, and cyberstalking. As of 2006, all fifty states have enacted separate statutes particularly on identity theft (Florida Department of Law Enforcement, 2001). In all the states, identity assumptions, and unlawful use, sale, and trafficking of identity information through the use of computer and the Internet are felony crimes, and they carry mandatory fines and prison terms.

Most of the states have enacted similar legislations on computer hackers and viruses, Internet child pornography, and stalking and harassment. California Penal Code 502, for example, states that any person who knowingly accesses a computer or a computer network, and damage, destroy, or steal data, or deny authorized computer services is guilty of a punishable offense. Any violation of the Penal code 502 is punishable by a fine up to $10,000 and prison term up to three years for first time offense. The Computer Crime Act of Maryland (7-302) describes that unauthorized access to computer materials is a felony crime punishable by up to 10 years of imprisonment. In Louisiana (Statute 14.73.7), computer tempering is punishable by a prison term up to 15 years. In Vermont, theft and destruction of computer materials carry a prison term up to 10 years. An Internet safety policy study, commissioned by the Attorney General of the

Commonwealth of Virginia in 2006, recommended for mandatory sentencing up to 30 years in prison for child pornography producers and laws to seize the computers of individuals convicted of downloading child pornography. In compliance with federal cyber crimes laws, many states have enacted legislations to criminalize the use of the computer and the Internet for threats, stalking, and harassment. "Forty-four states now have laws that explicitly include electronic forms of communication within stalking or harassment laws. State laws that do not include specific references to electronic communication may still apply to those who threaten or harass others online" (National Conference of State Legislatures, 2007, p. 1).

Within the general category of cyber crime statutes, many states have also adopted new and specific statutes on cyber terrorism and statutes for the protection of critical infrastructures (National Conference of State Legislatures, 2006). States such as California, Florida, Hawaii, Illinois, Kansas, Maryland, Massachusetts, Michigan, New Jersey, New York, South Carolina, and Virginia have specific statutes on cyber terrorism. Florida's H.B. 1430, signed by Governor Jeb Bush in 2002, for example, authorizes law enforcement to investigate attacks on protected computers owned by financial institutions and governmental agencies. Michigan's S.B. 942, signed Governor John Engler in 2002, and provided enhanced penalties for the use of the computer and the Internet to disrupt critical infrastructures and governmental operations. The Commonwealth of Virginia's S.B. 514, and S.B. 315 enactments, signed by Governor Mark Warner in 2002, define the use of computer and the Internet for terrorist activities as a class 5 felony (National Conference of State legislatures, 2003). According to California's Penal Code, any person who knowingly threatens to use a weapon of mass destruction to generate sustained fear in public minds through the use of the computer and the Internet is subject to a prison term of up to 6 years and fines up to $250,000. In 2006, Governor Edward Rendell of Pennsylvania launched a new cyber security website to promote public awareness and facilitate information sharing on cyber terrorism and cyber security. The state of Maryland published a *"Cyber Security White Paper: Defining the Role of State Governments to Secure Maryland's Cyber Infrastructure"* in 2006 (Ehrlich & Steele, 2006). The study recommended the implementation of some of the same measures suggested by the National Institute of Justice (2001) study on State and Local Law Enforcement Needs to Combat Electronic Crimes.

6.5 Judicial Policy-Making and Cyber Crime

Under different federal and state cyber crime statutes, thousands of individuals are being arrested, prosecuted, and convicted each year. The federal and state courts are becoming increasingly burdened with cyber crime cases. Cyber crime has posed new challenges for Congress and state legislatures. It has posed new challenges for courts as well. Some of the key legal issues raised by cyber crimes are the admissibility and discovery of digital data as evidence in the court (Leroux, 2004), scientific validity of electronic evidence, protection of privacy in the search and seizure of computer and digital data, protection of freedom and privacy in tracking Internet communications, expectation of privacy in the use of government computers, and prosecution of cyber criminals committing crimes from abroad. In recent years, a number of significant rulings came from federal courts that define the nature and directions of judicial policy-making in many of these areas of cyber crime.

Electronic evidence created in different forms and devices—word processing files, spreadsheet files, database files, browser history files, email programs and communications, electronic messages, and web pages—are now admissible in the court of law. The devices in which electronic evidence is stored—floppy disks, optical disk, network storage, remote internet storage, and handheld devices—are also admissible in the court (National Legal Research Group, 2002; Arkfeld, 2005). The Federal Rule of Evidence 1000 (3) states that "data stored on a computer or any similar device constitutes an original piece of evidence. Consequently, hard copy printout of documents, emails, and other digital data stored on computer hard drives qualify as originals under the Rules of Evidence" (American Bar Association, 2004, p. 77).

The case of *State v. Guthrie* litigated in South Dakota in 2001 is one of the examples of how electronic evidence is being increasingly used in criminal cases (American Bar Association, 2004). In 1999, Dr. William Boyd Guthrie, a Presbyterian Minister in South Dakota called 911 that his wife was dead and found naked with her face down in an empty bathtub. The forensic pathologist who performed the autopsy found evidence of prescription drugs in the blood system of the victim, but he could not confirm whether it was a suicide or a homicide. The law enforcement officers searched the home and the church of Dr. Guthrie, and seized his church computer for collecting evidence. In 2000, Dr. Guthrie was charged for first-degree murder of Sharon, his wife of thirty-four years. The defendant pleaded not guilty, and the defense argued in the court that Sharon committed suicide. After seven months, the defendant produced evidence of an unsigned suicide note, addressed to Sharon's daughter and written a day before Sharon's death. The note, according to the defendant, was found inside a liturgy book in the church. The state's computer forensic experts later found that the suicide note was in fact generated by Dr. Guthrie in his home computer after Sharon's death. The experts also discovered that Dr. Guthrie searched websites on prescription drugs, bathtub accidents, and household accidents. In the trial court, the jury found Dr. Guthrie guilty of first–degree murder, and he was sentenced to life in prison. There are many similar cases where electronic evidence received through computer forensic analysis enters into criminal trials (American Bar Association, 2004).

A number of cases in federal and state courts have also shown that electronic evidence is discoverable and the discovery of electronic evidence is admissible in the court of law. The courts made no sharp distinctions between the discoveries and legal significance of printed and electronic evidence. The Massachusetts Superior Court in *Linnen v. A. H. Robbins* Co. in 1999, for example, clearly stated that "A discovery request aimed at the production of records retained in some electronic form is no different in principle, from a request for documents contained in any office file cabinet" (American Bar Association,

2004, p. 19). In a number of cases in the past two decades, such as *Ford Motor Company v. Auto Supply Company* in 1981, *Touche Ross & Company v. Landskroner* in 1984, *United States v. Sanders* in 1984, *United States v. Catabran*, in 1988, *Kearly v. Mississippi* in 2002, *McCaninch v. Federal Express Corporation* in Iowa in 2005 and *Hutchens v. Hutchens-Collins* in 2006, the federal and state courts held the view that electronic evidence can also be regarded as "original evidence" and it needs no additional expert authentication. Under the "Best Evidence Rule," electronic evidence can also be considered as "original." In the cases of *United States v. Vela* argued by the 5th Circuit in 1982, and *United States v. Croft* argued by the 7th Circuit in 1984, the court clearly ruled that computer data can be presented as evidence for business records. Because of the increased use of electronic evidence in cyber crime cases, the courts also expect that electronic evidence is properly produced, restored, and respected by all parties. The spoliation and destruction of electronic evidence as shown in a number of recent court verdicts, such as in *Zubulake v. UBS Warburg LLC* in 2004, and *Coleman Holdings, Inc. v. Morgan Stanley & Co.* in 2005, can have serious and adverse legal consequences. For spoliation of evidence "the jury in the *Morgan Stanley* case returned with a 1.4 billion dollar verdict and in *Zubulake* the jury returned with a 29 million dollar verdict" (Law Partner Publishing, LLC, 2005, p. 1).

The recent growth in the science of computer forensics has made it possible to discover electronic evidence and bring them to the court for litigation in original forms. The Federal Criminal Code (18USC2703), the Electronic Communications Privacy Act of 1986 (ECPA), the USA PATRIOT Act of 2001, and a number of other related federal statutes have placed enormous power in the hands of law enforcement to search and seize private computers for electronic evidence. These developments of the increased use and admissibility of electronic evidence in the court and the extension of the power of law enforcement to access, disclose, intercept, search, and seize private electronic communications and computers raised a number of issues related to the First Amendment right to privacy and free speech, and the Fourth Amendment right of protection against unusual search and seizures (Kerr, 2006). Judicial opinions with respect to the protection of constitutional rights in the search of digital evidence, however, are still evolving. "The rules governing home searches and car searches are pretty clear by now. In contrast, the legal rules that govern computer searches are mostly a mystery. The Supreme Court hasn't decided a single case on when and how the police can search a computer" (Kerr, 2005, p. 1).

In a number of recent cases, the federal courts held the view that electronic evidence collected in violation of the First Amendment is not admissible in the court. In *United States v. Molina-Tarazon*, the Ninth Circuit Court in 2002, for example, recognized that search for electronic evidence is highly invasive and it is like an intrusion into the mind of an individual. In searching for electronic evidence, the privacy and the dignity of individuals, therefore, must be protected. In *Sony BMG Music Entertainment v. Arellanes*, the Federal Court of the Eastern District of Texas in 2006 ordered, at the request of the defendant, the appointment of an external forensic expert so that the privacy of the defendant is protected in retrieving case related electronic evidence. However, the Ninth Circuit Court, in another case, *United States v. Ziegler* in 2006, held the view that reasonable expectation of privacy doctrine cannot be applied in cases where employees are using office computers for downloading harmful and private materials.

In a number of cyber crime cases, the federal and state courts recently have also addressed issues related to the Fourth Amendment. In *United States v. Ickes* in 2005, the Fourth Circuit Court argued that the search of the defendant's computer at the border was not a violation of the Fourth Amendment in the broader context of national security interests. The court said that "We agree with the district court that the warrantless search of Ickes's van was permissible. Both Congress and the Supreme Court have made clear that extensive searches at the border are permitted, even if the same search elsewhere would not be" (United States Court of Appeals for the Fourth Circuit, 2005, p. 1). The Ninth Circuit Court in the cases of *United States v. Romm* in 2005 and *United States v. Arnold* in 2008 similarly argued that a computer search by law enforcement officers at U.S. borders without a warrant and a reasonable suspicion is not a violation of the Fourth Amendment.

CHAPTER SEVEN

CRIME AND JUSTICE POLICY IN AMERICA IN THE 21st CENTURY: THE EMERGING TRENDS

Crime policy is a huge and complex bundle of laws and statutes related to various aspects of crime and justice. This bundle is not made once and for all. It is an evolving document. It changes and evolves with change and evolution in politics, power, culture, and philosophy. The previous chapters have discussed some selected domains of that bundle focusing particularly on federalization of crime policy, crime and drugs, juvenile justice, sex crime, and cyber crime. Each of these areas of crime and justice has significantly changed during the last four decades of systematic policy-making in crime justice. But as a result of policy-making and policy developments in each of these areas, the system of crime and justice itself has significantly changed and evolved. The present system of crime and justice in America is vastly different from what was in the beginning of the 1960s. There are some core organizing themes and ideas that have been driving policy-making in crime and justice in general for the last four decades. This chapter will examine and reflect, by way of conclusion, on the role and significance of some of those organizing themes, ideas, and trends in policy-making in crime and justice in the beginning of the 21st century.

7.1 Crime and Justice:
Systemic Change and Transformations

One of the most remarkable developments that have happened, primarily as a result of the federalization of crime and justice policy, is that there has evolved a unique system of criminal justice in America. It is a system characterized by a complex of interdependent, interconnected, and differentiated actors, roles, and institutions responsible for policy-making in crime and justice at all levels of governments. One of the major concerns for the members of the President's Commission on Law Enforcement and Administration of Justice in 1965 was the lack of any national organizational structure of policy-making in criminal justice in America in the 1960s. The President Commission recommended the "systems approach" as a new paradigm for organizing crime and justice policy and administration. With the growth of hundreds of federal, state, and local crime policy actors and organizations during the last four decades—the actors and organizations that are highly interconnected through information technology— the vision of the President's Commission has been largely materialized. In each and every domain of crime and justice today, there are designated federal, state, and local actors and organizations, and nationally interconnected structures of crime control programs and strategies. All fifty states now have separate departments or agencies for crime and justice administration, and in each department or agency, there are again designated actors and organizations related to specific categories of crimes and crime control. Most of these developments in state criminal justice systems are mandated by federal laws.

Some of the major examples of nationally interconnected crime control strategies include such federal programs as the Combined DNA Index System (CODIS), Center For Sex Offender Management (CSOM), National Sex Offender Registry (NSOR), United States Computer Readiness Team (US–CERT), Internet Crime Complaint Center (IC3), National Innocent Images Initiative, Regional Computer Forensic Laboratory Initiative (RCFL), and Consumer Sentinel Program. The CODIS system developed by the Federal Bureau of Investigation in 1991 is the national DNA databank where DNA samples of various offenders are stored and analyzed. Through such federal laws as the DNA Backlog Elimination Act of 2000, Advancing Justice through DNA Technology Act of 2003, and the Justice for All Act of 2004, the CODIS system has evolved as a major national center for sharing and analyzing DNA samples collected from all federal and state crime scenes, crime victims, and criminal offenders. The NSOR website maintained by the Crimes against Children Unit of the Federal Bureau of Investigation is another major national program through which sex offenders' registration information is shared by different states and various agencies of the federal government.

There are also many state initiatives for strengthening the national system of crime and justice. The National Governors Association, the Council of State Governors, the National Conference of State Legislatures, the National Center for State Courts, National Center for Juvenile Justice, the Association of State Correctional Administrators, and a variety of other state-wide organizations make policy innovations and recommendations that have important impacts on crime and justice in the nation as whole. One of the recent notable examples of such state-wide policy innovations is the creation of State Prison Reentry Academies by the Center for Best Practices of the National Governors Association. The Center, with funding supports from the Department of Health and Human Services and the Centers for Disease Control, is currently running, as mentioned in Chapter I, twelve Prison Reentry Academies in twelve states including Georgia, Idaho, Indiana, Maine, Massachusetts, Michigan, Minnesota, New Jersey, Pennsylvania, Rhode Island, and Virginia. These academies study the problem of recidivism and make policy recommendations for effective policy-making in prison reentry initiatives. In 2001, the Council of State Governments created a state-wide Re-Entry Policy Council for similar reasons.

Two of the emerging trends that are observed in this evolving system of criminal justice, in addition to the rise of an expanding complex of nationally interconnected justice organizations and crime control programs, are its increased integration to information technology (Correl, 2004), and growing reliance on scientific methodology and evidence-based research for policy-making. The increased use of information technology is increasingly making the system more integrated, connected, and knowledgeable. The Office of Justice Programs of the Department of Justice has a number of information technology initiatives such as Global Information Sharing, Justice Standards Clearinghouse for Information Sharing, and Global Justice XML Data Model. These initiatives have created a central databank for criminal justice information that can be electronically accessed and shared by all federal, state, and local law enforcement agencies. A nationally integrated criminal justice information system is emerging also through such programs as the National Law Enforcement Telecommunication System (NLETS), the FBI's National Crime Information Center (NCIC), and the FBI's Criminal Justice Information Services' Wide Area Network (CJIS WAN). All federal, state, and local law enforcement agencies have access to NLETS, a computerized, high-speed information switching system chartered by the states through which a variety of criminal justice information can be obtained and exchanged. Some of the information that is nationally available from NLETS includes vehicle registration information, driving license information, criminal history records, parole and probation information, prison records, and sex offender registration information. NLETS links about 30,000 law enforcement agencies in the United States and Canada, and it has about 40 million transmissions per month (Correl, 2004). "Law enforcement and criminal justice agencies use NLETS more than 1,000,000 times everyday via nearly 327,000 terminals" (Dempsey, 2000, p. 2).

During the last decades, all fifty states have created separate statues for interstate sharing of criminal records and information, and many states have established separate Criminal Justice Information Centers or Integrated Criminal Justice Information Systems (ICJIS) within their criminal justice departments and agencies. Some examples of ICJIS will include the Alabama Criminal Justice

Information Center, Illinois Criminal Justice Information Authority, Connecticut Justice Information System, Iowa Criminal Justice Information System, Colorado Integrated Criminal Justice Information System, Justice Network of Pennsylvania, Unified Criminal Justice Information System of Kentucky, Integrated Criminal Justice Information System of Massachusetts and the Integrated Criminal History System of Florida. The various federal and state criminal justice information systems, linked to nationally integrated criminal justice information clearinghouses such as the Global Justice XML Data Model, have been fundamentally changing the modes of policy-making in crime and justice in America. Recently, Oracle has invented new software for developing a central repository of all criminal justice records and information produced by law enforcement agencies in the nation. The expansion of the Oracle model, described as Justice Information Hub and Justice Information Network, will bring a new era of integration and connectivity in criminal justice (see Table 34).

From the days of the Wickersham Commission in 1929, and the President's Commission on Law Enforcement and Administration in 1965, policy-makers in crime and justice began to demand an increased use of scientific research and methodology in policy-making. The Wickersham Commission report on criminal statistics provided scientific justifications for the need for data-based policy-making—a process that started through the organization of the Uniform Crime Reporting. The President's Commission in 1965 made a more elaborate demand for the integration of the science of criminology to criminal justice. The Omnibus Crime Control and Safe Street Act of 1968, passed on the basis of the recommendations of the President's Commission, created the National Institute of Justice (NIJ) and the Bureau of Justice Statistics (BJS)—the two institutions that have still remained as major centers for scientific research and information in crime and justice. Policy-making in crime and justice is not entirely based on scientific research and evidence. Social and economic interests, politics, and ideology of the policy-makers also shape policy-making in many complex ways. A trend, however, is growing for increased reliance on data-based management and evidence-based policy-making in crime and justice in general. During the last four decades, this demand has expanded and the use of scientific methods and evidence-based research for policy-making has rapidly increased (Shahidullah, 1996).

Almost all crime legislations enacted since the Omnibus Crime Control Act of 1968 emphasized the role of scientific research in crime policy and made provisions of federal grants for scientific research. The 1994 Stop Violence against Women Act, for example, clearly mandated that "The Attorney General shall request the National Academy of Science, through its National Research Council, to enter into a contract to develop a research agenda to increase the understanding and control of violence against women including rape and domestic violence." The Act instructed that the "National Academy shall convene a panel of nationally recognized experts on violence against women in the fields of law, medicine, [and] criminal justice" (Subchapter III, Subpart 2, The Violence Against Women Act of 1994). The Act further stated that the "Attorney General shall ensure that no later than 1 year after September 13, 1994, the study required under subsection (a) of this section is completed and the report describing the findings made is submitted to the Committee on the Judiciary of the Senate and the Committee of the Judiciary of the House of Representatives" (Subchapter III, Subpart II, Violence Against Women Act of 1994). Similar congressional mandates for conducting scientific research are made in almost all congressional enactments in crime and justice (Shahidullah, 2003).

Table 34: Selected Criminal Justice Information Systems and Telecommunication Networks

System Levels	Information Systems and Networks
National	CODIS (Combined DNA Index System) NLETS (National Law Enforcement Telecommunication System) NIBIN (National Integrated Ballistic Information Network) NDPIX (National Drug Pointer Index) NICS (National Instant Criminal Background Check System) IAFIS (Integrated Automated Fingerprint Identification System) ALIAS (Automated Law Enforcement Information Access System) LEO (Law Enforcement Online) IJIS (Integrated Justice Information System)
Federal	GJXDM (Global Justice XML Data Model) CJIS (Criminal Justice Information Services, FBI) NIPC (National Infrastructure Protection Center) FinCEN (Financial Crimes Enforcement Network) DRUGX (FBI/DEA Drug Intelligence Data Base) NSOR (National Sex Offender Registry) IC3 (Internet Crime Complaint Center) Consumer Sentinel Program, Federal Trade Commission
State	State Criminal History Record Systems State Correctional Information Systems State Driver and Vehicle Registration Systems State Court Systems Information

Source: Dempsey, J. X. (2000)

The National Institute of Justice (NIJ) is the major federal institution responsible for advancing scientific research and technology in crime and justice. The Institute's goal is to "marry science to criminal justice" (National Institute of Justice, 1999, p. 1). The Institute's budget has grown from $2.4 million to about $300 million in 2006. In 1995, the NIJ awarded 217 research grants. The number of grants increased to 483 in 2004 and 554 in 2005 (National Institute of Justice, 2006). More than 50 percent of NIJ funds are allocated for policy relevant research, evaluation, and developments. In 2000, the NIJ launched a new policy model for rethinking crime and justice described as COMPASS (Community Mapping, Planning, and Analysis for Safety Strategies). The COMPASS initiative was taken with the goals for developing a data infrastructure, convening an interagency policy group, developing evidence-based problem solving strategies, and evaluating programs on the basis of scientific methodologies. Many basic and applied research programs relevant to crime and justice policy are also funded by the Office of Juvenile Justice and Delinquency Prevention (OJJDP), Department of Homeland Security (DHS), Department of State (DOS) in areas of human trafficking and global organized crime, Department of Health and Human Services (DHHS) in areas of mental health and crimes, and the DEA on crime and drug connections.

The advance of scientific research and evidence-based policy-making are greatly aided by such criminal justice surveys as the Uniform Crime Reports (UCR), National Crime Victimization Survey (NCVS), and the National Incidence-Based Reporting System (NIBRS) funded and organized by the federal government. By storing, organizing, and analyzing these surveys, The Bureau of Justice Statistics (BJS), National Archive of Criminal Justice Data (NACJD), and the National Criminal Justice Reference Service (NCJRS) bring data and research more closely to policy-makers.

One of the recent examples of policy-makers' demand for scientific research in crime and justice is the Sherman Report on *"Preventing Crime" What Works, What Doesn't, What is Promising: A Report to the United States Congress."* The Department of Justice spends more than $3 billion a year to support crime prevention programs by state and local law enforcement agencies and other organizations. In 1996, the Congress required the Attorney General to review the scientific quality of those programs by an independent agency who will employ "rigorous and scientifically recognized standards of methodology." Accordingly, the NIJ commissioned a study by a group of criminal justice scholars headed by Lawrence W. Sherman of the University of Maryland. The group studied 500 different programs, examined their scientific merit, and presented a report to the United States Congress in 1997.

One of the primary conclusions of the report is that "Substantial reductions in national rates of crime can only be achieved by prevention in areas of concentrated poverty, where the majority of all homicides in the nation occur, and where the homicide rates are 20 times the national average" (Sherman, Gottfreedson, Mackenzie, Eck, Reuter, & Bushwa, 1997, p. 4). The report concluded that prevention programs must be developed simultaneously in seven institutional settings: communities, families, schools, labor markets, physical setting, police, and criminal justice. The *Sherman Report* presented a list of programs that have high and low scientific validity in preventing crimes. The report found that nurses visiting high-risk infants at home, Head Start programs, extra police patrols in high-crime spots, anti-bullying programs in schools, drug-treatment programs in schools, and rehabilitation focused on illiteracy had high scientific validity in preventing crimes. Boot camps, summer job programs for youth, home detention, electronic monitoring, neighborhood watch groups, and drug abuse education by police officers had low scientific validity in preventing crimes. The *Sherman Report* is about a decade old today, but it made major contributions in bringing the relevance of evidence-based research into policy-making for crime and justice (Sherman, Farrington, Welsh, & Mackenzie, 2002).

The Bureau of Justice Assistance (BJA) of the Department of Justice has an on-going initiative to study the crime control programs of different state and local governments that are funded under the Edward Byrne Memorial State and Local Law Enforcement Assistance Formula Grants Program. One of the key missions of this initiative is to gather knowledge about the programs that work and to disseminate that knowledge in the nation for more evidence-based policy-making in crime and justice. There is a clear mandate from the BJA that program evaluations must be based on experiments and scientific methodology. The first report published by BJA in 1997 was titled *"Improving the Nation's Criminal Justice System: Findings and Results from State and Local Program Evaluations."* The second report came in 2000 was titled *"Creating a New Criminal Justice System in the 21st Century: Findings and Results from State and Local Program Evaluations."*

The demand for the use of scientific methodologies and evidence-based policy-making has substantially increased in recent years also among state policy-makers. Crime and justice policy analysts in the states are increasingly using quantitative tools and methodologies for program development and assessments, particularly in such areas as prison management (Roberts, 2007), correctional growth projections, prison mental health, prison reentry programs, sentencing guidelines, sex offender classification (Shahidullah, 2007), and drug treatments. In recent years, many states have established separate sentencing commissions to study and make recommendations to state policy-makers on structures of sentencing guidelines, judicial compliance to sentencing guidelines, development of risk assessment instruments, prison population forecasting, projection of prison bed space, probation violations, community correction revocation trends, and many other criminal justice issues. These state sentencing commissions are increasingly using advanced quantitative methods and techniques for policy analysis and policy recommendations. As the Virginia Criminal Sentencing Commission (2003) noted in its methodological approach to sentencing guidelines: "For the decision whether to incarcerate the offender (the in/out decision), two statistical techniques known as logistic regression and discriminant analysis are used. For the sentencing length decision, a technique called ordinary least square (OLS) regression is applied" (p. 45). Such scientific approaches and methodologies are becoming common in most policy studies conducted by state sentencing commissions and other state policy-making agencies. These two trends—the rapid integration of information technology to criminal justice, and increasing reliance on scientific methodology and evidence-based research for policy-making—are likely to continue to grow in the coming decades.

7.2 Trends in Use of Technology for Crime Control

Along with the growing use of scientific methodology and evidence-based research for policy-making in crime and justice, there is currently growing a new trend to use science-based technology for crime control such as the use of the DNA, the use of crime mapping through the GIS (Geographic Information System), the use of biometrics, and the use of GPS (Global Positioning Satellite System) for offender tracking. In 1998, Congress passed the Crime Identification Technology Act to bring modern science-based technology into the center of crime control by federal, state, and local government agencies (Byrne & Rebovich, 2007). The Act made provisions to provide grants to: 1) centralize and automate adult and juvenile criminal record history; 2) establish automated fingerprinting identification system; 3) digitalize fingerprinting and images; 4) develop a nation-wide and even globally integrated criminal justice information system, and 5) upgrade and enhance the use of DNA for forensic analysis.

The discovery of the science of DNA opened up a new horizon in criminal investigation and identification analysis. The DNA can be traced and retrieved from a wide variety of artifacts that we use or that offenders leave in crime scenes such as blood stains, hairs, skin, bite mark, razor blades, jewelry, cigarette butts, cups and glasses, chewing gum, washcloths, eyeglasses, toothpick, and dirty laundry. DNA left in blood samples and body fluids are largely indestructible. The FBI's CODIS system contains DNA profiles of more than one million convicted felons. Very few policy-makers in crime and justice today challenge the use of DNA for forensic criminology, storage of DNA for cold case analysis, post-conviction analysis of DNA evidence, and the admissibility of DNA evidence in the court. New federal and state statutes are also growing for mandatory collection of DNA samples from all arrestees irrespective of the nature of offending, type of convictions, and age. Particularly noticeable are recent expansion of state policies for the collection of DNA from juvenile offenders (Shahidullah, 2006).

The science of DNA began to enter into policy-making in criminal justice from the beginning of the 1980s. In 1983, California made the first law in the nation to collect blood samples from violent and sexual offenders. In 1988, Colorado enacted a law to collect DNA samples from sexual offenders. In 1990, the Commonwealth of Virginia became the first state to make a law for the collection of DNA from all felons. The Federal DNA Policy in criminal justice came in response to these earlier state policy initiatives. In 1991, the Federal Bureau of Investigation developed the idea of a central data bank for criminal DNA—the project of Combined DNA Index System (CODIS).

In 1994, the Congress enacted the first DNA statute as a part of the Violent Crime Control and Law Enforcement Act of 1994 signed into law (PL 103-322) by President Clinton. The DNA Identification Act (Section XXI, Subtitle C of the 1994 Violent Crime Control and Law Enforcement Act) authorized the Attorney General to establish grants for the improvement of DNA laboratories and DNA analysis technology. It authorized the FBI to expand and improve the Combined DNA Index System and to establish a national advisory board with members from the National Academy of Sciences, National Institute of Justice, and experts from professional crime laboratories to make recommendations for expanding the federal DNA policy in criminal justice. The Act of 1994 authorized the expansion of the CODIS system with samples from crime scenes, crime victims, and unidentified human remains. The Act, however, did not require the collection of DNA samples from individuals convicted of federal crimes.

The first federal law to collect DNA samples from persons convicted of federal crimes was enacted as a part of the Anti-Terrorism and Effective Death Penalty Act of 1996 (PL 104-132). This statute was further extended through the enactment of the DNA Backlog Elimination Act of 2000, Advancing Justice through DNA Technology Act of 2003, and the Justice for All Act of 2004. The DNA Backlog Elimination Act of 2000 established the statutory basis to collect DNA samples from all persons convicted of federal crimes including murder, sexual abuse, kidnapping, and attempting or conspiring to commit any such offense or qualifying military offense. The Act required the Director of the Bureau of Prisons to collect DNA also from those who are under federal custody, and on parole and probation. The Act made it a federal crime to refuse to give DNA by persons convicted of federal crimes. The Director of the Bureau of Prison was authorized to collect DNA even by using reasonable force and restraints.

The DNA Backlog Elimination Act of 2000, for the first time, aimed to create a national system of DNA collection, analysis, and use in criminal justice. The Act authorized the Attorney General to provide grants to states to conduct DNA analysis and to make them a part of the national CODIS System, and to improve the DNA analysis quality and competence of the state and local DNA laboratories (National Institute of Justice, 2000). The Advancing Justice through the DNA Technology Act of 2003, and The Justice For all Acts of 2004 further expanded the scope of DNA collection (The White House, 2003). These Acts made it mandatory to collect DNA from individuals convicted of any federal felony, and also from those who were arrested but not yet convicted. The Debbie Smith Act of 2004, The DNA Sexual Act of 2004, and the Innocence Protection Act of 2004, that are included in the Justice for all Act of 2004, made more federal grants available for improvements in state DNA collection methods and analysis.

Systematic policy-making for integrating DNA in state criminal justice began in the early 1990s. By the end of the 1990s, a majority of the states enacted laws to collect DNA not only from sexual offenders but also from offenders of all violent crimes. In 1999, DNA database laws included sex offenders in all fifty states, violent crime offenders in twenty seven states, violent crime and burglary in fourteen states, and all convicted felons in six states. By 2003, thirty-one states had laws to collect DNA from all adult convicted felons. State DNA legislations further expanded after the enactment of the federal DNA Identification Act of 1994, the DNA Backlog Elimination Act of 2000, and the Advancing Justice through the DNA Technology Act of 2003. These laws brought a considerable amount of federal grants (about $1 billion was proposed by the Bush administration over five years) for states to improve their technology for DNA analysis, expand their DNA database, and strengthen their links with the CODIS system and the National DNA Index System (NDIS) of the FBI. There is wide consensus among the state legislatures to expand the state DNA database by including "as many people as possible" (National Association of Criminal Defense Lawyers, 2006, p. 1).

As of December 2004, thirty-eight states enacted laws to collect DNA from all adult felons, and forty-eight states had information links with the National DNA Index System. One of the recent trends in state policy-making is the inclusion of juveniles in the DNA database. As of 2004, according to a report of the National Conference of State Legislatures, thirty-four states have enacted laws to collect DNA samples from both violent and non-violent juvenile offenders. Twenty states have laws to collect DNA only from adjudicated juveniles. In Florida, requirements for juvenile DNA are the same as those of adult offenders. In Virginia, any juvenile, age 14 and over, is required by law to give DNA for a felony conviction. Alabama and Kentucky require DNA from juveniles adjudicated for sexual offenses (Edwards, 2002). As of 2002, four states—Texas, Virginia, California, and Louisiana—had laws to collect DNA from all adult arrestees. Proposition 69 passed in California in 2004 (The DNA Fingerprint, Unsolved Crime and Innocence Protection Act) will allow collecting DNA from all arrestees including juveniles by the year 2009. It is highly likely that by 2010, most of the states will have laws to collect DNA from both convicted and arrested juveniles, and hundreds of thousands of juvenile DNA profiles will be in the permanent storage of the CODIS system (Shahidullah, 2006). At present, the CODIS system does not take DNA of juveniles who are not convicted.

In 2006, according to the National Conference of State Legislatures, sex offender tracking through the GPS was one of the top ten topics in state crime policy agenda. As of 2006, "22 states passed legislation requiring or authorizing the use of Global Positioning Satellite (GPS) system to monitor some sex offenders following their release from custody (National Conference of State Legislatures, 2007, pp. 1-2). In California, Proposition 83, passed by voters in 2006, made it legal to use GPS monitoring of all registered sex offenders for life (National Conference of State Legislatures, 2007).

Biometric and crime mapping through the GIS system are also two of the rapidly evolving technologies in criminal justice. Biometrics is the use of digital information for criminal identification and offender tracking through the reading and observation of fingerprinting, hand geometry, retina scanning, facial recognition, voice recognition, signature verification, and keystroke analysis. And crime mapping is a technology that utilizes spatial data to analyze concentration of crimes in neighborhoods. The NIJ has a number of research programs for the advancement and the extension of biometrics and crime mapping in criminal justice. In 2000, NIJ, in cooperation with the Department of Defense, conducted a major technology demonstration project on the application of biometrics in criminal justice at the U.S. Naval Base in Charleston, South Carolina. In 2006, the NIJ, under its Sensor, Surveillance, and Biometrics Technologies for Criminal Justice Program, awarded a major grant to a private international company—International Biometric Group—for the development of high-accuracy and high-throughput multimodal biometric systems for justice applications (National Institute of Justice, 2006).

In the area of crime mapping, the NIJ has a continuing research program described as Mapping and Analysis for Public Safety (MAPS). One of the major activities of the program is the funding of research for crime mapping and the extension of crime mapping technology in criminal justice. The MAPS supported the development of a number of crime mapping technologies and software for use in criminal justice. Some of these technologies include CrimeStat III (a software package to analyze hot spots and offender movements), GRASP (online geospatial data repository), and School COP Software for tracking and analyzing school incidents (National Institute of Justice, 2007). In 1999, the NIJ conducted a survey of about 2,004 law enforcement agencies to study the extent of the use of computerized crime mapping in law enforcement. The survey found that about 75 percent of the departments who responded had computerized crime mapping capabilities. Even though the technology is still evolving, about eighty five percent of law enforcement agencies "reported that mapping is a valuable tool for the department" (National Institute of Justice, 1999, p. 3).

7.3 Trends in Policy-Making for Global Crimes

The rise of the information revolution and globalization has given birth to a new generation of criminal activities such as global terrorism, global money laundering, illegal human trafficking, global sex trade and prostitution, transnational organized crime, transnational drug trafficking, illegal trade of military weapons, smuggling of nuclear materials, trafficking of the weapons of mass destruction, cyber crimes, and "distant crimes"—crimes that can be done from thousands of miles away from the scenes of victimizations with the aid of information technology. One of the dominant trends in crime and justice today is the understanding of the nature and growth of these new crimes, and policy-making for their control and containment. The growth of intense connectivity between and among the different nations and cultures that came in the wake of the spread of the information revolution and globalization during the last three decades brought many positive developments by spreading democracy, market economy, modern education, modern science and technology, and the visions of a liberal society (Friedman, 2005; Nandi & Shahidullah, 1998; Fukuyama, 1992). But they also produced enormous complexities in governance and public safety by facilitating the rise and spread of a wide variety of global crimes (Shelley, 2003). These global crimes are fundamentally different from the traditional crimes of homicide, street violence, guns, drugs, and sex. The traditional crimes are domestic in nature, limited in scope, and do not pose any significant threats to public and national security in general. Global crimes pose significant threats to social and economic stability and national security (Finckenauer, 2000; Shelley, 1998; Shahidullah, 2000; 2001). There are rising concerns among crime policy-makers that global terrorists, in collaboration with transnational criminal groups, can unleash unprecedented attacks on American cities and critical infrastructures either through conventional attacks or through the means of bioterrorism, agro-terrorism, and nuclear terrorism—the attacks that can cause the death and destruction of millions of people.

According to the FBI, the Al-Qaeda, Abu Sayyae Group of the Philippines, Al-Gama's Al Islamia of Egypt, Al-Jihad of Egypt, Islamic Jihad of the Middle East, Hezbollah of Lebanon, Hamas of Palestine and Jordon, and Jamaah Islamiya of Indonesia are the major Islamic terrorist groups that are dedicated to harm and destroy the interests of the United States. America is fighting the present "war on terror" to control and contain the spread of activities of these Islamic radical groups both at home and abroad. Before the 2001 attack on the World Trade Center, global terrorism was perceived mainly to be a concern for U.S. foreign policy. After the 2001 attack on the World Trade Center, global terrorism became a concern also for policy-makers in crime and justice.

Some of the major transnational organized criminal groups that work in the United States include the Columbian Drug Cartels, South American Cocaine Trade Gangs, Mexican Heroine Trade Gangs, Orange Case of the Caribbean, Sicilian Mafia, Chinese Triads, Russian Red Mafia, Eurasian Organized Crime Groups, Japanese Yakuza, Nigerian Criminal Groups, Vietnamese Cyber Gangs, and La Cosa Nostra of the United States. These groups are engaged in global illicit drug trafficking, money laundering, trafficking of women and children, global sex trade, alien trafficking, contract killings, trafficking in stolen vehicles, diamond smuggling and trafficking, high technology theft, identity theft, securities fraud, telemarketing fraud, and a variety of other cross-border global crimes (Shahidullah, 2002) The crimes committed by these transnational organized criminal groups pose threats to the stability and expansion of the global economy, and the progress of democratization and liberalization in developing countries. What is alarming is that the global terrorists can make alliance with these transnational organized criminal groups and can get hold of chemical, biological, and nuclear materials and weapons. The National Intelligence Council's 2020 Project "Mapping the Global Future" recently concluded that the "Most worrisome trend has been an intensified search by some terrorists groups to obtain weapons of mass destruction. Our greatest concern is that these groups might acquire biological agents or less likely, a nuclear device, either of which could cause mass casualties (National Intelligence Council, 2004, p. 95). It is these concerns in recent years that brought the whole group of global crimes into the agenda for policy-making in crime and justice in America.

Congress has enacted several legislations to combat global terrorism and global organized crimes. Policy-making on global terrorism began through the ratifications of the 1963 UN Convention on Offenses and Certain Other Acts Committed on Board Aircraft, the 1970 UN Convention for the Suppressions of Unlawful Seizure of Aircraft, the 1979 UN Convention Against the Taking of Hostages, the 1999 UN Convention for the Suppression of the Financing of Terrorism, and the 1999 UN Convention against Transnational Organized crime. Congress enacted the Foreign Intelligence Surveillance Act (FISA) in 1978, the International Money Laundering Act in 1990 (as a part of the Crime Control Act of 1990), and the Anti-Terrorism and Effective Death Penalty Act in 1996. The Anti-Terrorism and Effective Death Penalty Act, enacted in the aftermath of the World Trade Center Bombing in 1993 and the Oklahoma City federal building bombing in 1995, created a legal category of foreign terrorist groups designated by the Department of State, and made new provisions to control terrorist funds and financing, and granting of visa and other material support to terrorist organizations.

The landmark legislation related to U.S policy on global terrorism, however, is the USA PATRIOT Act (Uniting and Strengthening America by Providing Appropriate Tools Required to Intercept and Obstruct Terrorism) signed into law in 2001. The Act was reauthorized in 2006. Title II of the Act—Enhanced Surveillance Procedures—made new provisions and provided law enforcement the authority to intercept wire and electronic communications, share terrorism investigation information, collect foreign intelligence, access computer and business records, install trap and trace device, and delay the execution of warrant. Title III of the Act—International Money Laundering—provided new power to law enforcement to search and seize bank accounts of suspected terrorists, access records of financial transactions, and track international wire transfers. The Act made it mandatory to take DNA samples from suspected terrorists and to use biometrics technology for identification analysis. Title V of the Act—Criminal Laws against Terrorism—provided mandatory sentencing of 20 years or life in prison for an attack on a mass transit system, destruction of national defense materials, destruction of an energy facility, sabotage of a nuclear facility, destruction of an aircraft, and destruction of Interstate gas facility. The Act provided a mandatory minimum of 10 years in prison for harboring or concealing terrorists and for use and possession of biological agents. The PATRIOT Act also made a number of new provisions to revitalize the Foreign Intelligence Surveillance Act and centrally coordinate all foreign intelligence gathering activities. The Intelligence Reform and Terrorism Act of 2004 created a new Office of National Intelligence within the Executive Office of the President.

The USA PATRIOT Improvement and Reauthorization Act of 2005, signed into law in 2006, made permanent fourteen out of sixteen sections of the USA PATRIOT Act of 2001. These permanent laws include wiretapping in terrorist and computer fraud investigations, law enforcement sharing of foreign intelligence information, seizure of stored voice mail by warrant, law enforcement access to computer trespassers' communication within the intruded system, and FISA wiretap or search orders with an accompanying law enforcement purpose.

The Reauthorization Act made misconduct at a "special event of national significance" a federal crime and authorized the United States Sentencing Commission to develop new sentencing guidelines with enhanced penalties for crimes of terrorism. The Act, however, made new provisions for greater congressional and judicial oversight on the implementation of the Act by law enforcement agencies (Congressional Research Service, 2006). The Reauthorization also created a new National Security Division within the Department of Justice for policy-making in global crimes related to terrorism.

Systematic policy-making to combat global organized crimes by the federal government began in the middle of the 1990s. In 1995, President Clinton issued a Presidential Decision Directive 42 (PDD-42), and it ordered the related executive branches of the governments, particularly the National Security Council, Department of Justice, and the Department of Treasury to formulate a national strategy to combat global crimes. In 1998, an International Crime Control Strategy was developed by the Clinton administration by integrating all related federal programs and initiatives (Congressional Research Service, 2006). The 1998 International Crime Control Strategy consisted of eight broad goals: 1) extension of the first line defense beyond U.S. borders through preemptive actions, prosecuting criminal acts committed abroad, and through engagement of U.S. law enforcement agencies in U.S. embassies and consular offices abroad; 2) protection of U.S. borders by attacking smugglers and traffickers; 3) denying of safe haven to international criminals; 4) combating of international financial crimes; 5) prevention of the criminal exploitation of international trade; 6) disruption of the activities of transnational criminal groups; 7) fostering of international cooperation to combat global crimes; and 8) the optimization of the full range of U.S. global crime control efforts. The internationalization of U.S. crime policy and law enforcement activities began primarily in the context of this International Crime Control Strategy formulated in 1998 (Shahidullah, 2003).

In the following years, the International Crime Control Strategy of 1998 led to a number of congressional enactments in areas of global organized crime. Some of the major legislations include the Trafficking Victims Protection Act of 2000 (TVPA), PROTECT Act (Prosecuting Remedies and Tools against the Exploitation of Children Today) of 2003, and Trafficking Victims Protection Reauthorization Act of 2005. The Trafficking Victims Protection Act of 2000 is one of the landmark legislations enacted by Congress to combat global crimes related to illegal human trafficking, trafficking of women and children for sexual exploitation, sex trade, and sex tourism both at home and abroad. The Department of State estimated that about 600,000 to 800,000 men, women, and children are illegally trafficked across international borders every year, and that "approximately 80 percent are women and girls and up to 50 percent are minors. The data also illustrate that the majority of transnational victims are trafficked into commercial sexual exploitation" (United States Department of State, 2005, p. 6). About 17,000 to 20,000 of those men, women, and children, as of 2003, are trafficked in the United States every year. The TVPA of 2000 made these trafficking activities federal crimes, and it instructed the United States Sentencing Commission to develop enhanced sentencing guidelines to prosecute those crimes. In addition, the TVPA made provisions for the creation of a separate task force for research and policy-making, assistance for the victims of trafficking, assistance to foreign governments to combat human trafficking, education and outreach programs, and training programs for state and local law enforcement agencies. The TVPA was reauthorized by Congress in 2003, 2004, and 2005 (The White House, 2002). The Trafficking Victims Protection Reauthorization Act of 2003 (TVPRA) "added responsibilities to the U.S. Government's anti-trafficking portfolio. In particular, the TVPRA mandated new information campaign to combat sex tourism, added some refinements to the federal criminal law and created a new civil action provision that allows trafficking victims to sue their traffickers in federal district courts" (United States Department of Justice, 2004, p. 5). The PROTECT Act of 2003 imposed enhanced penalties for child sex tourism and commercial sexual exploitation of children. It imposed a minimum of 30 years in prison for engaging in child sex tourism (United States Department of State, 2005).

The criminal prosecution of illegal traffickers with enhanced penalties was one of the major goals of the Trafficking Victims Protection Act of 2000, and the Department of Justice's Civil Rights Division was made responsible to implement the new directives. One of the sources shows that in between 2001 and 2003, there was nearly a three-fold increase in the prosecution of illegal human traffickers, and those cases involved victims who were trafficked in the United States from Bangladesh, Cameroon, China, El Salvador, Ghana, Guatemala, Honduras, Indonesia, Jamaica, Mexico, Russia, Thailand, Tonga, Uzbekistan, and Vietnam (United States Department of Justice, 2004). One of the studies made by the Bureau of Justice Statistics (2006) on federal prosecution of human trafficking noted that 555 cases were opened by federal prosecutors between 2001 and 2005. About fifty eight percent of them were investigated for the violation of laws made by TVPA of 2000. Out of fifty eight percent, twenty four percent were investigated for the violation of the statutes of forced labor, twenty three percent for sex trafficking of children, nine percent for trafficking slaves, and two percent for unlawful conduct or general provisions. Eighty five percent of those who were convicted received prison sentences. In addition to brining more prosecutions for illegal human trafficking in the United States, the TVPA of 2000 also created new U.S. initiatives to help foreign government to combat illegal human trafficking. In 2003, the U.S. government "supported approximately 234 international anti-trafficking programs totaling $90 million and benefiting over 90 countries, up from 118 programs in 55 countries in Fiscal Year 2001" (United States Department of Justice, 2004, p. 29).

The International Crime Control Strategy of 1998, the Trafficking Victims Protection Act of 2000, and the Trafficking Victims Reauthorization of Act of 2003 created a new set of federal organizations for global crimes. Congress, under the Intelligence Authorization Act of 1997, created a new Committee on Transnational Threats responsible for policy deliberations for a broader and coordinated approach to global crimes. The TVPA of 2000 required the President to set up a Task Force for policy-making in global crimes. Through an Executive Order (13257), President Bush established a President's Interagency Task Force to Monitor and Combat Trafficking in Persons in 2002. The Task Force included the Secretary of State, Attorney General, Secretary of Labor, and Secretary of Health and Human Services, Director of Central Intelligence Agency, Director of the Office of Management and Budget, and Director of the United States Agency for International Development. The Task Force was entrusted with the responsibility mainly of coordinating the implementation of the TVPA of 2000 and making policy recommendations to the President for more effective measures to combat global crimes (The White House, 2000). In 2003, the Interagency Task Force created a new Senior Policy Operative Group on Trafficking in Persons. The TVPA of 2000 also required the establishment of a separate office within the Department of State for policy-making in global crimes. The Department of State created a new office titled "Trafficking in Persons" in 2001 (TIP Office). The TIP Office is required by the Act to help the President's Interagency Task Force in policy-making and to produce a report on global human trafficking every year. "The TIP Office supported more than 240 anti-trafficking programs in over 75 countries in fiscal year 2003" (United States Department of State, 2004, p. 2).

The federal government's efforts to combat global crimes, however, are not confined to these three institutions created by the TVPA of 2000. There are programs to combat global crimes in almost all major federal agencies, particularly the Department of Justice, Department of Homeland Security, Department of Treasury, Department of Labor, Department of Agriculture, Department of Health and Human Services, Department of Defense, Department of Energy, and Drug Enforcement Administration. The State and Defense Departments, for example, have a collaborative program titled Proliferation Security Initiative to combat nuclear smuggling and reduce the proliferation of nuclear threats. The State Department's Bureau of Narcotics and Law Enforcement Affairs cooperates with the Department of Justice, Department of Homeland Security, Department of Defense and the Drug Enforcement Administration to develop programs for combating international drug smuggling. The Department of Treasury has a separate office—Office of Terrorism and Financial Intelligence—to combat international money laundering. The Department of Homeland Security's divisions of Science and Technology, National Protection and Programs, Transportation Security Administration, and Citizenship and Immigration have many programs related to combating global crimes. The National Institute of Justice's International Center supports a number of research projects and programs on global crimes. Some of the recent programs funded by the NIJ's International Center include 2005 World Drug Report, American Terrorism Study: Patterns of Behavior, Investigation, and Prosecution of American Terrorists, Asian Transnational Organized Crime and its Impact on the United States, Assessment of U.S. Activities to Combat Trafficking in Persons, Characteristics of Chinese Human Smugglers: A Cross-National Study, Human Trafficking: A Growing Criminal

Market in the United States, The Commercial Sexual Exploitation of Children in the U.S., Canada, and Mexico, and Sex Trafficking of Women in the United States: International and Domestic Trends (National Institute of Justice, 2007). The growth of these policy initiatives and policy organizations of the federal government related to global crimes have brought a new trend of globalization or internationalization to policy-making in crime and justice, and this trend is likely to continue to grow in the coming decades (Ward, 2000).

7.4. The Competing Policy Models: The Search for a Balance

In every age, there is a prevailing model—an overarching framework of thought and preference, or a paradigm—of crime and justice that remains dominant in the minds of policy-makers. With the change of time, crime control methods and strategies change because of a change in the prevailing model of thought about crime and justice. For the last three decades, the model that became and remained dominant in crime policy-making is described as the punishment model or the new penology—commonly described as get-tough approach. The approach that was dominant before the 1970s was described as the rehabilitative model or the progressive penology. Rehabilitation before the 1970s was the "dominant American theory of penal treatment" (Allen, 1987, p. 149). The report of the President's Commission on Law Enforcement and Administration of Justice "*The Challenge of Crime in a Free Society*" made 22 major recommendations for reforms in crime and justice. Most of those recommendations were made on the basis of the penal philosophy of rehabilitation (Gould & Namenwirth, 1971). "Until the 1970s retributism—the idea that criminals should be punished because they deserved it—was something of a dead letter in criminology ... During and since the Victorian era retributism had become increasingly disreputable" (Kaplan, Weisberg, & Binder, 2004, pp. 28-29).

From the beginning of the 1970s, the national mood for policy making in crime and justice in America, however, began to change, and the rehabilitative model—the progressive penology—began to be seriously challenged (Martinson, 1974). On the basis of his review of 231 correctional rehabilitative programs, Martinson stirred a new debate—"nothing works"—on the efficacy of the whole paradigm of rehabilitation. In the 1980s, rehabilitation was almost totally discarded as an approach to policy making in crime and criminal justice (Allen 1987). The change in perspective began to be seen not just among the policy makers but also in the academia. "Among the academicians, the conclusion that rehabilitative programs have been extensively tried and have been found wanting is generally accepted" (Gottfredson & Hirschi, 1990, p. 268). During the last three decades, while debates about the competing models of crime and punishment continued within academia, the new penology—get-tough approach—remained dominant in the arena of policy-making (Loader, 2007).

The ideas and assumptions of new penology are fundamentally different from those of progressive penology. Progressive penology was based on the notion of the social and economic roots of crime. Crime policy, for the advocates of progressive penology, is more effective when it is addressed to remove poverty, social and economic inequalities, and exploitation. The new penology does not actively participate in the discourse on the social and economic roots of crime (Dilulio, 1996; Bennett, Dilulio, & Walters, 1996). Thy advocates of new penology are "agnostic about the causes of crime" (Simon & Feeley, 1995, p. 164). For them, the roots of crime cannot be explained by social and economic factors alone. Crime is a function of rational choice. Those who commit crimes rationally choose to do so, and crime will increase if it does not bring swift and definite punishments (Wilson & Herrnstein, 1985). The new penology advocates claim that crime policy research and policy-making should "focus initially on the foreground, rather than the background of crime" (Katz, 1988, p. 4). Crime does not merely come from social and economic deprivations. Crime is constructed in the minds of the criminals for its rewards, interests, fantasies, and sensibilities (Katz, 1988).

The new penology looks at crime as a systemic problem—as a problem of control and management. "The language of the new penology is anchored in the discourse of systemic analysis and operation research. It conceives of crime as a systemic phenomenon and crime policy as problem of actuarial risk management" (Simon & Feeley, 1995, p. 148). The progressive penology's central goal was the transformation of individuals. "New penology reveals a shift away from the objective of transforming individuals. It embraces a new objective: risk management and the management of the system itself" (Simon & Feeley, 1995, p. 148). One of the major strategies of policy-making in criminal justice, the new penology advocates argue, is the incapacitation of the criminals, particularly the career criminals and repeat offenders (Blumstein, Cohen, Roth, & Visher, 1986).

The progressive penology was behind the justification and legalization of juvenile court, probation, parole, indeterminate sentencing, judicial discretion, prison education, and offender treatments in prison. It was a policy model that focused primarily on corrections, prison reforms, judicial autonomy, therapeutic interventions, behavioral modifications, offender rights, and ethics of sentencing. The policy strategies of new penology are based on the ideas of incarceration, incapacitation, deterrence, just deserts, determinate sentencing, truth-in-sentencing, high-risk offenders, judicial control, efficacy of sentencing, and science-based systemic management of crime and justice. It is on the basis of these notions of new penology during the last three decades that there has expanded a new science-based system of criminal justice in America with a whole new body of federal and state laws and statutes in juvenile justice, drugs and crime, sex crimes, cyber crimes, and many other areas (Greene, 2002).

From the middle of the 1990s, debates and discourses, however, have started both within the academic circle and by federal and state policy-makers about the effects and efficacy of the strategies of new penology (Clear, 1994; Mauer, 1999; Tonry, 2004; 2006). These debates and discourses (Culen, 2005) have raised two major issues related to criminal justice: economics of crime control, and ethics of crime and punishment. From the perspective of criminal justice, the main question is: do get-tough strategies help to reduce crime? Economically, the debate is about the cost of long term incarcerations, and its impact on state budgets and economics. Ethically, the questions are about the impact of long term incarceration on those incarcerated and on their families. Many argue that the get-tough strategies have disproportionately affected minorities, and many of their families are adversely affected (Tonry, 1995; 1996; Mauer, 1999)). In the context of the rise of these and other questions and concerns, many policy-makers today are revisiting get-tough strategies. The get-tough approach is not being abandoned, and policy-making is not returning to the old rehabilitative model. In the context of changing social, cultural, and economic transformations and the rise of new global crimes, the policy-makers are searching for an approach to balance between control and freedom, and order and progress. The search is for discovering balanced and innovative strategies remaining broadly within the get-tough model.

Crime Trends, 1960-2006

The control and containment of violent crime is one of the major goals of crime policy. About fifty percent of inmates in state correctional institutions are convicted of violent crimes including murder, manslaughter, rape, sexual assault, robbery, extortion, and criminal endangerment. About fifty percent of increase in state correctional population since 1995 was due to an increase for violent offense convictions. Crime data collected by various federal surveys show that violent crime in the U.S. has sharply increased between 1960 and 1990. In 1960, the violent crime rate was 160.9 per 100,000 population. The rate of violent crime increased to 596.6 in 1980, and 758.1 in 1991—the highest rate of increase in 30 years. However, from the middle of the 1990s, the rate of violent crime began to decrease. In 1995, the violent crime rate was 684.6 per 100,000 population. In 2000, it decreased to 506.5 and in 2004 to 463.2 per 100,000 population (Bureau of Justice Statistics, 2006).

Many attribute this crime drop to get-tough strategies (Blumstein & Wallman, 2000). The critics of the get-tough strategies, however, see this drop as a temporary trend, and they believe that the violent crime rate may go up again without major investments in social and economic growth for the poor. From 2005, violent crime has again started to increase in the U.S. particularly in midsize cities and in the cities of the Midwest (Justice Policy Institute, 2007). The FBI reports that "A breakdown of the 2005 data by population group revealed that all city population groups experienced increase in violent crimes when compared with those data reported for the previous year, with the exception of nation's largest cities, I million and over" (Federal Bureau of Investigation, 2005, p. 1). The report further adds that "cities with populations from 100,000 to 249,999 had the greatest increase in the number r of murders, up 12.5 percent" (Federal Bureau of Investigation, 2005, p. 1). According to a report from the National Law Enforcement Association, based on a survey of 56 cities and sheriff departments, "Overall from 2004 to 2006, homicides and aggravated assault with guns each increased 10 percent and robberies 12 percent" (The Virginian Pilot, 2007, p. A5). The report also found that homicides increased 20 percent or more in cities including Boston, Cincinnati, Cleveland, Hartford, Connecticut, Memphis, Tennessee, and Orlando. These recent trends of growth in violent crimes are forcing many policy-makers to revisit the get-tough strategies.

Trends in Incarceration, Parole and Probation

It is generally believed that incarceration and crime trends are connected. Higher rates of incarceration will lead to an increase in crime drops. Scientific research, however, does not show strong correlations between incarceration and crime drops. In a meta-analysis of 15 major empirical studies of relations between incarceration and crime trends, a study from the Vera Institute of Justice (2007) concluded that "The most sophisticated analyses generally agree that increased incarceration rates have some effect on reducing crime, but the scope of that impact is limited; a 10 percent increase in incarceration is associated with a 2 to 4 percent drop in crime" (p. 1). In 2005, there were about 7 million people who were under correctional supervisions in America including prison, jail, parole, and probation. Out of about 7 million, about 1.4 million were in state and federal prisons, and 747, 529 were in jails. Between 1980 and 2005, for 25 years in a row, the rate of incarceration under state and federal jurisdictions has consistency increased. In 1995, the total incarceration rate in state and federal prisons and jails was 601 per 100,000 population. In June 2005, the rate increased to 738 per 100,000 population. Between December 1995 and June 2005, prisoners in federal prisons grew at an annual rate of 7.4 percent and those in state prisons grew at a rate of 2.5 percent. During the same period, inmates in local jails increased at a rate of 3.9 percent (Bureau of Justice Statistics, 2006).

At the end of 2005, over 4.9 million adult men and women were under federal, state, and local probation or parole jurisdictions. Out of this number, about 784,400 were under parole and about 1.4 million were on probation. One of the noticeable trends is the slow but consistent rate of increase in parole and probation population under community supervision during the last fifteen years between 1990 and 2005. During this period, prison population grew 25.2 percent. But inmates on probation grew 53.3 percent and on parole grew 9.1 percent. During 1995 and 2005, the probation population grew at a rate of 2.5 percent and the parole population grew at a rate of 1.4 percent (Bureau of Justice Statistics, 2006). At the end of 2005, the states with the largest population under parole and probation included California, Illinois, Michigan, Ohio, Pennsylvania, and Texas. Some of the states that had the highest rate of increase in probation in 2004-2005 included Alabama, Arkansas, Kentucky, Mississippi, Montana, New Mexico, North Dakota, Virginia, West Virginia, and Wyoming. Some the states with highest rate of increase in parole population in 2004-2005 included Arkansas (22.7 percent), North Dakota (16.7 percent), West Virginia (16.4 percent), New Mexico (16.1 percent), Kentucky (15.8 percent), Vermont (14.9 percent), and Mississippi (12.1 percent). The annual rate of increase in probation population in the nation as a whole, however, is showing a downward trend from the beginning of 2001. The annual rate of increase in probation population was 2.8 percent in 2001. In 2005, the rate of increase dropped to 0.5 percent—the smallest rate of annual increase in probation population in last 26 years (Bureau of Justice Statistics, 2006).

Federal and State Sentencing Reforms

The surge in prison population both in federal and state prisons during the last three decades came primarily under the impact of mandatory sentencing guidelines, particularly related to drug offenses. The federal sentencing guidelines are guided mainly by the United States Sentencing Commission, Congress, the Department of Justice and the federal appellate courts. The state sentencing guidelines are guided, in most states, by state sentencing commissions, state legislatures, and the state court of appeals. During the last three decades, through the evolution of mandatory sentencing guidelines and a number of congressional enactments, sentencing trends rapidly moved from indeterminate to determinate and truth-in-sentencing structures, and the sentencing courts moved from practicing judicial discretions to judicial restraints and accountability. The sentencing guidelines were based on different get-tough sentencing philosophies, such as just deserts or retribution, deterrence, incapacitation, crime control, or structured sentencing. "Among states that have adopted desert-premised systems are Minnesota, Washington, and Oregon. Other states such as Virginia premised their guidelines on a philosophy of incapacitation or selective incapacitation" (National Institute of Justice, 2001, p. 3). In these philosophies and sentencing guidelines, the role of alternative sentencing methods or alternative systems of justice was largely ignored. In recent years, crime policy-makers, particularly the state policy-makers, have re-examined these get-tough methods of sentencing and punishment. The systems of sentencing guidelines that have evolved, based on many science-based methods of projections, are not being eliminated (National Center For State Courts, 1997), but policies are being made to accommodate alternative sentencing and judicial philosophies, and allow judicial discretions with accountability.

In 2000, under the federal sentencing guidelines, 81.3 percent of offenders from all categories of federal offenses received prison sentences. Of all federal offenders, 9.4 percent received probation, 5.4 percent received probation and confinement, and 3.9 percent received prison and community split. In 2006, the percentage of federal offenders who received prison sentences increased to 85.7 percent, and those who received probation decreased to 7.5 percent (United States Sentencing Commission 2000 and 2006 Data Files). In 2000, the average sentencing length for federal drug trafficking offenders and drugs-communication facility offenders respectively was 72.3 months and 40.6 months. In 2006, the sentencing length for the same offenders increased 82.0 months and 40.8 months respectively. In 2000, the average length of federal sentencing under the federal guidelines for sexual abuse was 56.1 months. In 2006, the length of sentencing for sex abuse increased to 100.8 months. The average length of sentencing given by federal courts for all categories of federal offenses in 2000 was 46.9 months. In 2006, it increased to 51.8 months.

In addition to increase in federal sentencing length, one also observes an increase in sentencing within the guidelines, and a moderate increase in downward departures from the guidelines, except in drug offenses, between 2003 and 2005. In 2000, 64.5 percent of sentencing from federal circuits remained within the federal guidelines. It increased to 70.9 percent in 2005. In 2000, 17.0 percent of federal circuits made downward departures. In 2005, downward departures from federal circuits increased to 28.4 percent. In 2000, 57.9 percent of drug offenders were sentenced within the federal guidelines, and 14.7 percent received downward departures. For crack cocaine, downward departures were received only by 8.5 percent in 2000 (United States Sentencing Commission, 2000 and 2006 Data Files). Between 2003 and 2005, downward departure was highest in the Ninth Circuit. The Ninth Circuit, in its sentencing made 40.3 percent downward departures from the guidelines in 2005. This was closely followed by the Second Circuit (39.9 percent) and the Third Circuit (32.1 Percent).

One of the major concerns about federal mandatory sentencing guidelines is about the sentencing disparities between powder and crack cocaine. As a result of enhanced mandatory sentencing guidelines for crack cocaine, more African-Americans are in federal prisons with drug convictions. About "81.8 percent of crack cocaine defendants in 2006 were African American .... Between 1994 and 2003, the average time served by African Americans for drug offenses increased 62 percent, compared to an increase of 17 percent for white drug offenders" (The Sentencing Project, 2007, p. 4). The United States Sentencing Commission recommended to Congress several times during the last decade to reduce this disparity in federal drug sentencing, but Congress, as of 2006, did not pass any major legislation to address the problem. The United States Sentencing Commission again in 2007 "issued recommendations that call on Congress to address the lengthy sentences for low-level crack offenses. Congress has responded with at least two bipartisan crack sentencing reform bills and a new Senate bill that would equalize penalties for crack and powder cocaine offenses (The Sentencing Project, 2007, p. 1). Legislative development in this area of removing disparities in federal drug sentencing remains to be seen.

Almost all states have enacted legislations in recent years to reform their sentencing guidelines and sentencing policies (The Sentencing Project, 2007). In the 1980s and 1990s, states introduced determinate sentencing structures, truth-in-sentencing laws, and mandatory sentencing guidelines, particularly for drug offenses. Many states abolished parole, introduced felony disenfranchisement laws, cut down mental health and substance abuse treatment opportunities, and restricted prison education programs. Between 1994 and 2002, the number of felony convictions increased 20 percent in state courts. About 70 percent of those convicted in state courts in 2002 were sentenced to incarceration under mandatory and structured sentencing guidelines (Bureau of Justice Statistics, 2006). The state of Washington enacted the first truth-in-sentencing law in 1984. By the end of the 1990s, truth-in-sentencing laws were enacted by most of the states under federal grants mandated by the Violent Crime Control and Law Enforcement Act of 1994 (Bureau of Justice Statistics, 1999).

The highest percentage of felony convictions in state courts is for drug-related offenses. In 1998, 33.9 percent of felons in state courts were convicted for drug offenses. In the same year, 17.8 percent were convicted for violent offenses, and 30. 5 percent were convicted for property offenses. In 2002, the felons convicted for drug offenses in state courts slightly decreased (32.4 percent). The mean maximum sentence length for drug trafficking in 2002 was 55 months, and for drug possession 35 months. Between 1995 and 2003, the percentage of drug offenders in state prisons decreased from 22 percent to 20 percent (Bureau of Justice Statistics, 2006).

The state sentencing reforms are progressing in three major areas: evidenced-based structuring of sentencing policy, proportionality in sentencing, particularly related to drug offenses, and more emphasis on treatment, reentry and rehabilitation (Vera Institute of Justice, 2004). In the area of drug sentencing, many states are revisiting their mandatory sentencing guidelines, making new provisions of parole for drug offenders, and introducing legislations to offer more treatments and after-prison care program for drug offenders. A report from the Drug Policy Alliance (2003) found that over 150 drug policy reforms were "enacted by voters and legislators in 46 states in between 1996 and 2002" (p. i). During that period, "voters approved seventeen of nineteen proposed statewide drug policy ballot initiatives to legalize marijuana for medical purposes, reduce asset forfeiture abuses, and divert nonviolent drug possession offenders from prison to treatment" (Drug Policy Alliance, 2003, p. ii). In addition, many states enacted legislations to change drug sentencing guidelines, offer mandatory drug treatments, and restore welfare benefits and voting rights for ex-felons. Between 2004 and 2006, nine states including Connecticut, Hawaii, Indiana, Maryland, North Dakota, Pennsylvania, Texas, and Washington expanded laws for sentencing diversions for drug offenders. In California, Proposition 36, passed in 2006, mandated the diversion of drug offenders from incarceration to treatments. A number of states such as Georgia, Michigan, Montana, Utah, Virginia, and Illinois passed laws to give drug offenders increased access to drug courts (The Sentencing Project, 2007).

From 1996 to 2002, legislations for drug sentencing reforms were enacted by 18 states including Arizona, California, Iowa, Michigan, Minnesota, Nevada, Oregon, Texas, and Virginia. During the same period, 10 states reformed asset forfeiture laws; and 4 states restored voting rights for convicted drug offenders (Drug Policy Alliance, 2003). The states that initiated drug sentencing reforms have reduced sentencing lengths for drug offenders, changed the mandatory sentencing guidelines, offered more treatment and alternative sentencing options, increased judicial discretions, and eliminated mandatory life time probation for low-level drug offenders (see Table 35).

Table 35: Selected State Sentencing Reforms, 2004-2006

State	Reforms
California	Expanded community supervision options to reduce parole and probation revocation (2005)
Hawaii	Expanded diversion to treatment for certain drug offenses (2004)
Illinois	Mandated treatment for certain inmates prior to early merit release (2005)
Indiana	Extended drug diversion programs for certain drug offenses (2004)
Louisiana	Established drug diversion courts (2004)
Maryland	Introduced laws for early release from prison to community treatment for certain types of offenders; established diversion programs for treatment (2004)
Michigan	Established drug courts and extended diversion programs (2004)
Minnesota	Introduced laws for early release for offenders convicted of a crime committed as a result of an addiction (2005)
Montana	Authorized district courts to establish drug treatment programs (2005)
New York	Reformed Rockefeller Drug Laws and revised drug sentencing structures (2004); declared reentry as a goal of sentencing (2005)
Oklahoma	Established intermediate sanction programs (2005)
Pennsylvania	Extended drug treatment programs (2004)
Texas	Expanded drug court programs (2005)
Virginia	Expanded drug court treatment programs (2004)
Washington	Expanded drug offender sentencing alternative program to include community supervision program (2005)

Source: The Sentencing Project, 2007

Legislations were passed by almost all states in recent years to reform sentencing provisions, change mandatory sentencing guidelines, and extend alternative sentencing provisions and community programs, including parole and probation, also for other categories of offenders. Arizona, for example, passed a law that established a Community Accountability Pilot program to deal with parole and probation violators in the community instead of returning them for incarceration. California and Washington passed laws to deal with probation and parole violators in the community with electronic monitoring. In 2001-2002, Colorado, Delaware, Indiana, Michigan, and North Dakota repealed their mandatory sentencing guidelines. Iowa, Indiana, and Michigan made laws to increase judicial discretions in felony sentencing, and Louisiana and Massachusetts repealed and revised their truth-in-sentencing laws (Vera Institute of Justice, 2002). In between 2000 and 2006, many states such as Alabama, Connecticut, Delaware, Maryland, Massachusetts, Pennsylvania, Texas, and Virginia made laws to remove restrictions on felony disenfranchisement.

Policy-making related to federal and state mandatory sentencing guidelines in general, however, has entered into a new era in the context of the U.S. Supreme Court rulings in *Blakely v. Washington* in 2004 and the *United States v. Booker* in 2005. In *Blakely v. Washington*, as mentioned in Chapter 2, the Supreme Court made a ruling that in following state mandatory sentencing guidelines, a sentence greater than the maximum can only be given, within the limits of the Sixth Amendment of the Constitution, by a jury and not by judges. The *Blakeley* decision brought a new turning point in the state sentencing system through the ruling that sentences given by judges higher than those recommend by state mandatory sentencing statutes are in violation of the Sixth Amendment's right of jury trial.

In the *United States v. Booker* in 2005, the U.S. Supreme Court applied the same argument to federal mandatory sentencing guidelines. Justice Stevens, in delivering the majority opinion, said that the Sixth Amendment principles are also applied to federal sentencing guidelines. "The Government's arguments for its position that *Blakely*'s reasoning should not be applied to the Federal Sentencing Guidelines are unpersuasive." The *Booker* decision brought a more fundamental issue about the nature of the enforcement of federal mandatory sentencing guidelines. Justice Breyer, in delivering the majority opinion, said that the system of federal mandatory sentencing guidelines "is incompatible with today's Sixth Amendment 'jury trial' holding and therefore must be severed and excised from the Sentencing Reform Act of 1984" (Legal Information Institute, 2005, pp.2-3). He further added that federal sentencing guidelines should be seen as advisory and not mandatory. If they are mandatory, they are in violation of the Sixth Amendment right of jury trial. The United States Sentencing Commission and all state sentencing authorities are still reading the implications of *Blakely* and *Booker* decisions.

How these two landmark decisions are going to affect the nature and the enforcement of federal and state mandatory sentencing guidelines remains to be seen. The United States Sentencing Commission (2006) in its report on the Impact of *United States v. Booker* on Federal Sentencing noted that the *Booker* decision "had an immediate impact on federal criminal justice system .... The uniformity that had been the hallmark of mandatory federal guideline sentencing no longer was readily apparent as courts began to address new issues raised by *Booker*" (p. iv). In response to *Blakely* decision, six states including Arizona, North Carolina, Oregon, and Washington enacted new laws to revise their mandatory sentencing guidelines. "In Alaska, lawmakers replaced presumptive terms with ranges, allowing for judicial adjustment for aggravating and mitigating factors. An action in Indiana similarly replaced fixed terms for felons with advisory sentences that a court may voluntarily consider midway between maximum and minimum sentences" (National Conference of State Legislatures, 2006, p. 4). In Alabama in 2006, a new law has adopted "voluntary guidelines of a sentencing commission that has been at work there for several years, with more truth-in-sentencing standards expected for legislative review within the next two years" (National Conference of State Legislatures, 2007, p. 8).

Correctional Policy Trends: The Reentry Initiatives

The policies of determinate and mandatory sentencing guidelines, truth-in-sentencing laws, juvenile transfer laws, revocation of parole and probation—all impacted on the rate of incarceration and the number of prison population in correctional institutions, particularly of the states. Between 1982 and 2003, as mentioned before, federal correctional expenditures increased 925 percent. During the same period, correctional expenditures for state governments increased 550.9 percent and local governments 519.6 percent. In 2003, the state governments spent about $39.2 billion for corrections (Bureau of Justice Statistics, 2006). One study on Maryland's Mandatory Drug Sentencing Laws estimated that in 2006, it cost about 17.3 million to keep 94 prisoners who received mandatory drug sentencing for a term of about seven years ((Justice Policy Institute, 2007). From the late 1990s, state policy-makers began to reexamine the growth of their correctional budgets in particular, and their strategies of correctional policy and management in general. More than twenty five states reduced their correctional budgets in the fiscal year 2002 through closing prisons, reducing staff, and cutting nonessential programs. Correction budgets in 2002 decreased $54.9 million in Michigan, $53.7 million in South Carolina, $37.4 million in California, $36.86 million in Oregon, $35.4 million in Illinois, and $25.5 in Virginia. The states of California, Florida, Illinois, Massachusetts, Michigan, New York, Ohio, South Carolina and Virginia closed many prison facilities and reduced the number of prison beds (Vera Institute of Justice, 2002).

In addition, concerns also began to be addressed to reduce recidivism and re-incarceration. About 650,000 inmates are released from federal and state prisons every year. It is estimated that about 95 percent of all state prisoners will be released at some point, and about 80 percent will be released to parole supervision (Bureau of Justice Statistics, 2003). Between 2000 and 2002, the number of prisoners released increased about 4.5 percent, and this trend is likely to continue. One of the significant challenges for correctional policy is that about 67 percent of those who are released from prison are rearrested within two years and about 50 percent are re-incarcerated within three years (National Governors Association Center for Best Practices, 2007). A study on recidivism done by the Office of Justice Programs, that tracked 272,111 prisoners for three years after their release from prisons in 15 States in 1994, found that the rate of recidivism among homicide offenders was about 40.7 percent. Out of 19, 268 homicide offenders released 3,051 committed homicides again within three years (Bureau of Justice Statistics, 2002). In order to address these issues of correctional budgets and high rate of recidivism, many policy-makers from the late 1990s began to think about innovative correctional strategies. Out of these concerns, a national prison reentry initiative as a new model of corrections has recently emerged.

The reentry model is based on assumptions different from that of the justice model. It is a model that seeks to bind prison and communities together to address the issues of corrections and reintegration. The reentry model brings new demands on corrections to plan for offender reintegration from the early days of incarcerations through objective assessments of inmate categories, treatment requirements, skill enhancement, and mental health development. It is based on the assumption that the communities—families, friends, neighbors, schools, businesses, and faith-based groups—also have a role to play in corrections and reintegration (Shahidullah, 1994). Hundreds of reentry programs currently exist in the country with the help of a number of major federal and state reentry initiatives and in the context of two major congressional enactments—the Community Solutions Act of 2002 and the Second Change Act of 2004.

Some of the major federal and state initiatives include the Transition from Prison to Community Initiative, Going Home: The Serious and Violent Offender Reentry Initiative, Reentry Court Initiative, Center for Sex Offender Management of the Department of Justice, Faith-Based and Community Initiative of the White House (Shahidullah, 2004), Re-Entry Policy Council of the Council of State Governments, and the Prisoner Reentry Policy Academy of the National Governors Association. In 2003, the National Governor Association, as mentioned before, created a Prisoner Reentry Policy Academy for research and training on prison reentry initiatives. The National Conference of State Legislatures (2007) noted that "The trend in states to better prepare inmates for and supervise them during reentry to the community continued in 2006; more than a dozen states added to or expanded laws in this area" (p. 7). The Commonwealth of Virginia, for example, "requires the Department of Corrections to provide to inmates, upon discharge, documentation of work, education and treatments programs completed while in prison (National Conference of State Legislatures, 2007, p. 7). The Virginia Department of Housing and Community Development is required by a new law "to create and implement housing programs for offenders who are returning to the community from prison" (National Conference of State Legislatures, 2007, p. 8). In 2006, the State of Washington created a joint legislative task force to examine prison-based programs and recommend strategies for effective prison reentry. A new law in California requires the California Department of Corrections to establish a Reentry Advisory Committee to make policy recommendations for reentry programs. Similar statewide reentry initiatives have been created in many states in recent years. In 2005, the Governor of Florida created a Governor's Ex-Offender Task Force to recommend measures for successful prison reentry. The Task force made fifteen recommendations in its report in 2006. One of the key recommendations was "Successful reentry and the rehabilitation of inmates must be made an explicit part of the mission of the Department of Corrections" (Governor's Ex-Offender Task Force, 2006, p. 5).

Federalization, the Congress, and Get-tough Policy Trends

The get-tough perspective began to be dominant in crime control from the beginning of rapid federalization in crime and justice in the 1970s. In the context of the evolving national system of crime and justice, the growing role of science and technology for crime control, and the rise of new global crimes, it is likely that the federal government will become more involved in policy-making in crime and justice, and the trend of federalization will further expand in the coming decades. The impacts of the major federal crime policy institutions such as the Department of Homeland Security, Office of Justice Programs, Office of Justice Statistics, National Institute of Justice, Drug Enforcement Administration, Office of National Drug Control Policy, and Office of Juvenile Justice and Delinquency Prevention on crime and justice policy of the states will further grow.

The get-tough policy strategies of Congress that began with the federalization of crime and justice are also likely to continue to expand in the coming decades, particularly in areas of sex crimes, cyber crimes, and global organized crimes. Some of the recent enactments such as the Children's Internet Protection Act of 2000, Victims of Trafficking and Violence Protection Act of 2000, USA PATRIOT Act of 2001, Cyber Crime Security Enhancement Act of 2002, PRO-TECT Act of 2003, Illegal Drug Proliferation Act of 2003, Advancing Justice Through DNA Act of 2003, Violence Against Women Act of 2005, the USA PATRIOT Improvement and Reauthorization Act of 2005, and the Adam Walsh Child Protection Act of 2006 show that Congress is still expanding, with broad bipartisan support, its get-tough strategies for crime control. These and other recent enactments created many new categories of federal crimes, developed many new federal crime control programs, and made new provisions for enhanced mandatory sentences. The Adam Walsh Child Protection Act of 2006, for example, made a new sentencing provision of life imprisonment for violent and repeat sex offenders. The PROTECT Act of 2003 removed the statute of limitations for child sexual abuse cases, authorized the use of wiretaps for investigating cases where children are lured through the Internet, and made new provisions for judges to provide explanations for downward sentencing in child sex abuse cases.

Crime policy has also remained as one of the areas of dominant policy interests for Congress. A number of new crime bills have been proposed and debated in the 109th and 110th Congresses. Some of the major crime bills proposed in the 109th Congress included Methamphetamine Act of 2005, Child Pornography Prevention Act of 2005, Comprehensive Identity Theft Protection Act of 2005, DNA Database Completion Act of 2005, Hate Crimes Prevention Act of 2005, Jessica Lunsford Act of 2005, Narco-Terrorism Enforcement Act of 2005, Sex Offender Registration and Notification Act of 2005, Criminal Restitution Act of 2006, Increased Penalties for Methamphetamine Traffickers Act of 2006, Data Theft Protection Act of 2006, and Sexual Predator Sentencing

Act of 2006. One of the controversial crime bills proposed in the 109th Congress is the Gang Deterrence and Community Protection Act of 2005 (HR 1279) sponsored by Republican House of Representative John Forbes of Virginia. The Act has proposed to make participation in street gangs a federal crime and gang control, a federal responsibility. It provides enhanced penalties for crimes related to street gangs, imposes twenty-four new mandatory sentences, and authorizes death penalty for a number of violent street gang crimes. The Act proposed a minimum mandatory sentencing of 30 years in prison for kidnapping by street gangs, and life imprisonment or death penalty for violent street gang crimes, including those committed by juveniles that result in death. The Gang Deterrence Act has received bipartisan support from both Houses of the Congress, and it has passed the House of Representatives in 2005.

Some of the major crime bills proposed in the 110th Congress include the Criminal Terrorism Improvement Act of 2007, Cyber Security Enhancement and Consumer Data Protection Act of 2007, Combating Money Laundering and Terrorist Financing Act of 2007, Gang Abatement and Prevention Act of 2007, Violent Crime Reduction Act of 2007, Second Chance for Ex-Offenders Act of 2007, Crack-Cocaine Equitable Sentencing Act of 2007, Gang Elimination Act of 2007, Sex Offender Visa Loophole Elimination Act of 2007, and Trafficking Victims Protection Reauthorization Act of 2007. The Criminal Terrorism Improvement Act of 2007 (HR 855) proposed to impose the death penalty for terrorist activities related to the use of weapons of mass destructions, missile systems to destroy aircraft, and automatic weapons. The penalty for providing material support to terrorists was increased from 15 years in prison to not less than 30 years in prison, or life in prison. The Cyber Security Enhancement and Consumer Data Protection Act of 2007 (HR 836) proposed a minimum penalty of 30 years in prison, or life in prison for unauthorized access and damage to protected computers. These recent legislative activities on crime policy in Congress suggest that the federal policy-makers are likely to expand, with bipartisan support, the get-tough strategies in the coming decades, particularly in areas of sex crimes, cyber crimes, high-tech crimes, and global crimes.

The U.S. Supreme Court and Get-tough Policy Trends

The U.S. Supreme Court is the guardian of the constitution, and it does not directly decide how crime has to be defined and punishment has to be devised. But its decisions, by implications, significantly shape the nature of policy-making about crime and punishment. A large number of decisions given by the Supreme Court in recent years in areas of police search and seizures, drug law enforcement, juvenile justice, sex offender registration and notification, and sentencing laws and guidelines upheld the get-tough policy strategies. The 1970s—the time of the beginning of the federalization of crime and the dominance of get-tough approach to crime control—was also a time of the ascendancy of the Rehnquist Court at the top of judicial power in America. William Rehnquist, a man deeply respected by many in America for his conservative judicial philosophy, was appointed in the Supreme Court by President Nixon in 1971.

President Reagan appointed him as a Chief Justice in 1986. During the last two decades, the Rehnquist court made a number of judicial decisions that strengthened and expanded the get-tough strategies in crime control and justice. This trend is likely to continue to remain in the judicial policy-making in the Roberts Court where the majority of Justices are also known for their conservative judicial philosophy (Wicker, 2002).

The Rehnquist Court made some significant decisions in the area of police search and law enforcement. The decisions made in *Michigan v. Sitz* in 1990, *Illinois v. Wardlow* in 2000, *Illinois v. McArthur* in 2001, *Maryland v. Pringle* in 2003, *Illinois v. Lidster* in 2004, and *Illinois v. Caballes* in 2005 have redefined the nature and vastly expanded the authority of police search. In these and many other cases, the Supreme Court ruled that police search on the basis of a probable cause, and not necessarily a reasonable suspicion, is not a violation of the Fourth Amendment's right of protection against unreasonable search and seizure and the Fourteenth Amendment's due process clause.

In the area of drug law enforcement, some of the landmark Supreme Court decisions, as mentioned in chapter 3, included *Oliver v. United States* in 1984, *Skinner v. Railway Labor Executives' Association* in 1989, *Veronica School District v. Acton* in 1995, *HUD v. Rucker et al.* in 2002, *Virginia v. Hicks* in 2003, and *Gonzales v. Raich* in 2005. In these cases the Supreme Court upholds the view that drug testing through urine analysis taken in a non-invasive way and regulations protecting public housing and public places from drug crimes do not violate the Fourth Amendment. In *Oliver v. United States* in 1984, the Supreme Court upheld the "open fields doctrine" that suggests that police can search a privately owned field, house, or papers without a warrant and without being constrained by the Fourth Amendment. The decision in *Skinner v. Railway Labor Executives' Association* was that the Fourth Amendment does not prohibit governmental authorities to develop drug and alcohol testing regulations for employees. In *HUD v. Rucker et al.* in 2002, the Supreme Court unanimously decided that the policy of eviction of people in public housing who abuse drugs, or even live close to people who abuse drugs, is consistent with the intent of the relevant statute made by Congress. In *Gonzales v. Raich* in 2005, the Supreme Court ruled that Congress, under the Commerce Clause and the Controlled Substance Act of 1970, has the right to regulate the production, trafficking, and use of medical marijuana.

A separate system of juvenile justice was central to the rehabilitative ideal and progressive penology. In a number of recent decisions, as discussed in Chapter 4, the Supreme Court held the view that adults and juveniles are to be governed by the same constitutional rules and principles. Under the Constitution, juveniles do not receive any special treatments. In a number of rulings such as in *Kent v. United States* in 1966, re *Gault* in 1967, in re *Winship* in 1970, *McKeiver v. Pennsylvania* in 1971, *Breed v. Jones* in 1975, *Boyd v. State* in 1993, and *Yarborough v. Alvarado* in 2004, the Supreme Court ruled that the constitutional principles of due process, unusual search and seizures, privilege against self-incrimination, and open trial are equally applicable to juveniles. In *Harmelin v. Michigan in 1991*, the Court said that mandatory sentencing for juveniles is not a violation of the Eighth Amendment's clause of cruel and unusual punishment. The defendant Harmelin received a mandatory sentencing of life in prison without the possibility of parole, under a Michigan mandatory minimum statute, for the possession of 650 grams of cocaine. In delivering the majority opinion, Justice Scalia, as mentioned in Chapter 4, said: "Harmelin's claim that his sentence is unconstitutional because it is mandatory in nature, allowing the sentencer no opportunity to consider 'mitigating factors,' has no support in the Eighth Amendment's text and history."

In areas of sex crimes, the Supreme Court is generally in agreement with the policy strategies of sex offender registration, notification, and involuntary civil commitment. In two recent cases, *Smith et al. v. Doe et al. of Alaska* in 2003, and *Connecticut Department of Public Safety et al. v. Doe* in 2003, as discussed in Chapter 5, the Supreme Court upheld the view that sex offender registration and notification laws are not in violation of the due process clause and the liberty clause of the Fourteenth Amendment. In *Kansas v. Hendricks*, the Supreme Court in 1997 made a ruling that Kansas's civil commitment statute was not in violation of the constitution's due process, double jeopardy, and *ex post facto* clauses.

During the recent years, the Supreme Court, however, has also decided a number of cases that were generally not in favor of get-tough strategies. Some of these cases are related to sex crimes, mandatory sentencing, and the death penalty. In the area of sex crimes, one of the landmark liberal decisions came in *Lawrence et al. v. Texas* in 2003. In a 6-3 decision, the Supreme Court made a ruling that the Texas homosexual statute violated the due process clause of the constitution. The *Lawrence* decision has made a significant impact on state sodomy laws, same-sex marriage, and adoption by gay parents. In *Reno, Attorney General of the United States et al. v. American Civil Liberties Union* in 1997 and in *Ashcroft v. the Free Speech Coalition* in 2002, the Supreme Court ruled, as discussed in Chapter 5, that the efforts to regulate Internet Child Pornography by the federal government, through the Communications Decency Act of 1996, the Child Pornography Prevention Act of 1996, and the Child Online Protection Act of 1998, were in violation of the First Amendment's right of free speech. The Supreme Court's *Blakely* and *Booker* decisions related to state and federal mandatory sentencing guidelines made in 2004 and 2005, *Atkins* decision related to the death penalty for the mentally retarded made in 2002, and *Roper* decision, made in 2005, related to juvenile death penalty are significant departures from that Court's traditional conservative judicial philosophy.

The social and economic contexts and the nature of crimes in America in the 21st century are very different from those of the 1970s when crime became a major domestic social concern for America's policy-makers. Today, crimes are not merely the problems of drugs, guns, and gangs. Today's concerns about crimes are intimately connected to the broader issues of public safety, economic security, critical infrastructure protections, national security, and globalization. The rise of global terrorism, global organized crime, and cyber crimes have permanently changed the scope and nature of policy-making in crime and justice in America, particularly from the beginning of the first decade of the 21st century (Muraskin & Roberts, 2004). The rise and expansion of the Internet has given birth to an entirely different set of crimes that can bring not just massive economic devastations, but also unimaginable moral and social chaos. It is in these contexts of the rise of new crimes and the new modalities of criminality that the core of policy focus in crime and justice today is moving away from the idea of correcting or rehabilitating an offender to the creation and expansion of an organizationally and technologically integrated system of control, supervision, and surveillance. The rise of a "culture of control" seems to be an inevitable process related to modernization in advanced industrialized countries (Foucault, 1977; Blomberg & Cohen, 1995; Dumn, 1987; Garland, 1990; 2001; Lucken & Blomberg, 2000). The advance of modernization and globalization has created new complexities for governance in post-industrial societies. The rise of new complexities in governance has brought new tensions between politics of growth and politics of control, particularly in policy-making in crime and justice (Simon. 2007). The process of American modernization, however, is also a process of expansion of American experiment—the experiment for a "good society" based on freedom, democracy, justice, and equality, or as Thomas Jefferson put it "life, liberty, and the pursuit of happiness." The search for a balance between progressive penology and new penology—between offender rehabilitation and systemic control—in America's crime policy will continue. But it will continue within the contexts and the realities of crimes in the 21st century.

REFERENCES

Abner, C. (2006). Waging war on sexual crimes. *State News*, 49 (4), 12-14.

Ackard, D. M., Neumark-Sztainer, D. (2002). Date violence and date rape among adolescents: Associations with disordered eating behaviors and psychological health. *Child Abuse and Neglect*, 26, 455-473.

Adler, J. S. (2006). *First in violence, deepest in dirt: Homicide in Chicago, 1875-1920.* Cambridge. MA: Harvard University Press.

Administrative Office of the U.S. Courts. (2006). *Judicial Business of the United States Courts* (Annual Report). Washington DC: The Government Printing Office.

Administrative Office of the U.S. Courts. (2007). *Fiscal year 2006 caseloads remain at high level.* Retrieved on August 7, 2007 from www.uscourts.gov

Alexander, P. C., Anderson, C. L., Brand, B., Schaffer, C., Grelling, B. Z., & Kretz, L. (1998). Adult attachment and long term effects in survivors of incest. *Child Abuse & Neglect*, 22, 45-61.

Allen, F. A. (1987). The decline of rehabilitative ideal in American criminal justice. In K. L. Hall (Ed.). *Police, prison, and punishment: Major historical interpretations* (pp.1-10). New York: Garland Publishing.

Allen G. (1995). *The courage of our convictions: Abolition of parole will save money* and *lives.* Washington DC: The Heritage Foundation.

American Bar Association. (2004). *Electronic evidence and discovery: What every lawyer should know* (by M. C. S. Lange & K. M. Nimsger). Washington DC: ABA.

American Bar Association. (1998). *The federalization of criminal law* (Task Force Report). Washington DC: Criminal Justice Section, ABA.

Anbinder, T. (2001). *Five Points: The nineteenth century New York City that invented tap dance, stole elections, and became the world's most notorious slums.* New York: Free Press.

Anderson, M. J. (2002). From chastity requirement to sexual license: Sexual consent and new rape shield law. *George Washington Law Review*, 51, 1- 46.

Arkfeld, M. R. (2005). *Electronic discovery and evidence.* Phoenix, AZ: Law Partner Publishing LLC.

Atwell, M. W. (2004). *Evolving standards of decency: Popular culture and capital punishment.* New York: Peter Lang Publishing.

Baker, J. S. Jr. (2005). Jurisdictional and separation of power strategies to limit the expansion of federal crimes. *American University Law Review*, 54, 546-576.

Baker, J. S. Jr., & Bennett, D. E. (2004). *Measuring the explosive growth of federal crime legislation.* Washington DC: The Federalist Society for Law and Public Policy Studies.

Beccaria, C. (1995). *On Crimes and Punishments* (Trans. by R. Davies). New York: Cambridge University Press.

Becker, H. S. (1977). The marijuana tax act. In P. E. Rock (Ed.). *Drugs and Politics* (pp. 55-66). New Brunswick, NJ: Transaction Books.

Beckett, K. (1999). *Making crime pay: Law and order in contemporary American politics.* New York: Oxford University Press.

Belenko, S. R. (2000). *Drugs and drug policy in America: A documentary history.* Westport, CT: Greenwood Press.

Bennett, W. J., Dilulio, J. J., & Walters, J. P. (1996). *Body count: Moral poverty and how to win America's war against crime and drugs.* New York: Simon & Schuster.

Berger, P. L., Kellner, H., & Berger, B. (1973). *The Homeless Mind: Modernization and Consciousness.* New York: Random House.

Bertram, E., Blachman, M., Sharpe, K., & Andreas, P. (1996). *Drug war politics: The price of denial*. Berkeley: University of California Press.

Blomberg, T. G., & Cohen, S. (Eds.). (1995). *Punishment and social control*. New York: Aldine De Gruyter.

Blumstein, A., & Wallman, J. (Eds.). (2000). *The crime drop in America*. New York: Cambridge University Press.

Blumstein, A., Cohen, J., Roth, J. A., & Visher, C. A. (1986). *Criminal careers and "career criminals."* Washington DC: National Academy Press.

Bonnie, R. J., & Whitebread, C. H. II. (2005). *The forbidden fruit and the tree of knowledge: An inquiry into the legal history of American marijuana prohibition*. Retrieved April 5, 2005 from www.druglibrary.org/schaffer

Booth, M. (2004). *Cannabis: A history*. New York: Thomas Dunne Books.

Boswell, J. (1994). *Same-sex unions in premodern Europe*. New York: Villard Books.

Braithwaite, J. (2000). The regulatory state and the transformation of criminology. In D. Garland and R. Sparks (Eds.). *Criminology and Social Theory* (pp. 47-70). New York: Oxford University Press.

Braswell, M., Pollock, J. M., & Braswell, S. (2005). *Morality stories: Dilemmas in ethics, crime, & justice*. Durham, NC: Carolina Academic Press.

Bremner, R. H. (1970). *Children and youth in America: A documentary history*. Cambridge, MA: Harvard University Press.

Brown, S. (2003). *Crime and law in media culture*. Philadelphia: Open University Press.

Brundage, J. (1987). *Law, sex, and Christian society in medieval Europe*. Chicago: Chicago University Press.

Bureau of International Information Programs. (2006). *U.S. Senate vote to ratify cyber crime convention* (by C. Walker). Washington DC: Department of State.

Bureau of Justice Statistics. (2007). Expenditure and Employment Statistics. Washington DC: Office of Justice Programs, Department of Justice.

Bureau of Justice Statistics. (2006). *Identity theft, 2004* (by K. Baum). Washington DC: Office of Justice Programs, Department of Justice.

Bureau of Justice Statistics. (2006). Justice Expenditure and Employment in the United States. Washington DC: Office of Justice Programs, Department of Justice.

Bureau of Justice Statistics. (2006). *Identity Theft, 2004* (First Estimate from the National Crime Victimization Survey). Washington DC: Office of Justice Programs, Department of Justice.

Bureau of Justice Statistics. (2006). *Probation and parole in the United States, 2005*. Washington DC: Office of Justice Programs, Department of Justice.

Bureau of Justice Statistics. (2006). *Federal prosecution of human trafficking, 2001-2005* (by M. Motivans & T. Kyckelhahn). Washington DC: Office of Justice Programs, Department of Justice.

Bureau of Justice Statistics. (2006). *Courts and sentencing statistics*. Washington DC: Office of Justice Programs, Department of Justice.

Bureau of Justice Statistics. (2006). *Reported crime in the United States*. Washington DC: Office of Justice Programs, Department of Justice.

Bureau of Justice Statistics. (2005). *State court sentencing of convicted felons, 2002*. Washington DC: Office of Justice Programs, Department of Justice.

Bureau of Justice Statistics. (2005). *Criminal victimization, 2004* (by S. M. Catalano). Washington DC: Office of Justice Programs, Department of Justice.

Bureau of Justice Statistics. (2005). *Sexual violence reported by correctional authorities, 2004* (by A. J. Beck & T. A. Hughes). Washington DC: Office of Justice Programs, Department of Justice.

Bureau of Justice Statistics. (2005). *Prisoners in 2005* (by P. M. Harrison & A. J. Beck). Washington DC: Office of Justice Programs, Department of Justice.

Bureau of Justice Statistics. (2005). *Violent crime trends, 1973-2004.* Washington DC: Office of Justice Programs, Department of Justice.

Bureau of Justice Statistics. (2005). *Prison and jail inmates at mid-year 2004* (by P. M. Harrison & A. J. Beck). Washington DC: Office of Justice Programs, Department of Justice.

Bureau of Justice Statistics. (2004). *Law enforcement management and administrative statistics, 2000.* Washington DC: Office of Justice Programs, Department of Justice.

Bureau of Justice Statistics. (2004). *Homicide trends in the United States* (by J. A. Fox & M. W. Zawitz). Washington DC: Office of Justice Programs, Department of Justice.

Bureau of Justice Statistics. (2004). *Justice expenditure and employment in the United States, 2001.* Washington DC: Office of Justice Programs, Department of Justice.

Bureau of Justice Statistics. (2004). *Cyber crime against business* (by R. R. Rantala). Washington DC: Office of Justice Programs, Department of Justice.

Bureau of Justice Statistics. (2003). *Reporting crime to the police, 1992-2000* (by T. C. Hart). Washington DC: Office of Justice Programs, Department of Justice.

Bureau of Justice Statistics. (2003). *Local police departments, 2003.* Washington DC: Office of Justice Programs, Department of Justice.

Bureau of Justice Statistics. (2003). *Reentry trends in the United States.* Washington DC: Office of Justice Programs, Department of Justice.

Bureau of Justice Statistics. (2003). *Intimate partner violence, 1993-2001* (by C. M. Rennison). Washington DC: Office of Justice Programs, Department of Justice.

Bureau of Justice Statistics. (2003). *Recidivism of sex offenders released from prison in 1994* (by P. A. Langan, E. L. Schmitt, and M. R. Durose). Washington DC: Office of Justice Programs, Department of Justice.

Bureau of Justice Statistics. (2002). *Correctional population in the United States, 2000.* Washington DC: Office of Justice Programs, Department of Justice.

Bureau of Justice Statistics. (2002). *Intimate partner violence* (by C. M. Rennison). Washington DC: Office of Justice Programs, Department of Justice.

Bureau of Justice Statistics. (2002). *Recidivism of prisoners released in 1994* (by P. A. Lingam & D. J. Levin). Washington DC: Office of Justice Programs, Department of Justice.

Bureau of Justice Statistics. (2001). *Intimate partner violence and the age of victim, 1993-1999* (by C. M. Rennison). Washington DC: Office of Justice Programs, Department of Justice.

Bureau of Justice Statistics. (1999). *Prior abuse reported by inmates and probationers* (by C. W. Harlow). Washington DC: Office of Justice Programs, Department of Justice.

Bureau of Justice Statistics. (1999). *Women Offenders.* Washington DC: Office of Justice Programs, Department of Justice.

Bureau of Justice Statistics. (1999). *Truth in sentencing in state prisons* (by P. M. Ditton & D. J. Wilson). Washington DC: Office of Justice Programs, Department of Justice.

Bureau of Justice Statistics. (1997). *Sex offenses and offenders: An analysis of data on rape and sexual assault.* Washington DC: Office of Justice Programs, Department of Justice.

Bureau of Justice Statistics. (1995). *Weapons offenses and offenders* (by L. A. Greenfield and M. W. Zawitz). Washington DC: Office of Justice Programs, Department of Justice.

Bureau of the Census. (1975). *Historical statistics of the United States: Colonial times to 1970.* Washington DC: Department of Commerce.

Burns, K. J. (1999). A chronicle of death penalty in Massachusetts (part one). *Lawyers Journal,* January (Massachusetts Bar Association, Criminal Justice Section News).

Bush–Cheney '04. (2004). *President signs nationwide Amber Alert Law.* Retrieved May 10, 2005 from www.georgebush.com

Bush, G. W. (January 20, 2001). *Proclamation 7403—National Day of Prayer and Thanksgiving, 2001* (Public Papers of the President). Washington DC: Government Printing Press.

Bush, G. W. (January 29, 2001). *Remarks on faith-based initiatives* (Public Papers of the President). Washington DC: Government Printing Press.

Bush, G. W. (February 1, 2001). *Remarks at the national prayer breakfast* (Public Papers of the President). Washington DC: Government Printing Press.

Bush, G. W. (March 3, 2001). *Remarks at the White House conference on faith-based and community initiatives in Los Angeles, California* (Public Papers of the President). Washington DC: Government Printing Press.

Butts. J. A. (2005). Can we do without juvenile justice? *Criminal Justice Magazine* (American Bar Association), pp. 1-10.

Butts, J. A. (2004). *Too many youths facing adult justice*. Washington DC: The Urban Institute.

Butts, J. A., & Mitchell, O. (2000). Brick by brick: Dismantling the border between juvenile and adult justice. *Criminal justice, 2000*, 2, pp. 167-213.

Byrne, J. M., & Revovich, D. R. (Eds.). (2007). *The new technology of crime, law and social control*. New York: Criminal Justice Press.

Cable News Network (CNN). (2005). *Record bad year for tech security*. Retrieved November 8, 2006 from money.cnn.com

Calder, J. D (1993). *The origins and development of federal crime control policy: Herbert Hoover's Initiatives*. Westport, CT: Praeger

California Amber Alert. (2003). *Save a child with an Amber Alert*. CA: Highway Patrol Commission.

Carnevale Associates. (May, 2005). *Improving state drug laws: Information brief*. MD: Darnestown.

Carpenter, C. L. (2006). The constitutionality of strict liability in sex offender registration laws. *Boston University Law Review*, 86 (2), 295-369.

Carpenter, T.G. (2004). The U.S. campaign against international narcotics trafficking. *Cato Policy Analysis Paper, No. 63.*

Centers for Disease Control and Prevention. (2004). *Costs of intimate partner violence against women in the United States*. Atlanta: Department of Health and Human Services.

CERT Coordinating Center. (2004). *2004 e-crime watch survey: Summary of findings*. Pittsburgh, PA: Carnegie Mellon Software Engineering Institute. Retrieved November 3, 2006 from www.cert.org/archive

Chiang, C. N., & Lee, C. C. (1985). *Drug exposure: Kinetics and dynamics*. Washington DC: National Institute on Drug Abuse.

Clear, T. R. (1994). *Harm in American Penology: Offenders, Victims, and their communities*. Albany, NY: State University of New York Press.

Clear, T. R. (1998). *Societal responses to the President's Crime Commission: A thirty-year retrospective*. Retrieved March 5, 2005 from www.usdoj.gov

Cluster, D. S. (1992). *Bad guys and good guys: Moral polarization and crime*. Westport, CT: Greenwood Press.

Clausen, J. A. (1963). Drug use. In R. K. Merton and R. Nisbet (Eds.). *Contemporary* Social Problems (pp. 185-226). New York: Harcourt Brace Jsvanovich Inc.

Clinton W. J. (January 13, 2001). *The President's Radio Address*. Washington DC: Presidential Document Online.

Clinton, W. J. (June 9, 1996). *Remarks in roundtable discussion on juvenile crime in Los Vegas* (Public Papers of the President). Washington DC: Government Printing Press.

Clinton W. J. (June 22, 1996). *Weekly Radio Address* (Public Papers of the President). Washington DC: Government Printing Press.

Clinton W. J. (January 24, 1995). *Address before a Joint Session of the Congress on the State of the Union* (Public Papers of the President). Washington DC: Government Printing Press.

Clinton, W. J. (June 29, 1995). *Remarks announcing community policing grants* (Public Papers of the President). Washington DC: Government Printing Press.

Clinton, W. J. (October 5, 1994). *Proclamation 6733—crime prevention month* (Public Papers of the President). Washington DC: Government Printing Press.

Clinton, W. J. (August 22, 1994). *Letter to members of the Senate on crime legislation.* Washington DC: Presidential Documents Online.

Clinton, W. J. (April 11, 1994). *Remarks to law enforcement officers* (Public Papers of the President). Washington DC: Government Printing Press.

Clinton, W. J. (August 11, 1993). *Remarks announcing the anticrime initiative and exchange with reporters* (Public Papers of the President). Washington DC: Government Printing Press.

Clinton, W. J. (July 1, 1993). *Remarks on the swearing-in of National Drug Control Policy Director Lee Brown* (Public Papers of the President). Washington DC: Government Printing Press.

Cohen, J. L. (2002). *Regulating intimacy: A new legal paradigm.* Trenton, NJ: Princeton University Press.

Cohen, P. J. (2004). *Drugs, addition, and the law: Policy, politics, and public health.* Durham: North Carolina Academic Press.

Collins, R. L. (2004). Watching sex on television predicts adolescent initiation of sexual behavior. *Pediatrics* (Electronic Journal), 114 (3), 280-289.

Colorado Department of Corrections. (2000). *State sex offender treatment programs – 50 state survey* (by M. West, C. S. Hormas, & P. Wenger). Colorado Springs, CO: Colorado Department of Corrections.

Congressional Budget Office. (2001). *Cost estimate: HR 2215—21st Century Department of Justice Appropriations Authorization Act.* Washington DC: CBO.

Congressional Research Service. (2006). *USA Patriot Improvement and Reauthorization Act of 2005: A legal analysis.* (by B. T. Yeh & C. Doyle). Washington DC: The Library of Congress.

Congressional Research Service. (2006). *Transnational organized crime: Principal threats and U.S. responses* (by J. R. Wagley). Washington DC: The Library of Congress.

Congressional Research Service. (2005). *War on drugs: Legislation in 108th congresses and related developments* (by M. Eddy). Washington DC: The Library of Congress.

Congressional Research Service. (2005). *Internet: An overview of key technology policy issues affecting its use and growth.* Washington DC: The Library of Congress.

Congressional Research Service. (2005). *Internet privacy: Overview and pending legislations* (by M. S. Smith). Washington DC: The Library of Congress.

Congressional Research Service. (2005). *Remedies available to victims of identity theft* (by A. A. Wellborn). Washington DC: The Library of Congress.

Congressional Research Service. (2002). *The USA Patriot Act: A sketch.* Washington DC: The Library of Congress.

Congressional Research Service. (2002). *Terrorism, the future, and the U.S. foreign policy* (by R. Lee & R. Perl). Washington DC: The Library of Congress.

Congressional Research Service. (2001). *Violence against Women Act: History, federal funding and reauthorization legislation* (by A. Siskin). Washington DC: The Library of Congress.

Congressional Research Service. (2000). *National information infrastructures: The federal role* (by G. J. Mcloughlin). Washington DC: The Library of Congress.

Connelly, M. T. (1980). *The response to prostitution in the Progressive Era.* Chapel Hill: University of North Carolina Press.

Constitutional Law Center. (2005). *Supreme Court: Landmark Decisions: A Century of Change.* Retrieved March 10, 2005 from http//supreme.findlaw.com

Correl, S. (2004). *National law enforcement telecommunication system.* Retrieved March 15, 2007 from www.iacptechnology.org

Covington, S. (1998). How conservative philanthropies and think tanks transform U.S. policy. *Covert Action Quarterly,* winter, pp. 1-13.

Cowin, A. J. (1991). Fighting crime: Assessing the Bush and Biden approaches. *Heritage Foundation Bulletin*, 164, pp. 1-8.

Crank. J. (1995). The Community-Policing movement of the early twenty-first century. In J. Klofas & S. Stojkovic (Eds.). *Crime and justice in the year 2002* (pp. 107-126). New York: Wadsworth Publishing Company.

Critical Choices. (2001). *Mandatory minimum sentencing and the state's drug incarceration boom.* Retrieved June 24, 2006 from www.drugstrategies.org

Culen, F. T. (2005). The twelve people who saved rehabilitation: How the science of criminology made a difference. *Criminology*, 43, 1- 42.

Currie, E. (1994). *Reckoning: Drugs, the cities, and the American future.* Chicago: Lawrence Hill.

Currie, E. (1986). *Confronting crime: An American challenge.* New York: Pantheon Books.

Daly, K., & Maher, L. (Eds.). (1998). *Criminology at the crossroads: Feminist readings* in *crime and justice.* New York: Oxford University Press.

De Bellis, M. D. (2005). The Psychobiology of Neglect. *Child Maltreatment*, 10 (2), 150-172

DeGrieff, P. (1999). *Drugs and the limits of liberalism: Moral and legal Issues.* Ithaca, NY: Cornell University Press.

Dempsey, J. X. (2000). *Overview of current CJUS information systems.* Washington DC: Center for Democracy and Technology.

Denson, J. V. (2001). *Reassessing the Presidency: The rise of the executive state and the decline of freedom.* Auburn, Alabama: Ludwig von Mises Institute.

Dilulio, J. J. (1996). Fill churches, not jails: Youth crime and "Superpredators." *Hearing before the Subcommittee on Youth Violence, Senate Committee of the Judiciary.* Washington DC: United States Senate.

Drug Policy Alliance. (2003). *State of the states: Drug policy reforms 1996–2002.* Retrieved March 7, 2007 from www.drugpolicy.org/doc

Dubin, J. M., & Hutt, P. B. (2001). *Rapist discovers new weapons: The problem of and response to drug-facilitated sexual assault.* Cambridge: Harvard Law School. Retrieved March 10, 2006 from www.leda.law.harvard.edu

Dumm, T. L. (1987). *Democracy and Punishment: Disciplinary origins of the United States.* Madison, Wisconsin: The University of Wisconsin Press.

Dunn, W. N. (1981). *Public policy analysis: An introduction.* Englewood, NJ: Prentice Hall.

Edwards, D. M. (1992): Politics and pornography: A comparison of the findings of the *President's Commission and the Meese Commission and the resulting response.* Retrieved June 10, 2006 from www.scireview.de/efs

Ehrlich, R. L., & Steele, M. S. (2006). *Cyber security White Paper: Defining the role of state government to secure Maryland's cyber infrastructure.* Retrieved March 10, 2007 from www.gov.state.md.us

Ekstrand, L. E. (1996). *Juvenile justice: Selected issues to OJJDP's Reauthorization.* Testimony before the Senate Subcommittee on Youth Violence. Washington DC: The U.S. Senate Committee of the Judiciary.

Epstein, J. C. (2001). *Understanding the Jeanne Clery Disclosure Act.* Washington DC: The Department of Education.

Epstein, J. N., Saunders B. E., Kilpatrick D. G., & Resnick H. S. (1998). PTSD as a mediator between childhood rape and alcohol use in adult women. *Child Abuse and Neglect*, 22 (3), 223- 234.

Erlen, J., & Spillane, J. F. (2004). *Federal drug control policy: The evolution of policy and practice.* New York: Pharmaceutical Products Press.

Fagan, J. (1996). *The criminalization of domestic violence: Promises and limits.* (National Institute of Justice Research Report). Retrieved June, 15, 2006 from www.ncjrs.gov

Faravelli, C., Giugni, A., Salvatori, S., & Ricca, V. (2004). Psychopathology after rape. *The American Journal of Psychiatry*, 161(8), 1483-1485.

Farber, D. (Ed.). (1994). *The sixties: From memory to history.* Chapel Hill, NC: University of North Carolina Press.

Federal Bureau of Investigation. (2006). *Innocent images national initiative: Online child pornography/ child sexual exploitation investigation.* Washington DC: The Department of Justice.

Federal Bureau of Investigation. (2006). *The Internet Crime Complaint Center* (IC3). Washington DC: The Department of Justice.

Federal Bureau of Investigation. (2005). *Preliminary crime statistics for 2005* (Press Release). Washington DC: The Department of Justice.

Federal Bureau of Investigation. (2004). *Uniform Crime Reporting (UCR): Frequently asked questions.* Washington DC: The Department of Justice.

Federal Bureau of Investigation. (2004). *History of the FBI: Rise of international crime.* Washington DC: The Department of Justice.

Federal Bureau of Investigation. (2004). *History of the FBI: Rise of a wired world, 1993-2001.* Washington DC: The Department of Justice.

Federal Bureau of Investigation. (2004). *Crime in the United States, 2004: Uniform Crime Reports.* Washington DC: The Department of Justice.

Federal Bureau of Investigation. (2003). *10 years of protecting our children: Crackdown on sexual predators on the Internet.* Washington DC: The Department of Justice.

Federal Communications Commission. (2004). *Children's Internet Protection Act.* Washington DC: FCC.

Federal Law Enforcement Training Center. (2006). *International Training and Technical Assistance.* Glynco, Georgia: FLETC.

Federal Register. (2003). *Presidential document: Executive Order 13286.* Washington DC: Federal Register.

Federal Trade Commission. (2005). *National and state trends in fraud & identity theft, 2004.* Washington DC: FTC. Retrieved November 8, 2006 from www.consumer.gov/idtheft

Federal Trade Commission. (2004). *Consumer Sentinel.* Washington DC: FTC. Retrieved November 10, 2006 from www.consumer.gov/sentinel.about.htm

Federal Trade Commission. (2003). *Identity theft survey report.* Washington DC: FTC. Retrieved November 4, 2006 from www.ftc.gov

Federal Trade Commission. (2003). *False claims in SPAM* (A report of the Division of Marketing Practices). Washington DC: FTC. Retrieved November 4, 2006 from www.ftc.gov/opa/2003/04/spamrpt.shtm

Feeley, M. M., & Rubin, E. L. (2000). *Judicial policy-making and the modern state: How the courts reformed American prisons.* New York: Cambridge University Press.

Feeley, M. M., & Sarat, A. D. (1980). *The policy dilemma: Federal crime policy and the Law Enforcement Assistance Administration, 1968-1978.* Minneapolis, Minn.: University of Minnesota Press.

Fellman, D. (1986). *Criminal procedure.* Encyclopedia of the American Constitution. New York: Macmillan.

Finckenauer, J. O. (2000). Meeting the challenges of transnational crime. *National Institute of Justice Journal,* July, 1-7.

Finer, J. (2004). Efforts to clear out Blue Laws in Massachusetts. *Washington Post,* April, pp. 1-2.

Finkelhor, D., & Ormrod, R. (2004). *Prostitution of juveniles: Patterns from NIBRS.* OJJDP Juvenile Justice Bulletin, June.

Fischer, F (2003). *Reframing Public Policy: Discursive Politics and Deliberate Practices.* New York: Oxford University Press.

Fisher, B. S., Cullen, F. T., & Turner, M. G. (2000). *The sexual victimization of college women.* Washington DC: National Institute of Justice

Florida Department of Law Enforcement. (2004). *State budget funds FDLE's top priorities, 2004-2005* (News Release). Tallahassee: FDLE Public Information Office.

Florida Department of Law Enforcement. (2001). *Governor Bush holds ceremonial bill signing for identity theft.* Tallahassee: FDLE Public Information Office.

Foucault, M. (1990). *The history of sexuality: An introduction.* New York: Vintage.

Foucault, M. (1977). *Discipline and punish: The birth of the prison.* London: Allen Unwin.

Freud, S. (1989). *Civilization and its Discontent* (Trans. by J. Strachey). New York: W. W. Norton & Company.

Freidman, L. M. (1985). *A history of American law.* New York: Simon & Schuster, Inc.

Friedman, L. M. (1993). *Crime and punishment in American history.* New York: Basic Books.

Friedman, T. L. (2005). *The world is flat: A brief history of the twentieth century.* New York: Farrar, Straus and Giroux.

Fukuyama, F. (1992). *The end of history and the last man.* New York: The Free Press.

Garland, D. (2001). *The culture of control: Crime and social order in contemporary* society. Chicago: University of Chicago Press.

Garland, D. (1990). *Punishment and modern society: A study in social theory.* Chicago: University of Chicago Press.

Gaubatz, K. T. (1995). *Crime in the Public Mind.* Ann Arbor, MI: The University of Michigan Press.

Gest, T. (2001). *Crime and politics: Big government's erratic campaign for law and order.* New York: Oxford University Press.

Gilfoyle, T. J. (1991). Prostitution. In E. Foner and J. A. Garraty (Eds.). *Reading Companion to American History.* New York: Houghton Mifflin.

Gilmore, J. (1998). *Making criminal pay: Jim Gilmore's plan to make criminals pay the cost of their incarceration.* Retrieved March 30, 1998 from www.gilmorenet.com

Gist, N. E. (1997). *Edward Byrne memorial state and local law enforcement assistance* (Bureau of Justice Assistance Fact Sheet). Washington DC: The Department of Justice.

Goldberg, P. (1980). *The federal government's response to illicit drugs, 1969-1978.* Retrieved April 5, 2006 from http://www.drugtext.org.library.reports

Gottfredson, M. R., & Hirschi, T. (1999). *A general theory of Crime.* Stanford, CA: Stanford University Press.

Gould, L. E, & Namenwirth, J. Z. (1971). Contrary objectives: Crime control and the rehabilitation of criminals. In J. D. Douglas (Ed.). *Crime and justice in American society* *(pp. 237-267).* Indianapolis: The Bobs-Merrill.

Governor's Ex-Offender Task Force. (2006). *Final report to the Governor.* Tallahassee, Florida: Office of the Governor.

Greene, J. (2002). Getting tough on crime: The history and political context of sentencing reform developments leading to the passage of the 1994 Crime Act. In C. Tata & N. Hutton (Eds.). *Sentencing and society: International perspectives* (pp.1-33). England: Ashgate Publishing Limited.

Greenberg, D. (1976). *Crime and law enforcement in the colony of New York, 1691-1776.* Ithaca: Cornell University Press.

Greenberg, M.A. (1999). *Prohibition enforcement: Charting a new mission.* Springfield, Illinois: Charles C. Thomas.

Greiff, D. P. (Ed.). (1999). *Drugs and the limits of liberalism: Moral and legal issues.* Ithaca: Cornel University Press.

Griffin, P. (2003). *Trying and sentencing juveniles as adults: An analysis of state transfer and blended sentencing laws.* Washington DC: Department of Justice, OJJDP.

Griffin, P. (2001). *Evaluation of Juvenile Accountability Incentive Block Grant Program in Pennsylvania.* Pittsburgh: National Center for Juvenile Justice.

Hallahan, K. M. (1986). Why so violent? *Foundation News,* May-June, pp. 1-5. Retrieved April 4, 2004 from http://www.eisenhowerfoundation.org

Hanson, G. R. (December, 2001). *Looking the other way: Rave promoters and club drugs.* Hearing before the Senate Caucus on International Narcotic Control. Washington DC: NIDA.

Harrison, L. D., Backenheimer, M., & Inciardi, J. A. (1996). *History of drug legislation.* Retrieved April 5, 2005 from http://www.cedro-uva.org

Harvard School of Public Health. (2006). *Study finds M-rated video games contain violence, sexual themes, substances and profanity not labeled on game boxes.* Retrieved January 25, 2007 from www.hsph.harvard.edu

Harvard School of Public Health. (2004). *Study finds "Rating Creep": Movie ratings categories contain more violence, sex, profanity than a decade ago.* Retrieved January 25, 2007 from www.hsph.harvard.edu/press/releases

Helderman, R. S. (2006). *Law tells schools to teach students about online safety.* Retrieved February 3, 2007 from www.washingtonpost.com

Healy, G. (February 12, 2003). *Ehrlich errs with Project Exile.* Washington DC: Cato Institute.

Hemmens, C., Steiner, B., & Mueller, D. (2004). *Criminal justice case briefs: Significant cases in juvenile justice.* Los Angeles, CA: Roxbury Publishing Company.

Holmes R. M., & Holmes, S. T. (Eds.). (2002). *Current perspectives on sex crimes.* Thousand Oaks, CA: Sage Publication.

Hopper, J. (2003). *Child Abuse: Statistics, Research, and Resources.* Retrieved April, 4, 2004 from www.jimhopper.com

Hopkins, L (April 24, 2004). *Warner restoring rights of felons at quick pace:* Warner making history. Norfolk, VA: The Virginian Pilot.

Horowitz, H. L. (2002). *Rereading sex: Battles over sexual knowledge and suppression in nineteenth- century America.* New York: Alfred A. Knopf.

House Committee on Education and the Workforce. (November 4, 2002). *President signs legislation to help reduce juvenile crime* (Press Release). Washington DC: The House of Representatives.

Hunter, J. D. (1992). *Culture wars. The struggle to define America.* New York: Basic Books.

Husak, D., & Peele, S. (1998). One of the major problems of our society: Symbolism and the evidence of drug harms in U.S. Supreme Court decisions. *Contemporary Drug Problems,* 25, 191-233.

ImpacTeen Illicit Drug Team. (2002). *Illicit drug policies: Selected laws from the 50 states.* Retrieved on July 20, 2007 from http://www.drugpolicy.org

Inciardi, J. A., & Harrison, L. D. (Eds.). (2000). *Harm reduction: National and international perspectives.* Thousand Oaks, CA: Sage.

International Telecommunication Union. (2005). *Harmonizing legal approaches to cyber crime* (by S. Schjolberg & A. M. Hubbard). Geneva: International Telecommunication Union.

Internet Crime Complaint Center. (2005). *IC3 2005 Internet crime report.* Washington DC: FBI, DOJ.

Jennings, R. (April 20, 2003). Laci Peterson case tied to Roe debate. *Daily Record News.* pp. 1-3.

Johnson, K. N. (2006). *Brothel Drama in America, 1900-1920.* New York: Cambridge University Press.

Jones, W.T. (1952). *A history of western philosophy.* New York: Harcourt, Brace and Company.

Justice Policy Institute. (2007). *Fact sheet: Response to FBI Uniform Crime Report.* Washington DC: JPI

Justice Policy Institute. (2007). *Maryland's mandatory minimum drug sentencing laws.* Retrieved March 10, 2007 from www.justicepolicy.org

Kaiser Family Foundation. (2005). *Sex on TV 4: A Kaiser Family Foundation report* (by (D. Kunkel, K. Eyal, K. Finnerty, E. Biely, & E. Donnerstein) California: Menlo Park.

Kaplan, J., Weisberg, G., & Binder G. (2004). *Criminal law: Cases and materials* (5th ed.). New York: Aspen Publishers.

Katz, J. (1988). *Seductions of crime: Moral and sensual attractions of doing evil.* New York: Basic Books.

Kendel, E. (1992). *Physical punishment and the development of aggressive and violent behavior: A review.* Durham, NH: Family Research Laboratory, University of New Hampshire.

Kerr, O. S. (2006). Searches and seizures in a digital world. *Harvard Law Review,* 119, 531-585.

Kerr, O.S. (2005). *Orin Kerr and Susan Brenner debate on search and seizure in a digital world.* Retrieved March 10, 2007, from www.legalaffairs.org

Kilpatrick, D. G., Saunders B. E, & Smith D. W. (2003). *Youth victimization: Prevalence and implications.* Department of Justice, National Institute of Justice.

King County Bar Association Drug Policy Project. (2005). *Drugs and Drug laws: Historical and cultural contexts.* Washington: Seattle.

King, R. (2007). *The regulatory state in an age of governance: Soft words and big Sticks.* Hampshire, UK: Palgrave Macmillan.

King, R. (1974). *The drug hang-up: America's fifty-year folly.* Springfield, Illinois: Charles C. Thomas Publisher.

King, R. (2005). *The 1970 Act: Don't sit there, amend something.* Schaffer Library of Drug Policy. Retrieved July 10, 2006 from http://www.druglibrary.org

Kingdon, J. W. (1995). *Agendas, alternatives, and public policies.* New York: Harper – Collins.

Kirsch, J. (1997). *The harlot by the side of the road: Forbidden tales of the Bible.* New York: Ballentine Books.

Koch, W. (May 23, 2006). States get tougher with sex offenders. *USA Today,* pp. 1-2. Retrieved February 4, 2007 from www.reentrypolicy.org

Krisberg, B (2004). *Juvenile justice: Redeeming our children.* CA: Sage Publications.

Kurian, G. T. (1994). *Datapedia of the United States, 1790-2000.* Lanham, MD: Bernan Press.

Kyle, A. D., & Hansell, B. (2005). *The meth epidemic in America.* Washington DC: NACo.

LaFree, G., Bursick, R. J., Short, J., & Taylor, R. B. (2000). The Changing nature of crime in America. *Nature of Crime: Continuity and Change,* 1, 1-49.

Lakoff, G. (1996). *Moral politics: What conservatives know that liberals don't?* Chicago: University of Chicago Press.

Lane, R. (1997). *Murder in America: A history.* Athens, Ohio: Ohio University Press.

Lane, R. (1979). *Violent death in the city: Suicide, accident, and murder in the nineteenth-century Philadelphia.* Cambridge, MA: Harvard University Press,.

Langeluttig, A. (1927). *Department of Justice of the United States.* Baltimore: Johns Hopkins.

Law Partner Publishing LLC. (2005). *Electronic discovery and evidence: Court sanctions for spoliation intensity.* Retrieved March 10, 2007 from www.lawpartnerpublishing.com

Legal Information Institute. (2007). *Murbary v. Madison* (U.S. Supreme Court Decision No. 5 U.S. 137). Ithaca: Cornell University Law School.

Legal Information Institute. (2007). *Scott v. Sandford* (U.S. Supreme Court Decision No. 60 U.S. 393). Ithaca: Cornell University Law School.

Legal Information Institute. (2007). *Plessy v. Ferguson* (U.S. Supreme Court Decision No. 163 U.S. 537). Ithaca: Cornell University Law School.

Legal Information Institute. (2005). *Illinois v. Roy I. Caballes* (U.S. Supreme Court Decision No. 03-923). Ithaca: Cornell University Law School.

Legal Information Institute. (2005). *United States v. Booker* (U.S. Supreme Court Decision No. 04 -104 and 04 -105). Ithaca: Cornell University Law School.

Legal Information Institute. (2005). *Roper v. Simmons* (U.S. Supreme Court Decision No. 03-633). Ithaca: Cornell University Law School.

Legal Information Institute. (2004). *Yarborough, Warden v. Alvarado* (U.S. Supreme Court Decision No. 02-1684). Ithaca: Cornell University Law School.

Legal Information Institute. (2003). *United States et al. Appellants v. American Library Association Inc. et al* (No. 02-361). Ithaca: Cornell University Law School.

Legal Information Institute. (2003). *Delbet W. Smith and Bruce M. Butelho, Petitioners v. John Doe et al* (U. S. Supreme Court Decision No. 01-729). Ithaca: Cornell University Law School.

Legal Information Institute. (2003). *Connecticut Department of Public Safety et al. Petitioners v. John Doe et al* (U.S. Supreme Court Decision No.01-1231). Ithaca: Cornell University Law School.

Legal Information Institute. (2003). *Lawrence et al. v. Texas* (U.S. Supreme Court Decision No. 02-102). Ithaca: Cornell University Law School.

Legal Information Institute. (2002). *Board of Education of Pottawatomie County v. Lindsay Earls* (U.S. Supreme Court Decision No. 01-332). Ithaca: Cornell University Law School.

Legal Information Institute. (1997). *Reno, Attorney General of the United States, et al, V. American Civil Liberties Union et al* (U.S. Supreme Court Decision No. 96-511). Ithaca: Cornell University Law School.

Legal Information Institute. (1997). *Kansas v. Hendricks* (U.S. Supreme Court Decision No. 95-1649). Ithaca: Cornell University Law School.

Legal Information Institute. (1986). *Bowers v. Hardwick* (U.S. Supreme Court Decision No. 478 U.S. 186). Ithaca: Cornell University Law School.

Legal Information Institute. (1967). In *re Gault* (U.S. Supreme Court Decision No. 116). Ithaca: Cornell University Law School.

Legal Information Institute. (1957). *Roth v. United States* (U.S. Supreme Court Decision No. 582). Ithaca: Cornell University Law School. .

Leroux, O. (2004). Legal admissibility of electronic evidence. *International Review of Law, Computers, and Technology,* 18 (2), 193-220.

Leshner, A. I. (July, 2000). *United States Senate Caucus on International Narcotics Control: Statement for the record.* Washington DC: NIDA.

Levenson, J. S. (2004). Civil commitment: A comparison of selected and released offenders. *International Journal of Offender Therapy and Comparative Criminology,* 48 (6), 638-648.

Levinson, D., & Ember, M. (Eds.). (1995). *Encyclopedia of cultural anthropology (Vol. 4).* New York: Henry Holt & Company.

Leyden, J. (2006). *Cyber crime costs biz more than physical crime.* Retrieved August 27, 2006 from www.channelregister.co.uk/2005/11/29/cybercrime

Lindenmeyer, K. (1977). *A right to childhood: The U.S. Children's Bureau and child welfare, 1912-1946.* Chicago: University of Chicago Press.

Loader, I. (2007). *Has liberal criminology "lost"?* (Eve Saville Memorial Lecture). England: University of Oxford: Center for Criminology.

Lucken, K., & Blomberg, T. (2000). *American penology: A history of crime control.* Piscataway, NJ: Aldine Transaction.

Lyons, D. (2002). *States enact new terrorism crimes and penalties* (Legislative Report). Denver: National Conference of State Legislatures.

Lyons, D. (2003). *State crime legislation in 2002* (Legislative Report). Denver: National Conference of State Legislatures.

MacCoun, R. J., & Reuter, P. (2001). *Drug war heresies.* New York: Cambridge University Press.

Marijuana Policy Project. (2006). *State-by-State Medical Marijuana Laws: How to remove the threat of arrest.* Washington DC: Capitol Hill.

Marion, N. E. (1994). *A history of federal crime control initiatives, 1960-1993.* Westport, CT: Praeger.

Marion, N. E. (2007). A Primer in the politics of criminal justice. New York: Criminal Justice Press.

Martin, J. K., Robert, R., Mintz, S., McMurry, L. O., & Jones, J. H. (1989). *America and its people.* Glenview, Illinois: ScottForesman and Company.

Martinson, R. (1974). What works? Questions and answers about prison reform. *The Public Interest,* 35, pp. 22-54.

Matthews, M. K. (2006). *Lawmakers crusade against molesters.* Washington DC: The PEW Research Center.

Mauer, M. (1999). *Race to incarcerate.* New York: New Press.

McAfee, Inc. (2005). *McAfee virtual criminology report: North American study into organized crime and the Internet.* Santa Clara, CA.

McClendon, J. G. (1990). Puritan jurisprudence: Progress and inconsistency. *Antithesis* (A Review of Reformed Presbyterian Thought and Practice), 1 (1), pp. 1-11.

Meehan, E. J. (1981). *Reasoned argument in social science:* Linking Research to Policy. Westport, CT: Greenwood Press.

Meier, K. J. (1994). *The politics of sin: Drugs, alcohol, and public policy.* New York: M.E. Sharpe.

Midwest Office of the Council of State Governments. (2006). New sex offender laws attack crimes against children in a variety of ways. *Firstline Midwest,* 13 (6), pp. 1-4.

Mullen, P. E., & Fleming J. (1998). Long-term effects of child sexual abuse. *Issues in Child Abuse Prevention,* 9, 1-14.

Muraskin, R., & Robert, A. R. (Eds.). (2004). *Visions for change: Crime and justice in the 21st century (4th Ed.).* Upper Saddle River, NJ: Prentice-Hall.

Musto, D. F. (1987). *The American disease: Origins of narcotic control.* New York: Oxford University Press.

Musto, D. F., & Korsmeyer, P. (2002). *The quest for drug control: Politics and federal policy in a period of increasing substance abuse, 1963-1981.* New Heaven, CT: Yale University Press.

Naffine, N. (1998). *Feminism and criminology.* Philadelphia: Temple University Press.

Nandi, P. K. & Shaidullah, S. M. (1998). *Globalization and the evolving world society.* Leiden, The Netherlands: E. Brill.

Naphy, W. (2002). *Sex crimes from renaissance to enlightenment: Sex with man, beast, and satan.* London: Tempas Publishing Ltd.

Naraine, R. (2006). *Microsoft sounds malware alarm.* Retrieved on March 6, 2007 from http://www.eweek.com

National Alliance for Model State Drug Laws. (1993). *New economic thinking on addition and legalization* (by R. B. Charles). Virginia: Alexandria.

National Association of Counties. (2004). *Ending the cycle of recidivism—Best practices for diverting mentally ill individuals from county jails.* Washington DC: NACo.

National Association of Counties. (2003). *President's Initiative on diverting the non-violent mentally ill from jails.* Washington DC: NACo.

National Association of Criminal Defense Lawyers. (2006). *State legislators conference highlights hot issues for 2006.* Retrieved July 22, 2007 from www.NACDL.org

National Center for Juvenile Justice. (2006). *State juvenile profiles.* Retrieved September 10, 2007 from www.ncjj.org

National Center for Missing and Exploited Children. (2003). *President Bush to sign Amber into law.* Alexandria, VA: NCMEC.

National Center for State Courts. (1997). *Sentencing Commission profiles: State sentencing policy and practice research in action partnership.* Williamsburg, VA: NCSC.

National Conference of State Legislatures. (2007). *State crime legislation, 2006.* Denver. NCSL.

National Conference of State Legislatures. (2007). *State computer harassment or "cyberstalking" laws.* Denver: NCSL.

National Conference of State Legislatures. (2007). *Integrated Criminal Justice Information Systems* (by H. Morton). Denver: NCSL.

National Conference of State Legislatures. (2007). *Adam Walsh Child Protection and Safety Act of 2006.* Denver: NCSL

National Conference of State Legislatures. (2006). *Cyber terrorism.* Denver: NCSL. Retrieve March 10, 2007 from www.ncsl.org

National Conference of State Legislatures. (2006). Statutes of limitations for sexual assaults, adult victims, 2006. Denver: NCSL.

National Conference of State Legislatures. (2006). Sex offender registration— HR 3132, HR 4472, the "Children's Safety and Violent Crime Reduction Act of 2005. *Preemption Monitor* (An information service of the NCSL Law and Criminal Justice Committee), 2 (1), 1-10.

National Conference of State Legislatures. (2006). *State crime legislation in 2005.* Denver: NCSL.

National Conference of State Legislatures. (2006). *Children and the internet: Laws related to filtering, blocking and usage policies in school and libraries.* Denver: NCSL

National Conference of State Legislatures. (2005). *Juvenile justice state legislation, 2004.* Denver: NCSL.

National Conference of State Legislatures. (2005). *State crime legislation, 2005.* Denver: NCSL.

National Conference of State Legislatures. (2004). *Law and criminal justice: Key issues.* Denver: NCSL.

National Conference of State Legislatures. (2004). *Law and Criminal Justice Committee.* Denver: NCSL.

National Conference of State Legislatures. (2004). *Crime records and information sharing.* Denver: NCSL.

National Conference of State Legislatures. (2004). *NCSL hosts study tour of MATRIX Supercomputer System.* Denver: NCSL.

National Conference of State Legislatures. (2003). *Juvenile justice state legislation, 2002.* Denver: NCSL.

National Conference of State Legislatures. (2003). Cyber terrorism/computer crime legislation. Denver: NCSL.

National Conference of State Legislatures. (2002). *On first reading: States try to stymie child porn.* Denver: NCSL.

National Conference of State Legislatures. (2001). *State crime legislation, 2001.* Denver: NCSL.

National Governors Association. (2004). *Fast facts on Governors.* Washington DC: National Governors Association.

National Governors Association Center for Best Practices. (2007). *Prison Reentry Policy Academy.* Washington DC: NGA.

National Governors Association Center for Best Practices. (2004). *Governors Criminal Justice Policy Advisers Network.* Washington DC: NGA.

National Governors Association Center for Best Practices. (2003). *First time drug offenders in Texas get treatment, not jail.* Washington DC: NGA.

National Governors Association Center for Best Practices. (2002). *Substance abuse: State actions to Aid to Recovery* (R. J. Burns). Washington DC: NGA.

National Household Survey on Drug Abuse. (October, 2004). *Gender differences in substance dependence and abuse.* Washington DC: Office of Applied Statistics, DHHS.

National Household Survey on Drug Abuse. (August, 2003). *Racial and Ethnic Differences in youth Hallucinogen use.* Washington DC: Office of Applied Statistics, DHHS.

National Household Survey on Drug Abuse. (July 2001). *Pregnancy and illicit drug abuse.* Washington DC: Office of Applied Statistics, DHHS.

National Household Survey on Drug Abuse. (October, 2001). *Availability of illicit drugs to females aged 12-17.* Washington DC: Office of Applied Statistics, DHHS.

National Household Survey on Drug Abuse. (November, 2001). *Youth violence linked to substance use.* Washington DC: Office of Applied Statistics, DHHS.

National Survey on Drug Use and Health. (January, 2004). *Marijuana use and delinquent behaviors among youth.* Washington DC: DHHS.

National Institute of Justice. (2007). *Mapping and analyzing for public safety.* Washington DC: Department of Justice.

National Institute of Justice. (2007). *Completed projects.* Retrieved November 4, 2007 from www.ojp.usdoj.gov/nij/international

National Institute of Justice. (2006). *2005 Annual report to the Congress.* Washington DC: Department of Justice.

National Institute of Justice. (2003). *Arrestee drug abuse monitoring annual report. 2000.* Washington DC: The Department of Justice.

National Institute of Justice. (2001). *Electronic crime needs assessment for state and local law enforcement.* Washington DC: The Department of Justice.

National Institute of Justice. (2001). Sentencing guidelines: Reflections on the future. *Sentencing and Corrections: Issues for the 21st century,* 10, 1-7.

National Institute of Justice. (1999). *1998 Annual report to the Congress.* Washington DC: The Department of Justice.

National Institute of Justice. (1999). *The use of computerized crime mapping by law enforcement: Survey results.* Washington DC: The Department of Justice.

National Intelligence Council. (2004). *Mapping the Global Future* (Report of the National Intelligence Council's 2020 Project). Pittsburgh: Government Printing Press.

National Legal Research Group. (2002). *Discovery and admissibility of electronic evidence.* Retrieved March 6, 2007 from www.divorcesources.com

National Online Resource Center for Violence against Women. (2004). *Marital rape.* Harrisburg, PA: VAWnet.

National Research Council. (2003). *Critical information infrastructure protection and the law: An overview of key issues* (Eds. by S. D. Personick & C. A. Petterson). Washington DC: The National Academy Press.

Nelson, W. E. (1986). Fourteenth Amendment. *Encyclopedia of the American Constitution.* New York: Macmillan.

Newsletter of the Federal Court. (2005). *Filings climbed in federal court.* 37 (3), 1-6.

Nisbet, R. (1969). *The quest for community.* New York: Oxford University Press.

Nixon, R. (August 8, 1968). *Acceptance speech* (Republican National Convention). Retrieved on March 10, 2005 from www.vedh.virginia.edu

Nixon. R. (1973). *1973 State of the Union Address (Part-Message of Crime Control).* Retrieved on March 10, 2004, from www.janda.org

North Carolina Department of Justice. (2001). *The North Carolina sex offender registration program* (Report by Attorney General Roy A. Cooper). Retrieved February 3, 2007 from www.jus.state.nc.us

North Carolina Department of Justice. (2007). *The North Carolina sex offender and public protection registration program.* Retrieved July 10, 2007 from www. jus.state.nc.us

Nuckols, C. (May 28, 2004). *Tougher DUI laws official.* Norfolk, VA: The Virginian Pilot.

Nuckols, C. (May 22, 2004). *Bill protecting fetuses from crime signed into law.* Norfolk, VA: The Virginian Pilot.

Nuckols, C. (May 22, 2004). *Legally unbinding: New law will be most restricted in the United States*. Norfolk, VA: The Virginian Pilot.

Office of Homeland Security. (2002). *National Strategy for Homeland Security*. Washington DC: Office of the President, The White House.

Office of Justice Programs. (2002). *First annual symposium on violence against women* Retrieved January, 2007 from www.usdoj.gov/ovw

Office of Juvenile Justice and Delinquency Prevention. (2005). *Juvenile justice clearinghouse*. Washington DC: Office of Justice Programs, Department of Justice.

Office of Juvenile Justice and Delinquency Prevention. (2005). *OJJDP Annual Report, 2003-2004*. Washington DC: Office of Justice Programs, Department of Justice.

Office of Juvenile Justice and Delinquency Prevention. (2005). *Juvenile arrests, 2003*. Washington DC: Office of Justice Programs, Department of Justice.

Office of Juvenile Justice and Delinquency Prevention. (2005). *OJJDP 2003 report to Congress: Title V Community Prevention Grants Program*. Washington DC: Office of Justice Programs, Department of Justice.

Office of Juvenile Justice and Delinquency Prevention. (2004). *Highlights of the 2000 National Youth Gang Survey* (by A. Egley and M. Arjunan). Washington DC: Office of Justice Programs, Department of Justice.

Office of Juvenile Justice and Delinquency Prevention. (2004). *Prostitution of juveniles: Patterns from NIBRS*. Washington DC: Office of Justice Programs, Department of Justice.

Office of Juvenile Justice and Delinquency Prevention. (2004). *OJJDP Annual Report, 2000*. Washington DC: Office of Justice Programs, Department of Justice.

Office of Juvenile Justice and Delinquency Prevention. (2004). *Formula Grants Program* overview. Washington DC: Office of Justice Programs, Department of Justice.

Office of Juvenile Justice and Delinquency Prevention. (2003). *Delinquency cases waived to juvenile courts, 1990-1999*. Washington DC: Office of Justice Programs, Department of Justice.

Office of Juvenile Justice and Delinquency Prevention. (2003). *Best practices in juvenile accountability: Overview*. Washington DC: Office of Justice Programs, Department of Justice.

Office of Juvenile Justice and Delinquency Prevention. (2002). *OJJDP Annual Report. 2002*. Washington DC: Office of Justice Programs, Department of Justice.

Office of Juvenile Justice and Delinquency Prevention. (2002). *Protecting children in* cyber space: The ICAC Task Force Program (M. Medaris & C. Girouard). Washington DC: Office of Justice Programs, Department of Justice.

Office of Juvenile Justice and Delinquency Prevention. (2001). *Gang localities in the United States: A quarter-century survey*. Washington DC: Office of Justice Programs, Department of Justice.

Office of Juvenile Justice and Delinquency Prevention. (2006). *Juvenile offenders and victims: National report series*. Washington DC: Office of Justice Programs, Department of Justice.

Office of Juvenile Justice and Delinquency Prevention. (2001). Delinquency cases waived to criminal court, 1989-1998. Washington DC: Office of Justice Programs, Department of Justice.

Office of Juvenile Justice and Delinquency Prevention. (2000). *Systems change through State Challenge Activities: Approaches and products*. Washington DC: Office of Justice Programs, Department of Justice.

Office of Juvenile Justice and Delinquency Prevention. (1999). *Juvenile court processing of delinquency cases, 1987-1996*. Washington DC: Office of Justice Programs, Department of Justice.

Office of Juvenile Justice and Delinquency Prevention. (1998). *Juvenile female offenders: A status of the states report* (prepared by Community Research Associates). Washington DC: Office of Justice Programs, Department of Justice.

Office of Juvenile Justice and Delinquency Prevention. (1997). *The national juvenile court data archives: Collecting data since 1927.* Washington DC: Office of Justice Programs, Department of Justice.

Office of Management and Budget. (2006). *Implementation of the government Paperwork Elimination Act.* Washington DC: The Government Printing Office.

Office of Management and Budget (2004). *The Budget for fiscal year 2005.* Washington DC: The Government Printing Office.

Office of National Drug Control Policy. (2007). *The President's National Drug Control Strategy.* Washington DC: The Executive Office of the President.

Office of National Drug Control Policy. (2007). *Executive summary: Economic cost of drug abuse.* Retrieved August 10, 2007 from www.whitehousedrugpoliy.gov

Office of National Drug Control Policy. (2005). *The link between marijuana and mental illness: A survey of recent research.* Washington DC: Executive Office of the President.

Office of National Drug Control Policy. (2005). *Fact sheet: MDMA (ecstasy).* Washington DC: The Executive Office of the President.

Office of National Drug Control Policy. (2005). *National Drug Control Strategy, 2005.* Washington DC: The Executive Office of the President.

Office of National Drug Control Policy. (2003). *Drug data Summary.* Washington DC: The Executive Office of the President.

Office of National Drug Control Policy. (2003). *Juveniles and drugs: Fact sheet.* Washington DC: The Executive Office of the President.

Office of National Drug Control Policy. (2003). *Rohypnol.* Washington DC: The Executive Office of the President.

Office of National Drug Control Policy. (2002). *What America's users spend on illegal drugs.* Washington DC: The Executive Office of the President.

Office of National Drug Control Policy. (2001). *The economic costs of drug abuse in the United States, 1992-1998.* Washington DC: The Executive Office of the President.

Office of the Attorney General of California. (2005). *Annual juvenile justice report.* CA: Department of Justice.

Office of the Governor of Alabama. (March, 2006). *Governor Riley signs new law against child pornography* (Press Release). Alabama, Montgomery: Governor's Office.

Office of the Governor of Alabama. (2006). *Tougher child pornography legislation signed into law.* Retrieved January 28, 2007 from www.governorpress.state.al.us

Office of the Governor of New York. (2004). *Integrated municipal policy anti-Crime teams will assist local law enforcement* (Press Release). New York, Albany: Governor's Office.

Office of the Inspector General. (2005). *Deterring staff sexual abuse of federal inmates.* Washington DC: Bureau of Justice Statistics, Department of Justice.

Office of the New York State Attorney General. (2005). *Cyber gangs charged with Internet drug trafficking* (Press Release). Retrieved November 3, 2006 from www.oag.state.ny.us

Office of the New York State Attorney General. (2004). *Crime fighting philosophies, strategies and management techniques in New York City in the 1990s.* Albany: New York.

O'Keefe, M. (1998). Post-traumatic stress disorder among incarcerated battered women. *Journal of Trauma and Stress,* 2 (1), 71-85.

Oliver, W. M. (2003). *The law and order presidency.* Upper Saddle River, NJ: Prentice Hall.

Oliver, M. W. (2001). *Community-oriented policing: A systemic approach to policing.* Upper Saddle River, NJ: Prentice Hall.

Onishi, N. (1999). The Puritan origins of American taboo. *The Japanese Journal of American Studies,* 10, 33-53.

Peed, C. (March, 2002). *Statement before the Committee of the Judiciary of the House of Representatives* (Subcommittee on Crime). Washington DC: Department of Justice.

Perry, C.O. (2001). *Justice in colonial Virginia*. NJ: The Law Book Exchange, Ltd.

PEW Internet and American Life Project. (2004). *The Impact of CAN-SPAM legislation*. Retrieved November 8, 2006 from www.pewinternet.org

PEW Research Center. (2005). *Support for tougher indecency measures, but worries about government's intrusiveness: New concerns about internet and reality shows*. Washington DC: The PEW Research Center.

PEW Research Center. (2002). *PEW Global Attitudes Project: What the world thinks*. Washington DC: The PEW Research Center.

Pickler, N. (2006). *Bush signs broadcast decency law*. Washington DC: The Associated Press.

Project Vote Smart. (2000-2004). *Fetal Protection- Passage*. Retrieved January 2005 from www.vote-smart.org

Project Vote Smart. (2000-2004). *Virtual child pornography – Passage*. Retrieved on January 2005 from www.vote-smart.org

Putnam, F. W. (2003). Ten-year research updates review: Childhood sexual abuse. *Journal of the American Academy of Child and Adolescent Psychiatry*, 42(3), 269-278.

Quade, E. S. (1982). *Analysis for public decisions* (2nd ed.). New York: New Holland.

Raley, G. A. (1995). The JJDP Act: A second look. *Juvenile Justice*, 2 (2), 11-18.

Raub, W. (September, 2000). Is drug use up or down? What are the implications? *Testimony before the Subcommittee on Criminal Justice, Drug policy, and Human resources*. Washington DC: The U.S. House of Representatives.

Reynolds, G. H. (1994). Kids, guns, and the commerce clause: Is the court ready for constitutional government? *Cato Policy Analysis Paper*, 216.

Reynolds, M.O. (2000). *Crime and punishment in Texas in the 1990s* (Executive Summary). Washington DC: National Center for Policy Analysis.

Riesman, D., Glazer, N., & Denney, R. (2001). *The lonely crowd: A study of the changing American character* (Subsequent edition). Doubleday: Yale University Press.

Roberts, A. R. (Ed.). *Correctional counseling and treatment: Evidence-based perspectives*. Upper Saddle River, NJ: Prentice Hall

Roberts, A. R. (Ed.). (2003). *Critical issues in criminal justice* (2nd Ed.). Thousand Oaks, CA: Sage Publications.

Robertson, S. (2005). *Sexual violence and legal culture in New York City, 1880-1960*. Chapel Hill, NC: University of North Carolina Press.

Roe, K. J. (2004). *The Violence against Women Act and its impact on sexual violence policy: Looking back and looking forward*. Washington DC: National Alliance to end Sexual Violence.

Rosen, R. (1983). *The lost sisterhood: Prostitution in America, 1900-1918*. Baltimore, MD: Johns Hopkins University Press.

Rothman, D. J. (1995). Perfecting the prison: United States, 1789-1865. In N. Morris and D. J. Rothman (Eds.). *The Oxford history of prison: The practice of punishment in western history* (111-130). New York: Oxford University Press.

Rotman, E. (1995). The Failure of Reform, 1865-1965. In N. Morris and D.J. Rothman (Eds.). *The Oxford history of prison: The practice of punishment in western history* (169-197). New York: Oxford University Press.

Rubun, E. L., & Dilulio, J. J. (Eds.). (1998). *Minimizing harm: A modern crime policy for America*. Boulder, CO: Westview Press.

Sabine, G. H., & Thorson, T. L. (1937). *A history of political theory* (4th Ed.). Illinois: Dryden Press.

Schjolberg, S. (2005). *Law comes to cyber space*. Paper presented at the United Nations Criminal Congress, Bangkok, Thailand. Retrieved November 5, 2006 from www.cyberlaw.net

Schjolberg, S. (2004). *Computer related offenses.* Paper presented at the Octopus Interface 2004 Conference on the Challenges of Cyber Crime. France: Council of Europe. Retrieved November 7, 2006 from www.cybercrimelaw.net

Schmitknecht, D. A. (2004). Building FBI computer forensic capacity: One lab at a time. *Digital Investigation,* 1, 177-182.

Schwartz, B. (1993). *A history of the Supreme Court.* New York: Oxford University Press.

Schwartz, H. (Ed.). (2002). *The Rehnquist Court: Judicial activism on the rights.* New York: Hill and Wang.

Senna, S. (1994). *Juvenile delinquency: Theory, practice, and law.* New York: West Publishers.

Shahidullah, S. M., & Green, D. L. (2007). Sex offenders: Assessment and treatment. In A. R. Roberts (Ed.). *Correctional counseling and treatment: Evidence –Based Perspectives* (pp. 201-228). Upper Saddle River, NJ: Prentice-Hall.

Shahidullah, S. M. (November, 2006). DNA, Juvenile Offenders, and the changing contours of juvenile justice. *Paper presented at the Annual Meeting of the Academy of Criminal Justice Science.* MD: Baltimore.

Shahidullah, S. M. (November, 2004). The science of faith and faith-based corrections: Crime, economics, and morality. *Paper presented at the Annual Meeting of the American Society of Criminology.* TN: Nashville.

Shahidullah, S. M. (November, 2003). Post-positivist science and post-modern criminal justice: Towards a framework of analysis. *Paper presented at the Annual Meeting of the American Society of Criminology.* CO: Denver.

Shhaidullah, S. M. (November, 2002). Crime policy in America: The Changing paradigms. *Paper presented at the Annual Meeting of the American society of Criminology.* IL: Chicago.

Shahidullah, S. M. (November, 2001). The social growth of the violent brain: Brain research on teen violence. *Paper presented at the annual meeting of the American Society of Criminology.* GA: Atlanta.

Shahidullah, S. M. (2001). Globalization, the emerging social divide, and global organized crime. *Virginia Social Science Journal,* 36, pp.14-26.

Shahidullah, S. M. (November, 2000). Transnational organized crime: The U.S. policy developments and initiatives. *Paper presented at the Annual Meeting of the American Society of Criminology,* CA: San Francisco.

Shahidullah, S. M. (1998). Useful sociology: Can sociological knowledge be valuable in policy-making? *International Journal of Sociology and Social Policy.* 18, pp. 86-110.

Shahidullah, S. M. (1996). Policy-Making and the Manufacturing of Knowledge: The Role of Applied Social Science in the 21st century. *Futures Research Quarterly,* 12 (4), pp. 6-33.

Shahidullah, S. M. (1994). Emerging trends in crime policy in America: Problems of returning to the Gemeinschaft. *Proceedings of the New York State Sociological Association.* Fort Worth, Texas: Cyber space Publications.

Shelly, L. I. (1998). Transnational organized crime in the United States: Defining the problem. *Kobe University Law Review,* 32, 77-91.

Shelley, L. I. (2003). Organized crime, terrorism and cyber crime. In A. Bryden & P. Flurri. (Eds.). *Security sector reform: Society and good governance* (pp. 303-312). Nomos Verlagsgesellschaft: Baden-Baden.

Shepherd, R. E., Jr. (2000). Juvenile Justice—Collateral consequences of juvenile proceedings. *Criminal Justice Magazine,* 15 (3), 1-5.

Sherman, L. W., Farrington, D. P., Welsh, B., & Mackenzie, D. (Eds.). (2002). *Evidence-Based crime prevention.* London: Routledge.

Sherman, L. W., Gottfredson, D., MacKenzie, D., Eck, J., Reuter, P., & and Bushwa, S. (1993). *Preventing crime: What works, what doesn't, what's promising?* University of Maryland: Department of Criminology and Criminal Justice.

Simon, J. (2007). *Governing through crime: How the War on Crime transformed American democracy and created a culture of fear.* Oxford: Oxford University Press.

Simon, J., & Feeley, M. M. (1995). True crime: The new penology and public discourse on crime. In T. G. Bloomberg & S. Cohen (Eds.). *Punishment and social control* (pp. 147-181). New York: Aldine de Gruyter.

Smith, P. (Ed.). (1993). *Feminist jurisprudence.* New York: Oxford University Press.

Snyder, H. N. (2000). *Sexual assault of young children as reported to law enforcement: Victims, incident, and offender characteristics.* Washington DC: Office of Justice Programs, Department of Justice.

Sorokin, L. G. (1998). The trilogy of federal statutes. In *National Conference of Sex Offender Registries* (pp. 35- 39). Washington DC: Office of Justice Programs, Department of Justice.

StandDown Texas Project. (July, 2007). *Governor Perry Signs Jessica's Law.* Retrieved on August, 2007 from http://www.standdown.typepad.com

Stenson, K., & Cowell, D. (Eds.). (1991). *The politics of crime control.* London: Sage Publications.

Stolz, B. N. (2002). *Criminal justice policy-making: Federal roles and processes.* Westport, CT: Praeger.

Storrs, K. L. (1998). *Mexican drug certification issues: U.S. congressional action, 1986-1998.* Washington DC: Congressional Research Service.

Sussman. M. A. (1999).The critical challenges from international high-tech and computer-related crime at the millennium. *Duke Journal of Contemporary International Law, 9,* 451- 489.

Tafari, T. (2002). *The Rise and fall of Jim Crow: A century of segregation* (PBS series). New York: Educational Broadcasting Corporation.

Talbot, N. L., Duberstein, P. R., Cox, C., Denning, D., & Conwell, Y. (2004). Preliminary report on childhood sexual abuse, suicidal ideation, and suicidal attempts among middle-aged and older depressed women. *American Journal of Geriatric Psychiatry, 12,* 536-538.

Tarter, B. (1987). Virginians and the Bill of Rights. In J. Kukla (Ed.). *The Bill of Rights: A lively Heritage,* pp. 3-17. Richmond, VA: Virginia State Library and Archives.

Tarr, G. A. (2003). *Judicial process and judicial policy-Making.* New York: Wadsworth Publishing Company.

TechWeb News. (2004). *Operation firewall nets 28 suspects allegedly involved in online fraud and conspiracy.* Retrieved November 3, 2006 from www.informationweek.com.

The Associated Press. (2006). *Virginia man gets 150 years for child porn convictions.* Retrieved March 4, 2004 from www.wbz.com/topic.ap

The Associated Press. (2005). *Video game critics take aim at cannibalism: Group warns of danger to kids playing adult-rated games.* Retrieved January 25, 2007 from www.msnbc.msn.com

The Columbia Electronic Encyclopedia. (2003). New York: Columbia University Press.

The Council of State Governments—Eastern Regional Conference. (2005). States step up monitoring of sex offenders. *Weekly Bulletin, 74,* 1- 4. Retrieved February 3, 2007 from www.csgeast.org/pubweekly.asp.

The Encyclopedia of American Crime, Vol. 1. (2nd edition). (2001). New York: Facts on File.

The Sentencing Project. (2007). *Changing direction? State sentencing reforms, 2004 -2006* (by R. S. King). Washington DC: The Sentencing Project.

The Sentencing Project. (2007). *Federal crack cocaine sentencing.* Washington DC: The Sentencing Project.

The Illinois Office of the Governor. (January 2, 2004). *Governor reopens Sheridan correctional center* (Press Release). Illinois: Governor's Office.

The Virginian Pilot. (March 9, 2007). *Police report: Violent crime spikes across the nation* (by K. Zernike written for the New York Times). Norfolk: Virginia

The White House. (2004). *President Bush signs Unborn Victims of Violence Act of 2004.* Washington DC: Office of the President.

The White House. (2003). *The National Strategy to Secure Cyber Space.* Washington DC: Office of the President.

The White House. (2003). *Advancing justice through DNA technology.* Washington DC: Office of the President.

The White House. (2002). *Analysis for the Homeland Security Act of 2002.* Washington DC: Office of the President.

The White House. (2002). President's Interagency Task Force to monitor and combat trafficking in persons. *Federal Register,* 67 (33), 1-2.

The White House. (1998). *Presidential Decision Directive/NSC-6.* Washington DC: Office of the President. Retrieved November 10, 2006 from www.fas.org.irp

Tjaden, P., & Thoennes, N. (2000). *Full report of the prevalence, incidence, and consequences of violence against women* (Findings from the National Violence against Women Survey). Washington DC: National Institute of Justice.

Tonry, H. M. (2006). *Thinking about crime: Sense and sensibilities in American penal culture.* Oxford: Oxford University Press.

Tonry, H. M. (2004). *Punishment and Politics: Evidence and Emulation in the Making of English Crime Control Policy.* England: Willan Publishing.

Tonry, H. M. (1996). *Sentencing matters.* New York: Oxford University Press.

Tonry, H. M. (1995). *Malign neglect: Race, crime, and punishment in America.* New York: Oxford University Press.

Torbet, P., & Szymanski, L. (1998). State legislative response to violent juvenile crime, 1996-1997 update. *Juvenile Justice,* 6(2). Retrieved June 10, 2006, from www.ojjdp.ncjrs.org

Travis, J. (1997). *The mentally ill offender: Viewing crime and justice through a different lens.* (Speech to the National Association of State Forensic Mental Health Directors). Washington DC: National Institute of Justice.

Uhde, A. (July 16, 2004). 1680: *It was a very good year Jamestown excavation uncovers cellar, complete with wine bottles.* Norfolk: VA: The Virginian Pilot.

Uniform Crime Reports (1963). *Crime in the United States* (Issued by J. Edgar Hoover, FBI). Boston: Beacon Press.

United Nations. (2006). *World Drug Report, 2006.* New York: UN Office on Drugs and Crime.

United Nations. (2004). *World Drug Report, 2004.* New York: UN Office on Drugs and Crime.

United States Conference of Mayors. (2007). *Strong Cities, Strong Families for Strong America.* Washington DC: U.S. Conference of Mayors.

United States Court of Appeals for the Fourth Circuit. (2005). *United States v. John Woodward Ickes* (No. 03-4907). Retrieved March 10, 2007 from uscourts.gov

United States Department of Commerce. (2004). *A nation online: Entering the* broadband age. Washington DC: DOC.

United States Department of Commerce. (2002). *A nation online: How Americans are expanding their use of the Internet.* Washington DC: Economic and Statistics Administration and NITA, USDC.

United States Department of Defense. (2004). *Department of Defense Cyber Crime Center.* Washington DC: DOD.

United States Department of Health and Human Services. (2003). 2003 *National survey on drug use and health: Results.* Washington DC: SAMSA, Department of Health and Human Services.

United States Department of Homeland Security. (2003). *Fact sheet: Protecting America's critical infrastructures—Cyber security* (Press Release). Washington DC: Department of Homeland Security.

United States Department of Homeland Security. (2003). *Federal law enforcement training center: Performance and accountability report.* Washington DC: Department of Homeland Security.

United States Department of Justice. (2006). *Computing crime—latest news.* Washington DC: Computer Crime and Intellectual Property Section, Department of Justice.

United States Department of Justice. (2006). Field *guidance on new authorities that relate to computer crime and electronic evidence enacted in the USA Patriot Act of 2001.* Washington DC: Department of Justice.

United State Department of Justice. (2005). *2005 FBI computer crime survey.* Washington DC: Department of Justice.

United States Department of Justice. (2004). *Report to Congress: U.S. government efforts to combat trafficking in persons in fiscal year 2003.* Washington DC: Department of Justice.

United State Department of Justice. (2003). *The National Information Infrastructure Protection Act of 1996: Legislative analysis.* Washington DC: Computer Crime and Intellectual Property Section, Department of Justice.

United States Department of Justice. (1999). *On keeping America secure for the 21st century* (Remarks by President Clinton, National Academy of Sciences, January 22, 1999). Washington DC: Department of Justice.

United States Department of Justice. (1996). *National Information Infrastructure Protection Act of 1995: Report of the Senate Committee on the Judiciary.* Retrieved November 8, 2006 from www.usdoj.gov/criminal/cybercrime

United States Department of State. (2006). *United States joins Council of Europe Convention on Cyber Crime* (Press statement by S. McCormick). Washington DC: Department of Justice.

United States Department of State. (2005). *Trafficking in persons report.* Washington DC: Department of State.

United States Department of State. (2004). *Trafficking in persons report.* Washington DC: Department of State.

United States Drug Enforcement Administration. (2005). *Drug trafficking in the United States.* Washington DC: DEA.

United States Drug Enforcement Administration. (2003). *Speaking out against drug legalization.* Washington DC: DEA.

United States Drug Enforcement Administration. (2003). *Controlled Substance Act.* Washington DC: DEA.

United States Drug Enforcement Administration. (2003). *Drugs of abuse.* Washington DC: DEA.

United States General Accounting Office. (2003). *Federal law enforcement training center: Capacity planning and management oversight need improvement* (Report to the Congress). Washington DC: The Government Printing Press.

United States General Accounting Office. (2002). *Violence against Women: Data on pregnant victims and effectiveness of prevention strategies are limited.* Washington DC: The Government Printing Press.

United States General Accounting Office. (2002). *Critical infrastructure protection: Report to the Committee on Governmental Affairs, U.S. Senate.* Washington DC: General Accounting Office.

United States Office of the Inspector General. (2005). *Deterring staff sexual abuse of federal inmates.* Washington DC: Department of Justice.

United States Sentencing Commission. (2006). *Final report on the impact of United States v. Booker on federal sentencing.* Washington DC: The Sentencing Commission.

United States Sentencing Commission. (2003). *Increased penalties for cyber security offenses: Report to the Congress.* Washington DC: The Sentencing Commission.

United States Sentencing Commission. (2000). *Sentencing federal sexual offenders: Protection of children from Sexual Predators Act of 1998* (Sexual Predator Act Policy Team Report). Washington DC: The Sentencing Commission.

United States Sentencing Commission. (1999). *Identity theft: Final report.* Washington DC: U.S. Sentencing Commission. Retrieved November 8, 2006 from www.ussc.gov

Vera Institute of Justice. (2007). *Reconsidering incarceration: New directions for reducing crime* (by D. Stemen). New York: VIJ. Retrieved June 2007 from www.vera.org

Vera Institute of Justice. (2004). *Changing fortunes or changing attitudes: State sentencing and corrections reforms* (by J. Wool & D. Steman). New York: VIJ.

Vera Institute of Justice. (2002). *Is the budget crisis changing the way we look at sentencing and incarceration* (by D. Wilhelm & N. R. Turner). New York: VIJ.

Verton, D (2000). *"Crime Boy's go hack spree.* Retrieved March 2, 2007 from www.cnn.com

Vidich, A. J., & Lyman, S. M. (1985). *American sociology.* New Haven, CT: Yale University Press.

Virginia Criminal Sentencing Commission. (2003). *Annual report, 2003.* Richmond: VA Criminal Sentencing Commission.

Vorenberg, J. (May, 1972). The war on crimes: The first five years. *The Atlantic Monthly,* pp.1-15. Retrieved October 10, 2004 from http://www.theatlantic.com

Walker, S. (1997). *Record of the Wickersham Commission on Law Observance and Enforcement.* Retrieved June 10, 2005 from www.lexisnexis.com

Wall, D. S. (2007) *Cybercrime: The transformation of crime in the information age.* Cambridge, UK: Polity Press.

Walsh, N. (November, 2000). *Life in prison without the possibility of release* (excerpt from Juveniles and the Death Penalty). Washington DC: Coordinating Council on Juvenile Justice and Delinquency Prevention.

Ward, R. H. (2000). The Internationalization of criminal justice. *Criminal Justice, 2000: Boundary of Changes in Criminal Justice Organizations, 2,* 267-321.

Weems, R. J. (1995). *Battered love: Marriage, sex, and violence in the Hebrew Prophets.* Minneapolis: Fortress Press.

Weiner, R.S. (October 18, 2000). *Survey finds support for school filters.* Retrieved January 25, 2007 from www.nytimes.com

Weiss, C.H. (1991). Policy research as advocacy: Pro and con. *Knowledge and Policy,* 4, pp. 37-55.

Weiss, M., & Young, C. (June, 1996). Feminist jurisprudence: Equal rights or neo-paternalism? *Cato Policy Analysis Paper,* 256.

Wekerle, C., & Wall, A. (Eds.). (2002). *The violence and addiction equation.* New York: Brunner- Routledge.

Wellford, C. F. (1998). Changing nature of criminal justice system responses and professions (pp. 1-9). Retrieved March 10, 2004 from www.ojp.usdoj.gov

Whitehead, B. D., & Popenoe. D. (1999). *Changes in attitudes toward marriage, cohabitation, and children* (The National Marriage Project). Retrieved June 5, 2006 from www. rutgers.edu

Wicker, T. (2002). Reflections of court watcher (Forward). In H. Schwartz (Ed.). *The Rehnquist Court: Judicial activism on the right* (pp. 3-12). New York: Hill and Wang.

Wilson, A. D. (2000). *Rockefeller Drug Laws information sheet.* New York: Partnership for Responsible Drug Information. Retrieved June 6, 2005 from http://www.prdi.org

Wilson, J. Q. (Ed.). (1983). *Crime and Public Policy.* New Brunswick NJ: Transaction Books.

Wilson, J. Q. (1997). *Moral Judgment: Does the abuse excuse threaten our legal system?* New York: Basic Books.

Wilson, J. Q., & Petersilla, J. (Eds.). (2002). *Crime: Public policies for crime control*. San Francisco: Institute for Contemporary Studies.

Wilson, J. Q., & Herrstein, R. J. (1985). *Crime and human nature: The definitive study of the causes of crime*. New York: Simon and Schuster.

Zeese, K. (2002). *Once secret "Nixon Tapes" show why the U.S. outlawed pot*. Retrieved July 17, 2005 from www.alternate.org

INDEX